I & II KINGS

I & II KINGS

Albert McShane

JOHN RITCHIE LTD
CHRISTIAN PUBLICATIONS

40 Beansburn, Kilmarnock, Scotland

ISBN 1 904064 14 0

Typeset by John Ritchie Ltd., Kilmarnock
Printed at The Bath Press, Avon

Contents

II KINGS

Foreword

The reader is now holding in his hands the last full scale work we will have from the able pen of its highly esteemed author. This book constitutes another part of the spiritual legacy from the ministry of Mr Albert McShane. His passing into the presence of the Lord, on May 20th 2002, after a long, active and useful life, meant that, though he had finished his work on 1 and 2 Kings, he never saw the completed project in print. In this we are, once again, the beneficiaries of his labours in the Word of God.

Any commentator on these books has to meet the daunting challenge of history, chronology and archaeology, as well as theology. It is practically impossible in a single work to treat all of these areas exhaustively, so that an author has to be selective. In the pages of this volume the reader will notice that while the historical story line of 1 and 2 Kings has been carefully followed, adequate but less space has been given to matters of chronology and archaeology. Detail on such matters can be found in works which specialise in those areas.

Here the author's priorities lie elsewhere. At frequent intervals in these pages, Mr McShane pauses to note how the principles, which emerge from a consideration of the inspired record of the ancient history of the kingdom of Israel, have a practical bearing upon Christian living in the present time. In line with his previous work on the books of Samuel the author demonstrates how principles of assembly rule are likewise illustrated by the material of the Kings. This feature alone, which is not commonly found in expositions of 1 and 2 Kings, will give this volume a special place on the book shelf of the Old Testament student.

Another marked feature of the following pages is that the author, from time to time, draws attention to the prophetic significance of this material. He clearly shows how some of the events of history are a foreshadowing of things to come, and will be played out yet again on a larger scale in the unfolding drama of world events.

One further note of explanation is necessary. The author often indicated that in the course of producing this commentary he assiduously resisted the temptation to relate the material of Kings to its counterpart in Chronicles. This temptation was particularly strong, for example, in dealing with the record of the reign of Hezekiah, whose religious reforms are allocated only a few verses in Kings but three chapters in Chronicles. Mr McShane strenuously avoided making much comment on the Chronicles parallel, believing it was a distinct work, given by the Holy Spirit for a distinct purpose.

Commentaries on the books of Kings are not as prolific as on many other parts of Scripture. This is a work which makes a unique contribution to the elucidation of that part of the field of inspiration and may it please the Lord to use its contents to the enlightenment, encouragement and edification of many.

David Gilliland

November 2002

Introduction

The purpose of the books

Most are aware that what we know as the First and Second Books of Kings were originally one in the Hebrew language. The Greek translators, followed by the Latin writers, divided, what to them was a very large book, into two. They did the same with Samuel and also Chronicles. Some have suggested that the size of the scrolls they used in those days had a bearing on this, for when these became too long, they were cumbersome to handle, so it was thought convenient to divide the larger historical books, but for some reason the prophetic books, some of which were even larger, were not so treated. Of this we are sure, there was nothing in the text where the Book of Kings is divided, which guided them as to where the break should be made for it occurs in the middle of Ahaziah's reign, and also in the middle of Elijah's prophetic ministry. In light of this fact, we must, in this introduction, view the two books as one document. Perhaps it should also be pointed out that the same Greek translators called the Books of Samuel "First Kings" and "Second Kings", so that our Book in the Septuagint is called 'Third Kings", and is followed by "Fourth Kings'.

It is evident that the Books of Kings is a historical account of the

9

happenings in the nation of Israel during the reign of its different kings, yet it is history written from a religious view point. Strictly speaking there was no such thing as a secular history of Israel, for the nation was God's people, and its various vicissitudes are recorded to show how its relationship with Him was reflected in the conditions which prevailed at any particular time. It was His will that all future generations would learn, as they read the story of these various rulers, the importance of obeying God and walking in His ways, for the record will show that this leads to peace and prosperity, and it likewise shows that turning from Him, and turning to idolatry, leads to disaster. Interspersed in this history is the proof that even after departure, if there was a turning to God in true repentance, He would show mercy and bless His wayward people. Thus the ups and downs, which mark the events recorded, reveal His character, and both warn, and encourage those who read. The sad plight of the nation at the close of the history, might cause us great surprise, and raise the question in our minds, "Does God keep His promises and His covenants"? However, the provocation and rebellion of His people revealed in their history, and His longsuffering with them, prove Him to be altogether blameless for their disaster.

There is a clear distinction between the secular history of the nations, and that of Kings, for they wrote their annals as a memorial to their successes, and achievements, and practically ignored their disasters and failings; whereas, sacred history never ignores the failures, nor does it hide the corruptions which brought these about. Indeed, it goes far to prove that as sure as night follows day, so sure does disaster follow departure from God and His ways.

When the Lord was speaking to the two on the way to Emmaus it is stated that He began with "Moses and all the prophets", so in some way the historical books are included in the "prophets" (Lk 24.27), This would seem to give us encouragement to see the future typified in the history of the past. Most cannot fail to see in the history of the reign of Solomon, some shadow of the Millennial kingdom of Christ, and likewise realize, as they read of an earthly and material Temple, that they are viewing, at the same time, a type of the spiritual temple. History in Scripture is no less true, even though it is so written as to foreshadow future events.

The pen-man

There is no definite proof as to who wrote the books of Kings, but much has been said in favour of Jeremiah as being their author. If he were not the author, then someone close by him was most likely involved in the task. The main objection to his authorship is the fact that he, as far as we know, went down to Egypt, whereas the writer of Kings appears to have resided in Babylon. Not that the events narrated took place in his day, nor was he, or any other man contemporary with all of them. Whoever wrote the books must have searched the existing records of events which occurred during the former centuries, and compiled them into one volume. If Jeremiah was the compiler he must have been very old when he wrote the closing verses, or else these were added by another hand. Whoever was the pen-man, the divine intention was fulfilled, for the history of His people, under different kings, was not forgotten, nor were the lessons it taught, left in oblivion.

The plan

The first eleven chapters centre mainly on Solomon, even though David was still alive in chapters one and two. From ch.12-16 the division and decline of the Nation under the different kings is recorded, In these chapters, the writer alternates the history of the kings of Judah, and the kings of Israel. From ch.17 to ch.2 of 2 Kings, the deeds of Elijah are the leading theme, and this is followed by the deeds of Elisha until ch.13. From ch.14-17 the history is resumed as formerly, with no mention of prophets. However, the evil deeds of the Northern kingdom reached a point when God's patience was exhausted, so He allowed it to be carried into Assyria, as recorded in ch.17, and this left only the kings of Judah and their doings as the subject of the remaining chapters. Alas! they soon followed the example of their Northern brethren and fell into idolatry, with the result that they too were carried away, not to Assyria, but to Babylon. In this section there were at least two revivals, one during the reign of Hezekiah, and the other during the reign of Josiah, but even these times of mercy could not permanently arrest the decline, so the City and Temple were burned, and the greatest centre of divine manifestations on earth, was left in a state of ruin. The Books of Kings, viewed broadly, trace from the time of the kingdom of Solomon with its world wide dominion, until the time the kingdom was devastated. In the early chapters the Temple, with all its splendour was built; in the closing chapter this same Temple was burned to ashes. In the crowning of Solomon (ch.2), we are shown the house of

David established, but how different in 2 Kings 25 when the throne was emptied of David's seed, with the result that not one of his descendants has ever sat on it since. Had David been allowed to see the House of God built, and it filled with the Shechinah, the visible symbol of the divine presence, he would have been overwhelmed with joy, but had he seen the same house burned to ashes, he would have been no less overwhelmed with grief.

The period covered

The history given in the two books extends to about 450 years, (from about 1012- 562 BC), so it was a period of the same duration as the days of the Judges, for it too, lasted 450 years. Both periods began with Israel in prosperity, and ended with Israel in bondage. At the beginning of the Kings period Israel was the envy of the world, for Solomon's wisdom was famous throughout it, but the passing of time proved the failure of man, be he ever so well favoured. In less than half a millennium the best nation the world has ever seen had so deteriorated as to be a scattered people, with neither king nor land that they could call their own. Not only were they politically destroyed, but religiously they had become no better than the heathen around them. Autocratic rule is ever the ideal form of government, but the one who exercises dominion must himself keep right with God. Indeed, he can only successfully rule others, if he himself is ruled by God. The divine plan from creation's morn has been that a man should rule the world. This was evident when Adam was set over creation, but he failed, and ever since, every kingdom ruled by man has likewise proved human failure. The history of this remarkable period written in the Books of Kings proves that even the most favoured Nation has fallen into apostasy. However, God has not abandoned His original purpose, for He has found a true ruler, and that One a man, but at the same time, His own Son. He shall not fail, but will establish a kingdom that will be filled with righteousness as the waters cover the sea.

Throughout the Kings period the plague of Israel was always idolatry. With all David's failings, he was never guilty of turning to false gods, but from the time of Solomon, who married heathen wives, some of whom brought their idolatry with them, until the captivity, this one evil marked the nation. Strangely, the captives were brought to Babylon, the land of idols, and their stay there seemed to cure them of this besetting sin.

The history opens with heaps of wealth. Most of these riches were the spoils of Israel's enemies which David had taken during his different campaigns. The quantity of these treasures was so great that our minds stagger as we consider it. In the Temple and its furnishings, the gold and precious stones alone were priceless, yet these books show us that in a comparatively short time, all these treasures were again back in the hands of the heathen, and the once prosperous people, either slain, or carried captive slaves to end their lives in the service of a heathen king. This is the sad story of this history, but just as it is about to close a little ray of sunshine appears, for the new king of Babylon, Evil-merodach, exalted the king of Israel, Jehoiachin, who had been in prison for 37 years, and allowed him to end his days sitting at his table. This is the one event that fixes the date of the composition of this history, for it occurred some time before the close of the captivity, but not long before the decree of Cyrus.

The parallel writings

Much that is recorded in Kings is also in Chronicles, but there are some distinctions between the two writings. In Kings it is history written by the prophets, who viewed things from a judicial standpoint; whereas in Chronicles the same events are viewed from the religious and priestly aspect. In Chronicles many of the failures of kings are not mentioned, but whatever they did according to the will of God is emphasised. For example, David's sin with Bathsheba, is passed over in Chronicles, but detailed in 2 Samuel. In Chronicles the sickness and recovery of Hezekiah is only mentioned, whereas in 2 Kings it is enlarged in detail. In 2 Chronicles his passover is given much space, but it is not mentioned in Kings. One clear distinction in these two writings is that several chapters are given to the prophets in Kings, but no such chapters are to be found in Chronicles.

Obviously the prophets in Israel were recorders as well as prophets, so as the events occurred, they noted these down, and kept them as treasures for future generations. The writer of Kings had access to at least three such documents. He mentions, "The book of the acts of Solomon" (1 Kings 11.41), "The book of the Chronicles of the kings of Judah" (I Kings 14.29), and "The book of the Chronicles of the kings of Israel" (1 Kings 14.19; 15.31). He refers to these as sources of further information some thirty times. These writings must have been available to most of the people, and they, along with others of a similar nature, were made use of by the writer of Chronicles. During David's time records were kept by Samuel, Nathan and Gad, all of whom were also prophets, so this practice was continued throughout the Kings period. The writer of Kings, not being alive during much of the time covered by this history, must have been indebted to earlier records in compiling his work.

In the early chapters of Isaiah we have reference made to Uzziah and Ahaz, and later the interesting historical section of the same prophecy, (chs.36-39), deals with events in the life of Hezekiah, so all these link together the prophecy and 2 Kings. To our surprise, Jeremiah, who was alive during the latter times of the kings, is never once mentioned in the Books of Kings.

There are some links with the Psalms and the Kings, and these will be noted as we make our way through the book. The most interesting would be the "psalm for Solomon" Ps 72, for it must have been composed near the time when 1 Kings takes up the history.

There are some links between Kings and the earlier Minor Prophets, for their messages were intended to arrest the decline which was fast approaching both in the Northern and Southern kingdoms. It is evident that as the departure from God by His people increased, He raised up more prophets to warn them of the inevitable consequences, and to arrest them on their disastrous course; so when the judgment fell, they could never claim that they had not been told.

The prophets' role

Those who rule are ever in need of counsel, and that of a spiritual nature, Samuel, Gad, and Nathan were invaluable aids to David, so that in every crisis in his life, one of these was directed to him with a timely message. The latter is the only one of these to play a part in the kingdom as recorded in Kings. After him we have the man of God and an old prophet (1 Kings 13), then Ahijah, Jehu, Elijah, Elisha, Jonah, and Isaiah, all of whom were instruments of God to communicate His message to the various kings. Those who heeded their message, were blessed and guided; and those who rejected their words suffered the sad consequences. The absence of prophetic ministry during the time of Solomon is a striking feature of his history. Possibly God communicated His will to him directly, especially in his earlier days. The prophets were not always enabled to bring about the recovery in the nation which they sought, but none can doubt that they did play a part in arresting its decay, even though they could not halt it.

Apparently the kings, who were anointed, were thus honoured by the prophets. We are not told that all kings were anointed, but it may have been the case even though not particularly mentioned. There were times when king and prophet were opposed to each other, as was specially true in the case of Ahab and Elijah, for if the king and his wife would have had their way, he would have filled an early grave. Much courage was required for humble servants of God, with no human protection, to venture into the presence of proud monarchs and at times rebuke them for their sins.

I & II Kings

I KINGS

CHAPTERS 1.1 - 2.10

THE CLOSING DAYS OF DAVID'S REIGN

CHAPTER 1, Verses 1-4

His Physical Weakness

The opening paragraph of this book makes clear that David had reached the time when he was no longer fit to govern the nation and was nearing his death. The news of his declining strength must have cast a cloud of sorrow over the entire land. Through his wise and God-fearing rule he had brought prosperity and wealth to the people, raised Israel to high national glory, and, what was even more important, to a high spiritual state. Since the days of Joshua, who established the people in their God-given inheritance and subdued their enemies, they had never been in a more secure position.

If this section is seen as a continuation of the events ending the books of Samuel, then David's health had deteriorated quite rapidly. In its closing chapter he appears to be fit and well. The account of his discovery of the site for the Temple, recorded there and in 1 Chronicles 21 and 22, is undoubtedly the record of one of the greatest thrills of his life. It must have encouraged him to intensify his efforts in accumulating the material for its erection.

Whatever the background to his weakness, he was about seventy years old at this time and so had reached the allotted span (Ps 90.10). He had endured many hardships in his life. They must have taken their toll though no doubt he was sustained by divine aid. His experience of the effect of passing years may be compared to that of Paul, who speaks of himself as "Paul the aged" (Phlm 9) even when he was probably only in his early sixties. Few of Israel's kings lived to be as old as David. In their cases at least, heavy responsibilities had an adverse physical effect.

However, the changes time can bring are here vividly displayed. The man whose brow had often been wet with sweat from the heat of exertion, was now so cold that no wrappings could warm him. The battlefield where he had displayed his strength and stamina is now exchanged for a bed where he lies in weakness. The royal robes that once marked his dignity are now replaced by heavy coverings that fail to restore warmth to his shivering body. The greatest of men are still only men. If allowed to die through natural causes, the nearer they come to their end the more they show their frailty. Often David had feared being slain and thought he would fill an early grave, but the Lord had delivered him and allowed him to go to his fathers in peace.

The scheme devised to bring warmth into the king's body may seem quite immoral to us, but in the time of David no such scruples crossed the thoughts of his attendants. They considered that a young woman full of life and energy could give her body-heat to him as she lay beside him. Throughout his lifetime David had had relations with a number of women, some of whom were alive at this time, but none of these was thought of as suitable on this occasion. After some searching, Abishag was found. She was chosen for her beauty and considered to be acceptable for this service.

The success or otherwise of the experiment is not revealed. She cared for the king. But she remained a virgin. While she may well have thought her task no small honour, in that she was the one chosen to comfort the king in his closing days, on the other hand her favour was short lived. It resulted in the rest of her life being ruined. The poor girl deserved the sympathy, not the envy, of all the women of her day. She was sacrificed to meet a passing need and never knew the simple joys of a normal life. In a sense Abishag died when David died, for after his death she was probably confined to the royal harem where she would spend the remainder of her days. Her name appears again in connection with the slaying of Adonijah.

These few verses also show David as one no longer troubled by one of his greatest weaknesses. Throughout his life his passion for women was a cause of stumbling, but now, through physical weakness, he could no longer indulge himself in this way. It was not at his request that Abishag was secured, but those who suggested the idea knew only too well that they were doing what in the past would have appealed to the king.

The sharp contrast between these opening verses and the history of the same time as recorded in 1 Chronicles 28 and 29 has puzzled commentators. In those chapters, there is not a hint of David's frailty, nor of Abishag. It could well be that he did recover from this bout of weakness, and that he regained sufficient strength to enable him, as related there, to counsel his officials vigorously regarding Solomon and the Temple.

The story of Abishag is one of a young life spoiled through the custom of the period.

Verses 5-10
The abortive coup of Adonijah

The natural accompaniment of the approaching end of one in high position is the question of who will be his successor. Absalom could not wait until his father was dying but attempted to dethrone him even while he was alive and well. Now another son attempts to force matters.

At this time, Adonijah may have been the oldest surviving son of the dying king, although originally he had had three older brothers – Amnon and Absalom who had been killed (2 Sam 13 & 18), and Chileab, of whom nothing is said other than that he was the son of Abigail. He may have died a young man, as there is no mention of his activities. Adonijah, conscious that soon the throne would be vacant, and that the crown was not always given to the oldest surviving son, could see that the time had come when, if he was going to be king, he must act immediately. There can be little doubt that all in the royal household knew that Solomon was expected to succeed his father to the throne. Despite this, Adonijah was determined to overturn the purpose of his father and so made this daring attempt to seize the crown.

Perhaps he assumed that because some leading figures, such as Joab and Abiathar, were on his side he would have no difficulty in achieving his objective. In fact he had no doubts about this, for he said, "I will be king" (v.5).

His outward pomp matched his inner ambition, so, like Absalom his half-brother before him, whose example he followed closely, he assembled the great company described which included the royal officials and his younger brothers. This latter group must have numbered nine or ten, even without Solomon, and possibly seldom came together. With so many different mothers, there would be little sense of family spirit. These, with his fifty runners, followed by chariots and horsemen, combined to display no small show of strength.

At no time did he seek the guidance of a prophet in the matter, nor had he any authority from his father for his action. The entire scheme originated out of the pride of his heart. In order to give the occasion a token of religion, he sacrificed the choicest of animals, possibly using the Stone of Zoheleth as a kind of altar.

The scene must have been impressive to those invited. None who gathered had ever before witnessed such an occasion. The festivities, together with all the eating and drinking, must have appealed to most of them and the united proclamation rang out, "Long live King Adonijah" (v.25, NIV). The majority may have grasped how serious and important was the event, but some may have been present of whom it could be said, as was said of some who followed Absalom, that "they went in their simplicity" (2 Sam 15.11).

Adonijah had two serious disadvantages. The first may not have seemed so. He was very handsome and so was able to draw people to him by that alone for man still "looks on the outward appearance". To the natural eye, he was all that could be desired in a popular ruler. Alas, this was a deceitful snare to him and to his admirers. Second, he was the spoiled child of his father for, according to v.6, David had never questioned him about what he did. He had a free hand, and could behave as he liked. With all the confusion brought about by so many wives and their children, it must have been all but impossible for David to rebuke the misconduct of any of his offspring. When the heavy responsibility of ruling the nation, and at times waging war with his enemies, is taken into account it can be readily appreciated that his private life must have been abnormal. However, even if allowance is made for these circumstances, he was not exempt from the duty of exercising his parental responsibilities. In this he failed.

The narrative is noticeable in that it emphasises the fact that there were some important omissions in those called to Adonijah's celebration. Neither Zadok the priest, nor the prophet Nathan, nor Benaiah, nor David's mighty men (probably his personal bodyguard) were invited to the grand function. As for Solomon, it is obvious why he was not called for Adonijah knew that he, in spite of his youth, was the son chosen to be anointed. Even more surprising is the conduct of Abiathar and Joab. Who would have imagined that the priest who had followed David through all his trials and hardships would now throw in his lot with a usurper? He could not have been ignorant of the divine choice for the throne, nor could he have claimed that he was unaware that his action would be a grief to the king. As for Joab, he had a great reputation for gallantry and had fought for David in many campaigns. In the slaying of Abner (2 Sam 3) and Amasa (2

Sam 20) he had deeply grieved the king and, as a result, lost his position as the head of the army. Although he was shrewd enough not to take sides with Absalom, he failed to see that success was no more likely on this occasion. In spite of all the exploits he had engaged in for David during his forty year reign, and even before it, there appears to have been little in common between the two men, especially toward the end. The story of Joab is one of cruelty and craft, and of one destitute of any trace of the fear of God.

For those interested in seeing prophetic pictures in OT events, Adonijah seems to be a clear type of the Antichrist. Just as Adonijah appears as the false king before Solomon the true king takes the throne, so will the Antichrist reign for a time before Christ, the rightful King, sits on His throne. Many of the nation in the future will be deceived and will imagine that they are supporting the rightful ruler. He will, like Adonijah, have a religious side to his activities, and the support of some of the nobles in the land (Dan 11; 2 Thess 2). However, there will be a faithful remnant, who, like Zadok and Nathan, will not be taken in by his false claims.

Verses 11-27

David learns of Adonijah's action

News of the momentous event at Zoheleth, where the new king was hailed by his supporters, must have spread quickly. Nathan the prophet, being an influential man in the kingdom, would, no doubt, have been one of the first to be informed of what had occurred. He was a faithful and true friend of David, even though, on at least two occasions, he brought unwelcome messages; first, when he revealed to him that God would not allow him to build the Temple (2 Sam 7), and second, when he rebuked him over the matter of Uriah (2 Sam 12). Notwithstanding these painful experiences, the friendship between king and prophet remained unbroken, and, indeed, seemed to become more dear as a result of them. Neither had any doubt as to who was to succeed to the throne, but the king's weakness and confinement meant that he was largely in the dark as to the happenings in the kingdom. Nathan would have failed in his duty if he had not told the king and Bathsheba what had transpired.

He handled the matter with great tact, for he told Bathsheba first and directed her to inform David, for, if the scheme of Adonijah succeeded, she and her son Solomon would probably be executed. It was often the case that a new king eliminated any rivals to the throne.

The tactic, that Bathsheba would go to the king with the news and hear his response with Nathan arriving to reinforce the story, was planned to compel the king to act quickly in spite of his weakness to ensure that Solomon, who was divinely chosen, would be given the crown. On the other hand, if Adonijah was reigning with the consent of his father, it would mean that the latter had broken the promise he had earlier made to Bathsheba.

The alarming news must have profoundly shaken and surprised the sick king. He could not have expected that the boy, whom he had never rebuked, would rise up and make himself king.

God always has those who are not deceived by outward show or worldly pomp. On this occasion the prophet in particular was fully aware that the claim of Adonijah was entirely wrong. There have always been those who seek high position who were never intended nor fitted by God for it. They will have support from some, but the discerning, like the prophet, will see through their falsehood and refuse to be identified with them.

Adonijah, if he had succeeded, might well have dealt with Nathan as a traitor, but the Lord overruled and preserved his servant. The fools, who were gulled by the usurper, must have felt ashamed as well as terrified when they discovered their folly.

These verses also draw attention to the reverence shown to the king, not only by his ordinary subjects, but also by those near to him. Bathsheba, although she was his wife, bowed when entering his bed-chamber and knelt before him. Likewise, Nathan, who was in a special sense the chosen link between God and the king, also bowed with his face to the ground.

Both the prophet and Bathsheba addressed the king repeatedly as "My lord", accepting that they were not on the same level as he. In addressing her husband, Bathsheba was like Sarah who spoke of Abraham as "lord" (1 Pet 3.6). However, it appears to have been the custom that when kings were addressed, especially in the presence of others, their full title was given, as, for example, Esther, when speaking to Ahazuerus (Est 5,7 & 9). Whether Abishag witnessed the interviews is not revealed.

In settling the heir to the throne the king had, according to v.20, the final say. The nation left the choice in his hands. The oldest son was not necessarily the one chosen. Jacob, the father of the nation, made Judah, his fourth son, the father of the royal tribe. David himself was the youngest of eight sons.

Bathsheba, having recounted the action of Adonijah and her concern for herself and Solomon, stressed the fact that the final decision as to who would be king rested with him.

Nathan entered and inquired whether Adonijah had the king's sanction for what he had done. Being the prophet of the Lord, and one who enjoyed the confidence of the king, he sought to learn whether or not it was on David's authority that this new king had been appointed. His implication was that it was unusual for the king to keep such a vital matter hidden from him.

Verses 28-40

David makes Solomon king

The fact that Bathsheba had to be recalled implies that she had withdrawn when the prophet entered the bedchamber. Without the slightest hesitation David assured her that her son Solomon would be Israel's next king. The oath he had formerly given her was repeated, so her mind was set at rest. She expressed her appreciation of his promise by wishing him the normal royal benediction, the one often offered to Persian kings, but only here used to a king of Israel: "Let my lord king David live for ever" (See Dan 2.4; 3.9; 5.10; Neh 2.3).

One might well wonder why the young son of one of David's wives should be chosen as king in preference to one of his older half-brothers, especially when the shameful way his mother became united to David is taken into consideration. Is this another case of God choosing "the base things of the world" (1 Cor 1.28)? Solomon was the chosen one of God as well as his father's choice (compare 2 Sam 12.24; Mt 1.6).

To the three great leaders among the people, Zadok the high priest, the prophet Nathan, and Benaiah the army general, was given the task of anointing Solomon and setting him upon his father's throne. The great event was held in the valley of Gihon, possibly because it was a suitable place for the congregation of a large crowd. Benaiah, could not refrain from shouting "Amen!", and from expressing his wish that, with the Lord's help, the son might even surpass his father (v.37). When the nobles had escorted the mule carrying the young prince to Gihon, Zadok the priest took a horn of oil from the tent where the Ark was placed and anointed his head. This oil was the special compound used in the service of the sanctuary. He will again be anointed (1 Chr 29.22), just as was his father, but in the latter's case he was anointed three times, not twice. The tabernacle mentioned here must be the tent that David had pitched at Zion and not the one at Gibeon. The latter was much too far away to be reached at such short notice.

The blast of the trumpet was the signal to the multitude that the great event had occurred, so, with pipes blowing and with the people shouting, "Long live King Solomon" (NIV), the coronation was celebrated. The noise was so great that it sounded as if there had been an earthquake. This response of the people to the choice of Solomon by far eclipsed the celebrations at Zoheleth when Adonijah thought he had secured the throne.

The anointing of a king by God's representative brought him into a special position which demanded respect in the eyes of the God fearing, who viewed them ever afterwards as "the Lord's anointed" (1 Sam 24.6). In a sense it linked them with the sanctuary, from which the oil used was obtained. All of Israel's kings may have been anointed, but it is chiefly recorded in cases where there was some doubt as to who should reign. The kingship of Solomon had the approval of his aged father. This was seen in his sitting on the king's mule. He also had the sanction of the priest and prophet, for they anointed him. Finally, he had the acceptance of the people who shouted and piped.

Verses 41-50
Adonijah learns of Solomon's anointing
There was nothing secret about the great event for the noise of the celebrations was heard as far away as the place where the followers of Adonijah were feasting. It may not be surprising that the guileful Joab was first to sense that something unusual had taken place in the city. Jonathan the son of Abiathar arrived and his terse statement, "Verily our lord king David hath made Solomon king", introduced the story of the happenings of that memorable day, and when it was finished all the sandcastles Adonijah and his followers had built had tumbled to the ground.

Clearly Jonathan was in favour in both circles. He was close enough to Solomon to know all that had transpired in Jerusalem and he could, on the same day, find a welcome in the presence of Adonijah. It would seem that he cared not which man sat on the throne. Being the son of Abiathar meant that he was tempted to take sides with his father, but he was not a guest at the feast of Adonijah.

His account of the events of Solomon's anointing was given in great detail and showed that he was a spectator of all that had happened.

The sharpest arrow in his quiver was the statement that "Solomon sitteth on the throne of the kingdom" (v.46).

The guests at the great banquet scattered in panic and were so alarmed that they left their leader to his fate, and he, fearing for his life, ran to the altar and held it by its horns. It is difficult to decide which altar is intended. There was one at the tent in Zion and one at the Tabernacle at Gibeon. Apparently it was believed that mercy could be found at the altar by all who were in danger (Ex 21.13, 14). In 2.28 Joab likewise resorted to it in order to save his life, but was slain in spite of his action. Solomon, on this occasion, allowed the usurper to live and return to his own home, but not until he had bowed the knee in his (Solomon's) presence. The door was also left open for Adonijah to be slain should wickedness be found in him in the future. Sadly the time came when this did occur.

In this account of the two sons of David there is a sharp contrast. All the activity and effort to become king in the case of Adonijah were exclusively his own. Even though the priest was there and he did ask to be anointed by him, he himself proclaimed, "I will be king" (v.5).

How different was Solomon, for in the account of his ascension he is entirely passive. His mother acts, the prophet acts, and David speaks, but not a word is recorded about his own part in the momentous event. He sat on the mule and, later, on the throne, with the assurance in his mind that his exaltation was not due to his own achievements. The words spoken of Christ; "God also hath highly exalted Him" (Phil 2.9), could be used of Solomon. On the other hand, Adonijah will for ever be remembered as an example of the words of Christ;, "For whosoever exalteth himself shall be abased" (Lk 14.11).

This chapter cannot be read without seeing in it shadows of things to come. As has already been noted, Adonijah illustrates the coming Antichrist, and Solomon the true King. As surely as Solomon was enthroned, so surely will God's anointed sit on His throne (Ps 72). The great celebrations at the coronation of Solomon were but a shadow of the rejoicing by the faithful when God will set His King on His holy hill of Zion (Ps 2.6). Solomon riding on the king's mule as he is led to the place of his enthronement is a reminder of the One who is Faithful and True and who will ride on His white horse. His head will be crowned with diadems, and on Him will be written the words, "King of kings, and Lord of lords" (Rev 19.11-16).

Notes

1. "Now" is a connective participle which is found at the beginning of several OT books, even when the connection is not apparent. However, in the historical books, it indicates that the story is advancing from the one preceding.

The word "clothes" (BEGED - 899) though normally used for garments may be used here for "bed-clothes".

2. The word "cherish" (SAKAN - 5532) used here and in v.4 is sometimes translated "profitable". It implies that Abishag took care of the king. She worked as his nurse (v.15) as well as fulfilling her chief responsibility, which was that of warming his body.

8. It has been suggested that Shimei and Rei are the same as the older brothers of David called Shimma and Raddai in 1 Chronicles 2.13-14. If so, they were very old, for David was the youngest in his family.

33. The Gihon spring was situated in the valley south of the Temple area below Jerusalem.

CHAPTER 2, Verses 1-9
David's charge to Solomon

In Scripture, from the days of Jacob, the last words of dying fathers have been cherished with deep respect. This charge to Solomon can be compared to that given by dying Jacob to Joseph and later to all his sons (Gen 48 and 49). Earlier, mention has been made of David's poor health (1.1); either he had revived sufficiently to give the charge to the people recorded in 1 Chronicles 28-29, or this may have taken place on an earlier occasion. However, in these verses he directly charges the young king and puts upon his shoulders some heavy burdens. Links with Joshua are evident. "I go the way of all the earth", is reminiscent of Joshua 23.14. Both the death of Moses and the death of David were accompanied with a charge to their successors. Joshua and Solomon were each pressed to be courageous in keeping the word of God. Joshua was leading the people into Canaan, which thing Moses was not allowed to do. Solomon was to build the Temple, which thing David was not allowed to do. Both were promised prosperity in their respective responsibilities. Both men had a special revelation from the Lord (Josh 5.13-15; 1 Kings 3.5-15).

Like not a few of those in touch with God, the aged king knew that his end was at hand. The lot of all mankind was about to be his, so it was fitting that he should pour into the ear of his son a parting message.

It is significant that one matter is   given the first place and singled out as of supreme importance - the keeping of the word of God. Solomon's prosperity would depend upon his walking in the path of whole-hearted obedience. Like Joshua, he would need courage to do this, so he must show (himself) a man. Similar injunctions were given to the Philistines (1 Sam 4.9) and the Corinthians (1 Cor 16.13).

Four words are used here to describe the Law: - "statutes", "commandments", "judgments" and "testimonies". The distinction between these terms is not easy to define, but "statutes" may imply that which is decreed or appointed; "commandments" suggests that which is set up or established; "judgments" tells of that which is upright or just; and "testimonies" denotes that which is repeatedly witnessed. This grand rulebook is to be the guide of the young king. Clearly David had obeyed the injunction to kings given by Moses in Deuteronomy 17.18-19, where they are commanded to copy out the Law and read it all the days of their lives. The secret of establishing an unbroken dynasty was for each successive king to walk before the Lord in obedience to His word.

In the original promise to David that his throne should be established forever (2 Sam 7.16) there was no stipulation that this would depend upon future kings being obedient to the word of the Lord. Here this is specified as a vital necessity, and later history proved the validity of this statement. There did come a time when successive descendants of David turned away from God and His word, with the result that eventually there was not one of them reigning in Israel, nor was there a throne upon which any of them could sit. However, the promise made to David in 2 Samuel has not been broken, for Christ his Son will be King forever. The opening words of the NT, "The book of the generation of Jesus Christ, the son of David", and the name written on His thigh, "King of kings, and Lord of lords" (Rev 19.16) show clearly that David will always have an heir on the throne. God's people can rejoice in the fact that human failure can never thwart His purpose.

The practical lesson of this paragraph is obvious. Those who desire prosperity in God's spiritual kingdom must understand that this comes through simple, but true, obedience to the Word of God. David's charge to Solomon brings to mind the charge Paul gave to Timothy his son in the faith. In each of the closing three chapters of 2 Timothy, which was his last letter, there is a reference to the Word of God. If Timothy was to prosper and fulfil the purpose of his service, he too, like Joshua, and Solomon, must give heed to the Holy Scriptures. In this present age, as in former times, the tendency to depart from the teaching of the Word of God is all too common and the sad consequence of this is evident in a lack of power. It is particularly important that those who have the burden of rule in assembly life be most careful that they walk in the way of truth.

The new phase of the kingdom over which Solomon was to reign must be established in righteousness. Thus every matter in it which demanded God's judgment must be dealt with in a fair and just way. David was very conscious that certain matters had been passed over during his own reign that he was unable to deal with because of personal weaknesses, and because of promises he had made. One of these was the case of Joab, his nephew, who had committed murder on at least two occasions, yet was not executed for his crimes. He had slain two captains, perhaps out of jealousy, and stained his girdle, cloak, and sandals with innocent blood. Had he done this in warfare, he would have been guiltless, but doing it by craft and subtlety left him without excuse. He carried out these acts in a time of peace and David felt as if they had been done against him. If the land was to be cleared of innocent blood, he must be executed.

The memory of the famine which resulted because of Saul's slaughter of the innocent Gibeonites may have been fresh in David's mind, so, to avoid a repeat of some such disaster, he directed that the righteous demands of God be met. The young king had to act with the wisdom David recognised was there (vv.6 and 9), and not shirk his responsibility in this matter.

The reign of David can be compared to this present period of grace. During it, much seems to be passed over without the judgment of God being executed. Not that His longsuffering means that He will not in His own time punish all unrighteousness. All men will be held accountable for their sins, but in the coming kingdom period there will be no delay in judgment being executed. The reign of Christ will be in righteousness and He will remove from His kingdom all that is unjust, and deal with all wrongdoers according to their desserts.

Atrocious deeds are perpetrated daily across the world. Men ask in astonishment, "Why does God allow such happenings, and apparently do nothing about them?" No such problem will arise in the Millennium, for, morning by morning, the King will bring His judgment to light (Zeph 3.5).

Sandwiched between two examples of evil men, Joab and Shimei, who were ripe for judgment, is the contrast in Barzillai. He is remembered by the dying king as the outstanding example of one who showed him kindness in a dark and needy time (2 Sam 17.27-29). The old man may have been dead at this time, for when he brought his bountiful gifts to David he was an octogenarian. The sons he left behind are to be rewarded for their father's thoughtfulness. It is left to Solomon to make sure that these had a place at his table, so that they might never be in want. In 2 Samuel 19 mention is made of only one of Barzillai's sons, Chimham, who returned with David, but others may have followed later. Apparently he established an inn at Bethlehem, where some stayed who were seeking to escape from the Chaldeans (Jer 41.17).

When Barzillai was gathering together the much-needed supplies for David in the day of his rejection he had no thought of the far-reaching consequences of his kindness. Had he brought the same provisions to David in the palace they would probably have been accepted, but their value would have been little compared with when they were brought to Jordan and met the deep need of the king and his followers. It is good for saints to remember that they are now living in the time of the rejected King. Though He is not in any personal need, yet some of His followers, who are suffering reproach because of their faithfulness to Him, can be shown kindness and sympathy, all of which will be rewarded in the day of His kingdom. He said, "Inasmuch as ye have done it unto one of the least of these my brethren, ye have done it unto me" (Mt 25.40). The need in the day of His rejection is not always material things, but it can be of a spiritual character. In such cases it is good "to sustain with words him that is weary" (Is 50.4 RV). Just as surely as there was reward in Solomon's glorious kingdom for the faithfulness of those who helped in a dark day, so too, in the kingdom of Christ there will be a public display of honour upon the heads of all those who have shared in His reproach.

Although David was physically very weak at this time and near the point of death, it is evident that his memory was not impaired. The passing of years had not erased from it the deeds of the past. There was another guilty man who must be dealt with by Solomon, Shimei the Benjamite. He had grievously cursed David, cast stones at him, and called him a worthless bloody man. Had Abishai been given his way, the railer would have been beheaded on the spot. But it was not then the time for David to fight for his rights, but rather to submit to the dealings of God, whom he acknowledged as the One who allowed the trial to come upon him. Later Shimei repented and attempted to be reconciled to him by confessing his wrongdoings. David accepted his apology and swore to him that his life was secure. So long as David lived he would not be slain (2 Sam 19.16-23). Cursing "the Lord's anointed" was more than cursing an ordinary person. It was a crime against the Lord whom he represented. Solomon was charged to rid the land of this criminal by putting him to death, which he did, but not without some delay. Shimei may have imagined that this foul episode was forgotten and that his dark past was buried in the grave with David, but in this he was mistaken. Men may forget their sins, but God "requireth that which is past". Though sentence against an evil work is not executed speedily it does not mean that it will not be executed later - "Whatsoever a man soweth, that shall he also reap" (Gal 6.7).

Verses 10,11
The death of David

At length the aged king died and his spirit joined the faithful in their blessed abode. It was a solemn day in Israel, for the man who began as a shepherd had not only reached great heights himself, but had turned the fortunes of the nation from humiliation to glory. Very few have done so much in a lifetime as he did. He had distinguished himself on the battlefield as a soldier. As a poet he had given his people their songbook. As a worshipper of the true God he had erected a sanctuary in Zion where divine order was established, and, though not allowed to build the Temple, he had made extensive preparation for it. His kingship is constantly referred to in later history as the standard example for succeeding kings to follow.

For seven years the scope of his kingdom was limited, but eventually the entire nation owned him as its king. He reigned forty years in all.

It does seem strange that despite all the great features of his reign there is no mention of mourning for David. Not even in the parallel passage in 1 Chronicles 29 is there a hint that the nation went into mourning for the great king.

His sepulchre may have been hewn out of the rocks of Zion, or one of the caves so common in that area could have been modified for the purpose. Apparently, it afterwards became the burying place for all loyal kings. However, there was one person buried in this honoured place who was not a king. He was Jehoiada the high priest, a man who had used his influence to turn the nation back to the right ways of the Lord (2 Chr 24.16).

Even down to the days of the apostles, David's tomb could be identified (Acts 2.29). It must have been treated with respect during the thousand years that intervened.

Notes

4 The word "fail" (KARAT - 3772) literally means "be cut off". See, for example, Psalm 37.9, where David says that "evildoers shall be cut off", Genesis 9.11, and Jeremiah 33.17 RV margin).

6 and 9 The references to "hoar head" suggest that both Joab and Shimei were older men at this time.

8 "Cursed me with a grievous curse"; compare Balaam (Deut 23.4,5)

CHAPTER 2.12 - 5.18

THE EARLY YEARS OF SOLOMON'S REIGN

CHAPTER 2, Verses 12-21
Adonijah asks for Abishag

Immediately after the statement that Solomon sat on the throne of David and that he was established in his kingdom, the historian proceeds to show how Adonijah's plot to disturb his rule was defeated. The young king had scarcely settled into his new position when he was confronted with an unexpected problem. To western minds the chief concern in the story might appear to be the sin of incest in the attempt of Adonijah to marry his stepmother. But this did not figure greatly in the thinking either of Adonijah or his brother Solomon. Strictly speaking she was neither David's wife nor concubine for it is stated that "the king knew her not" (1.4). Nevertheless, her close relationship with him gave her a special status. That she was one of the fairest young women in all Israel seems clear from the story, but again this was not the reason for her being sought as a wife by Adonijah.

One of the customs at that time among the heathen nations around was also a practice in Israel. It was deemed that whoever took possession of the throne had the right to claim the wives of its previous occupant. David was given the wives of Saul (2 Sam 12.8). Absalom took over the harem of his father and lay with the women in the tent, which was erected on the advice of Ahithophel, so that he might give a public display before all that he had displaced David as king (2 Sam 16.21,22).

It had come home to Adonijah that he had lost the kingdom. But no doubt he thought that if he could obtain Abishag as a wife he would at least have some opportunity to establish a link with the throne. He could claim that the last woman to lie in David's bosom was now his wife.

After all that is recorded of Bathsheba in ch.1 it must have been common knowledge that she had a great influence over her son Solomon. Adonijah knew that if he could obtain her help there was the possibility that his plan would succeed. Obviously there would not have been much contact between the two, more especially after all that had occurred at En-rogel. Nevertheless, he was bold enough to venture into her presence and ask her to use her influence to persuade her son to give him Abishag to wife. In his interview he still claimed that he was the rightful heir to the throne, and what is more, that all Israel endorsed his kingship. However, he confessed that Solomon was the Lord's choice, something he must have known even before he attempted to take the kingdom. The implication of his words is that, but for the Lord having His way, he would be reigning instead of her son. By telling her that her request would not be turned down by Solomon, he was flattering her regarding her influence with the king.

In response to Adonijah's plea she fulfilled her promise and had an interview with the king. She was received with dignity, and given a throne at his right side. In a sense he owed his position to her intervention, for she was the first to acquaint David of the usurpation of Adonijah, but apart from this she was highly regarded by her young son. He was fully aware that she had some special mission in mind when she asked for this interview, so he inquired what was upon her heart. In making the matter known she desired "one small petition", and so made the request, although a serious one, seem as if it were insignificant. She also sought an affirmative answer before she asked the question, and this she was assured would be granted.

Verses 22-25
Solomon's anger at Adonijah's request

In all probability Bathsheba did not apprehend the subtlety of Adonijah's scheme. Her son was not so naive, for he grasped immediately the import of the request. To him it was a crafty attempt to destabilize the kingdom, and to give the impression throughout the land that Adonijah had a claim to, and had already a share of, the throne. Immediately, he linked in his thoughts the two famous men who had helped the usurper, Abiathar the priest and Joab the captain of the army. He may have been suspicious that they too were involved in this scheme; indeed, some have thought that the priest and captain had suggested the idea to Adonijah as compensation for losing the crown and providing an opportunity to recover it. Without delay he swore that he would rid the kingdom of such an enemy. Benaiah was dispatched to execute Adonijah and dispose of a potential troublemaker. Thus another of David's sons filled an early grave, as did Amnon and Absalom before him. However, in this case David was not called upon to endure the sorrow he had borne when he heard of the earlier deaths. Three of the six sons born to him in Hebron were no credit to their father, and of the other three we are told nothing.

Verses 26,27
Abiathar is sent to Anathoth
Adonijah's plot revived in Solomon's mind the part played by Abiathar in associating with the rebel in his bid for the throne. As already suggested, asking for Abishag may well have been sanctioned by the priest. If this was so there was every reason why, for the security of the kingdom, he was dispatched to where he would have little or no influence. Had he not been closely associated with David and with the Ark, he too would have been executed at this time. His former service saved his life. In the providence of God, the blunder he made in following Adonijah was the basis for his dismissal from the priesthood, so fulfilling the words of 1 Samuel 2.31. He was the last of the descendants of Ithamar, and of the house of Eli, to hold high office. His position was filled by Zadok, a descendant of Eleazar an older son of Aaron.

It is interesting to note that in the future, prior to the establishing of the Millennial kingdom, the sons of Zadok will have proved more faithful than their brethren. They will be given, as a reward, the great privilege of serving in the inner sanctuary of the Temple (Ezek 44.15).

Verses 28-35
Joab is executed
The news of Solomon's treatment of Adonijah and Abiathar reached the ears of Joab and struck terror to his heart. Well did he know that he was next on the list for judgment. Conscience told him that he was wrong in supporting Adonijah, but perhaps he had forgotten his earlier crimes, and knew nothing of the charge David had given to Solomon concerning him. Many years had passed since he slew Abner, not so many since he slew Amasa, yet these killings, coupled with his more recent conspiracy with Adonijah, justly demanded that he should be put to death.

Adonijah, when he feared death by Solomon, fled to the altar and found mercy, so Joab no doubt imagined that, if he reached the altar, he too would be spared. Alas, he was mistaken. Benaiah, who was commissioned to slay him, was reluctant to do so at the altar. Perhaps he thought that in so doing he would in some way defile it. Although the king had commanded Joab to come forth, yet he would not leave, but said he would die at the side of the altar. On the instructions of Solomon he was executed there, so in a sense his blood was mingled with that of the sacrifices. If the altar referred to here was the one at Gibeon, he died near the spot where he slew Amasa, for it was at the great stone which was at Gibeon that the crime was committed (2 Sam 20.8-10).

Joab was a nephew of David, had accompanied him during almost all of his campaigns and had distinguished himself in the taking of the citadel of Jerusalem, but, throughout his lifetime, none of David's spiritual qualities were seen in him. Immediately after his execution he was removed from the Tabernacle and buried in his own house in the wilderness.

In these actions the leading thought is the establishing of Solomon's kingdom by removing from it all who deserved God's judgment because of their evil deeds. It would seem that God tolerated David's forbearance and allowed for his special circumstances, so that in his lifetime certain men were spared, who ought to have died.

Verses 36-46
Shimei is executed

There remained in Solomon's kingdom one more potential troublemaker, Shimei, who, though apparently not involved in the conspiracy of Adonijah, was very opposed to David at the time of Absalom's rebellion. He later came to David with 1000 servants and apologised for what he had said and done (2 Sam 19.16ff). Otherwise he would never have been spared to see Solomon on the throne. He was the last relation of King Saul to retain a measure of influence in Israel. He was not a man who could be trusted. It was in order to guarantee that Shimei would not use his influence to foment trouble that Solomon summoned him to his court and ordered him to build for himself a house in Jerusalem. He had to live the rest of his life within the confines of the city and so was put under "city-arrest". This meant that he would never again live among his own people and that all his movements could be carefully watched by those faithful to the king.

At the end of three years, when the test came, the fickleness of Shimei was shown. When two of his servants ran off to Achish of Gath, he was thoughtless enough to saddle his ass and follow after them. He apparently forgot the promise he had made to Solomon and may have imagined that the agreement was a mere formality. The servants probably knew that he was restricted in his movements and so they assumed that once they escaped they were free for ever. He recovered his servants, but at the expense of his life.

His kinsman, King Saul, failed to obey the charge given to him by Samuel, and, because of his disobedience, was told by the prophet that his kingdom would not continue (1 Sam 13.13 - 14). Similarly Shimei had acted contrary to his promise and had to pay the price for his disobedience. Before his execution he was told plainly the justness of it and reminded of earlier evil of which he was guilty when he railed on David and cast stones at him. Again Benaiah was ordered to carry out the sentence.

A look back over these cases of potentially dangerous men makes clear that in the death of Adonijah an end was put to any rivalry in the royal household. In the banishment of Abiathar his support for any treason was nullified. In the execution of Joab, the possiblity of military rebellion was reduced, and in the destruction of Shimei the last of the influential men of the house of Saul was removed. With this purging over it is no surprise to read, "And the kingdom was established in the hand of Solomon" (v.46).

In these executions there is a picture of the severe judgments that will mark the setting up of the future kingdom of Christ. While the Millennium will be a wonderful period of peace and plenty, its opening will be a time of great wrath. All who have taken sides with the Beast and with his associate, the Antichrist, will be slain, and all the living from every nation will be summoned to the throne of judgment where they will be sentenced according to their works (Mt 25.31-46). "The Son of man shall send forth His angels, and they shall gather out of His kingdom all things that offend, and them which do iniquity" (Mt 13.41).

Much that will seem to have been passed over during the lTribulation period, especially crime against the faithful remnant, will then be exposed and receive its due reward.

In the previous paragraph two prophetic periods have been referred to - the "Great Tribulation" and the "Millennium". The former refers to the period of three and one half years, or forty-two months, which will begin when the covenant between the Beast (the head of the revived Roman Empire) and the nation of Israel is broken (Dan 9.27). This treacherous breach of promise will bring about the "time of Jacob's trouble" (Jer 30.7), and will also commence a period of terrible judgment upon all mankind. It will also be marked by the persecution of those faithful to God. At its close the Lord will come to the mount of Olives (Zech 14.4), and, after destroying all His enemies, will proceed to set up His kingdom. This kingdom on earth will last in this particular form for one thousand years, or a Millennium. During these years Satan will be bound, and righteousness will rule throughout the world (Rev 20.2; Heb 1.8).

Notes

19 "Seat" (KISSE - 3678) is the same as the word throne

24 "A house" (BAYIT - 1004) is a posterity (a continuing family) that will retain the kingdom

34 "In his own house" does not mean that his grave was in his private dwelling, but that it was in the area where he lived.

CHAPTER 3, Verses 1-3
Solomon's wife, and worship

After stating that the kingdom was established, having been delivered from its potential internal enemies, the writer turns his attention to Solomon's personal and private life. First, he describes the new relationship between the king and Pharaoh and his subsequent marriage to the daughter of the latter.

Not since Israel left Egypt had there been a friendly relationship between the two nations, but now all is changed. Israel had become, through the achievements of David, a mighty power. There was mutual profit in the arrangement mentioned here for it meant that neither would fear attack by the other. Already, in David's day, a good relationship existed between Israel and Hiram king of Tyre, so there was no likelihood of trouble arising from the North and West. This confederacy with Pharaoh meant that the South was also secure.

The East then was the only other direction from which an attack might be made, but before Solomon was king he had already married Naamah an Ammonitess, whose land lay on the eastern side of Caanan. To her his only son, Rehoboam, was born (14.21). Therefore this quarter also presented no threat. If he was to enjoy a peaceful reign, and he did, it was vital that he and the surrounding nations were living in harmony.

There has been a great deal of speculation as to which Pharaoh is referred to in v.1. It is generally agreed that he was not of the same dynasty as Shishak who invaded Israel some forty years later (14.25,26). The most probable identification is with Siamun of the late twenty-first dynasty, who is known to have invaded Philistia and may at that point have captured Gezer (see 9.16). If, as is thought by many, Egypt had become weak at this time, joining with Israel under such a king as Solomon would have been an advantage well worth giving a daughter to secure.

It is strange that in all the references to Solomon's wives there is no account of him having married one of his own people. Among his 700 wives and 300 concubines some Israelite women would almost certainly be included, but they are not specifically mentioned. This daughter of Pharaoh is the first reference to his choice of a partner. Although she was not the mother of an heir to the throne, she seemed to be given preference over all his other women. She may have become a proselyte since there is no record of any form of Egyptian idolatry being introduced by her. Of the idols mentioned in ch.11, there is no reference to any from Egypt, and, indeed, it was toward the end of his life that he turned to idolatry (11.4). It was not necessarily unlawful for an Israelite to marry an Egyptian – Joseph had an Egyptian wife. However in Solomon's case it was the beginning of his spiritual downfall.

At this early time of his life, when he was living in his first love for the Lord, he may have been able to convert this stranger to the true faith. Later, when he loved many strange women, (11.1), they turned him from the Lord and led him into contact with idolatry.

Probably because of her dignified position as a princess in the house of Pharaoh, Solomon felt it his duty to accommodate her in a suitable palace. This he did later (2 Chr. 8.11), but she was, for the time being, obliged to dwell in the city of David, i.e. Jerusalem. After he had built his own palace he brought her up to her own quarters, which were situated behind his Hall of Judgment.

It has been suggested that in the marriage of Solomon to the Egyptian bride there is a picture of Christ and the Church. It has also been thought that the bride in the Song of Songs was none other than Pharaoh's daughter. However, the stress in the history of Solomon is not on the favour he showed to his Gentile brides, but rather on the evil influence they had on him. That the Gentiles will share the kingdom with Christ is beyond question, but whether or not this is typified in Pharaoh's daughter is less clear.

There are practical lessons to be learned from these verses. One is that affinity with Egypt, which is a type of the world, brings bitter disappointment, for though it did for a time preserve good relations between the two nations, Egypt was never a friend of Israel. Later, when Solomon's son had reigned only five years, Shishak king of Egypt came to Jerusalem and stripped the Temple of much of its wealth and so was the first to destroy what Solomon had built up (14.25-26).

Again, though it may have been lawful for Solomon to marry Pharaoh's daughter, it reveals a weakness in his character, which, instead of curbing, he developed. This weakness was shown in his taking so many foreign wives. Initially these alliances were perhaps mainly for political ends but later seem simply to have reflected failure by Solomon to exercise self-control.

Every believer has some natural failing, which can be mastered if detected in youth and if grace from God is sought to overcome it. But if it is allowed to develop it will dominate and may well ruin their testimony.

This policy of making treaties with surrounding nations and confirming them through marriage brought idolatry into Israel. At the same time it reduced dependence on the Lord.

With all this political and private activity there was still one great lack in the land. No fixed centre of worship had been established at that time. The Tabernacle was at Gibeon, but the Ark (symbol of the Lord's presence) had been removed from it. David had found it at Kirjathjearim and brought it into the tent he had erected in Zion (2 Sam 6).

Thus there were two centres with neither of them recognized as the exclusive place where sacrifices should be offered. This confusion led to the setting up of many high places throughout the land. Care should be taken to distinguish these from the idolatrous high places so often mentioned in this book. Once the Temple was erected all this confusion ended, for the Lord stamped that building with His presence through the cloud of glory that filled it. In Exodus 20.24 there is given the authority for offering in any place in the land. An altar of earth or of unhewn stone could be built and sacrifices acceptable to God offered on them. The reason for siting these on high places may have been that such elevated parts were thought to be nearer heaven and so closer to God who dwelt there. Even the site divinely chosen for the Temple was the hill of Zion.

The brief reference to Solomon's devotion to the Lord at this time, is worthy of note: "Solomon loved the Lord, walking in the statutes of David". However, there was this difference between him and his father, in that he frequented high places whereas his father never went to such centres, not even to the most famous of these at Gibeon. Nor, when David was exercised to bring back the Ark, did it enter his mind to return it to the Tabernacle where it originally belonged. Psalm 78.67,68 records that God "refused the tabernacle of Joseph...but chose the tribe of Judah, the mount Zion which he loved". God bore patiently with the people at this time of confusion and apparently did not blame them for having so many places of worship.

Verses 4-15
Solomon asks the Lord for wisdom
One of the most outstanding times in the early life of king Solomon was this occasion when he went, along with the leaders of the congregation (2 Chr 1.3), to Gibeon. He and they offered to the Lord a thousand sacrifices on the brazen altar that had been with the Tabernacle from the days of Moses. This must have been an abnormally busy time for the priests. It may have taken longer than one day to burn all the offerings.

The Scriptures do not reveal why or when the Tabernacle made by Moses was transferred from Shiloh in the territory of Ephraim to Gibeon in the territory of Benjamin, a place twenty miles nearer Jerusalem. It remained there until dismantled and brought to the Temple (8.4) where it was probably stored.

During the visit, Solomon had a revelation of the Lord in a dream. This form of divine communication was granted to Jacob, Joseph, and Gideon, and is referred to by Elihu: "For God speaketh once, yea twice...in a dream, in a vision of the night" (Job 33.14,15). He had freely offered to the Lord, and in his dream he was told by the Lord to ask what he desired and it would be granted to him. His request was for a wise heart to rule the nation, and this request pleased the Lord. Only a wise man would ask for this favour. The virtue of this request lay in the fact that it was for the good of others rather than for his own glory. He had sufficient understanding to know that ruling so many people was no light matter and that he was inexperienced, even as a "little child", and unfitted for the great responsibility involved.

This feeling of helplessness marks most of those who are charged with the burden of leadership. Moses, Joshua, Gideon, and even the Apostles all felt their weakness.

Solomon was not over-estimating the difficulty confronting him, for the thousands of Israel were not likely to be free from disputes, nor were they exempt from the attacks of Satan. He would need divine help in his conduct as well as his understanding for he would be under scrutiny by the people. Thus he sought help so as to "know "how to go out [and] come in" (v.7).

That the Lord had shown favour to David, not only in blessing him while alive, but also in giving him a son to sit on his throne, he freely acknowledged. The memory of the good example set him by the king remained vividly before his mind, and shows that the closing years of David's life were perhaps the best. Solomon was possibly unaware of some of the earlier breakdowns that blotted the otherwise good life of the one whose shoes he had to fill. The same Lord who had upheld his father David in the past could be trusted now to meet his need and prove to him that He was all that He claimed to be.

The response of Solomon to the Lord's offer was very acceptable to Him. So much so, that not only was he promised what he asked, but he was also given all the other things he might have requested. Riches, honour, length of days, death of enemies and supremacy among the kings of earth were all to be his. However, the promise of long life was conditional on him walking in the ways of the Lord as did his father, David.

When the dream was over and he awoke, he immediately returned to Jerusalem where he again offered sacrifices and peace offerings. No doubt he felt the importance of attending the altar erected by his father. He possibly also had some doubts in his mind as to whether it was appropriate for him to go to Gibeon, the place which the Lord had forsaken, and which, as already pointed out, his father never visited.

It is surprising that the Lord should manifest Himself to the young king at Gibeon since the Ark was no longer there. Apparently the ritual carried on as if all was normal, so the brazen altar was still in use and the sacrifices continued. However, instead of the Tabernacle being the only centre of worship, Gibeon was classified as "the great high place" (v.4), and thus was just one amongst the many others.

A good number of years had passed since the Lord appeared to Samuel by night at Shiloh. Even then, conditions were exceedingly bad because of the evil doings of Eli's sons. It is well that the failings of men do not block the streams of blessing from the Lord, for if they did, their flow would seldom be enjoyed.

There are occasions when God's course of action perplexes His people. They cannot understand why some places, where His ways seem to be neglected or ignored, are blessed, and other places, where there is great respect for His Word, seem to be left barren and fruitless. It should never be forgotten that none deserve His favour and that every blessing and benefit received is due to sovereign grace. He is free to dispense His blessings according to His sovereign will.

Verses 16-28
Proof of Solomon's wisdom

When the Lord bestows a gift or special endowment on any of His servants, He always brings about circumstances for it to be used. How long it was after the revelation and promise given at Gibeon until this case of the two harlots is not known, but it could not have been very long, for not until this time did the fame of Solomon's wisdom begin to spread abroad. Those God uses to accomplish His purpose are often surprising. Who would imagine that two evil women would be the first cases coming to Solomon for judgment? That two immoral women lived together no doubt suited their illicit lifestyle but was not without its difficulties. How was it to be determined to whom the living child belonged? The problem was difficult for there was no third party in the house to bear witness to what had happened; it was one person's word against another. The two women appeared before Solomon. The false claimant agreed that the little one be cut into two, but the real mother offered to let the other woman have it. The child was then returned to its rightful owner and the other woman was left a manifest thief and liar. The wisdom of Solomon is seen in his having an understanding of a mother's love for her own son.

It is little wonder that news of this wise verdict, as it quickly spread throughout Israel, convinced the nation that the new king was indeed endowed by the Lord with unusual wisdom.

Wisdom is surely needed in judging differences between individuals, especially when there is no substantiating evidence. Many problems have to be left unresolved because there are not two or three witnesses. Yet where there is wisdom even such cases may find a true verdict.

The false can be detected, even though they cannot be dealt with because of lack of evidence.

The "sword" here has been connected with the Word of God, and it has been suggested that the statement in Hebrews 4.12 regarding the Word of God being "sharper than any twoedged sword" with power of "dividing asunder" is a reference back to this passage.

Division and death in this incident were closely tied together. It is true that where division comes amongst the saints spiritual deadness often ensues. Those who have a real love for their fellow believers will not want to see them divided. There were the Judaizers in the Galatian assemblies who wanted to claim the saints as their own property, and to cut them off from Paul and others who had begotten them through the Gospel. He, like the true mother, yearned over them, and wished that those who troubled them might be cut off (Gal 4.19; 5.12).

Notes

1 The word "affinity" (CHATAN - 2859) means "to contract affinity by marriage" (See Deut 7.3; 1 Sam 18.21; 2 Chr 18.1).

9 An "understanding heart" is a heart that listens to God's voice and responds to it. This enabled Solomon to "discern" or "hear". Both words are also in v.11, but the word here translated "understanding" (SHAMA - 8085), is there translated "discern", and the word here translated "discern" is there translated "understanding".

26 In the OT the strongest feelings are associated with the lower inwards, especially the womb, here translated "bowels" (RACHAMIM - 7356), which were viewed as their seat. When tender mercy or compassion was expressed this figurative language was adopted. Now these are spoken of as arising from the heart, e.g. "Did not our heart burn within us...?" (Lk 24.32), though originally the expression involved both heart and mind in the sense in which they are now used.

The word "yearn" (KAMAR - 3648) "to shrivel up as with heat", occurs only here and in Gen 43.30, Lam 5.10 (translated "black") and Hos 11.8 (translated "kindled").

CHAPTER 4, Verses 1-6

The officials in Solomon's kingdom

Already the wisdom of Solomon has been described in a variety of circumstances, but now it is shown in his administrative arrangements for Israel. With such a large population and with so many problems likely to arise amongst them, it was vitally important that the kingdom should be administered by trustworthy men whose capability to assist the king would be beyond question. It was evidence of Solomon's wisdom that he delegated responsibility to others and thus avoided the mistake of other rulers who tried to do the impossible, namely, deal personally with every matter that demanded attention. It speaks well for Israel that at this time there were competent men, who had the confidence of the king and of the people, and who could be left in charge of the various affairs of state. Without such help the kingdom would have sunk into confusion. Even Moses, who in many ways had to act as though he was a king in the wilderness, was instructed to appoint seventy elders to share with him the burden of judging the people (Num 11). Wisdom was needed, not only to appoint men to specific responsibilities but to appoint those who were competent to undertake the duties.

There is always the temptation, whether in the business world or in the assembly, for those with outstanding ability to confine all responsibility to themselves. They often over-estimate their own qualities and underestimate the virtues of others. Learning to detect and to give opportunity to latent and undeveloped talent in younger men is not easy but is important.

God's kingdom, like Solomon's kingdom, has those whom He qualifies to lead, and there is the majority that ought to be content with the God-given leadership. Even in the coming kingdom of Christ, which will be ruled with perfection, there will be delegated authority. This the Lord Himself made clear in the parable of the pounds (Lk 19.12-27).

After this look at the private and personal life of Solomon together with a sample illustration of his ability to judge, it is fitting that the historian draws attention to his court and to the wisdom shown in the way it was administered. Unlike his father, who for seven years in Hebron had only a limited kingdom, and unlike some of his descendants, who were kings of Judah only, he reigned over all Israel. Perhaps this opening statement of the chapter is made to show the need for the officers mentioned. Such an expanse of country and people required these men to have access to the king and to act as a channel of communication to him, especially when serious matters, needing royal decisions, arose. The larger the territory the greater the need for representatives to be appointed.

A careful reading of the two lists of names in this and the following paragraph makes clear that they refer to the middle of Solomon's reign. The fact that two of his daughters are said to be married to two officers (vv. 11,15) indicates that the period in question is not during his youth.

The first officer named is Azariah the son of Zadok. Like the following officials he is a "prince" or "captain" and so had authority, but whether he was a prime minister or a (high) priest cannot be easily determined. The words, "the priest" (KOHEN – 3548), have been understood in two different ways. One view is that the title here refers to the religious office of priest and is the same as in v.4 where we read of Zadok and Abiathar the priests. In this view Azariah was appointed to the priesthood to be a successor to these two high priests, especially as Abiathar was banished to Anathoth and thus was no longer functioning in Zion. This may indicate that these references are to times later than the early days of Solomon's reign. However, the Hebrew word for "priests" is used of David's sons in 2 Samuel 8.18 where it is translated "chief rulers". Similarly it is used of Zabud in this chapter (v. 5), where it is translated "principal officer" and it is generally agreed that in these latter cases the reference is to secular authority.

If Azariah was priest in the religious sense, he must have been named priest here in anticipation. In the view of some the definite article before "priest" seems to give support to the idea that he was "high priest". There were already two high priests (v.4), so if he was already functioning as high priest, this would mean that three men held that position. In light of this abnormality, the second view is that the reference here is to a secular position as the "prime minister". The two views are not wholly incompatible with one another since high priests had considerable authority not only in the religious sphere but also in secular matters. Indeed Jehoiada, a high priest, had such influence that, when he died, he was buried among the kings (2 Chr 24.16). The fact of Azariah being the first person named in this list of officials indicates the importance of his position, and marks him out as having high authority.

The next officials to be named are Elihoreph and Ahiah whose duty was that of "scribes". Their work included writing letters on behalf of the king to his own people and to foreign nations. They were his private secretaries. That two were needed to do this work implies that it was extensive. Probably they had also to interpret foreign correspondence.

Shisha (also called Shavsha) the father of Elihoreph and Ahiah was scribe to David and so the sons followed in their father's footsteps. Throughout the history of Israel, even until NT times, the art of writing was highly regarded. Although kings and prophets did on occasion write personally, they usually employed men skilled in writing for official correspondence. Bearing in mind that there was no technological equipment to help in this task it is not surprising that men like these secretaries were necessary.

The entire OT bears witness to the fact that official historians were employed to record important events for future generations. This was a common custom. For example, in Esther there are several references to this practice in Persia. Solomon appointed Jehoshaphat to this position. In so doing he had chosen one who had already served in this capacity for David (2 Sam 8.16) and so was no novice. As pointed out in the introduction the prophets also kept records and so the history of the nation was well documented.

That Benaiah was made "commander in chief" of the army is no surprise. His name occurs often in ch. 2 in relation to official executions. As early as 2.35 we are told that "the king put Benaiah in his (Joab's) room over the host." He was not appointed to this position without proof of his ability to fill it. Earlier he had killed a lion in a pit in a time of snow and had also killed two "lionlike" men of Moab. He had killed an Egyptian armed with a spear, which he took from him, when he himself had only a staff (2 Sam 23.20-21). Some of these feats of courage echo those of David. Both David and Solomon had confidence that he was no ordinary soldier. Like some of the other officers mentioned above he had served David and had been appointed by him as officer over his bodyguard (2 Sam 23.23). In the dark days of the Absalom and Adonijah rebellions he remained faithful to David. With this catalogue of achievements he was a worthy occupant of the distinguished post assigned to him here. It may appear surprising to read that his father was a priest (1 Chr 27.5). If the term "priest" is a reference to a sacrificing priest and not to a principal officer (see v. 5 above), it would have been expected that he would have followed the calling of his father and served at the altar rather than in the army. However, it is most unlikely that his father was a sacrificing priest and therefore his son's choice of an army career was almost certainly not out of keeping with his background.

The two centres of worship, one at Gibeon the other at Jerusalem, meant that there was need for more than one chief priest. Here Abiathar, though earlier in this position than Zadok, is named second.

His banishment to Anathoth had removed him from his place of dignity. Whether he still exercised the priest's office or not, he is listed here as a priest. Not until the Temple was built did the order of worship return to normality. Then there was only one high priest.

Solomon was very conscious of the importance of order. Whether in the religious, military or social sphere he was aware of the need for clear lines of responsibility. Later he appointed twelve officers over Israel but before they are named Azariah is identified (v.5) as their overseer. He was the son of Nathan, but which of the two Nathans associated with the kingdom at that time there is no way of knowing. The majority view is that he was not the son of the prophet of that name but the son of Solomon's brother, born to David in Jerusalem, and mentioned in the genealogy of Christ (Lk 3.31). Zechariah refers to the same person when he writes of the "family of the house of Nathan apart" (Zec 12.12).

Closely linked with Azariah was his brother, Zabud, whose position was that of "principal officer" or "priest" as in v.2. His responsibilities were akin to those of Hushai who is also described as the king's friend with respect to David (2 Sam 15.37; 16.16). Today he might be called a "privy counsellor", an adviser to the king on various matters. One should not think that a wise man like Solomon would despise the advice of one less endowed with that virtue than himself. Two heads are better than one, even though one of these be wiser than the other.

The last in the list of officers are Ahishar and Adoniram the latter of whom was responsible for the tribute or "levy". He had to ensure that all those who were required to give free labour to the king did their duty. The extensive building programme devised by Solomon and completed during his lifetime demanded a great number of workers. Some of these were skilled and some were simply labourers to the craftsmen. Some were foreigners and others were Israelites. Conscripting men to hard work would have been difficult and the officer responsible would have been very unpopular. After the death of Solomon, at the beginning of Rehoboam's reign, this man was stoned to death (12.18). It was said that compelling them undertake such work brought men into slavery.

Verses 7-19

Solomon's purveyors

The household and court of Solomon must have been extensive, especially when we include in it all his officials and servants. It was partly the sight of this which impressed the Queen of Sheba when she visited his house (1 Kings 10.4,5). Ahishar was given the task of controlling the household, so all the cooks, waiters, and kitchen staff were under his control. Later the scale of the provision for each day is described and it clearly needed a large number of people to prepare and serve it.

It was imperative that Solomon had some arrangement to obtain from his citizens the essentials for the maintenance of his household and army. Great quantities of grain and cattle together with wood for fuel had to be provided daily. In order to spread this burden over the entire nation, Solomon divided the land into 12 areas, each supplying the needs of the king's court for one month. To operate this plan he appointed twelve men, each to take charge of one area. It is surprising that the boundaries of these were not exactly according to the allotment of the land to the twelve tribes. It appears that the early division of the inheritance, which gave each tribe its portion, was no longer strictly maintained and that the intermingling of the tribes had, to some extent, obliterated the clear lines of demarcation. The grouping together of certain areas was meant to level out the burden. Some parts of the country would be more productive than others.

Another apparently strange feature of this paragraph is that in five cases the officer is not personally named. Instead the name of the father is given. However, it may have been that both father and son bore the same name or that the father was so well known that the son was identified through him.

It is interesting that Gilead was not exempt from supplying its portion. Just as in the case of the choice of the cities of refuge, the east side of Jordan was not excluded. Three of the districts mentioned were in that area.

The order in which the various divisions are named is neither that of any list which names the tribes, nor is it according to geographical position. The first is Mount Ephraim, which was a most fertile part in the centre of the land. The man appointed over it was the son of Hur. Nothing more is known of him or of his father.

The second district was south-west of Ephraim and was part of the inheritance of Dan. It was much smaller than the first and the man in charge of it was the son of Dekar. Again nothing further is known of him.

The third district lay along the Mediterranean coast and in charge of it was the son of Hesed, only mentioned here in Scripture.

The fourth area was also on the sea coast. Over it was the son of Abinadab a son-in-law of Solomon. This district was one of the smallest described and so must have been particularly fertile.

The fifth area lay north of Ephraim. Baana the son of Ahilud was its officer and is the first to be personally named. His father was probably the same man who was father of Jehoshaphat the recorder (2 Sam 8.16).

The sixth officer was the son of Geber, and his district was on the east side of Jordan in the land of Gilead. This was the largest of the portions and had its sixty important cities protected by walls and bronze bars.

The seventh district was also in Gilead but south-west of the preceding district. It was under the control of Ahinadab of whom nothing more is known.

Another son-in-law of Solomon is named, Ahimaaz, and to him was allocated the eighth and most northerly area.

The ninth was Baanah the son of Hushai who was given the area west of the former portion but extending slightly more to the south. His father was the friend and adviser of David (2 Sam 15.37; 16.16).

The tenth portion was in the territory of the tribe of Issachar, and over it was Jehoshaphat the son of Paruah. It was a small area and so must have been productive.

The eleventh portion was also small while the twelfth takes us again to land beyond Jordan and to the most southern allotment. It was given to Geber the son of Uri. This is the second time the name Geber appears in this list. Possibly the father's name is mentioned here to suggest that he was a different man from the one named in v.13. If, on the other hand, he was the same person then father and son had each a portion assigned. His territory had once belonged to Sihon and Og, and though it was extensive he was appointed on his own to oversee it.

One odd feature of the list is the absence of any mention of the territory of Judah. Many explanations have been given for this. Being so near to Jerusalem it may have been considered as directly under the command of the King.

That all the districts were able to supply the required goods at the right time, either fresh or from store, is assumed. The king would not have put upon his subjects an unbearable burden and so what was asked was within the bounds of their capability.

It might be asked, "Was it not a serious burden on each area that a month's production was taken from it simply to cater for the luxury of the king's court?". The answer is fairly clear. But for the good government of Solomon they would not be enjoying the goods they possessed. Indeed if they had been forced to pay tribute to a foreign nation, as at times did happen, then a much more extensive levy would have been demanded. They would have been left in poverty like slaves. They were only giving to Solomon what was owed. Like David they could say, "Of thine own have we given thee" (1 Chr 29.14).

By this arrangement the entire land was united in supplying provisions for the palace. No area could say, "We are of no account, and all the king's supplies are gathered from his favourite areas". The most remote corner was, in this respect, as important as the great centres of influence.

Later however, when Rehoboam began to reign, the levy was considered by the people to be a heavy burden (12.4), and because of this the kingdom was divided.

It should not be forgotten that this reference to Solomon's purveyors is recorded here to give further evidence of his wisdom. Those in authority must be on their guard lest anyone subject to them has cause to believe that he or she is of no account. All are needed to supply those things necessary for the health of the king's servants. While the responsibility of leadership does not fall on all, this does not mean that those being led have no opportunity to show their indebtedness and loyalty to the Lord. In an assembly especially, the principle that each member has a role to play is vitally important.

Verses 20-28
Solomon's daily provisions

After listing the purveyors and the areas under their supervision, information is given as to why such men were appointed and the extent of the provisions they had the duty to supply. The population had greatly increased under the good reign of David so that it had become like the grains of sand on the seashore. It was also as happy as it was numerous. Every man sat under his own vine and fig tree without the slightest fear of any enemy disturbing him. The language gives us a shadow of the Millennium. Israel may at this time have come closer to that utopian state than ever it did in the rest of its history.

The bounds of Solomon's kingdom were extensive, for he ruled from the Euphrates to the Mediterranean, and from Lebanon in the north to Egypt in the south. Nations which formerly had impoverished Israel were then under Solomon and so had to bring tribute. By so doing they enriched his kingdom. This abundance of peace and prosperity was very different from the former days of the judges, and even the time of Saul, when Israel was often subdued and spoiled by its enemies. Later in the history of the northern kingdom it was brought so low that the prophet cried out "By whom shall Jacob arise? for he is small" (Amos 7.2).

Details of the daily requirements of the palace indicate the large number of people associated with it. However it is not possible to calculate in equivalent weights the exact amounts specified here. The "measure" or cor was used for both liquids and solids, so the idea of weight is not involved. It is said to have contained about 340 litres, so the amount of flour used in one day was 10,200 litres, and the amount of meal was 20,400 litres. It has been suggested that this supply would make almost 13,000 kilos of bread, sufficient to feed 15,000 persons. This bread was supplemented by a large quantity of meat that included ten fattened, or store-fed, bullocks and twenty others which were fed on pasture. To these were added 100 sheep together with a variety of deer, and fattened fowl. Thus delicacies were not omitted nor was the diet without variety.

The absence of fish in the provisions is noticeable. The fact that Jerusalem is some distance from the sea may account for the exclusion, but the "fish gate" of the city suggests that the fishmongers used that entrance when they were selling their catch. Whether the king ate fish or not is unclear. But one of the subjects on which he spoke was "fishes" (4.33).

The amount to be supplied for each month was some thirty times the daily demand and therefore very great. It is little wonder that collectors were necessary to ensure an even flow of these foodstuffs throughout the year. Once again (v.24) the extent of the kingdom is mentioned as including everywhere west of the Euphrates. That is from Tiphsah, which was on its north-west bank, to Azzah, which was Gaza, in the extreme south-west where the Philistines lived. Not only was the kingdom extensive but peace was enjoyed from Dan to Beersheba.

In v.25 Judah and Israel are mentioned separately before the division in the kingdom had taken place. No doubt the historian is referring to the kingdom as he later knew it at the time of writing.

The mention of Solomon's horses in this part of his history (v.26) is no doubt to call attention to his military power. As in the case of his wives, (chs.3 & 11), these were another evidence of his departure from the instructions given to Israel's kings in Deuteronomy 17.16. Just as the multiplying of wives was a feature of the wealthy, so the multiplying of horses and chariots was a display of power. God purposed that His people, when engaging the enemy, should be dependent upon His help. They were not expected to be charioteers but rather foot soldiers. "Some trust in chariots, and some in horses: but we will remember the name of the Lord our God" (Ps 20.7), is the testimony of the faithful in Israel. They had to view any battle as the Lord's, so, whatever their weaponry, their trust had to be in Him. David neither trusted Saul's armour nor his own sling.

The large number, 40,000, given here differs from the 4,000 stated in 2 Chronicles 9.25. It is sometimes suggested that the latter is the correct number and that the former is an error made in transcription. However, there is a slight orthographical difference in the Hebrew word used in each place and so they may refer to two different types of things. In Kings the total number of horses may be given. In 2 Chronicles the number of chariots with associated horses may be recorded. The 12,000 horses (AV "horsemen") mentioned at the end of v.26 were the cavalry as distinct from chariot horses.

The officers mentioned earlier supplied the food for the king's household. In addition to food for human consumption they were responsible to provide fodder for the many horses. Apparently all the animals were "stall-fed" and not put out to graze in the open fields. The amount of straw and barley required for each day must have been very great indeed.

Verses 29-34
Solomon's wisdom

A description of Solomon concludes this section. Again his wisdom is shown to be exceptional. A number of men reputed for their wisdom are mentioned but only to show that he surpassed even the most famous of them. He had the wisdom to decide what was best to do in every circumstance. He had the keenness of understanding to solve every problem and the breadth of intellect to embrace every department of knowledge. Whether one looks eastward and thinks of the shrewd Arabians or southward and considers the wisdom of the Egyptians or to any other of the wise of that day, he excelled them all. Four men are named who were all sons of Mahol, a son of Zerah, and who must have been renowned for their wisdom. Two of these, Ethan and Heman are mentioned in the titles of the Psalms, the former in the title of Psalm 89, and the latter in the title of Psalm 88. All four are mentioned in 1 Chronicles 2.6, "Darda" and "Dara" being the same person.

Only a selection of Solomon's compositions have been preserved for us in the Scriptures. Some of his sayings are found in the book of Proverbs and one of his songs in The Song of Solomon. Every branch of nature study was given his attention not only great beasts and the mighty trees but even insects and the simple hyssop were not beyond his close attention. His studies took him to consider the sea and its fish life as well as the birds that fly in the heavens.

It might have been expected that there would be some reference to astronomy among the subjects studied by Solomon. His father David often turned his thoughts to the heavens. Minding sheep day and night gave him time to gaze at these particular aspects of creation. Solomon, living mainly in houses and palaces, may not have been as likely to be attracted by them.

Given all this it is no wonder that the fame of his wisdom reached the corners of the then known world and that all who heard of him sought to meet him and learn from him, the Queen of Sheba being perhaps the most striking example.

Notes

2 In 1 Chronicles 6.10 a man of the same name "executed the priest's office in the temple". Whether he was the same person as the man here is doubtful. When a name in Scripture is used for over twenty different persons as "Azariah" is, there will always be opportunity for confusion.

28 The animals here termed "dromedaries" (REKESH - 7409) were not camels but more likely swift horses or chasers. The horses used in the chariots were probably heavier and not as suited as these when fast transport was needed. They are called "mules" in Esther 8.10, 14, and "swift beast (s)" in Micah 1.13.

CHAPTERS 5-7

SOLOMON BUILDS THE TEMPLE

CHAPTER 5, Verses 1-12

Solomon procures the timber for the Temple

This chapter begins what is perhaps the most important part of Solomon's history. In erecting the Temple in which God was pleased to dwell he showed his wisdom and devotion to Him in a way that he had never done before. It is probable that during its construction and shortly afterwards that Solomon rose to his highest spiritual heights. Had he retained the standard then reached he would, without question, have been the greatest king in all Israel's history. It was a mammoth task for one so young as he, but the Lord, who had purposed the entire project, fitted him for its accomplishment.

David had given instructions regarding this house, had made extensive preparations for it (1 Chr 28 and 29), and had received from the Lord the blueprint for it which, before he died, he had given to his son (1 Chr 28.11,12). This meant that in its construction there was no place for human imagination or even for the wise king to exercise his natural judgment by putting into it what specially appealed to his taste. If God were to make this house His dwelling place, and He did, He must have the exclusive right to determine its design.

Notwithstanding the considerable amount of material accumulated and set apart by David for the building, there were still great quantities of timber needed for its construction. The two woods chosen were cedar and fir (cypress). The most famous place for these large trees was, of course, Lebanon. Naturally Solomon's mind turned to that area as the source of supply.

In the providence of God the king of that region, Hiram, was on friendly terms with David and on no less friendly terms with Solomon. He expressed his joy at learning of the latter's enthronement and sent his congratulations to him. This opened the door for the messengers of Solomon to ask for the timber required for the Temple. Payment for it was in kind, as was usual at that time, so 20,000 cors of wheat along with 20 measures of beaten oil were promised as compensation (v.11 - see note).

Apparently Hiram was in constant need of grain. His territory may not have been well suited to growing crops since much of it was rocky. On the other hand, the land of Israel was capable of producing not only sufficient grain for its own people but such a surplus as to be able to supply the needs of surrounding nations. It was indeed the land of corn and wine.

The limited amount of wood needed to make the Tabernacle was evidently easily obtained in the wilderness, but Solomon could not find in Canaan the timber essential for the Temple. Not only were the trees lacking, but men skilled to fell and dress them were also lacking. Therefore the request for wood was accompanied with another for men of appropriate experience. Thus Hiram's workers were as needful as his wood.

It was no small request that Solomon made. In sacrificing so many choice trees, some of which may well have taken a century to mature, Hiram was parting with the basic wealth of his land. In one respect these trees were unlike the grain sent as payment for them. The grain could be produced annually, not so a forest. Once it was stripped it could not be replenished during the lifetime of those who felled it. The fact that Hiram was able to fulfil his promise is an indication of his power as a king. One with lesser authority might have faced objections and rebellion from his people.

Before asking for Hiram's help, Solomon gave the reason why his father had not built the house. The will was present but enemies around and the absence of peace combined to make fulfilment impossible. This is the circumstantial reason. The moral reason is given in 1 Chronicles 22.8 and 28.3. There it is explained that David could not build the Temple because he had shed so much blood and was a man of war. What was also true was that the Lord had revealed to David that his son would do what he was forbidden to do. Thus, when Solomon asked for timber, he was asking what his father would have sought had he been allowed to do so. It follows that in granting the timber to the son Hiram was in a sense giving it to his friend David of former days.

In the correspondence Solomon laid great stress on "the Lord" and so made clear that this structure was not a mere palace for man but a sanctuary for God.

Much has been written as to the exact kind of trees asked of Hiram. If it is accepted that the "cedars" were the normal cedars of that name then the wood was most suitable for inside and outside use. Though not a hard wood, it is able to withstand the ravages of the weather. When something lofty and proud was being described it was often likened to these stately trees of Lebanon.

Along with the cedar trees were "fir trees", which may have been cypress. Their tall slender trunks had a variety of uses. The LXX has "pine", which accounts for the translation, "fir", in the AV.

Hiram knew that trees felled in Lebanon were of no use to Solomon unless they were transported to the site of the Temple. It was a long way from Lebanon to Jerusalem but Hiram was no less skilful in their haulage than he was in their hewing. His plan entailed three journeys; first, from the forest to the sea, perhaps some 20 miles (32km), second, from somewhere near Sidon to near Joppa, another 100-120 miles (160-190km) and third, from the sea to Zion, another 40-50 miles (65-80km). In all about 200 miles (325km) were covered before these cedars were at their destination. There is no information given as to how such large trunks were transported by land, but their sea journey is described. During it the trees were banded together into floats, and, probably by the use of long poles, were steered and pushed along the sea-coast. Transporting timber by water continues to the present day. When trees are being floated in water their natural resins are to some extent washed out and this helps to hasten the seasoning process.

Apparently, the trees while in the water formed a large raft on which those in charge could walk freely At the end of their voyage the trees were separated and carried individually to mount Zion. In these three stages of their journey the first was perhaps the easiest for it was mainly downhill. The next stage by sea was somewhat more difficult. The last was by far the most laborious for it was uphill from the sea-coast to a height of around 800 metres above sea-level. It is an interesting problem how, in those days when there were no machines, heavy weights were moved from one place to another. There was no scarcity of help, for Solomon provided the labourers, but how heavy beams were carried to the heights of Zion is not explained in the passage. Some of the terrain over which they passed must have been very rugged. Pulling heavy loads must have entailed much sweat and labour for those who were given this task. However, God as Ceator has given men engineering skills that have enabled the accomplishment of great work. Solomon was given detailed instructions for that part of the work which he either was not allowed to or could not deduce from his own wisdom, but was left to use his natural gift in doing things which were within his engineering skill.

It is not possible to decide on the spiritual condition of Hiram, but, if his confessions are noted, these come very near to the assertions of one who believed in the God of Israel. Here in v.7 he praises the Lord, and in 2 Chronicles 2.12 he goes further and says, "Blessed be the Lord God of Israel, that made heaven and earth". Even the wisdom of Solomon, he concludes, is a gift from the Lord and not merely a natural possession. If his contacts with David had enlightened him regarding the true God then his confessions are understandable. On the other hand, if these were made just out of courtesy to Solomon, and were mere formalities, then they cannot be taken as evidence of his true state.

Throughout these chapters there are constant reminders of the links, and at times contrasts, between the Tabernacle and the Temple. When Moses was erecting the former structure he did not need to send to any foreign land in order to obtain material for it. The shittim wood was beside him in the desert and possibly was even felled by storms some time before it was needed. It would thus be seasoned and ready for use. Only very dry timber could be overlaid with gold and not subsequently shrink away from the metal.

Nor had he to ask, as did Solomon, for anyone to send him skilled workers to make even the most intricate parts of it for God fitted men of Israel for all the work. When the early sanctuary was finished those who looked upon it could say, "This is our workmanship, and no stranger made even a peg or a piece of cord for it". Not so in the case of the Temple, for here, at the beginning of its history, Gentiles are brought in and are seen working with the children of Israel. It was humiliating for Solomon to admit to a Gentile king that he needed his help not only to provide the material to build the house but also to provide the skilled men to work with it. These experts were joined by the thousands of Israel who were sent to the mountain to help the Sidonians and to learn from them the art of handling timber.

The great structure described in Ephesians 1-3 is here seen in type. That spiritual building which will be God's dwelling place throughout eternity is composed of Jew and Gentile. It began when the Lord "ascended on high" and after he had put all enemies under His feet (Eph 1.22; Heb 2.8; 10.13) just as the Temple was built after David had put all enemies under his feet. Whether it be the "holy temple" (Eph 2.21), or the peace which results from the breaking down of the middle wall (v.14), or the absence of "enmity" (v.16), or being "no more strangers and foreigners" (v.19), all of these are foreshadowed in this passage. In a future day when a greater than Solomon sits on His throne then, too, will Jew and Gentile live together and God's house will be a house of prayer for all nations (Is 56.6,7; Mic 4.2).

Verses 13-18
Solomon's levy

From the time the Israelites were freed from bondage in Egypt nothing was more repugnant to them than slavery. However, in order to build the Temple great numbers of labourers were required and these could not be found among the foreigners in the land, so a recruitment of Solomon's own people, which may have seemed akin to the work in Egypt, became inevitable. Those involved were only in servitude as long as they were needed in Lebanon for the forestry work relating to the building of the Temple. The number of them is given as 30,000, but only 10,000 were actually in the forest at any one time. Two out of every three months were granted as home leave. This levy on manpower was only a small fraction of the available workforce. How they were selected is not explained but because the work was for God's house many of them may have volunteered their services.

The major difficulty in this work was that it entailed leaving home, travelling some 150 miles (240km) and remaining there for a month at a time. Already in 4.6 we have been told that Adoniram was in charge of this levy. Helping in this great task was another band of labourers numbering 70,000. These were not Israelites, but Canaanites. They were men of other nationalities who were such as were sentenced to bondage from the days of Joshua (Josh 9.23). To them were given the more arduous and menial tasks. With so many workers employed it was essential to have a number of overseers otherwise the entire project would have been in utter confusion. The number of these was 3,300, and we are told that they "ruled over the people". The term used may suggest that the rule was firm, for it is often translated "have dominion". The workers in the forest and in the quarry provided the wood and stone to build the house.

The stones for the foundation were large. Some were 8 cubits and some 10 cubits long (7.10). Studies of the Temple site have led to the discovery of stones 9 metres long. The "stone-squarers" were from Gebal (Byblos) near Tyre and were skilled stone-masons. All the various classes of worker were united in providing and preparing the basic materials for the building.

Notes

1 The city of Tyre was a rock fortress which was considered almost impregnable. It was constantly linked with its sister city Sidon. In the 15th century BC it was under Egypt. In the time of Solomon it was independent and had its own king. Some 30 years earlier Hiram had sent cedar to David for his palace (2 Sam 5.11). If this Hiram was the same person, which the expression "ever a lover of David" implies, he must have been an old man at this time.

3 The idea of "enemies under the soles of feet" springs from the practice of putting the foot on the head or neck of a defeated enemy before slaying him as seen in Joshua 10.24. In a special way it is used of Christ in His exalted position now, (Eph 1.22), of His kingdom dominion (Ps 8.6), and of His final victory at the end of the millennial kingdom (1 Cor 15.27).

4 "occurrent" (PEGA - 6294) is used only here and in Ecclesiastes 9.11 and means "happening" or "accidental occurrence".

6 Though Hiram was king of Tyre, his workmen are called "Sidonians". Originally Sidon was the more important place so the Phoenician population took their name from that city.

8 The "fir tree" (BeROSH - 1265) which grows alongside the cedars of Lebanon is a conifer and can reach 22 metres in height. Its wood is reddish yellow and is durable. The marginal reading "cypress" represents its most likely identification. Apparently musical instruments were made from it and so it must have been a wood suited to cabinet work (2 Sam 6.5).

9 "floats" (DOBROT - 1702), a word which occurs only here, were rafts of timber. A different word is used in 2 Chronicles 2.16, where it is (RAPSODA - 7513), but with a similar meaning.

11 The small quantity of oil compared with the large quantity of wheat may seem strange. Oil which was "pure" or "beaten" (KATIT - 3795) was much more expensive than that obtained from the oil press. It was of the same quality as was used for the lamps of the Tabernacle.

12 The "league" or "covenant" (BERIT - 1285) between Solomon and Hiram was "made" or "cut" (KARAT - 3772). The original speaks literally of "cutting a covenant" because of the killing of a "covenant animal" that was often part of the covenant ritual.

16 In 2 Chronicles 2.2 and 18, the number of overseers is recorded as 3,600 while here it is 3,300. However, to the figure of 3,300 must be added the 550 chief officers of 1 Kings 9.23, making a total of 3,850. To the number in 2 Chronicles 2 must be added the 250 chief officers mentioned in 2 Chronicles 8.10, also making a total of 3,850. Thus both accounts are in harmony.

CHAPTER 6, Verses 1-10
The specification of the Temple

Before giving the dimensions of the Temple, the writer notes the exact date when building commenced. A special day in the history of the nation had been reached for now a permanent dwelling place for the Lord was being established for the first time. Unlike the Tabernacle built by Moses and unlike the tent erected by David, both of which were portable structures, this building was founded upon a rock and was fixed in one location.

The period from leaving Egypt until the foundation of the Temple is given as 480 years. However a total of 573 years can be reckoned from Judges and Samuel. In Judges 11.26 it is stated that from the entrance to Canaan to the days of Jepthah was 300 years. If to this is added the remaining 5 years of his judgeship and all the periods mentioned afterwards until Samuel the 450 years mentioned by Paul in Acts 13.20 is reached. If there is then added to this the 40 years of Samuel, the 80 years of Saul and David and the 3 years of Solomon then the total is 573, which is much greater than the number given in this chapter.

A number of suggestions have been made to solve the problem. One is that the periods of servitude given in the Book of Judges are not reckoned here. They amount to 93 years which, if subtracted from the total of all the periods given in Judges and Samuel, leaves all in agreement, and there is something attractive about this view.

Another solution is to take into account that there are occasions when overlaps occur. For example the servitude of the Philistines and the judgeship of Eli overlap. The times of each of them cannot then be added to give the total time elapsed. Similarly the judgeship of Samuel and the reign of Saul overlap.

As a final possibility, the reading in Acts 13 in the RV puts the 450 years at the close of v.19 rather than into v.20. This would remove the 450 years from the period of the Judges.

The size of the Temple may come as a surprise. Given that it was to be the place where the God who is the only true God would make his presence known it might have been expected to be very extensive. Instead it was less than 30 metres long and 12 metres wide. Its main purpose was not as a place of assembly for a great congregation. It was a dwelling place for God. Apart from the pillars and the doors there was nothing particularly attractive about its appearance. To the casual passer-by it probably looked like a large stone box. Its beauty was mainly internal and was seen only by those who were allowed to enter.

A careful examination of the dimensions given shows that they were taken from the Tabernacle but that its measurements were doubled. The Holy Place here is 40 x 20 cubits and the Most Holy Place is a cube of 20 cubits. The height of 30 cubits might seem to imply that the Tabernacle was 15 cubits high. The Tabernacle boards were only 10 cubits. If the strict proportion is maintained then those who have suggested that the Tabernacle had a ridgepole over which the roof curtain was draped see these extra 5 cubits as confirmation of that idea.

Along the entire front of the house was a porch 10 cubits wide. There is no mention of a porch in the details of the Tabernacle, but again it has been suggested that the extra covering at the front, which could be folded back, served this purpose when necessary.

High up above the side chambers were narrow windows which, being wide inside and narrow outside, allowed the light of the sun to shine in during daylight and also helped to ventilate the building. Clearly daylight could not penetrate the stone walls and the wooden doors. These were unlike the curtain door of the Tabernacle that may have allowed some daylight to shine into the Holy Place. The windows were designed to ensure that during the day those who served God in His house could see where they were moving and what they were doing.

An interesting feature of this building is the side chambers. Just as the Tabernacle had a space between the gold covered boards and the pegs that pinned the curtain that formed its roof so these side chambers surrounded the three sides of the Temple. Eli and Samuel slept in this space in the Tabernacle and from it they arose and opened its curtain door every morning. The side chambers in the Temple were small apartments 3 storeys high and varied in width from 5 cubits to 7 cubits. They rested against the outside wall of the house but were not built into it. Though they were not part of the sacred building they were closely associated with it.

As the wall of the house rose it was reduced in width by a cubit at the height where the floor of the middle chamber rested. It was reduced by another cubit at the height of the floor of the third storey. By adding to the 15 cubits given as the combined height of these chambers the thickness of their floors and their roof the total height was probably about 20 cubits. This left about 10 cubits from the roof of these chambers to the roof of the main building. It was possibly in this area that the windows mentioned in v.4 were placed. These side rooms were used mainly by the priests who were at any particular time serving in the Temple. They appear also to have been used for storage and were like treasure chests for the wealth of the kingdom.

One can apply this as a picture to the house of God today. Whether viewed as the Church in its universal sense or as a local assembly it is surrounded by stores of spiritual treasure which are the fruits of the victory of Christ. These rooms in the Temple were entered by a door on the right side of the house and a stairway led from one storey to the next. The third storey could only be reached through the second. In entering fully into the treasures of truth the believer must be prepared to climb and advance to spiritual higher ground (1 Cor 3.1,2).

The roof of the Temple is not described in detail. The wood was cedar and if the roof was pitched the beams were its main strength and the boards filled the spaces between them. If however the roof was flat then the beams across must have been very strong or the roof would have sagged in the middle. Whatever form the outside of the roof may have taken the ceiling inside was flat and must have been beneath the cedar roof.

In the middle of the description of these features of the house it is said that in its erection there was a notable absence of noise. Unlike other building schemes where all is noise and din, this had all its material cut to size and ready to be placed in position. The quarry and sawmill were full of sound and bustle, but on the actual building site all was quietly erected without the use of either axe or hammer.

Preparing material for God's house today also requires toil and labour for both evangelists and teachers. All those who are saved are built into God's house as it is seen in Ephesians.

In spite of the craftsmanship of the stone-squarers, who skilfully cut with precision every stone, their handiwork was covered over on the inside of the house with boards of cedar. Only on the outside were the stones seen. If the stones are taken as being locally quarried and the trees of cedar as being from Lebanon, then the boards closely covering the stones provide a picture of Jew and Gentile being made one in God's house. Had it not been that the Temple was being built these boards and stones would never have been united. While, of course, every believer is a stone in the spiritual temple God is building, initially those saved were mainly Jews. Not until later were Gentiles brought into the great building.

Beautiful as the cedar wood sheeting may have been, especially after it had been carved, it was not the final covering for the stones. Over it were placed the sheets of gold (vv. 20-22) so that the wood, as well as the stone, was concealed. Both compartments of the Temple were entirely overlaid with gold; not only was it put on the side walls, but it was spread on the floor and ceiling as well. The relief carvings would still be seen but were now gilded.

The typical significance of this feature is to show that what is natural and attractive to human observation has no place in God's presence. All is covered with gold that speaks of His glory. Even the nails fastening the gold to the boards were gold. Iron or copper had no place in the sanctuary. In the great spiritual structure being built today the same principle is revealed. What men are by nature is no longer seen. Just as God, dwelling in the Temple, saw only what reflected His glory, so as He looks at His own people in Christ, He sees in them the reflection of His Son who is the brightness of His glory.

Verses 11-13

God's message to Solomon

Again the details of the building are interrupted by a special message from the Lord to Solomon which apparently came to him during the course of its erection. The importance of obeying the word of the Lord, impressed upon him by his father, is again brought home to him by the Lord Himself. If he follows the commandments and decrees of God he is assured that the house he is building will become the dwelling place of the Almighty. The promise made to David before he died that his son would build the Temple and that it would indeed be God's house was conditional on obedience to the law of God. Its later history demonstrated this solemn fact. When Israel forsook the word of the Lord, He forsook His house and it was destroyed. The most important word for Solomon was that, when the house was finished, God would take up His abode in it. In spite of all the labour and skill, together with the great expense involved in its erection, without His presence it would have been only an empty shell and a waste of effort, time and wealth.

The principle illustrated here has a special bearing on local assembly testimony. The local church is called the "house of God" in 1 Timothy 3.15. There it is seen as "the pillar and ground of the truth". It is a base for all who seek the truth, and it upholds the truth for all to see. Such companies need to covet the presence of the Lord and ought to fear departure from His Word lest He no longer grants them this precious favour.

Verses 14-22
The two compartments

The historian resumes his account of the building in v.14 with the statement that the stonework was finished. Then follows the detailed account of the inside. The floor was of different wood to that used to line the side walls. It was "pine" or "cypress", and the ceiling was covered with this same wood (2 Chr 3.5).

At the back of the Temple, that is at its western end, a partition went across which separated the Holy Place from the Most Holy. The larger compartment extended 40 cubits from the front of the house, and the smaller sanctuary was a cube of 20 cubits. The partition was made of cedar and extended from floor to ceiling, 30 cubits. The Holy Place was 40 x 20 cubits and this meant that, apart from the entrance into the Most Holy Place, it was entirely covered with cedar boards. No stone was seen inside it.

The cedar boards were decorated with carving which was possibly in the form of relief work (that is cutting away of the wood so as to leave raised the palm trees, the cherubim, the knops (gourds), and the open flowers. If this was so, it meant that the embroidery work of the Tabernacle, which was raised above the cloth, was followed as closely as possible. These decorations were a constant memorial of the wilderness, for, apart from the cherubim, all the other objects were plentiful there, and were intended to remind the priests who served in the Holy Place of that time when the nation was in less favourable circumstances.

In the future when the saints as kings and priests sing in heavenly glory, they too will remember the past when they were redeemed by the blood of the Lamb. The care of the Lord and His faithfulness toward us will never be forgotten.

The ark of the covenant (v.19) contained the two stones on which were written the ten commandments. These are called the "tables of the covenant" (Deut 9.11). The Ark was designed to hold the two tables and the Tabernacle was made to hold the Ark, as was the Temple. The covenant was the centre of both structures.

In a brief statement, the only reference to the altar of incense is of it being also overlaid with gold (v.22). Its dimensions are not given, nor is it included in the account in 2 Chronicles. It has been suggested that it was made of stone and then covered with cedar overlaid with gold. Although the wording in the original may allow this, it was in all probability a wooden pedestal covered with gold. While not placed in the Most Holy Place it belonged to that quarter. It was positioned in front of the entrance to the Most Holy Place so that the fragrance rising from it not only filled the larger compartment but also penetrated into the inner sanctuary. Of all the vessels of the Holy Place it was the most used. The priest burned incense on it morning and evening.

In the Temple to be built in the future, described by Ezekiel, the altar, or table is the solitary piece of furniture in the Holy Place (Ezek 41.22). By comparison with both the Tabernacle and Solomon's Temple, this must be an altar or table from which God will receive sweet incense from it throughout the coming kingdom age. Today the devotions of God's people, whether in prayer or praise, rise up as fragrance before Him as they come boldly to the throne of grace and enjoy fellowship with him.

Verses 23-30
The cherubim of glory

The introduction of two large cherubim into the oracle may appear to be a departure from the pattern of the Tabernacle. Nothing corresponding to them was present in the Most Holy Place of that structure though, of course, there were two smaller cherubim on the Mercy Seat. However, since the Ark was only one eighth of the width of the Most Holy Place there was a lack of proportion. These two cherubim filled the room from wall to wall. They stood about ten cubits apart with outstretched wings of ten cubits.

They demonstrated the importance of the guardianship of God's glory. They overshadowed the Ark and, at the same time, looked toward the larger Holy Place. The two smaller ones on the Mercy Seat gazed down upon it, but these soared to a height of ten cubits and stood like two sentinels keeping guard over the sacred vessel. The fact that their wings touched each other, and also touched the side walls of the house, suggests the unity that befits the presence of God. What their faces were like is not stated, nor the shape of their bodies. It has been suggested that they are connected with the living creatures of Revelation 4. They were made of olive wood overlaid with gold. This oily wood may have been chosen for its suitability for carving. The body of each must have been the large trunk of a tree. The wings may have been attached to each side of the figure. They could not have been made from one piece of a tree.

The wood in the Ark below them was shittim, so in the one compartment four woods met; cedar round the walls, fir on the ceiling, olive in the doors and the cherubim and shittim in the Ark. All of them were covered with gold.

Verses 31-36
The doors of the Temple

Unlike the Tabernacle, where the Most Holy Place was entered through the veil, in the Temple there were two doors that led into it. These were a fifth part of the width of the house and so were 4 cubits wide and possibly the same in height. If they did extend to the ceiling then they were almost twenty cubits in height. Like the cherubim they were of olive wood overlaid with gold. In keeping with the rest of the house, they had carved upon them cherubim, palm trees, and open flowers. They turned upon hinges and opened toward the Holy Place.

In these verses there is no mention of a veil, but it is referred to in 2 Chronicles 3.14. If the entrance to the oracle is taken as being a square of 4 cubits, rather than extending to the ceiling, the height seems quite low for a structure of twenty cubits high. A tall man would have to stoop as he went in. However, it seems probable that the High Priest had to lift the veil while entering and so would already be stooping. Taking together the three barriers into the oracle, the gold chains, the doors and the veil, it can be seen that all was designed to prevent intrusion into the sacred abode of the Ark.

The entrance into the Holy Place from outside was also by doors, but these were different in that they were folding doors. They were wider, for they were a fourth part of the width of the house, and so were 5 cubits wide. The wood used in their making was fir, but olive was used for their posts and the same decorations were carved upon them as were upon the inner doors. Like them, they were overlaid with gold. This gold was later stripped off by Hezekiah and given to the king of Assyria to buy off his attack on Jerusalem (2 Kings 18.16).

Apparently these doors opened outwards and each one had two halves which folded back so that there were four doors with two on each side hinged together. Their height may have been the same as their width and so the entrance would have been a square of 5 cubits. Again this still seems low in relation to a building which was 30 cubits high.

On the Day of Atonement the high priest had to pass through the outer doors, the veil and the inner doors before he could reach the Mercy Seat on the Ark. This again emphasises that the way into the presence of God was not then open as it is today (Heb 9.8).

Possibly adjacent to these doors, and close by the front of the Temple, was the court of the priests, here called "the inner court". It was surrounded by a stone wall built of three rows of hewn stone. Upon this was a coping of cedar wood planks. Just as the Tabernacle was surrounded by a court so too was the Temple. In the latter case there were at least two courts for the "inner court" implies an outer one which, in fact, was the court of the congregation and was much larger (7.12). There were doors at the entrance to these courts which were covered by bronze according to 2 Chronicles 4.9.

It is noticeable that this chapter progresses from the Most Holy Place, at the back of the Temple, then to its doors, then to the outer doors, and finally to the court. The order of description is from the immediate presence of God outward.

Verses 37,38
The completion of the Temple

These verses show that the Temple was built in a little over seven years. The foundation was laid in the second month of Solomon's fourth year on the throne, and the building finished in the eighth month of his eleventh year. Never before in Israel was so much valuable material and so much craftsmanship concentrated in one place. The labour involved and the skills exercised must have been a matter of wonder to the known world at that time. It is likely that the preparation of the stone and timber began some years before the foundation was laid while the making of the great number of vessels needful for its functioning may have occupied some months after it was finished.

Notes

4 The word "narrow" (ATAM - 331) when not used of windows is translated "stopped" and "closed".

5 The term "oracle" (DeBIR - 1687) occurs here for the first time, and is used as the name for the Most Holy Place of the Temple. It may be derived from the word "speak" (DABAR - 1696) and, if so, the sanctuary was the place from which God spoke.

6 The fact that the side and back walls of the Temple could have recesses of a cubit for each of the three storeys means that the base of the walls must have been at least 5 cubits thick. This with the outer wall of the rooms means that the extreme width of the Temple was about 44 cubits and that its extreme length was about 74 cubits.

7 The original word for "made ready" (SHALEM - 8003) is translated "perfect" in 8.61; 11.4; 15.3 and 15.14 .

8 If the idea of "shoulder" (KATEP - 3802) for "side" is adopted here then the door of the chambers was on the south side of the Temple.

21 The chains of gold passed from one side to the other either of the house or of the doors into the oracle. The word translated "made a partition" (ABAR - 5674) means "to pass". The fact that chains are mentioned as part of the decorations (2 Chr 3.5) has led to conjecture that these were decorations across the top of the entire oracle and that they were not a fence to guard the entrance to it.

38 The word "fashion" (MISHPAT - 4941) is the normal word for "judgment" as in v.12. Here it is used in the sense of "specification" and indicates that there was a settled pattern to which it conformed.

CHAPTER 7, Verses 1-12
Buildings adjacent to the Temple

The historian now interrupts his description of the Temple by giving details of other buildings Solomon constructed at a later time. The reason for this diversion is that these buildings were erected near the Temple site and were closely associated with it. As long as the kings of Israel were walking in the ways of the Lord it was an advantage for them to live near the Temple. It was the centre to which the Nation came to worship. Also if any of his subjects had some matter to bring before the king he could attend to it while at Jerusalem.

However, according to Ezekiel, having the king's palace close by the Temple meant that when the later kings, and indeed, Solomon himself, turned aside from God and introduced idolatry into their homes it defiled the sanctuary. To avoid the possibility of this in the Millennial Temple no such arrangement will be allowed. The whole area around will be "most holy" (Ezek 43.7-12).

The buildings now mentioned are the house of the forest of Lebanon, the two porches, the royal palace, the house of Pharaoh's daughter, and the great court. All these were situated close by the Temple and were viewed as a combined range of majestic buildings, so that the entire group is simply referred to as the king's house (9.1,10,15; 10.12). Evidently the Temple was on higher ground than the palace, for Solomon ascended to it (10.5).

What became of the "house of cedar" (2 Sam 7.2) which David had built, and in which he lived, is not recorded. It appears that when Solomon came to the throne he did not take over this house. He seems not to have been satisfied with a wooden house and built one of stone. He probably started it immediately after the Temple was finished but did not finish it until he had reigned twenty years. Thus half of Solomon's reign was spent in building work. In this he differed from his father. David's earlier years were spent in conflict.

There are widely different views of this work. Some authors have concluded that the thirteen years he spent on his own house show that he thought more of his own comfort than he did of the Lord. Others suggest that the long time taken indicates that the same zeal had not characterised him in building his own palace as had marked him when working at the house of the Lord. If it had he would have finished in less time. However, the simple fact is that these buildings were more numerous and the area they covered far more extensive than the Temple, therefore more time was involved in their erection.

The house of the forest of Lebanon was not a summer residence erected in the forest of that name. It was a building near to the Temple. The reason for giving it this name was because many pillars of cedar were clustered in it. Anyone looking at them might have imagined themselves to be looking into a forest. It was 100 cubits long and 50 cubits broad, and, like the Temple, it was 30 cubits high. The brevity of the description of this building makes the details difficult to reconcile. Apparently it was three storeys high with the upper two floors for storage. It had a cedar roof which covered its forty-five chambers, fifteen on each level. Possibly these followed the pattern of the Temple chambers, so that six were on each side and three were at the back of each level. There is no mention of stairs, but only of doors and windows, and again, like the Temple, the doors were square, as high as they were broad. The description of windows facing each other has led to the suggestion that the building had an open courtyard in its centre. If the cedar pillars reached the roof and between them was an open space, then the chambers on each side would allow the windows to be internal and those looking out of one window would be looking into the window of the chamber on the other side. The same arrangement held for the doors.

The next structure mentioned is the porch, but whether this was the porch in front of the house of the forest of Lebanon or whether it was a separate building is not clear. If a parallel is drawn with the Temple, then it may have been an entrance porch for the former building. It consisted of rows of pillars with a roof over them and measured 50 cubits by 30 cubits.

The porch where the throne was placed is described next. Whether it was attached to those buildings already referred to or whether it was separate is again not recorded. It was not an open porch but a stone structure lined from floor to ceiling with cedar. No dimensions are given for the throne room, but it was probably the same as the porch previously described. To this room those who came to the king seeking his judgment, or bringing to him information, had ready access. From it his decrees radiated to every corner of the land. It was, in measure, like the oracle of the Temple. As the Lord dwelt between the cherubim, and was at the heart of the worship of His people, so the king sat on his throne and was at the heart of his kingdom.

Despite the greatness and grandeur of the king's palace, a brief reference to it is all that is made. Evidently it was near the throne room but not attached to it, and was probably a distinct building set further back than those already considered. It would have had its own entrance and therefore would be more private.

These buildings were in many respects similar in design and, to some degree, took their pattern from the Temple.

Of his many wives none seemed to hold as high a place in the estimation of Solomon as Pharaoh's daughter. Close by his own palace, and possibly behind it, was the palace specially built for her. She had lived in the City of David from the time of her marriage.

Chapter 3.1 records that she had to wait until after the Temple was built before she could have her own private house. As the daughter of a wealthy king, presumably she was accustomed to luxurious accommodation. Solomon must have felt duty bound to provide her with a palace in keeping with her pre-marriage status.

The materials used in addition to the cedar, were hewn stones of great size. These must have been reasonably soft (possibly limestone), to allow them to be sawn to size. Surrounding these buildings were walled-in courtyards, like that which surrounded the Temple, to give an inner and an outer court. The three rows of large stones with their cedar capping preserved the privacy of the palace.

As suggested earlier, all these large halls and houses were designed after the pattern of the Temple, even to the detail of their courts. In approaching the king, one had to pass through the outer court and through the inner court before reaching the porch and throne room.

A connection can readily be made between these buildings close by the Temple and the New Testament "house of God" (1 Tim 3.15). Just as the building of the king's palace is closely connected to the building of the Temple, so the instructions regarding the "house of God" are related to instructions regarding "overseers" (ch. 3.1). There is a close connection between the assembly as a dwelling place for God, and its government by those fitted by the Holy Spirit to care for it. It has already been pointed out that the palace of the Prince will not be close to the future earthly temple. Yet it will be close to its court, part on the North and part on the South, thus maintaining the principle that worship and rule are never far apart.

Verses 13,14
The artificer from Tyre

Not only did Solomon send to Tyre for the timber to build the Temple, but he also sent to the same city for a workman, Hiram, to mould the brass pillars and other items that stood outside. Apparently the fame of Hiram as a craftsman had spread abroad, so the king sent for him, took advantage of his skill, and gave him the responsibility of making all the great works of brass. This man, like Bezaleel and Aholiab who made the Tabernacle and its furniture, and like Solomon himself (4.29) was filled with "wisdom, and understanding". According to 2 Chronicles 2.7-14 he was a master of a variety of trades. Like some other famous men in Scripture, he was the son of a widow who, according to 2 Chronicles 2.14, was a daughter of Dan. If "Dan" there refers to the town of that name, it was situated in the tribe of Naphtali, and was originally called "Laish", or "Leshem" but when the Danites took it over they called it "Dan" (Josh 19.47). Like Timothy in the N T, he was the son of a mixed marriage for his mother was an Israelite and his father a man of Tyre, yet grace triumphed over human failure and made their son a chosen vessel to furnish the courts of the Lord.

He learned his trade from his father, who was also a worker in brass. Although he had a variety of skills, in this chapter most, if not all, of his handiwork was in brass. This metal was not what is now called brass, an alloy of copper and zinc. It was entirely copper. The value of this metal lay in its strength to resist the ravages of the weather and to endure the heat of fire.

The combination of Gentile and Israelite symbolized in Hiram is in perfect keeping with the combination of those involved with the stone and timber of the Temple. Neither the building nor its associated vessels were the exclusive work of the people of Israel. This is a reminder of the New Testament truth that Gentiles are to be fellow heirs with Israel as members of the one body (Eph 3.6). While Hiram was a master workman, it was not left to him to design the things he made. Solomon remained the architect, and he, in turn, had received from his father David the God-given pattern of the house and its vessels.

Verses 15-22
The two pillars

The most spectacular sight greeting the eyes of those who approached the Temple was its two brass pillars. These were placed on either side of the doorway into the Holy Place and stood like two sentinels. Their respective names, Jachin and Boaz, mean "He will establish", and "In him is strength". Thus they testified that God has established His house, and has strength to support what He has established.

Apart from the priests, who could enter the Holy Place, no one in Israel was allowed to see the beauty and ornamentation of the inside of the Temple. But in these pillars most of the internal decorations were reproduced and in this way some understanding of its internal grandeur could be conceived. Probably they stood apart from the Temple and were not supports for any part of it. They served to inspire the worshippers and at the same time relieved the dullness of the stone structure they fronted.

Although there are five references to these pillars in 2 Kings 25.13-17; 2 Chronicles 3.15-17; 4.12-13 and Jeremiah 52.20-23, as well as here, it is almost impossible to determine their design or to be dogmatic as to their appearance. The main shaft seems to have been a round plain pillar 18 cubits high and 12 cubits in circumference. There is no mention of a base. All the decorative work was at the top, on the capitals or "chapiters". Each of these was in the form of a bowl covered with a network and with hanging chains. Two rows of pomegranates (either fruit or flowers) were on the network, one hundred on each row. On top of the bowls was lily-work 4 cubits high. This may imply that the total height of each was 27 seven cubits, though it has been suggested that the 4 cubits were not additional to the 5, but were included in them. This would reduce the height to 23 cubits. With the lily-work on the top, the pillars looked like two giant flowers growing in front of the Temple.

They were hollow, but not light. The thickness of the brass used was 4 fingers or a handbreadth (Jer 52.21). According to 2 Chronicles 3.15 the pillars were 35 cubits high. However, the word "high" used there is normally translated "long", and so it may refer to the combined length of the two stems of the pillars and suggests that each pillar had a base of half a cubit. With this base the overall height of 18 cubits (v.15) leaves 17 $1/_2$ cubits for the stems.

It should be noted that the decorations of these pillars were copied from earlier well-known features associated with the high priest and with the house of God. For example, there were chains on the shoulders of the high priest to hold the breastplate in place, and there were also chains at the entrance to the oracle. There were pomegranates on the hem of the high priest's garment of glory and beauty, and there were lilies in the porch of the Temple.

Whatever difficulties surround understanding the exact design of these master-pieces of brass, there can be no mistaking their spiritual significance. The apostle Paul refers to three leading men, James the Lord's brother and two apostles, Peter and John, as "pillars" (Gal 2.9). The pillars can reasonably be considered as pictures of leaders of the church.

There is much of the inward beauty of an assembly, the house of God, unseen and unknown by those outside. Just as these pillars were a revelation of the inner features of the Temple, so the lives of those who lead the saints ought to manifest the character of the company to which they belong. Note, too, that the main stress in the description of them is on their heads. The heads of leaders should be like bowls filled with wisdom and understanding. The network echoes the girding of the loins of the mind (1 Pet 1.13); the pomegranates suggest fruitfulness of thought, and the chains restraint and submission as well as the linking together of that which is beautiful. The lilies speak of the pure mind (2 Pet 3.1). The many references Paul makes to the "mind" in Philippians indicate its importance. The references to self-control, vigilance, sobriety, holiness, not being soon angry and not being violent in his qualifications for those aspiring to be overseers emphasise how vital are the virtues of the mind for those who are leading others (1 Tim 3.1-6 and Tit 1.7-9).

It is surprising that no reference to the altar or its dimensions is given in 1 Kings. However it is described in 2 Chronicles 4.1. The four references to it in ch.8 show that it was made at this time (vv. 22, 31, 54, and 64).

Verses 23-26
The brass sea

The laver in the Tabernacle was reproduced in the large vessel here called the "molten sea". It was circular, like a huge bowl. The measurement across it, from outer edge to outer edge, was 10 cubits. The inside of the vessel had a circumference of thirty cubits. The width of the rim, like the thickness of the material of the pillars, was a handbreadth which is about 10cm (4 inches). These dimensions satisfy the formula relating radius to circumference.

It was 5 cubits high and could hold 3,000 baths, but normally only 2,000 were kept in it. Thus when full it contained approximately 113,500 litres of water, and, when in use over 75,000. Underneath the rim were two rows of knops, or gourds, and these were placed ten to a cubit. It was supported by twelve oxen, three of which faced each point of the compass; thus all their hindquarters were inwards. Like the laver in the court of the Tabernacle it was situated between the altar and the Holy Place so that the priests could wash at it before entering the sanctuary. In all probability the mouths of the oxen were the outlets for the water and served as taps.

The copious supply of water in this sea was essential because the priests, while serving in the Temple, wore neither shoes nor gloves and so were in need of washing lest they brought in with them anything which would defile that sacred place. Obviously the height of the sea, 5 cubits (2.3 metres), meant that the priests could not reach into it to dip their hands and feet. Washing was carried out by pouring the water from it upon them.

The first of the spiritual lessons apparent in this vessel is that God requires holiness to characterize all who approach Him. The second, which follows immediately, is that He has made ample provision for the removal of defilement. If the brazen altar, (not mentioned here) typifies atonement, the brazen sea speaks of sanctification and the lily flowers at the lip of the sea are a reminder of the purity demanded by God of all who enter His presence.

There are two aspects of sanctification in the N T. Firstly, that once-and-for-all sanctification which occurs at conversion. This corresponds to the bathing of the priests at the time of their inauguration. Then there is the practical and daily sanctification that comes by the application of the Word of God in the power of the Holy Spirit. This corresponds to the washing of the hands and feet of the priests. The oxen speak of those who carry the burden and labour to bring the Word of God to the people of God that it may be applied to all who appreciate their need for holiness of life. The washed hands are a reminder of the works and the cleansed feet a reminder of the walk of the people of God. The words of Psalm 119.9 are relevant in this context "Wherewithal shall a young man cleanse his way? By taking heed thereto according to thy word". That the oxen faced the four corners of the earth emphasises that defilement can be removed no matter from whence it comes.

Verses 27-39
The brazen washstands
The introduction of these portable lavers was something entirely new. nothing resembling them was used in the Tabernacle. The quantity of burnt offerings Solomon expected to be offered on the large altar led him to think that much water would be needed to wash all the inwards and legs of the animals sacrificed as burnt-offerings. To bring the necesssary water for such an abundance of sacrifices by carrying it in earthenware vessels to the altar would have been all but impossible and so portable bases on which lavers were placed were made to overcome this difficulty.

He may have remembered that when there were heavy parts of the Tabernacle to be carried God directed Moses to accept the wagons brought to him (Num 7). Thus Solomon felt free to assist in this task by making these trolleys. They were rectangular boxes 4 cubits square, and 3 cubits high. They had panelled sides which were decorated on the upper part with lions, oxen, palm trees and cherubim, and four corner stays or uprights. Underneath were four wheels, each a cubit and a half high, turning on axles, and supported by brackets from the upright stays. Inside the square box was a circular "mouth" one half cubit high, and surmounting it was a chapiter or capital a cubit high. The latter was designed to receive the laver. This base was supported by "undersetters" which rose from the bottom corners, where the wheels were attached. Most likely there was on the bottom of the bowl-shaped lavers a ring which fitted into the chapiter of the bases and held them in their place. The lavers held forty baths of water, which is about 1,500 litres. When not in use they were set, five on the north side, and five on the south side of the Temple.

As for the typical teaching of these portable lavers, they, like the brazen sea, are reminders of God's holiness. The sea emphasised the need for cleanliness to enter His house; the lavers pointed out the need for all that is put on His altar to be clean.

The water portrays "the washing of water by the word" (Eph 5.26). In the burnt offerings the inwards and legs were washed before being put on the altar. Christ, the true burnt offering, had no defilement, but His inner being, with all its desires and emotions, as well as His outward walk, were both subject to the Word of God. Since the burnt offering represented the offerer and died in his place, so he was, as it were, on the altar. God expects all His people to present their bodies as living sacrifices, holy, acceptable unto God (Rom 12.1). If these are to be a sweet savour to Him, they must know the application of the Word of God to their inward yearnings and also to their walk. "Thy word have I hid in my heart, that I might not sin against thee" (Ps 119.11) is appropriate to the lesson of the lavers.

Verses 40-47
Hiram's works of brass

Although Hiram was a master-worker in all metals, as regards the Temple his work seemed to be confined to brass. This summary includes not only the larger vessels which have been considered but also those smaller, yet essential, vessels used in the sacrificial ritual including pots, shovels and sprinkling bowls. The pots were for boiling parts of the peace-offerings, the shovels were for removing the ashes and the sprinkling bowls were to catch the blood so that it could be sprinkled round the altar. The metal used was bright or furbished brass, which seems to imply that it was polished after being moulded. The quantity used was so great, and the pieces so varied, that no attempt was made to estimate their total weight.

Apparently there was no place near Jerusalem where suitable clay ground could be found for the moulding of these vessels. Hiram had to go to the Jordan valley to carry out his work. It is surprising that the two places mentioned, Succoth and Zarthan, were on different sides of Jordan, the former on the east, the latter on the west. However, the work was probably carried out on the west side, but no town was near the place to help identify it, so Succoth on its other side had to be mentioned. The foundry where such artistic work was moulded was no doubt primitive by current standards nevertheless the quality of the finished pieces must have been very high. How the stems of the pillars and their decorated heads were formed remains a mystery. The labour involved, the heat endured, and the transport of the finished articles all demanded exceptional skill and energy and were executed to the highest standard of precision.

There was no relationship between the stiff clay and the burnished brass, yet one was as essential as the other in the making of those things which God had planned for His house. He still uses vessels in the church to-day which are fitted by His power and wisdom to function in His house as and when they are needed. Sometimes the fiery trials of life are the moulds wherein they are shaped for His service. It was a wonderful change for these vessels to be lifted out of the miry clay and set up upon the Temple site. From the most humble conditions in earth have been produced the choicest of instruments God has used in His work. The brass was brought down to Jordan, a type of death and judgment, before it was brought up to adorn the Temple courts. Many would like to be chosen vessels for God's service but fail to realize the humbling experiences essential to their making.

Verses 48-51
The vessels of gold and silver

After giving a summary of the work in brass, a detailed account is given of the articles of gold. It would appear that all the gold work was supervised by Solomon himself and so he is credited with making all the vessels of the Holy Place. Most of these are simply mentioned with no details given of their size. The golden altar has already been described, but here the table for the shewbread, and the candlesticks are added. In the Tabernacle there was only one candlestick, but in the Temple there were ten, five along each side. According to 2 Chronicles 4.8, ten tables for the shewbread, as well as ten lampstands were made, but only one table is mentioned here. It may have been that though there were ten tables only one was used at any particular time. (See 2 Chr 13.11; 29.18). In the case of these articles the gold used is said to be "pure", but the hinges of the doors were evidently made of gold of somewhat lesser purity. This may have been necessary to increase their strength.

Unlike the brass used for the outside vessels which was not weighed, the gold for all these internal vessels was not only provided by David, but, for each of them, he allocated a distinct weight (1 Chr 28.14-18). The pattern for all these was given to him and so he knew exactly the amount of precious metal needed. It has often been noted that no sizes were given for the golden candlestick of the Tabernacle, but its weight was one talent of pure gold. This settled, indirectly, its dimensions (Ex 25.39). Similarly the amount of gold set apart for these vessels decided their size.

There were also candlesticks, tables and basons made of silver in the Temple, (1 Chr 28.15-17), but where they were placed is not revealed. They may have been used either in the porch or in the side chambers. The latter is the more probable as silver is not an ideal metal for outside use. The first mention of silver being used in the Temple is a reminder of the great quantity of it, 7,000 talents, given by David for use in its construction (1 Chr 29.4). In 1 Kings no account is given as to how the walls were overlaid with silver, nor which walls were so treated. Neither is there a record of the precious stones being inserted into the gold plating around the house.

Now that the building work was finished (6.38), and the outside essentials completed, the house was ready for the reception of the ark. First the treasure accumulated by David was brought in and stored (7.51). The surplus of precious metal shows that there was more than enough to furnish the Temple. Moses had to restrain the people in giving for the Tabernacle, so on both occasions nothing had to be abandoned because of lack of material. The side-chambers, no doubt, were where the excess was deposited. An earlier, but miniature example of this was seen when the sword of Goliath was placed in the Tabernacle. Instead of keeping that special treasure David apparently deposited it for safe keeping with the priest. However, he had it returned to him by Ahimelech when he fled from Saul (1 Sam 21.9).

Notes

3 The word "beams" (TSELA - 6763) is literally "ribs" and is used of the side chambers of the Temple (6.5). It has a similar meaning here.

6 The word "thick beam" (AB - 5646) has been translated "threshold" or "steps" or "overhanging roof". Which ever is correct, it appears to be a feature at the entrance of the porch, although its true meaning is uncertain.

16 "chapiter" (KOTERET - 3805) is used only of the heads of the pillars and of the heads of the portable trolleys for the lavers. It seems to have derived from "crown" as a similar word is so translated in Proverbs 14.18.

28 The "borders" (MISGERET - 4526), from a word meaning "close up" were evidently the panels at the sides which enclosed the trolley.

32, 33, 35, 36 The word translated "axletrees" and "ledges" (YAD - 3027) is the ordinary word for "hand" and is used here for the brackets from the bases which reached out like hands and laid hold of the wheels.

34 The "undersetters" (KATEP - 3802) were "shoulders" which carried the weight of the lavers.

38 It is difficult to decide whether the 4 cubits mentioned refers to the height of the lavers or to their diameter. It could well be that it covers both measurements. If they were circular, which seems correct, then they were the same width as the trolleys on which they rested. If the 4 cubits refers to their height, then the entire height of the laver would be eight and a half cubits.

41 This is the first mention of "bowls" (GULLA - 1543) for the pillars. The word is also translated "spring" (Josh 15.19; Judg 1.15) and "pommel" (2 Chr 4.12,13). The bowls were covered by the networks and pomegranates.

49 The "flowers" were for the candlesticks where the branches joined the main stem.

50 The word translated "spoon" (KAP - 3709) is usually translated "hand" or "sole". The palm of the hand can be made hollow and become a spoon-like container. The spoons were used to lift the incense (Num 7.86).

CHAPTER 8

THE DEDICATION OF THE TEMPLE

CHAPTER 8, Verses 1-11
The removal of the Ark and the Tabernacle to the Temple

It might have been expected that, as soon as the Temple and its vessels were finished, Solomon would have immediately dedicated and confirmed it as the centre of worship for the nation. This did not happen. A delay of at least eleven months intervened before the great event took place. The use of the word "Then" in v.1 seems to link back to the storage of the treasures described in 7.51. These cannot have been put into the Temple before it was finished. The month Ethanim would have been eleven months after the Temple was finished (6.38).

However, a number of different opinions exist as to when exactly the dedication did occur. It has been suggested that it took place before the building work was finished. Again, because the statement in 9.1-2 implies that the answer to Solomon's prayer did not come until all his buildings were completed, it is claimed that it did not occur until the end of the twenty years. Others suggest that there were two dedications, one of the Temple, and the other of the palace. The most probable of these is the first, which views the ceremony as planned to coincide with the Feast of Tabernacles, when the nation would not only be gathered together, but be rejoicing in memories of the past. This feast of the seventh month had ended by the time the Temple was finished in the eighth month (6.38). Solomon was prepared to wait until it came round again.

Even though all the work was finished, time was needed to place everything in order and to arrange for the Tabernacle to be dismantled and transported to its new site. The delay of thirteen years (9.1-2) to include the palace buildings may have had in view the Lord's answer to Solomon's prayer.

The tables, the altar and the lamps seem to have been put in place without any ceremony. But the Ark, symbol of the Lord's presence, was different. Representatives of the entire nation were called to Jerusalem to witness its movement from Zion to the house built for it. This assembly was a repeat of that under David when he brought home the Ark (2 Sam 6.1).

The "elders" were the appointed rulers, the "heads" were the leading men of each tribe, and the "chief of the fathers" were the heads of the houses. Thus the nation, tribes and families were all represented. Had David been spared to witness this event he would have rejoiced, for this was his wish before he died. It would appear that normally the Levites carried the Ark, but on special occasions, as in this case, the priests bore it through the Holy Place, through the doors and veil, and set it under the spread wings of the cherubim. The priests undertook this service since the Ark had to be brought into the Most Holy Place, and the Levites were not allowed to enter there in order to lift the Ark, even in the wilderness, until it was covered by the veil (Num 4.4-6).

The ark had been carried through the wilderness, over the bed of Jordan (Josh 3), round the city of Jericho (Josh 6), into the houses of Dagon (1 Sam 5), Abinadab (1 Sam 7.1), and Obed-edom (2 Sam 6.10), into the tent David had erected in Zion (2 Sam 6.17), and now, at length, to its final resting place in the new sanctuary. Never before had it been in such a palatial setting. Even in the Most Holy Place of the Tabernacle, with its gold covered wooden sides and its beautiful curtain ceiling, it had the earthen floor to rest on, but from this time until the Captivity it was completely surrounded by gold. For about one hundred years the Ark had been separated from the Tabernacle, but from now on, both were under the same roof. There is no note of any repairs being needed for this temporary structure. Most, if not all of it, was the original handiwork of those who built it under Moses shortly after the exodus from Egypt. Strangely, the Tabernacle was in use longer than the Temple, even though it was a portable structure.

There is no mention of the vessels from the court of the Tabernacle, such as the laver and altar, being brought up. These may not have been considered either suitable for, or in keeping with, the magnificent interior of the new temple.

However, the Tabernacle and the holy vessels from Gibeon were carried up. There were probably few, if any, vessels in the Zion tent, but the original ones, which were made for the Tabernacle, may well have been preserved.

Great care was taken that no disaster should befall any who carried the Ark. Instead of it being carried directly into the Temple, time was taken during the journey to offer a great number of sacrifices both of sheep and oxen. These were almost certainly peace offerings that provided food for the crowds as well as giving God His due. There was no provision here for a portable altar so these sacrifices must have been killed on the ground. The parts for the Lord could have been burned on the new altar in the court of the Temple.

David had set the example for this procedure when he brought the Ark from the house of Obed-edom to the tent he erected for it at Jerusalem (2 Sam 6.13). On that occasion, for every six paces the priests took a sacrifice was offered. The death of Uzzah, at the time when he touched the Ark on the cart, had left a deep impression on the king's mind and on that of his son.

The long staves of the Ark would have stretched a good part of the width of the Most Holy Place so that the ends of them could be seen from the Holy Place but not from outside the Temple. Both here, and in 2 Chronicles 5.9, the AV implies that they were drawn out so as to be visible. The more probable idea is simply that they were long. In the original instructions they were not to be withdrawn (Ex 25.15), but that may not have applied to the entirely new conditions described here.

The contents of the Ark were, at this time, exactly as they were when it was first made. It contained nothing but the two tables of stone. The wording in the OT regarding the two other items, the rod of Aaron (Num 17.10), and the pot of manna (Ex 16.33), might imply that these two things were merely placed beside the Ark, but in Hebrews they are said to be in it (9.4). The golden pot may have been stolen by the Philistines when they captured the Ark. The stones would have appeared to them to be of little value and would have been left. The golden emerods and golden mice they sent as a trespass offering may have been intended as compensation for the loss of the golden pot. The fact that the contents of the Ark had been checked suggests that it had been opened at this time.

As soon as the Ark rested in the Most Holy Place and the priests had withdrawn, the most important feature of the great event occurred. The glory of the Lord filled the house. This confirmed that He had made it His dwelling place. Not that He had left heaven to live in it! Solomon was aware that heaven is God's abode (v.34) and was conscious that "the heaven and heaven of heavens" could not contain him (v.27).

Though He is omnipresent, yet there have been places where His presence, in a special sense, has been granted. Just as the cloud filled the Tabernacle after it was erected, so here this new dwelling, which was more substantial, was likewise filled.

While there was a close association between the "cloud" and the "glory", the latter appears to refer to the bright shining through the cloud of the light-like fire which accompanied it. In this context it is relevant to make a comparison with the great cloud and fire in Ezekiel 1.4.

God dwelling in darkness or in a cloud did not change with the new Temple, for like the Most Holy Place of the Tabernacle, which had no natural light, the same was true here. The larger compartment, the Holy Place, was different, for it had windows. However, the cloud on this occasion filled both compartments. One unusual feature of this grand event is the absence of any reference to the high priest having a part in it. There is no mention here of any role he played in the transportation of the Ark. Seeing he alone could enter, on the day of atonement, the Most Holy Place where the Ark rested, he above all others, even above the king himself, should have been deeply involved in this whole transaction, yet his name never appears in the story. No doubt he was included in the "priests", but there is no one person marked out as "the priest", which is often the term used when the reference is to the high priest.

Many spiritual lessons could be taken from these verses. However, pointing out a few of the more obvious ones will suffice. Establishing the Ark in glory in the Temple is suggestive of the Lord being seated in heaven after His time on earth had ended. Just as the Ark's period of humiliation had passed, so had His.

The staves being seen by those allowed into the Holy Place illustrates that, even in glory, none will forget the One who journeyed down here. The wood in its construction is a reminder of the Lord's humanity, and here there is pictured the fact, that, though He is in the highest place in heaven, He has taken with Him His previous human body. The tables of stone in the Ark would identify the place the Law has in the heart of the glorified Lord. The overshadowing cherubim illustrate the hosts of heaven who are ready to execute the Lord's commands and guard His glory (Is 6.2,3).

There can be no doubt that this triumphant entrance of the Ark into the Temple is also a foreshadowing of the appearing of the Lord in His Temple, when He comes to set up His kingdom. The sounds of music and the trumpets referred to in 2 Chronicles 5 which accompanied the Ark are but a foretaste of the rejoicing of that future day. The language of Psalm 24.7 "Lift up your heads, O ye gates; and be ye lift up, ye everlasting doors; and the King of glory shall come in", will then be fulfilled.

If the Temple is viewed as a type of a local church, for both are called "the house of God", then the lesson it teaches is that the presence of the Lord is the most important feature of it. When the gifts were exercised under the Lordship of Christ in the church at Corinth, Paul expected that a stranger coming in would fall down and worship with the confession on his lips, "God is in you of a truth" (1 Cor 14.24,25). It is not enough to claim the promise of Matthew 18.20, there ought to be evidence that He is in the midst and that His authority is being acknowledged by all in the company. Just as Solomon desired above all else that the Lord would accept the Temple as His abode, so all who labour to plant assemblies have one special yearning in their hearts, which is that the Lord will make His presence known when His people gather together.

Verses 12-21
Solomon blesses the people, and recounts the past

Although much of Solomon's wisdom and of his great works has already been recorded perhaps it is not until this passage that his ability as a public speaker is seen. He must have had, not only the substance of his address in mind, but also the words to express it and the power of voice so clear that the large congregation could hear what he said. The burden of his address was, not only to bless the people, but to recall the Lord's dealings which had resulted in his building of the Temple. The cloud in the house gave him the assurance that the Lord had indeed come to dwell in His new abode. Perhaps the passage he referred to here is Leviticus 16.2 where the Lord promises to appear in the cloud over the mercy seat. In many of the crises in the wilderness the cloud appearing was the evidence that the Lord had drawn near to speak to Moses. On this occasion no voice was heard, nor did Solomon receive any communication from heaven. He confessed that he built the Temple for the habitation of the Lord. Having spoken to the Lord with his face toward the Temple, he proceeded to address and bless the people and turned toward them.

In these verses Solomon goes over in some detail the dealings of

God with his father regarding the building of a house for the Lord. His mind goes back to the time when Israel was delivered from Egypt and he shows how the idea of building a settled dwelling in any city in Israel was never mentioned by the Lord. His father was the first to think of this. Though David was the initial planner of this house he was not allowed to build it. However, in choosing him to be king, the Lord knew the exercise of his heart and fully endorsed it in the words, "thou didst well that it was in thine heart" (v. 18). Although forbidden to build himself, he was assured that his son would, by the help of the Lord, have the honour of building it, and now this promise had been duly fulfilled, for the house was erected. The substance of these verses is a rehearsal of the words of Nathan to David as recorded in 2 Samuel 7.5-13.

The Ark and its precious contents, the tables of the covenant, was the most important of all the great treasures in the Temple. This sacred chest was the symbol of the Lord's presence and the centre from which He communed with His people. No cloud nor outshining glory would have been seen in the Temple had these things been absent. The stones were not made for the Ark, but it was made for them, and they were secreted in it beneath the mercy seat, and could only be seen when this lid was removed. It was the only vessel in God's house which was used for permanent storage.

Verses 22-53
Solomon's prayer

This prayer by Solomon is one of the longest in Scripture. It begins with an appreciation of the One to whom he prays, and a plea that the care already experienced will continue. After this introduction, seven different supplications are put before the Lord, all of which would be needed during the history of the nation. Solomon stood for a short time before the people, but then kneeled down with his hands upraised (v.54) as he poured out his soul to the Lord. Throughout this prayer he made constant reference to the Pentateuch, especially to the book of Deuteronomy. He was very conscious that the principles laid down for the nation after its deliverance from Egypt had not changed, nor had the God who gave them altered in His character. He regards Him as the great, supreme, the only true, God, and the One who is covenant-keeping and merciful. He recalls the special evidence of this as seen in his father's case, for all the promises made to David had been completely fulfilled. That his posterity should sit on the throne of Israel in perpetuity had also been promised, but not without conditions, for it depended upon their walking before the Lord as did their father. This example is also referred to in 3.6,14 and at 9.4.

The wonder that God would take up His abode in an earthly dwelling still staggered Solomon's mind, for he was conscious that the highest heaven was not fit to confine Him in its bounds. How much less, then, could this Temple accommodate Him. Nothwithstanding this, the plea of Solomon was for Him to watch with the eye of pity over the house where He had placed His name. When, from this time, any would pray toward the Temple, they were not looking to the building for their help, but to the Lord, who, though dwelling in heaven, had placed His name in it.

Before looking in detail at the several requests which Solomon made on this memorable occasion, it should be noted how deep was his understanding of the special needs that were likely to arise in the nation. A study of its later history reveals how appropriate his pleas were, for examples of every one of the difficulties he foresaw can be found in its pages. His prayer was almost a prophecy of coming events, and indicates that the Spirit of God was operating in his mind as he poured out his soul to the Lord. Equally clear is the fact that all the distresses visualized by him were the outcome of sin and failure, and likewise, because of this, repentance and confession were essential if prayers were to be heard and answered.

The first special request concerned anyone who sinned against his neighbour (vv. 31,32). In some cases the offender would be asked to confirm his evidence by an oath. When such an oath was taken before the altar of the Temple, then God was called upon to decide the case and show His approval for the righteous, and His condemnation of the wicked. This first request calls to mind Deuteronomy 25.1, and Exodus 22.11. In the former passage the importance of righteous judgment is stressed, and the latter deals with an occasion when the necessity of an oath could arise. The swearing here is not "by the altar", but at the altar, and by the name of the Lord. Such an oath attests the fact that the one swearing believes in the Lord in whose name he swears. It was at once a confirmation of the truth of his statements, and a confession of his conviction that all he had done, or was doing, was seen by the One who is omniscient.

The second plea concerned the people when defeated by the enemy, and some were taken captive (vv. 33, 34). This was not by any means an unlikely possibility. The reason for such a calamity befalling the nation was no secret. Sin, and particularly the sin of idolatry, which involves departure from God, would bring this result. The curses of Deuteronomy 28 envisaged such a condition, and the warnings regarding disobedience in Leviticus 26 elaborated more fully upon it. Thus Solomon realized that such a sad day could come again and pleaded for the repentant captives to be heard and for those still in the Temple, that is in its courts, also to be heard by the Lord. The outcome of these prayers being heard would be the return of the captives to their own land. In a special way this was fulfilled in the prayers of Daniel and the return of the remnant in the days of Ezra.

The possibility of drought and, as a consequence the land becoming barren, is the third matter about which he prayed (vv.35,36). Unlike Egypt, the land of Canaan was totally dependent upon God for its supplies of water. He had the key of the heavens and could turn off the supply as He willed. Again the cause of the drought is traced to sin. The possibility of such a disaster had been already mentioned by Moses (Lev 26.19; Deut 28.23). Should those suffering drought turn in repentance to the Lord, then, in such a case, Solomon asked that they be heard and the needed water supply restored. The case of Elijah at Carmel is an obvious example of God giving rain after a long period of drought (1 Kings 18.41). God's purpose in chastening His people in this way was to lead them into His ways, so that no such punishment would be necessary in future.

The fourth subject of His prayer concerned famine, pestilence, blasting, mildew, locust, or caterpillar, any one of which would leave the land in a state of devastation (vv. 37-40). A further, but similar situation could arise if an enemy were to besiege one of the cities and this would result in famine and plague distressing the inhabitants. Most if not all of these were also mentioned by Moses in Leviticus 26 and in Deuteronomy 28. They demonstrated the variety of instruments that God had at His disposal, any one of which He might use to chastise His people. Solomon took for granted that in such circumstances the afflicted would pray to the Lord with outstretched hands, and so he asked that God would hear and deliver. He acknowledged that each would understand that God knows the hearts of all and can therefore see the reality of repentance. In the previous request the outcome was to be learning the ways of the Lord, here the outcome is to be a reverential fear of Him. In v.36 the land was given to the people for an inheritance, but here it is the land given to the fathers.

The fifth plea was for something entirely different. It is not the distress of his own people that it concerned but the wonderful possibility of one who was not an Israelite turning in his time of need to the true God and praying to Him (vv. 41-43). The fame of God's name will move some to travel to Jerusalem in order that they may come to know Him as did the Queen of the South. The reverential fear of the Lord, expected in the Israelites who would pray (v.40), is also expected in the much wider sphere in the hearts of all who learn of Him, even to the ends of the earth.

At no time in a nation's history was help more needed than at the time when it was engaged in warfare, whether it be when attacking the enemy, or when defending against an invader. The sixth prayer was that on such critical occasions God would hear the cries for help from His weak and needy people (vv. 44,45). The invasion by the Assyrians in the days of Hezekiah was a special occasion of distress, but he prayed to the Lord (Is 37.15), and the angel of the Lord, in answer to his request, smote 185,000 of the enemy. Had Israel kept right with the Lord and obeyed His word, no such invasions would have succeeded, for just as He had fought for them at the Red Sea, so would He have done throughout their history.

The seventh and last supplication applied to the people when carried into captivity by an enemy (vv. 46-53). Such a disaster, like the others, could come about as the result of God's anger because of their sin. Moses had warned of this when he wrote, "The Lord shall bring thee, and thy king...unto a nation which neither thou nor thy fathers have known" (Deut 28.36). In the lands to which they would be brought, they would have time to think and reflect on the cause of their plight. When repentance had been fully wrought within them, then they would turn to the Lord who dwells in the Temple. He, in this prayer is asked to hear them and show them compassion. From the time the children of Israel were delivered out of Egypt, which was a strong and cruel persecutor of the nation in its infancy, God had in mind to give the land of Canaan to His people as their inheritance. At the same time He purchased them to be His own inheritance. The implication of this plea is that it is altogether out of keeping with this original purpose that these people languish in a foreign land. Their restoration would be in harmony with God's original intention. One could not fail to link this closing supplication with the experience of Daniel, who, possibly thinking of these words, opened his window toward Jerusalem and did what is expected here, prayed to his God. Jonah, looking towards

God's holy Temple, is another example of what is anticipated here. Just as the prayer opened with a reference to the covenant with David, so it closed with a reference to the covenant of Sinai.

Verses 54-61
Solomon blesses the congregation
Apparently Solomon stood briefly before the congregation beside the altar, and then, when he began to pray, kneeled down. He is the first in Scripture to adopt this posture, though there are several references to it later. When he had finished praying he again stood up to bless the people, and did so with his hands stretched out and with a loud voice. While he might not have pronounced the priestly blessing (Num 6.24-26), yet he went as near to doing so as possible. He referred in a special way to the words of Moses, who spoke of the day when Israel would be at rest, and when God would select a fixed place to put His name (Deut 12.5-11). Those promises, made to Israel, had all been duly kept, for God was faithful to His word, as Joshua proved when he led the people into the land (Josh 21.45). Following his confession of the faithfulness of God, Solomon pleaded that the people would continue to have God with them as had their fathers. In a special way Jacob was the first to have the promise, for in his dream he heard the words from the Lord, "I am with thee, and will keep thee for I will not leave thee" (Gen 28.15). Solomon further pleaded that the hearts of the people would be inclined by divine power to obey the word of God and walk in His ways. He was aware that it required more than good resolutions for the people of God to fulfil His will in their lives. Without further detail, he asks in a general way, that, whatever needs may rise in the experience of the people, the help of the Lord will be granted accordingly. Once again he widened his horizon and thought of the effect their good testimony would have on the heathen. The name of the Lord would become so famous that He alone would be acknowledged as the true God. The visit of the Queen of Sheba subsequently proved the truth of this. He closed his blessing with a plea to the people to be careful to obey the Lord with a perfect heart.

The lessons in this wonderful dedicatory ceremony are many. One outstanding fact stamped upon the prayer is the tendency for those favoured by God to go astray. All can sing, "Prone to wander Lord we feel it, Prone to leave the God we love". Possibly the saints of the present age have had to make every one of the supplications expressed here, albeit in a spiritual sense. Problems still arise. Often defeat is experienced, as when wrestling against the powers of darkness, and there are times when those engaged in the struggle feel parched and dry. Equally clear is the unchanging principle that the way to recovery is by repentance. When sin is confessed and forsaken the way is open for God to show mercy and for Him to use His power to deliver.

Saints do not turn their faces to a building on earth in which the Lord has placed His name, but to the throne of grace, where the Lord is seated. Sins are confessed to God, and Christ the advocate pleads their cause and restores the fellowship which has been temporarily broken (1 Jn 1.9; 2.1).

Just as the prayer of Solomon is studded with references to the Pentateuch, so the value of God's Word, whether in warnings or in promises, should characterize all prayer. The cry of Jonah is almost entirely quotations from the Psalms and other OT writings.

Supplications should be based on the promises of God, and, if so, they will rise to Him as sweet incense.

Verses 62-66
The dedication sacrifices and feast
Before this consecration, workmen, whether Israelites or Gentiles, could walk through the Temple as they would through any other building, but from this time onward it was holy ground which could only be entered by those fitted to do so. Later Uzziah, even though a good king, ventured into it, and was smitten by leprosy (2 Chr 26.16-21).

The immense number of animals sacrificed on this occasion as peace-offerings, 22,000 oxen and 120,000 sheep, meant that the large altar was too small to burn on it the fat that was the Lord's portion of these as well as the other offerings. So the centre of the court became, for the time being, a huge altar. The feast lasted fourteen days so as to allow time for the killing of so many animals. The thousands of Israelites who assembled for this great function would no doubt be fed by the flesh of these animals. Solomon did not provide all the victims, for the people joined with him in sacrificing. While the sacrifices showed the people's devotion to the Lord, at the same time they celebrated a feast lasting two weeks. It was the time of the Feast of Tabernacles, so there was a combination of dedicating the temple, possibly during the first week and keeping of the feast of booths on the second week. Thus the dedication began on the 8th day of the month Ethanim, and all were sent home on the evening of the 22nd day of the same month.

Probably there never was as large a gathering of the people at any other time in their history. The heads of the households came from far and near to enjoy this unique occasion. The heights reached at this time were the nearest the earth has seen to what the world will be like when the King, of whom Solomon is but a type, establishes His kingdom. The people were so delighted with all that the king had done, that they wished him God's blessing, or saluted him, before they returned with glad hearts to their own homes.

Some may find it difficult to grasp that the way to rejoicing is by giving the Lord His portion of all that is acceptable to Him. Complete consecration may seem costly, but those who put their all upon the altar for God never regret their action. The eleven references to "heart" in this chapter emphasise the importance of that great centre of will and feeling. The nine references to "sin" in the chapter show that most needs arise because of it.

Notes

8 The AV translation gives the impression that the staves were drawn out of the Ark, now that its travels were over, but the word translated "drew out" (ARAK - 748) is often translated "prolong" or "lengthen", so its meaning here is that the staves were long. The reason for their length may have been to preserve those who carried it from judgment through accidentally touching the ark. Perhaps these staves could have been seen from the Holy Place only when the high priest was going into the oracle, and had to open the doors and pull back the curtain in order to do so.

28 The three words, "prayer", to request from God, "supplication", when a special need was involved, and "cry", the loud call for help, are combined here. The word "supplication" (TeHINNA - 8467) is used seven times in this chapter, and at 9.3.

38 The "plague" (NEGA - 5061) of his own heart is often thought of as the personal evil of the heart, but it refers rather to that which pains him, or smites him, so the reference is to the anguish he feels under the dealings of God.

51 The "furnace" (KUR - 3564) as a picture of Israel's bondage in Egypt is taken from Deuteronomy 4.20.

63 The word "dedicate" (CHANAK - 2596) means to inaugurate, or set apart. It is used in "train up a child" (Prov 22.6), and of the dedication of a new house (Deut 20.5).

64 The middle of the court was "hallowed" (QADASH - 6942) which meant that it was set apart for holy use on this occasion. It seems probable that this was the smaller court of the priests, but of this we cannot be sure.

65 The most northerly boundary of the land was Hamath (Num 34.7,8), and the most southern boundary was "the river (or brook) of Egypt". This river must not be confused with the Nile. It is mentioned in Num 34.5, and in Josh 15.4.

CHAPTER 9

SOLOMON'S RELATIONSHIP WITH THE LORD, AND WITH THOSE ABOUT HIM

CHAPTER 9, Verses 1-9

The Lord appears to Solomon a second time

If this second appearing was in the middle of Solomon's reign then it is noteworthy that little detail is given of his activity since he began to build the Temple. However, this chapter reveals many of the matters to which he attended during, and after, the time of his two great building projects. As has been stated earlier there is a problem in deciding whether this second appearance of the Lord occurred immediately the Temple was dedicated or was delayed until his palace also was completed. The chief reason given in support of the view that the Temple was not dedicated until Solomon had finished his own house and was granted this appearance of the Lord is that the words, "I have heard thy prayer", and, "I have hallowed this house", must have come immediately after he had prayed. However, the Lord could have been reminding him that his prayer of thirteen years earlier had not been forgotten. Those who take the view that the Temple was dedicated immediately it was finished point to the cloud filling it as evidence of God's presence and approval for its use from that time forward.

The tone of the Lord's words on this occasion seems to indicate that a period had elapsed from the time the prayer was offered until this answer was given.

Unlike the first appearing of the Lord in ch.3, there is no mention of a dream here, unless it is implied in the words "...as he had appeared unto him at Gibeon". The message brought to him at this second appearance of the Lord is also different in character from the first at Gibeon in that it is more exhortatory and less commendatory. At the first appearance, the building of the Temple and of the palace still lay ahead, but now his dreams have become realities.

As long as one is struggling for a goal there is a conscious sense of need. Once the goal is reached there is a danger of pride entering the heart. There is no doubt but that the Lord not only foresaw the coming apostasy but was uttering a warning so as to leave no excuse for either Solomon or those who succeeded him should they turn away from the true God.

Broadly speaking the Lord's message divides into three parts. First, a word of assurance regarding the Temple (v.3); second, a word concerning his throne (vv. 4,5); third, a word of warning on the consequences of departure from God (vv. 6-9). Already the cloud of glory, which appeared at the dedication of the Temple, had assured all who saw it that the Lord had accepted the house as His dwelling place. However, on this occasion, the fact is put into words of promise. The cloud did not remain on the Temple, but the promise given here remained permanently. The Lord had put His name on the building. He would watch over it as His own treasure and His heart would always be toward it. There was no other structure like it on earth at that time, in a unique way it was God's holy house.

Having assured Solomon regarding the Temple, the Lord proceeded to speak directly to him on the establishment of his throne.

Again the example of his father is set before him. Only by walking in his father's footsteps could he, and his posterity, retain the throne. The commendation given to David by the Lord may seem, in the light of his failures, to be more than was warranted, but, whatever the sins in his life, he had never turned to idolatry. Solomon was to imitate his father's virtues, but this did not imply that he was to look lightly upon his father's failings. The promise to David that "There shall not fail thee...a man on the throne of Israel" (2.4) would be honoured provided each succeeding heir kept God's commandments and judgments.

The serious consequences of turning to idolatry were pressed upon Solomon. The nation, so highly favoured, would be cut off out of the land. The Temple also would be destroyed and the surrounding nations would mock the worshippers who would be helpless to save it. They would even hiss as they passed by the ruins of what was once a glorious palace. To the question of why such a special people could be so devastated the answer would be given, even by the heathen, that this destruction was the result of the people and their king having turned away from their God who had earlier made them to prosper.

In this appearing of the Lord to Solomon there were not only words of warning but words which proved to be prophetic of the ultimate fate of the Temple. Not that they were given as a prophecy, but the rest of the record of the kings is a sad revelation of the fact that the things warned against were the very things that did take place. The destruction, so unlikely at this time, did eventually occur. Just as, in the prayer of Solomon, the evils which he foresaw as possible became, in the course of time, actual, so here the dangers of departure, disobedience to God's word and idolatry, later became history. It would have been difficult for Solomon to imagine that the Temple, which was a masterpiece and his delight, would one day be a heap of ashes.

In this there is a weighty lesson. The most spiritual assembly, which, according to the NT, is a house of God, can be brought to ruin as was the Temple. Equally true is the fact that even though the founders of an assembly were careful to obey the Word of God, this does not guarantee that their successors will be equally obedient. There can be various reasons for once prosperous assemblies to die out, but, in not a few cases, the real cause can be traced to one factor, namely, departure from the Word of God.

Verses 10-14
Exchange of cities

Already reference has been made to the great amount of wood and gold contributed by Hiram for the building of the Temple. Now these verses show how Solomon sought to repay him for these. Although grain and oil had been constantly forwarded during the years of building, something more permanent was considered necessary in order to "balance the books".

In Galilee, which lay close to Hiram's territory, and was probably at this time occupied by Canaanites, there were twenty cities or villages. These were offered as a gift to Hiram. When he came to see them he was disappointed and spoke of them in a slighting manner. It would appear from 2 Chronicles 8.1- 2 that these cities were returned to Solomon who had no right, in the first place, to give them away. They had to be rebuilt before the children of Israel could live in them. Clearly no offence was taken for Hiram gave Solomon a handsome gift of 120 talents of gold. If this came after all the building work was practically completed, it was a much needed bonus and helped to fill the coffers which by this time must have been drained to a low level.

Verses 15-24
Solomon's cities and levy

When the Temple was finished those Israelites engaged in building it were, in all probability, freed from the work. However, with more buildings designed by Solomon, and situated in different places, a large contingent of men was needed for their erection. Here there is evidence showing how he obtained his workforce. Just as Joshua put the Canaanites to slave labour so Solomon also made slaves of the remnant of those who had survived over the intervening centuries. They were forced to toil at these buildings. While he had a large number of workers who were Israelites, they were not slaves. Rather they were like officers in the army and civil servants.

His success in building the Temple and the palace gave him an appetite to use his skills in many corners of the land. A study of the places where he erected forts shows that he was not putting up buildings at random, but rather that he was building defences which would withstand any attacks that might be made by enemies seeking to penetrate his kingdom. One of these was Millo which had already been built by David (2 Sam 5.9) and must have been enlarged by Solomon at this time. It was the great fort of Jerusalem and seems to have been a citadel included in the wall surrounding the city. Later it was strengthened by Hezekiah to ward off the Assyrians (2 Chr 32.5).

The second defence mentioned is Hazor which was in the north of Palestine, and, being in a high position, was a vital fort and one which protected the surrounding area from any northern invasions. Originally it was a capital city, the seat of Jabin in Joshua's time (Josh 11.1) and the seat of another king Jabin in the days of Deborah (Judg 4.2). Megiddo was situated in the area of the tribe of Manasseh (Josh 17.11), and it too was a much needed defence point on the way from the Sea to the plains of Jordan. It is mentioned at the overthrow of Sisera (Judg 5.19), but is specially remembered as the place where king Josiah was killed (2 Kings 23.29-30).

Yet another of these fortified cities was Gezer which was near to Lachish on the border of Ephraim. It was a levitical city which was given to the Kohathites (Josh 21.21). Its Canaanite inhabitants had not been expelled by Israel. However, during Solomon's reign, Pharoah's army captured and burnt it, and he then gave it to his daughter, Solomon's wife. Solomon now re-built it, and so added another outpost to his defences.

Two cities bore the name of Beth-horon, one the upper and the other the lower, with less than 2 miles separating them. The one mentioned here is the lower town which was 800 feet below its sister. The armies of the five kings of the Amorites fled through this area in the days of Joshua (Josh 10), and the Philistines fought from it in the days of Saul (1 Sam 13.18). Its situation between Benjamin and Ephraim meant that it was an important fortified city able to act as a defence against any invasion from either Philistia or Egypt.

In the territory of Dan, and not far from the land of the Philistines, Solomon built another fortress called Baalath. The Philistines were always ready to invade Israel, especially at times of the nation's weakness. Thus it was wise to build the city to block their path.

The last of the cities mentioned here is "Tadmor" or "Tamar". It was a most important place to fortify for it lay on the road to Babylon and on the north-east of Palestine. It is said here to be "in the land", which implies that Solomon's kingdom extended beyond the normal bounds of Israel as far as to the area of that city.

These and other cities were built, not only as forts, but also as depots for the surplus grain that the land produced. The many horses Solomon acquired were also in need of stabling and so there was almost no end to the demand for buildings. The first person recorded in the OT to build "cities of store" was Pharaoh (Ex 1.11). Solomon imitated Egypt in this as well as in acquiring chariots and horses. The influence of his Egyptian wife may have had a bearing on his actions at this time. Added to these essential cities were a number, including the one at Lebanon, which were built for his own personal pleasure. The shade and vegetation of the forest of that area would be pleasant in the heat of summer. Some of the pleasing features of Lebanon are described in his Song (4.11,15; 5.15).

The levy mentioned in v.15 is described in detail in vv. 20-21. It is surprising that such a variety of the descendants of the Canaanite nations still existed in the days of Solomon. Though Joshua conquered them and captured their cities, he did not exterminate them, nor did their distinct identity disappear in the intervening years. Alas, quite a number of them were married into the families of Israel. They could not be treated as slaves. But some had no such connection to Israel, and these were the subjects of this bondage. Already the part played by Gentiles in the building of the Temple has been noted. Once more it can be seen that in the other great building schemes of Solomon they likewise had a major part. Again there is a reference to the entrance of Pharaoh's daughter into her new home, but here it is linked with the building of Millo. The reason for this is probably to show that, though she had left the City of David, she was no less secure in her new home.

Before leaving this section, attention must be drawn to the horses and chariots referred to (v.19). Neither in the matter of these, nor in the matter of wives, did Solomon take heed to the instructions in Deuteronomy 17.16,17. His later experience proved the costliness of this neglect.

These verses make plain that the defence of a kingdom is vital and that this should be put in place before it is needed. Believers should be aware of potential dangers and should fortify their minds and hearts with the Word of God, so that when attacks are made upon them they will be able to overcome.

Another lesson is that the passing of time does not change the nature of the enemies. The Canaanite nations picture the powers of darkness which seek to prevent the saints entering into their spiritual inheritance, and against which they are expected to wrestle (Eph 6.12). There is to be no yielding to the influence of these spiritual forces.

There was great wisdom in Solomon's effort to build defences to protect the land from its foes. This, however, did not guarantee its safety. The danger has always been that when a sense of security is felt, then dependence on the Lord tends to decline. It is well to remember that "except the Lord keep the city, the watchman waketh but in vain" (Ps 127.1).

Verse 25
Solomon's offerings

According to law, the males in Israel were to appear before the Lord three times in the year (Deut 16.16). As a true Israelite, Solomon attended to this demand and offered his burnt offerings and peace offerings on the great altar he had made. The three visits to the Temple were on the feasts of Passover, Pentecost and Tabernacles.

The statement that, "he burnt incense upon the altar that was before the Lord" has been interpreted to suggest that he entered the Holy Place and burnt incense as though he were a priest. This is a misunderstanding of the passage. The idea is that, along with his sacrifices, incense was offered. He was not the bearer of it into the Holy Place any more than he was the one who put the burnt offerings on the altar or that he built Millo with his own hands. By using the

Temple in this way he demonstrated to the people that it was the only centre of worship and that it fulfilled all that was intended of it.

Verses 26-28
The naval expeditions of Solomon and Hiram

Palestine had no natural harbours and so the Israelites were not noted as seafarers. Nevertheless, there were many goods that had to be imported by sea. Already the floating of the timber for the Temple has been mentioned. In these verses reference is made as to how the wealth of Solomon, much of which had been expended on costly buildings, was replenished. Ships were built at Ezion-geber in Edom at the head of the gulf of Akabah which opens into the Red Sea. The Israelites on their journey from Egypt were near this place before they entered the wilderness of Zin (Num 33.35). It is possible that the timber for these ships was obtained from Lebanon and brought to Ezion-geber where Hiram's men not only helped in their building but taught the Israelites the art of seafaring.

Apparently, when the ships were ready, both Solomon's and Hiram's sailors went to Ophir. It is not clear where exactly this place was located. It could be in Arabia, but the length of time occupied in the return trip, three years (10.22), seems to suggest that it could be even further away. India has therefore been suggested as its possible location. Another possibility is that it was in Somaliland. However, the time factor should not carry too much weight. At that time procuring the cargoes, bartering with the traders and waiting for favourable winds may have taken longer than would be expected.

The large quantity of gold, 420 talents, about fourteen to fifteen metric tonnes, which was brought home on the first expedition, is a staggering amount. One thing is certain, this huge cargo of gold so filled the coffers of Solomon, that, though he had earlier lavished almost all of his wealth on the Temple and other buildings it restored to him his former affluence.

Notes

1 The word "desire" (CHESHEQ - 2837) is used only of Solomon except in Isaiah 21.4 where it is translated "pleasure". It implies personal interest. The kindred word "pleased" (CHAPETS - 2654) is used in 10.9 and there translated "delighted". It is also used of the Lord, "I delight to do thy will" (Ps 40.8).

4 The "integrity", (TOM - 9537), or ""complete sincerity" of David's heart is often mentioned in the psalms he wrote, and, at times, is used as his plea to be heard by God (Ps 7.8; 25.21; 26.1,11; 41.12; and 101.2).

7 A "byword" (SHeNINA - 8148) is a term always used of the "taunt" of the nations when they see Israel humiliated (Deut 28.37; Jer 24.9).

8 The word "hiss" (SHARAQ - 8319) is first used here, and means to make a shrill call in scorn, or to whistle in scorn.

9 Israel "taking hold upon" (CHAZAQ - 2388) other gods is an interesting expression. It implies that they gripped them firmly, as did Adonijah and Joab the horns of the altar (1.50; 2.28).

21 The original inhabitants of Canaan were sentenced to "utter destruction" (CHARAM - 2763) which means that they were considered as "devoted to God" as were the spoils of Jericho (Josh 6.17; 7.1).

28 In 2 Chronicles 8.18 the number of talents is 450, but here only 420. Solomon may have given the thirty talents to Hiram for the service rendered by his men.

CHAPTER 10

THE GLORY AND FAME OF SOLOMON'S KINGDOM

CHAPTER 10, Verses 1-13
The state visit of the Queen of Sheba

This chapter recounts the zenith of Solomon's wise administration. His kingdom had no equal in the then known world and his divinely given wisdom had made him the most famous man on earth. After telling of his building programmes and his maritime fleet the historian shows his universal fame which the visit of the Queen of Sheba personified. The general traders, who constantly passed through the land and sold their wares in the best markets, would have spread abroad the news of the wonderful prosperity of Israel under the wise rule of its king. In all probability, however, it was the adventures of the navy which introduced his fame into Sheba, so that it reached its Queen. This land, though sometimes mentioned as modern Ethiopia, was more probably in the south east of Arabia, and was famed for its trading in gold and spices. In those days the prosperity of a kingdom was attributed to its gods, and they, in turn, were judged by the success of their worshippers. Equally it was believed that when a nation fell it could be attributed to its people having offended their gods.

Solomon was not only famed for the success of his rule, but especially for his unique wisdom. It is possible that the Queen of Sheba herself had a flair for sharp thinking, for it takes wisdom to think out riddles, (for that was what her "hard questions" were) as well as to solve them. For such an erudite woman to learn of one who could excel her in this domain was no small surprise to her. In spite of the distance involved and the slow means of transport, she was prepared to travel the long journey in order to have a personal interview with the reputed philosopher. To her amazement he was able to solve all her enigmas. It is to be hoped that he went further than merely untying the knots of worldly wit and that he did indeed introduce her to the Lord, the great source of all wisdom. As has already been admitted regarding Hiram there is no certainty regarding the Queen's spiritual state. However, the Lord's reference to her when He said, "The queen of the south shall rise up in the judgment" (Mt 12.42), raises great hopes in that domain. One thing is certain, she could have travelled the then known world, but nowhere else, save at Jerusalem, could she have seen such impressive sights. Whatever her impressions were of the name of the Lord of whom she had heard in her own land, these object lessons left her in no doubt as to His surpassing greatness. Indeed she was so overwhelmed that she exclaimed, "The half was not told me". She reckoned that it was a privilege to be in Solomon's presence, and to hear his wisdom. It is still no small privilege to be in close contact with leaders who have been enriched with wisdom. Possibly some who met the king daily did not value his counsel as much as did the Queen.

As well as opening her ears to learn the depths of Solomon's wisdom, she opened her eyes and particularly noted six of his court arrangements. She was deeply impressed by the great palace he had built; by the banquet table with its variety of food; by the guests, who were his ministers of state, in their dignified positions; by the attending servants in their uniforms; by the cupbearers who served out the wine; and by the wonderful stairway which led from the palace to the house of the Lord. Reports often exaggerate and when they are investigated the expectations of those who hear them are disappointed, but, on this occasion, the report she had heard before fell far short of the reality.

In her outburst of appreciation of all that she had proved of Solomon's wisdom and wealth she voiced her personal wonderment. She also proceeded to speak of the blessedness of those who had the privilege of being his servants, and who therefore could listen daily to his wisdom. She went further, and expressed her appreciation of the Lord, the God of Israel, who had so loved His people as to give them such a wise king to sit upon the throne. These statements have led many to conclude that she was a true convert to Jehovah. On the face of her words, this is a fair assumption, but almost the same words were used by Hiram (5.7), without convincing the reader that he was one who had turned from idols to serve the living and true God. Possibly it was common courtesy to extol the gods of other nations when speaking to their worshippers.

When people are poor, even the smallest gifts are appreciated, but to bring an acceptable gift to a king as wealthy as Solomon was no easy matter. However, she did not need to feel embarrassed. Her present was indeed massive. The 120 talents of gold, the gems and the large quantity of spices were most acceptable gifts and were in keeping with her status as a queen. All of these treasures were products of her own land, which at that time, particularly because of its spice trade, was one of the richest in the world. Solomon did not only attempt to repay her generosity by gifts chosen by himself, but allowed her to ask what she desired. As it were, he gave her a blank cheque that she could fill in as she pleased. Doubtless she did not leave empty-handed, for her benefactor had much which she may not have been able to obtain in her own country.

Her return home, like her journey to Jerusalem, must have been arduous, with the heat of the sun above and the sand of the desert beneath, but her heart must have rejoiced as she reflected on all that she had heard and seen. Since she could spend so much time away from her throne there must have been those able to be left behind to hold the reins until she returned. The train of servants that accompanied her would, no doubt, make conditions as comfortable for her as was then possible, but she must have had more than normal stamina to endure the hardships of the journey.

The visit of the Queen and her comments teach some important lessons. One is that when the Lord has His rightful place in a nation or even in an assembly, the fame of His presence will spread abroad. Where He is working and blessing His own, there will be a centre to which strangers will be drawn. When Israel is restored in the future, and when His presence will again be manifest in Jerusalem, then the Gentiles will bring their gifts, and call it "The city of the Lord, The Zion of the Holy One of Israel" (Is 60.1-14). Though Israel was never a missionary nation with messengers travelling to other lands to spread abroad the fame of their Lord, yet it was always intended by God to be a centre of light for any Gentile wishing to learn of Him.

Often complaints are made by believers that it is all but impossible to gather strangers into meetings, but it must be realized that it takes more than invitations to bring people to hear the Gospel. News spreads abroad of the Lord working and the interests of most men are stirred when they hear of it. They will then seek to investigate the reason as did the Queen of Sheba. This can result in their hearts being opened to the way of salvation.

Another important lesson from the passage is that strangers are observant. Just as the Queen noted all that was transpiring in the palace of Solomon, so visitors to any new environment will invariably watch with critical eyes all that comes before them. How vital it is that all should be as God would have it, so that there is nothing introduced which could stumble strangers. Had the Queen come to Jerusalem some time later than she did, what confusion would have filled her mind, for she would have been forced to ask which of the gods worshipped by the king's household was the true one. Not far from the Temple the wives of the king were by then attending the shrines of idols, were offering their sacrifices and were burning incense to their false gods.

This story also teaches another lesson. Giving to someone who already has much is not so absurd as many might think. When a believer gives to the Lord he or she is giving to One who owns the cattle on a thousand hills. Had the Queen of Sheba asked herself before she left home, "What does Solomon need?", she could have truthfully answered, "Nothing". Yet she came with all the precious gifts she could afford. Likewise, those who give to the Lord, know that they do not give to Him because of His need, but rather as an expression of their appreciation of Him. Equally true is the fact that just as she received from Solomon all that she desired, so the Lord is no one's debtor, for He supplies all the needs of His people (Phil 4.19).

Quite often there is little thought given to the fact that people have different responsibilities and different interests. This visit by the Queen shows that she specially noted the order of the King's palace. Being a ruler herself, she had a deep interest in how he ran his establishment. Had she been an architect she would no doubt have surveyed the buildings and barely noticed the ministers of state. Those to whom the gospel is preached have different backgrounds and different interests, so it ought to be presented to them in a way that they can understand and in a way that will make it acceptable to them. The preaching of Paul in Acts 13 and in Acts 17 illustrates this principle. The Lord in His parables is the greatest example of this.

The historian breaks the story of the Queen of Sheba with a parenthesis in which he tells of the cargo of gold, precious stones and almug trees which the ships built by Hirman's men brought home to Solomon. In these two verses (11 and 12) the link with the main story is that they show that the wealth he received by sea was additional to that which he had received from the hand of the Queen or through traders who travelled by land. The almug trees which they brought with them were native to India and of special interest. Not only were they hitherto not used by Solomon, but their fragrant wood proved suitable for a variety of purposes including being burnt to perfume temples and houses. The wood was also used to make musical instruments. It has been thought to be the modern sandlewood, but it may have been either a harder type of this timber, or some other wood, for it was suitable for external use as well as for the most delicate work. The use of this wood in the Temple courts is problematic for all the buildings were finished before this time. However, if we combine the reference in 2 Chronicles 9.10,11, where the word "algum" is used, with this passage, the conclusion could be reached that two staircases with handrails had been constructed with it, one for the Temple court, and the other for the court of the palace.

Verses 14-29
Solomon's glory

The historian in these verses reaches a climax. In a sense it would have been well if his history had ended with this chapter. Apart from his revenue collected from traders, kings and governors, his annual income of 666 talents of gold was immense. It must have taxed his mind to its limit to think of ways in which such an amount of gold could be used. He thought of making shields of it. These were of two sizes, the two hundred larger ones, called "targets" in the AV, were made of just over 3.25 kilos of gold, and the three hundred smaller ones were made of over 1.5 kilos of gold. The house of the forest of Lebanon must have been an arms depot as well as being a barracks for the king's bodyguard, for these shields were deposited in it. They were probably hung upon the walls for display rather than for use in the battlefield, and were tokens of great wealth. Later, in ch.14, their removal is recorded.

Already details of Solomon's porch where he met and judged the people have been given (7.7), and now the throne on which he sat when dealing with the affairs of the kingdom is described (vv. 18-20). While many references are made to the "throne of David", yet there is no description of an actual seat. Eli appears to have had a particular seat (throne) near the Tabernacle (1 Sam 1.9), but possibly not until Solomon did any ruler in Israel have a throne room and an ornate throne. It is possible that this throne was made of wood overlaid with ivory, but it could have been made of ivory itself. It is referred to as if constructed of that material. Intermingled with the ivory, and possibly inlaid into it, was a special kind of gold here called "the best gold". It was reached by climbing six steps. On each side of these stood a lion symbolising the strength of the authority of the throne. Two armrests were also provided, and these, too, had lions supporting them. The circular head which rose from the back may have been a kind of canopy. This would have been in keeping with the king's crown.

A further evidence of Solomon's glory was seen in the vessels on his table, for these were of gold. Even his elite body-guard in the house of the forest of Lebanon was supplied with similar precious vessels. The rare and costly metal, with universal value, had become so plentiful in Jerusalem as to be used for the most common utensils. Silver, though highly valued elsewhere, was counted of little worth in this kingdom. Later it is said that it was as common as stones in the street (v.27). The more we have of any commodity the less it is valued, so the large quantities of imported cedar wood made it as common as the sycamore which was an indigenous tree of Canaan (v.27).

The reason given for this large amount of precious metals is that every three years a cargo of valuables was brought to Solomon by his fleet of merchant ships. Some suggest that the term "navy of Tarshish" was used for trading ships irrespective of where they sailed. It is more likely that Solomon had two fleets, one operating in the Red Sea and the other in the Great Sea. If the latter of these did exist then the port of Tyre was the most probable landing place for both his and Hiram's ships. If the Tarshish mentioned here is in Spain, the difficulty raised is that it was famed for silver, but not for gold, ivory, apes and peacocks. Indeed, some have gone as far as to claim that the names given to these creatures here are more like Indian names than Hebrew. Why Solomon wanted apes and peacocks, apart from curiosity, is difficult to say. No doubt their rarity made them more valuable.

Another source of Solomon's wealth is given in vv. 23-25. His fame had spread abroad to the entire known world. Kings from distant lands came, as did the Queen of Sheba, to receive from him counsel and benefit from his God-given wisdom. None came empty handed. They brought of their best to him, and did so annually. Precious metals, together with armour, clothing and spices were all acceptable gifts. Earlier, it was stated that he had horses, but here there is the first reference as to how he obtained them. They were included in the gifts brought to him by various kings.

Solomon's riches and fame were a serious temptation to him. He had so much to spend he scarcely knew what to buy with it. Had he pondered the Book of Deuteronomy he would have learned that he was not to multiply horses (Deut 17.16), yet this was the very thing he did. These animals were not draught horses but war horses as the mention of chariots makes plain. A great deal of expense was involved in buying 1,400 chariots and the horses to pull them, together with maintaining the 12,000 horsemen to attend to them. Egypt was known for its horses, so from there he augmented his equine stock, together with their chariots. The cost of a chariot was four times that of a horse, and the two together amounted to 750 shekels of silver.

It is evident that the Hittites, who were Canaanites, were still present in the land, but no doubt under the authority of Solomon. They also bought horses and chariots from the traders.

The "full cup" of Solomon is a reminder that even the wisest of men find great difficulty in carrying it. When wealth is rolling in from every quarter and every adventure is successful, there is a strong temptation to depart from the path of faith and from a life lived daily in dependence upon God. His riches were as great a test for him, and all like him, as was poverty to his father when he and his followers were thankful to eat the stale loaves of shewbread (1 Sam 21.4ff).

There is something incongruous about a king becoming a horse dealer. However they were the emblem of his military strength. It is instructive that the failure at Corinth in the NT was, in great measure, because they imagined that worldly wisdom was of value in the church. However this, like Solomon's horses, was never intended by God to displace dependence on Him and the wisdom that is from above.

Similarly the Ephesian church was the most enriched with spiritual wealth of all those that are mentioned in the NT, yet this did not keep it from falling as Revelation 2 shows. This is a solemn reminder that God's blessings were never intended to develop pride or cause dependence upon Him to wane.

Another lesson from these verses is the danger of imitating the world. The things Solomon gathered were the very things that every king in his day would have aimed at. Israel's wealth was mainly material, but, in a sense, it was only loaned by the Lord. This meant they were stewards of all that they possessed. Likewise the believer to-day is a steward, not just of material wealth, but also of those spiritual riches which the Lord has entrusted to him. Wisdom is needed, not only to obtain them, but to use them for the honour of their true owner.

The links between Solomon's reign and the coming reign of Christ have already been pointed out. Again it must be stressed that in this, the peak of his kingdom glory, is the closest resemblance to that wonderful future day that has yet been seen. In the day when that wise King, the Lord Himself, takes the throne the prosperity of the world will be so great that it is impossible even to imagine it. The long-standing enmity between Jew and Gentile will be ended and Gentiles will come from every corner of the earth to worship God in His holy Temple, and to bring to the King their choicest presents (Ps 45.12). If the shadow given here is so great, what will be the substance? How wonderful to share the kingdom with Him!

Notes

1 The "hard questions" were "enigmas" (CHIDA - 2420) translated "riddle" eight times in Judges 14, and "dark saying" in Psalms 49.4; and 78.2.

2 Her "train" (CHAYIL - 2428) indicates a "strong force" whether of men or means, and in this case refers to her bodyguard.

3 All her "questions" (DABAR - 1697) here were the words spoken to him, and not the riddles of v.1.

12 The "pillars" (MISAD - 4552) are mentioned only here in the OT. They were props or supports, but neither house needed props, so they are believed to be railings or balustrades.

18 The word translated "ivory" (SHEN - 8127) is the ordinary word for "tooth". The throne must have been made of tusks, or else it was overlaid with material made of these. Either way, it was far from comfortable as a seat.

28 It is suggested by some authorities that rather than Egypt (also known as Mizraim), the true rendering is Misra, which referred to Cilicia/Cappadoccia, and which was the place from which the horses actually came.

CHAPTER 11

SOLOMON'S FAILURE AND DEATH

CHAPTER 11, Verses 1-8
Solomon and his Gentile wives

The height of Solomon's glory having been traced, there follows the sad story of his downfall and its causes. It is hard to believe that such a wise king could prove to be so foolish. In later times when some of the returned remnant married Gentile wives Solomon was held up as a solemn example of the serious nature of this evil. Nehemiah is recorded as saying there was "no king like him, who was beloved of his God...nevertheless even him did outlandish women cause to sin" (Neh 13.26).

The many heathen wives he took were instrumental in turning him aside. Until this time the implication is that he had one wife, the daughter of Pharaoh. Even later she is distinguished from the rest and apparently held an unique place in his life.

There were three particular warnings given in Deuteronomy 17 to any future king of Israel. He was not to "multiply horses...nor cause the people to return to Egypt, to the end that he should multiply horses" (v.16); he was not to "multiply wives to himself" and he was not to "greatly multiply to himself silver and gold" (v.17). Solomon ignored all three to the ruin of his house.

At that time among the nations one measure of the greatness of a king was the number of his wives and concubines. Since Solomon was one of the most wealthy, the size of his harem was almost unlimited. What appears even more surprising in this matter is that he evidently had little interest in the women of his own nation but had many foreign wives. In direct defiance of the teaching of the Law (Ex 34.16; Deut 7.3,4), which warned of the danger of such unequal yokes, he drove on in his reckless course and had to suffer the consequences. These wives were mainly from the neighbouring nations. The first three of those mentioned in v.1 were related to Israel through Abraham, while the last two were of the original stock of Canaan. The reason they are brought together is that they all engaged in idolatry. While the prohibition of v.2 originally applied only to the nations of Canaan, all of them are said to be "strange" because of their idolatry.

Particularly in the earlier part of his reign Solomon was anxious to forestall any attempt by neighbouring nations to invade his kingdom. As time passed he judged that if he took wives of these potential enemies he would be safe. They would be unlikely to attack their own flesh and blood. The marriages were of political value.

It would have been utterly impossible for him to give personal attention to each of these women since there are said to have been a thousand of them.

A second motive in taking them was to enhance his fame. It is not explained how he dealt with them. Perhaps like the king of Persia, he had only brief and limited relationships with them (Est 2.14). However it is sadly made plain that, instead of him converting them to the knowledge of the true God, they retained their idolatrous religion, and even turned his heart away from the Lord. None of them was heard to say, as did Ruth, "Thy people shall be my people, and thy God my God" (Ruth 1.16).

In many cases youth is the time when folly is most likely to mark a man, but for Solomon it was his early years that were characterized by wisdom. He was especially endowed with it from the Lord. His prosperity was the blessed outcome of it. But in old age he became the "old and foolish king, who will no more be admonished" (Eccl 4.13). Not that he is to be thought of as being particularly elderly for at his death he was about sixty years old and must have been turned away in heart from the Lord some years before this.

It would be good to think that he had no serious interest in idols but merely obliged his wives by building them shrines at which to worship. However, the reference to his being turned away in heart to other gods seems to go further than this. Whatever may have been his motive in having so many foreign wives it appears that they turned his heart away from the Lord. The four references to "his heart" in the chapter show the deep-seated nature of his departure. He could not love the women without becoming, to some degree, attracted to their gods.

How far he went into idolatry is not entirely clear, but he did retain his practice of worshipping the Lord. His greatest error was in erecting shrines for the heathen gods, and doing so in close proximity to the holy Temple.

Whatever David's failings he never engaged in idolatry. He was always a worshipper of the God of his fathers. While it is wrong for us to try to grade sins as major and minor, it is evident that the one most detested by God is idolatry. He is a jealous God and will not tolerate any rival. Even though Solomon may not have bowed and worshipped the gods of his wives the very fact that he helped them by building high places for their devotions was viewed by God as seriously as if he had whole-heartedly turned himself to be an idolater.

Notwithstanding all that the Lord did for Israel, it is very probable that throughout the history of the nation there never was a time when it was fully clear of idolatry. Even in the wilderness, as well as the golden-calf, it was charged with bearing "the tabernacle of your Moloch and Chiun your images" (Amos 5.26). The remainder of Israel's history in these books of the Kings bears testimony to the consequences of this evil.

It is not difficult to understand why "Ashtoreth" the goddess of the Zidonians heads the list of the heathen gods. The extensive trade between Hiram and Solomon must have brought the Israelites into close contact with the worshippers of this idol. It, being a female deity, has been connected with the moon or another heavenly body such as Venus. The planets and stars of heaven, created to display the glory of God, have often been turned into objects of worship. Fallen man would rather worship the works of God than their Creator.

The trading relationship between Hiram and Solomon opened the door for other relationships. Just as the friendship between Pharaoh and Solomon led to the daughter of Pharaoh becoming his wife, so the dealings between him and Hiram resulted in Phoenician wives being brought to Jerusalem. These heathen kings and their associates may have thought it a great honour to have their daughters as princesses in the kingdom of the greatest ruler of the day.

Even though Solomon loved these women he could not bring them into the Temple court to worship God. Rather than them having no religious exercise he assisted them to worship as they had done in their own land.

While the Lord sanctioned the importing of timber to build the Temple, He could not approve bringing wives with their idols into the precincts of His house.

The god of the Ammonites, "Milcom" (also called "Molech", or

"Malcham") is next mentioned. To this god human sacrifices were offered. There were those who made their children "pass through the fire to Molech" (2 Kings 23.10). This meant that the child became a human sacrifice (Jer 7.31). Even Ahaz, the father of Hezekiah king of Judah, burnt his children in the fire (2 Chr 28.3). Topheth, one of the "high places" was a noted centre for this hideous form of worship. No wonder it is called "the abomination of the Ammonites".

The Zidonian wives came from the north, the Ammonite wives came from the east. It is hard to understand why Solomon thought of taking an Ammonitess to be his wife. The Ammonites were consistently the inveterate enemies of Israel. That the smoke from burning children who were offered at shrines built by him should have risen from the same mount as the sweet incense from the altar he had made to the Lord is astonishing. The deceitfulness of the human heart is shown here and confirmation given to the statement, "The heart is deceitful above all things, and desperately wicked: who can know it?" (Jer 17.9). Time has not changed it. Until heaven is reached there should be deep exercise before God regarding it.

Like the Ammonites, the Moabites were also descended from Lot. They had their own god, here called "Chemosh". Though distinct, to it also were offered human sacrifices. For example to it the king of Moab offered his son as a sacrifice (2 Kings 3.27). Moab lay to the south-east of Canaan. Solomon sought friendship in that quarter also by taking wives from there. Though Ruth, his distant relative, came from that area and married Boaz she did not bring her gods with her as did these women.

Solomon built shrines for the worship of all three of these gods, and did so in the mount of Olives. The high places dedicated to them remained in existence until almost the end of the kingdom when Josiah defiled them (2 Kings 23). Whether this meant that they were totally destroyed or that they were merely polluted so as to be unfit for use is not made clear. It is sad that the evil introduced by Solomon could continue so long and that none of the kings who reigned before Josiah, even though some of them were God fearing men, seemed to have the will, or the power, to deal with the matter.

These verses emphasise important lessons. For example one learns that the greatest of men are still but men and are not exempt from failure. Indeed the fact is that for most of the outstanding men in biblical history failure is recorded in Scripture. Adam, Noah, Abraham,

Moses, David, Solomon and even Peter in the NT all excelled, yet they all failed. It appears that those who reach a high standard in divine things are special targets of Satan. An especial danger is pride, as was true of the Evil One. Those who, while pressing toward the mark, are conscious that they have not attained their goal are more likely to be both humble and watchful.

Again there is demonstrated here the evil of the unequal yoke. His people were taught by God to pity strangers and to spread His fame throughout the world. At the same time they were to remain a distinct people and not to intermingle with idolaters. If they married into heathen families it followed, as was the case with Solomon, that the partners would not necessarily leave their religious beliefs behind them but would continue their idol worship after they were married. Paul's words "Be ye not unequally yoked together with unbelievers" (2 Cor 6.14) is a warning that never goes out of date.

Wives in Scripture can, as parables, represent "principles" as shown in Galatians 4.21-31. Thus, taking these foreign wives suggests the danger of embracing strange principles. The Galatians are an example of this. They embraced Judaism, which was a denial of the gospel, and this departure was a grief to Paul. Had they clung to the principle of faith, represented by Sarah, they would never have turned to the principle of legality, represented by Hagar. Many good men have been swept off their feet by strange doctrine. There is a very serious feature of this form of departure, for few who have imbibed strange doctrine have later renounced it and been restored to the truth.

Had Solomon been charged with idolatry he would have declared his innocence. He would have vowed that he was a worshipper of the true God of his fathers. Yet God condemned him for turning from Him. Some may suggest that there is no real harm in having fellowship with things contrary to the Lord so long as those who do so are not wholly committed to them. That this is a delusion is illustrated in this passage. Had Solomon told each new wife that she must forsake her idols or not come with him perhaps he would have had fewer. Indeed, their fathers, who gave them to him, might well have refused to let them go with him under such conditions. The advice of Paul is the only safe way to behave: "Touch not the unclean thing" (2 Cor 6.17).

A further lesson is that evil, once introduced, can persist a long time. These shrines were not removed when Solomon died but lasted almost as long as the kingdom. Tolerance of evil is not grace, nor is it helpful to the recovery of those involved in it. But even more sinister and baneful is providing the means to assist others to practice evil. It is dreadful to consider that Solomon left behind him two very different monuments to his work, one the Temple of the Lord, the other the high places of idolatry.

Verses 9-13
The consequences of Solomon's fall

That Solomon turned to idols was all the more inexcusable because the Lord had appeared to him twice. To have direct contact with God is the highest favour man can be shown. Idols do not speak to their worshippers for they are dumb but the living God can communicate His mind to those to whom He appears. The very evil Solomon had been specially warned against in the Lord's second appearing to him was the one into which he fell. He may have deceived himself by thinking that his limited association with idolatry would go unnoticed by God, and that so long as he continued to attend the Temple three times each year whatever else he did was of little account. But he is told here of the judgment that would come upon him. The kingdom promised to him and his seed would be torn out of his hand and given to his servant. However, two gracious limitations were added, first that this would not happen in his day, and second that a tribe would be retained over which his seed would rule. These alleviations of his sentence were granted, not because of his own goodness, but for his father's sake, and because God had placed His name in Jerusalem. The suspension of the sentence until he was dead is like a later suspension granted to Hezekiah who likewise did not experience judgment in his lifetime (Is 39.8).

How he felt after hearing such a message is difficult to imagine. When at length the weight of it sank into his mind he must have been disturbed that so many of his great achievements and extensive territory could be so dramatically torn away from his posterity so that only a fraction of it would remain in their hands. What was even more painful for him to accept was the fact that much of his kingdom, with the fortified cities he had built, would be inherited, not by his sons but by one of his common servants.

Benjamin and Judah alone remained to his family. They were so closely linked that they stayed together and, moreover, the Temple was built on the border between them so that neither could claim it as being in its territory. It might have been thought that, on the basis of natural ties, the two contiguous tribes who were descended from Rachel, Ephraim and Benjamin, would remain together, but this did not happen. Benjamin was so small a tribe that it was scarcely reckoned as distinct from the one powerful tribe of Judah. Along with these two tribes was the dispersed tribe of Simeon which was also in Judah. In addition a number of the tribe of Levi no doubt continued with the house of David so that they could serve in the Temple as God had appointed.

Even after the great divide in the nation, the faithful among the ten tribes went to Jerusalem to worship. This was an annoyance to Jeroboam who succeeded in hindering it. Despite this, from time to time numbers from the ten returned to the southern kingdom and worshipped in the place where God had placed His name.

It is vital to learn the serious nature of turning away from the Lord. A consideration of Solomon, the heights he reached and the costliness of his departure from God, demonstrates that those who are more highly favoured are more responsible and so will receive heavier judgment in failure. "For unto whomsoever much is given, of him shall be much required" (Lk 12.48).

Preserving right relations with the Lord should be the greatest concern of His own. If any object comes between them and Him then this is idolatry and will have serious consequences. Attendance at the various meetings of the saints may be kept up and daily devotions may continue. Yet it is conceivable that occupation with earthly relations and material things can gain control so as to leave little place in the heart for the Lord. Some of the last words of the NT to be written, "Little children, keep yourselves from idols" (1 Jn 5.21), are more appropriate than one might realize.

Verses 14-40
Solomon's adversaries

After the consequences of Solomon's link with idolatry are recorded, attention is drawn to those adversaries who troubled the king in the latter part of his reign. The first of these was an Edomite, the second was a Syrian, and the third was from the tribe of Ephraim. Thus disturbance was brewing in the south, in the north, and in the centre of the land. None of these succeeded in destroying his kingdom, nor indeed is there any record of them attacking his kingdom during his reign. Yet they were thorns in his side and took away from him that rest of mind and freedom from anxiety he had enjoyed in his early life. After his death they were more active and stripped much he held dear from his son.

Hadad the Edomite is the first to be named. That "adversaries" (Satan in the LXX) were stirred up is a reminder that there had been a time when no such enemies were apparent. Solomon had been able to say, "The Lord my God hath given me rest on every side, so that there is neither adversary nor evil occurrent" (5.4). Here the same Lord stirred up a son of one of the kings of Edom to trouble him. Long before Israel had kings the Edomites had "dukes" or leaders (Gen 36). By now they too had kings and evidently a royal line. No account is given of what Hadad did in opposing him, except that he had the courage to return to his native land, something he would have been afraid to do during the lifetime of David, or in the earlier days of Solomon. Evidently Hadad had not the same dread of Solomon that he had of David and Joab. This may imply that Solomon no longer had his former military strength.

The army of David under Joab had mastered Edom and almost wiped it out. Hadad had escaped into Egypt where he remained until some time after the death of both David and Joab. According to the record given of his time in Egypt he and his family were well treated by Pharaoh. Yet Hadad was determined to return and felt it was now safe for him to do so. This decision was not so much the result of national pride but rather the work of God in his heart. By daring to return Hadad showed that he did not fear Solomon. God was teaching the king that he was no longer the feared monarch he had once been.

The next adversary noted was Rezon of Syria, that northern country which often produced enemies of Israel. Again, like Hadad, this man came from a place formerly conquered by David who had gained such a victory at that time that the vanquished Syrians became his servants and brought to him their tribute (2 Sam 8.5,6). During this conflict Rezon escaped but later returned, gathered an army and became king in Damascus.

These things are mentioned here in order to show the change that had come upon the kingdom of Israel. Instead of the Syrians being subjects to Solomon, as they had been to his father, they had become independent, and a potential threat.

Throughout the history of Israel there was rivalry between Judah and Ephraim. The Tabernacle was in the territory of the latter, but God gave up the tribe of Ephraim and placed His name in Jerusalem, which belonged to Judah, and established David and his posterity as kings (Ps 78.59-72). During Solomon's reign the nation was united but after his death that unity ended. These verses tell how this came about. The previous two adversaries of Solomon were external, but this third one, Jeroboam, was internal and so by far the most dangerous. He was the son of Nebat, who was dead by this time and so his mother, Zeruah, was a widow. He had distinguished himself in the building of Millo and in the completing of the wall around Jerusalem. His overseeing of this great project was so well performed that Solomon made him head of all the affairs of Ephraim. Little did the king think that he was opening the door for his servant to win the hearts of the Ephraimites and thus lay the foundation for him to become leader in the approaching rebellion.

Suddenly the prophet Ahijah, dressed in a new robe, confronted Jeroboam on his way from Jerusalem. The introduction here of a prophet is important to note. Throughout the reign of Solomon there is no record of prophets bringing messages to him. Unlike his father, and future kings, he seemed to have no need for such men to bring him a word from God, or to guide him in his administrations. The Lord spoke directly to him on at least two occasions, and even when reprimanding him regarding his idolatrous ways, we are told "The Lord said unto Solomon", although no mention is made of the means by which He did this (v.11).

Ahijah conveyed his message from the Lord to Jeroboam, privately, in a field outside the city. Like many other prophets he gave a sign, or demonstration, to illustrate his message. The scene before Jeroboam was startling. He saw a man tear into pieces a brand new cloak, an action more like the work of a lunatic than a servant of God. Even when handed ten pieces of the torn garment he would still have been bewildered. However the explanation given made clear that the twelve pieces represented the twelve tribes. Ten of these pieces given to Jeroboam showed to him that he would reign over these tribes and that the two others would remain in the hands of the descendants of David. The two remaining pieces of the garment are desribed as one tribe, for Benjamin, as already pointed out, was small and not considered worthy of naming as a tribe.

The rending of a garment to demonstrate the rending of a kingdom was not new. Samuel used his torn mantle to show Saul that the kingdom was being rent from him (1 Sam 15).

The prophet gave Jeroboam an elaborate outline of what God was about to do, and why He was doing it. The words are almost a repeat of what was said to Solomon himself. This has led to the suggestion that it was this very prophet who spoke the message to him recorded in vv.11-13.

The promise to Jeroboam was great. Not only would he be made king but, if he followed the Lord and obeyed His commandments as did David, his posterity would also reign over Israel. All was made so plain that only a fool could have failed to grasp the message. It opened a door of opportunity for him, one which very few were ever given. Later it became clear that this offer fell on deaf ears. He failed to fulfil the conditions involved and the promise made to him of a "sure house" was short lived. His son, Nadab, reigned over Israel for less than two years. This was the extent to which his posterity reigned in Israel.

The prophet's message to Jeroboam must have reached the ears of Solomon, whether by the prophet himself, or by those who had heard it from Jeroboam. The king sought to kill his rival, just as Saul sought to kill David, but he escaped to Egypt.

Usually in Scripture the title "Pharaoh" is all that is used to describe rulers in Egypt. However on this occasion the personal name "Shishak" is noted. This may be due to the fact that he was the first of a new dynasty. Having just come to power himself he might have looked favourably on Jeroboam as a potential king of Israel and founder of a new royal house. Later Shishak invaded Israel and plundered its treasures (14.25).

These verses show more of God's ways of working, especially with regard to those who rule. Though Jeroboam was assured of the honour of reigning over ten tribes, he was told that the reason for this was that the former king, Solomon, had turned to idolatry. If he did the same, his house, too, would be rejected, for God's standards do not change.

Responsibility to rule the saints at this present time is not handed down from father to son. Each overseer is to be appointed by the Holy Spirit. However spiritual leaders, who obey God's Word, do produce sons in the faith, as Paul did Timothy, who can continue God's testimony. Sometimes the full result of the departure of those who have failed in their duties as guides, as in the case of Solomon, is only seen after they have gone.

God's appreciation of the faithfulness of His servants is seen in His remembrance of David and in the maintenance of his house. The "man after his own heart" had obtained promises that will never be broken. His greater son and true seed the "King of kings", will reign forever. The affliction of the house of David is not final, but temporary. The promised heir to his throne is the One who cannot fail and who delighted to do the will of God.

Verses 41-43
The death of Solomon
Before concluding the story of this great king, the writer states that a more detailed account exists. The "book of the acts of Solomon" is probably the source from which the events in the scriptural history were drawn. Chronicles may refer to this in naming three prophets who recorded his activity (2 Chr 9.29).

Though Solomon had many wives he had only one son, Rehoboam who, unlike his father, was far from wise. Solomon must have been disappointed that the daughter of Pharaoh, his favourite, had no son and that his heir was the son of an Ammonitess.

Solomon, like David, reigned for forty years. Since he came early to the throne he was only about sixty years old at the time of his death, not reaching the allotted span of seventy. Especially in his earlier years he accomplished more than any other king of Israel. There may have been none wealthier, certainly there were none wiser. Men leave their wealth behind. Solomon also left his writings, an enduring legacy. But at death some things of value do not remain. Solomon's wisdom and ability passed away with him.

From this history it is clear that wealth and wisdom cannot extend life or diminish the effects of age. Unlike his father Solomon was never in the heat of battle, nor did he ever have to sleep beneath the open sky, but, in spite of all the comforts he enjoyed, he did not have an especially long life. Though not being particularly advanced in years he is called an old man. His many wives and rich living might suggest an unhealthy lifestyle. The cause of his death is not given but in Ecclesiastes 12 he provides a wonderful insight into the frailty of old age (Eccl 12.1-7). Whether he was referring to his own experience or to that of others his vivid imagery is very apt.

Notes
3 Concubines were greatly inferior to the "princesses", and were not included in the royal household. The numbers stated are greatly in excess of those in the Song of Songs (sixty queens and eighty concubines - 6.8). This may indicate that the Song was written early in his reign.

36 Had the kingdom been entirely removed from the house of David then his "light" or "lamp" (NIR - 5216) would have been extinguished. But this would have been a breach of the promise made to him (2 Sam 7.16). During his lifetime his faithful followers viewed him as the "lamp" of Israel (2 Sam 21.17). Even when his descendants did evil, and were removed, as in the case of Abijam, the lamp was still to burn, (1 Kings 15.4). Later, when Jehoram's evil ways corrupted the house of David, the Lord still kept the lamp of David burning because of that same promise (2 Kings 8.19). This use of a lamp to illustrate life is first introduced by Bildad (Job 18.6), and this figure of speech is elaborated on by Solomon (Eccl 12.6,7).

41 The three prophets who recorded the history of Solomon were Nathan, Ahijah, and Iddo. The first of these was involved in his anointing and so would cover the early period, the second described his kingdom being divided and the third, who may have been the youngest, had more to do with his son, Rehoboam.

CHAPTERS 12-22

THE KINGDOMS OF JUDAH AND ISRAEL

CHAPTER 12, Verses 1-19
The accession of Rehoboam, and the revolt of ten of the tribes

This chapter introduces an entirely new situation in Israel. Until now the history of a single, united, kingdom has been traced. From now to the end of the book two kingdoms are in view. One is comprised of two tribes ruled from Jerusalem, the other of ten tribes ruled from Samaria. Later the ten tribes were carried into captivity and again the history returns to one kingdom.

Unlike his father who was crowned at Gihon on the outskirts of Jerusalem Rehoboam travelled some thirty miles to Shechem where the nation assembled to make him king. The choice of this place was possibly because it was in the centre of the land and on the northern border of Ephraim. He would have been aware that there was the potential for disruption due to jealousy arising from that quarter and so the place of assembly removed one cause for complaint. Rehoboam was not the first to be crowned at Shechem. Abimelech was crowned there in the days of the Judges (Judg 9.6).

Throughout the history of Israel there was great rivalry between Judah and Ephraim. Jacob had made plain which tribe would have the supremacy saying "The sceptre shall not depart from Judah" (Gen 49.10). Despite this, Ephraim, because of its size and its central position in the land, was always jealous of Judah and sought excuse, whenever possible, to assert its authority. As far back as the days of the Judges both Gideon and Jephthah were confronted with complaints from this tribe, and David, himself, had to wait seven years before it would accept him as king (Judg 8.1;12.1; 2 Sam 5.5).

News of the death of Solomon and the anointing of his son would soon have spread to Egypt through his wife, the daughter of Pharaoh. Jeroboam, who was in exile there would learn of the change. Evidently he had no fear of the new king nor had he any problem in gaining the confidence of the northern tribes. The fact that they called him to return showed their high estimation of his qualities as a potential leader. He became their spokesman and proved fully competent in presenting their case. Even though the whole nation had joined to make Rehoboam king, the ten tribes only accepted him as such under certain conditions. To have their allegiance he was not to be absolute ruler like his father, who did as he saw fit. He would have to rule in line with the wishes of the people. Otherwise they would rebel. Until this time the kings of Israel reigned autocratically. Now they would have to be more democratic in behaviour. The complaint of the people was about his father's heavy yoke. In spite of the fact that Solomon did make a great distinction between the slave labour of the Canaanites and the more supervisory work of the Israelites, they still thought this a heavy burden. It did not seem to dawn on them that if they had not had good kings they might well have been the slaves of a foreign oppressor. It does also seem that they exaggerated their burdens and made them out to be more grievous than they were.

One notes that though Rehoboam had not inherited the wisdom of his father he was wise enough to ask for time to consider the matter. His two privy councils, one the old men who had served under his father and the other young men inexperienced like himself. The complaint of the older group over Solomon's building schemes suggests that some of the hard physical work had to be done by Israelites under the pressure of his levy system. While he thought it honourable employment they felt it as a heavy yoke. Naturally, when the new king began to reign they wondered whether he would continue on the same course. The advice given by the senior advisers was sensible, and if taken, could have preserved the kingdom. However, Rehoboam would accept their judgment only if it tallied with his own and so adopted the very different plan of the younger group. One might wonder why he chose the second course. No doubt it appealed to his pride and could extend his authority. It even made him feel that he was stronger than his father. This attitude opened the door for the ten tribes to rebel against him and make their spokesman their own king. Thus the great divide in the nation had begun and a breach made that will not be healed until the true heir to the throne, the Son of David, Christ Himself, reigns.

Behind this division, of course, lay the sovereignty of God and the fulfillment of His word as spoken by the prophet Ahijah. Truly He has the hearts of kings in His hand and can turn them to do those things that fulfil His purpose. This does not diminish their responsibility but nonetheless shows the overruling hand of God.

The time had now arrived when the proud Ephraimites were no more in second place behind Judah. The language they used revealed their hearts; "What portion have we in David?" They had no regard for Psalm 78 which made clear that David was the Lord's choice for Israel (v.70). They returned to their homes without the slightest remorse or grief for what had happened. Little did they care that their new king would lead them into idolatry and cut them off from the chosen centre at Jerusalem.

Apparently Rehoboam failed fully to grasp what had happened, otherwise he would not have sent Adoram his servant and representative into the camp of his rival. No doubt he had in mind his wish to sustain the levy of workers as in previous times. This slave-master paid dearly for his visit. It cost him his life. How could he, or the king, have imagined that the head of the evil complained about could possibly be welcome where the practice was so detested? On his eventual return from Shechem to Jerusalem Rehoboam must have felt bewildered. For a king to lose five-sixths of his dominion in a matter of days is surely abnormal.

Verse 20
Jeroboam made king

No time was lost by the northern tribes in selecting their king. Already they had pinned their hopes on Jeroboam who had so ably presented their case to Rehoboam. They had found a man who was after their own hearts and one who would submit to their demands. How unlike David who was a man after God's heart! The Lord, through the prophet, could say, "They have set up kings, but not by me: they have made princes, and I knew it not" (Hos 8.4). In a similar way Saul was the one desired by Israel. God granted him to them. He said, "I gave thee a king in my anger, and took him away in my wrath" (Hos 13.11).

It might well be true that none of the kings of the northern kingdom was the Lord's choice. How different when the true King reigns, for then God will say, "I (have) set my King upon my holy hill of Zion" (Ps 2.6)

There are practical lessons to be learned from this account. It is especially important to note that the painful loss suffered by the new king was the result of his father's sin and failure. Men leave a legacy behind them both of good and evil. We all suffer because of our own mistakes, but no one should wish to do anything that would mean that those coming after have to suffer. David sowed a harvest of good that was reaped by Solomon. Solomon sowed a harvest of evil that was reaped by his son. Surely all ought to maintain a close walk with God, not only for their own blessing but also for the good of those who may follow.

When leaders are removed their power and authority may not be retained by those who succeed them. Much can remain suppressed while leaders are alive, but once they depart these problems soon surface. The word to the Ephesian elders is relevant: "After my departing shall grievous wolves enter in among you" (Acts 20.29).

The man who divided Israel had spent a considerable time in Egypt. Egypt is a type of the world and wordly-minded men are often at the root of division.

This section also illustrates that when people are discontented they often find fault with the manner in which they have been guided and ruled. The "levy" of service may not have been an ideal practice but was a common means of taxation at that time. The kingdom had to be maintained and this was costly. Some means had to be adopted to gather the necessary revenue. Murmuring in Israel against leaders began in the wilderness. There the people, turning against Moses, said, "Let us make a captain, and let us return into Egypt" (Num 14.4).

Again it is all too common for people to seek advice, but, when given it, refuse to act upon it. The old men had a wealth of experience in the court of the wisest man on earth. Their counsel should not have been refused lightly. Often men accept the guidance of those who flatter them, especially if it fits their preconceived ideas. There is no substitute for experience and it is wise to listen to its voice.

Verses 21-24
Rehoboam attempts to make war with Jeroboam

Once Rehoboam came back to his own tribe and to his own city he immediately set out to regain, by means of military action, the part of his kingdom he had lost. He mustered a sizeable army of men out of Judah and Benjamin and must have been confident that it would be sufficient to overcome the more numerous army which supported the new king Jeroboam. This is the first reference to the tribe of Benjamin as part of the southern kingdom. These two tribes were always considered the best warriors among the tribes. It seems probable that David chose most of his bodyguard from these two tribes. However, their military skills were never put to the test. The word of God came by the prophet Shemaiah: "Ye shall not go up, nor fight against your brethren the children of Israel". The repeated references to the divine word show the influence it had and the respect it was given. The battle was over before it had begun. What, to Rehoboam, seemed to be a rebellion to be quelled, was shown to him to be the operation of God. In view of this there was nothing else he could do but obey the message and disperse the army. To continue the attack against the word of the Lord would have been a disastrous act of folly. Had this war not been stopped the nations around Israel would have witnessed a nation destroying itself. Those who were enemies would have rejoiced. Those favourably disposed would have been amazed.

The mention of the relationship between the two parts of the nation, even though they had different kings, is important for the war was between "brethren". The same idea was prominent in the strife between the herdsmen of Abram and the herdsmen of Lot. The former's words were, "Let there be no strife...between thee and me...for we be brethren" (Gen 13.8).

Men are, at times, slow to accept their reversals as being in the purposes of God, and, like Rehoboam, are tempted to try to change matters to suit their own preconceived ideas. To accept humiliations meekly, and to do so without retaliation, is contrary to human nature. There is much in life that cannot be changed and so it is wise to submit even when the reason for the disappointments may not be fully understood.

It should also be borne in mind that attacks from within are far more disastrous than attacks from outside. Fighting amongst brethren is most unbecoming and ruinous. When difficulties do arise, as they will, it is good when someone has a word from the Lord that ends the strife as did the prophet in this case.

Victories are not always as great as they may seem to be. Jeroboam and the ten tribes thought they had won the day. In a sense they did, but the far-reaching consequences, particularly for the spiritual condition of the rebellious tribes, were extremely sad. Refusing Rehoboam as king was nothing compared to giving up Jerusalem, the divinely chosen centre of worship. It would be well for those who may strive for power in assembly life to ask themselves, "What will be the outcome if the change in leadership is as I demand?" Jeroboam, fresh from Egypt, represents those who introduce worldly principles amongst the people of God. As will be seen, he lost no time in doing so.

Verses 25-33
Jeroboam's reign and apostasy

The experience and skills developed in the nation through the building programme around Jerusalem were no doubt a great help to Jeroboam in his own building programmes. Shechem became his first headquarters. There he built a city and possibly his palace. His next project was at Penuel, a place Gideon had destroyed (Judg 8.8-17). It lay to the east of Jordan. Having a fortified city there was important for his kingdom. Like Shechem it had sacred memories for the Israelites for it was where Jacob, their father, saw God face to face (Gen 32.30).

A problem confronted Jeroboam. The divine centre of worship was at Jerusalem and was adjacent to the residence of his rival king. He therefore had to make sure no visits from his kingdom would be made to that place lest those who worshipped in the Temple also returned to loyalty to the king there. Those who climb to positions of power by popular choice are always in fear that another might steal the hearts of their followers. Those who suddenly make a choice for one man can just as suddenly change to another.

Knowing the hearts of his people, he was convinced that they would not dispense with worship since it was part of their lives. Therefore, he decided to introduce his own form of religious ritual. From his experience in Egypt, golden calves seemed to him appropriate. He was like Aaron, who made the gold calf in the wilderness (also copied from Egypt) and declared, "These be thy gods, O Israel, which brought thee up out of the land of Egypt" (Ex 32.4). Jeroboam knew that they would be accepted by the majority of the people and worshipped as their gods. Therefore the calves were made and one placed in the south at Bethel, near the border with Judah, and the other at Dan, in the extreme north, near Lebanon.

Jeroboam had complained about the grievous yoke of Solomon (v.4). Now he implied that another burden put on the people was the long journey to Jerusalem. They must have judged him to be very thoughtful. How sad that Bethel, the house of God, became the shrine of a golden calf and a centre of idol worship.

These new gods required temples and so he had to build shrines for them and for the worshippers who came to them. If sacrifices were to be offered altars were needed upon which to burn them. Next a priesthood to conduct the ceremonies was also needed. He formed this from the lowest of the people, possibly even some from the heathen shrines were appointed. No longer was priesthood confined to the sons of Aaron. It is to be hoped, in any event, that few of them would have accepted such a shameful post. The three great yearly feasts, when thousands went up to Jerusalem held a special place in the heart of the nation. So Jeroboam devised a feast day for his shrines in the eighth month, some weeks later than the Feast of Tabernacles which was in the seventh month, and he set the example for the people by making an offering on the altar he had made. They would thus conclude that their new king was truly religious.

A review of these arrangements illustrates that imitation is a hallmark of false religion. Everything Jeroboam introduced was meant to be a substitute for the pattern commanded by God. Great changes were brought in but this was done in such a way as to shock the people as little as possible. The ready acceptance by them of such falsehood is still amazing. Could it have been, due to Solomon's involvement in the religion of his heathen wives, that the people no longer regarded idolatry as something hated by God?

The greatest weakness of the nation lay in its being prone to turn to idolatry. From the time of the golden calf made by Aaron until the end of their national history with the commencement of the "times of the Gentiles", this one evil more than any other stained the pages of their history. To give golden calves, recently made, the credit for delivering them from Egypt seems so illogical that only fools would speak of it. Yet all these lies were swallowed as if they were the truth.

Of course one must recognise that Jeroboam and the people may have understood the calf to be only an object of gold. They might have seen it as a symbol of an unseen "god". If this was the case they were worshipping a demon or demons without understanding what they were doing. Falsehood has a charm for fallen human nature and only the light that shines from God can reveal the truth.

Notes

1 Shechem was at the end of the narrow valley which lay between

Mount Ebal and Mount Gerizim It was an ancient gathering place for the nation. The altar of plastered stone on which the Law was written was erected there. The blessings and the curses were shouted from these two mounts. The first of the curses concerned idolatry. This was the very evil introduced by Jeroboam who had no fear in making his palace near the place where these curses were heard.

10 There is no word for "finger" in the original. But "little finger" suits better than toe.

11 The painful sting of the scorpion is presumably spoken of figuratively.

13 "roughly" (QUASHEH - 7186) means "hard" or "grievous", and refers, not to his manner of speech, but to what he said.

16 The words of the people, "What portion have we in David..." echoed the words of Sheba, the man of Belial (2 Sam 20.1).

"To your tents" is simply another way of saying "go home". In v.24 the people of Judah are told to return to their "houses".

CHAPTER 13, Verses 1-10
A prophet from Judah visits Bethel

While Jeroboam was engaged in his devotions at Bethel, possibly at the time mentioned in 12.33, he was unexpectedly visited by a man of God from Judah. Earlier in his life he had been visited by another man of God who brought him good tidings (11.29). Had he heeded the first messenger he would not have been worshipping a gold calf, nor would he have heard the solemn word from this latest prophet. It is important to note that God was showing that He had not forsaken Judah, but had a prophet there ready to carry His message even to the seat of idolatry. Jeroboam was not merely a tolerator of idolatry in his kingdom, but was wholeheartedly devoted to it. He was offering incense as a priest might do.

He must have been surprised that someone dared to intrude on his devotions. The stranger from Judah directed his words against the altar, apparently ignoring the king. It is noteworthy that his prophesy not only spoke of the time when this very altar would have on it the bones of the priests of the high places but also the name of the one who would do it, Josiah, of the house of David. This is another instance of a person being named before he was born. "Isaac" (Gen 17.19), "Solomon" (1 Chr 22.9) and "Cyrus" (Is 44.28) are other examples of this. However, the last of these is the nearest parallel in that a long time intervened between the mention of the name and the birth of the one named. Of course it is true that by the time this book was compiled the prophecy had been fulfilled. This does not mean that the writer simply inserted Josiah's name because he knew who had carried out the act. A record of the word spoken by the prophet had no doubt been preserved in some form and from this the historian was able to draw. One feature that distinguishes the Lord from all false gods is that He can tell the future as though it were already the past.

It was surely unwelcome to Jeroboam to hear from a man from Judah that one of his chief centres of worship would have its altar so desecrated. Not only so but that it would be so by a king of the house of David. Just as Moses, who confronted Pharaoh and told him of coming disasters, had his word confirmed by signs, so this solemn message was confirmed by a sign. The broken altar and dispersed ashes spoke loudly of the pending disaster. The calf god was powerless to defend its altar and equally powerless to rebuke the man who had spoken against it. Little wonder that the agitated king lifted up his hand to smite the prophet. Had not God intervened to touch the king's arm, the prophet's life would have been taken. He was taught, as was Pharaoh, that the God of Israel has power to protect His own, and has power to hurt those who would harm them.

Though Jeroboam was not a true believer in the unseen God, he acknowledged His supremacy by asking for healing. The Lord who withered could heal and did so at the request of his servant. In this second miracle Jeroboam was taught the mercy of God.

It might have been expected that with such evidence of divine power and mercy he would have said, "This God shall be my God", but no such conversion took place. However, he did feel indebted to the prophet and sought to pay by inviting him to the palace and promising a reward.

The prophet had been forbidden to receive hospitality in Israel, nor was he to return home by the way that he came. How could a man of God sit down at the table of an idolater and have fellowship with him? Though he may have been hungry at this time his orders were clear. Hence his blunt refusal. He used words similar to those of Balaam who said, "If Balak would give me his house full of silver and gold, I cannot go beyond the word of the Lord" (Num 22.18).

Jeroboam must not be viewed as a mere idolater. He was a true Israelite, of the tribe of Ephraim, and must have had some knowledge of Jehovah. In addition, the word of the Lord had not only come to him but had been fulfilled in his experience. He was thus an "apostate".

He deliberately turned to falsehood despite his knowledge of the truth. He had been enlightened yet refused the light.

Had he been reared an idolater and continued to worship the god of his fathers this could be understood. However, he was an idolater by choice, not merely nominally, but wholly given to his false devotions. From the time of the first golden calf in the wilderness, Israel's tendency to drift into idolatry was seen. But for ten tribes to so suddenly turn away from the God of their fathers is surprising. However, not all in these tribes were swept off their feet, for many of them, especially the priests and Levites, came to Jerusalem and worshipped the Lord (2 Chr 11.13-17).

Verses 11-32
The seduction and death of the man of God

True history can be stranger than fiction. The story in these verses of the fate of the man of God, is almost striking. How one so courageous in the presence of Jeroboam the king, and so dogmatic as to the terms of his mission, could be deluded and snared into his death is hard to understand. If triumph marked the happenings at Bethel, tragedy is stamped upon the scene here.

The old prophet at Bethel is one of those characters in Scripture whose true condition is not easily determined. His motives in bringing about the death of the man of God are not clear. Whether he was another Balaam, or whether he was a true prophet but away in heart from God, is not revealed. One thing is sure, he was not chosen by the Lord to denounce the idolatry of Jeroboam. Not that he should have needed any special commission to do so. If he knew the law he knew God's hatred of idols. Apparently he was quite content to let the people slip into idolatry and say nothing against the evil.

Whether the prophet's son who was present at the denunciation by the man of God was also involved in the worship of the calf is not said, but he was in the company of those who assembled to do so. The news of the broken altar and the scattered ashes must have been the topic of the day. The report reached the old prophet and roused him to contact this strange intruder and to entertain him in his home. His invitation was refused just as firmly as had been that of the king. However, the claim that an angel had spoken to the old man "by the word of the Lord", though a lie was sufficiently plausible that it swayed the mind of the man of God. To associate the Lord and an angel by such a lie was evil in the extreme.

When the true message from the Lord came to the old prophet and pronounced judgment, the man who had posed as a friend was the first to condemn the man of God for his disobedience and to sentence him, on divine authority, to an early grave. However, the prophet did not accept his own responsibility for the deception of his guest.

In order to help him on his journey to Judah, the old prophet provided him with an ass, but before he had travelled very far he was met by a lion and slain. A strange feature of the story is that the ass was spared and the body of the man of God was not mutilated or devoured. The great Creator controlled the creatures involved, so, while the lion slew the man and remained beside the dead body and the ass, it made no attempt to satisfy its appetite by eating the flesh of either. The lion was under divine control, not only as the instrument to slay the man of God, but also as a sentinel beside the ass and the dead body.

After the old prophet had recovered and buried the corpse and mourned, it is to be hoped that he felt guilt at being the one who brought about the disaster. The death of the prophet was final proof of the truth of the message brought to Jeroboam.

This strange story speaks loudly for it illustrates principles that demand careful attention. One of the most telling of these is that when success comes in a work for the Lord there is always the danger of temptation overtaking and overcoming those who experience it. Often the temptation will come from an unexpected source.

The old prophet proved more dangerous than the angry king. The enemy often repeats the principles of the Fall. He approaches as a friend, tells lies and deceives by offering what seems desirable. The man of God repeated the experience of Eve in the Garden. Both had been given plain instructions as regards eating, both had clear recollections of what they had been told, both were led to believe that what they had been told was not to be strictly obeyed, and both responded to the enemy's deceit and died as a result.

Another principle demonstrated here is that when God gives clear directions He does not change them. There is an interesting parallel in the case of Paul. He had clear guidance from the Lord that he should go up to Jerusalem, and had to overcome the pressure of friends who were determined to stop him from going. There are still those who contend that he was wrong to venture into such a dangerous place.

It is also the case that some have difficulty in believing that a man can receive communications from the Lord and yet not be one of His true servants. Though Balaam spoke sublime and true words, this did not sanctify his soul, for he remained an enemy of Israel to the bitter end. The same lips that spoke of Israel's portion and destiny were later used to convey to the king of Moab how he could bring about the destruction of the nation. God, who could speak through an unclean ass, could also speak through an unclean man.

Perhaps the most unusual feature of this story is that the true servant of the Lord was judged, whereas the lying prophet, who lured him to his death was left unharmed. One might be tempted to think that the lion that slew the man of God should have slain the old prophet when he was on his way to do mischief. However, there is a principle in God's dealings well expressed in the words of Amos, "You only have I known of all the families of the earth: therefore I will punish you for all your iniquities" (Amos 3.2). Those who are closest to Him are the more responsible for their actions. He will not wink at their wrong doings. His children will not lightly be allowed to do evil practised by the world, but will feel the weight of their Father's chastening hand.

Those who, like the old prophet, condone evil and are content to dwell in the midst of it are not fit company for those who are true to the Lord. Separation should not only be from evil and worldly men but from all who are associated with them. Many maintain that we cannot reach the lost unless we mingle with them and share their way of life, but God's message is clear; "Come out from among them...and touch not the unclean thing" (2 Cor 6.17).

Some men have imagined that if they show respect to the dead, this in some way atones for any ill treatment they may have inflicted upon them when they were alive. This is false. Neither bringing home the body of the man of God nor providing it with a grave could in any way diminish the serious nature of the original crime that brought about the tragedy.

Verses 33-34

Jeroboam persists in evil

Notwithstanding the warning from the Lord and the strange circumstances surrounding the death of the man of God, no impression was made on the heart of Jeroboam. He was determined to proceed in his wicked ways and was prepared to employ anyone who would sell himself to become a priest of the high places. Not only did he make priests of those outside the house of Aaron, but even the meanest were considered by him to be good enough for this office (12.31). The entire idolatrous system was exclusively ruled by him. The gold calves, the places where they were put, the feast day, and the priests who attended the altars all conformed to his will. How unlike this was to the true centre of worship where everything required divine sanction.

Earlier, God promised Jeroboam a sure house like the house of David. But this was a conditional promise that would be fulfilled only if he walked in God's ways and kept His commandments (11.38). Here it is stated that his house would be cut off from the face of the earth since he had regard neither for God nor for His commandments. His turning to idolatry robbed his posterity of the crown of Israel

Notes

1 The altar was for sacrifices not incense, as is implied by the ashes. It is probable that while the sacrifices were burning Jeroboam had a censer burning incense close by.

3 The "sign" (MOPET - 4159) or "wonder" was a symbolic confirmation of the future disaster. The signs in Egypt (Ex 4.21; 7.3,9; 11.9,10) were, in a similar way, performed by Moses to convince Pharaoh of the power of the Lord.

4 The "dried up" (YABESH - 3000) hand left Jeroboam powerless to act, not only against the man of God, but also in any other way. The idol shepherd of the future will suffer a similar judgment, for of him we read that "his arm shall be clean dried up" (Zec 11.17).

CHAPTER 14, Verses 1-20
Judgment on Jeroboam and Israel prophesied by Ahijah

These verses give an insight into the Lord's dealings with Jeroboam, and are closely connected with the close of ch.13. Just as God smote the first-born of Pharaoh so here Jeroboam's son, Abijah, is smitten with a deadly sickness. Whether he was the heir to the throne is not stated, but the fact that all Israel mourned his death implies that this was so. He was not necessarily a little child, but more likely a young man.

Though determined to go on in his idolatrous ways, Jeroboam knew that only true prophets could foretell the future. The man who had given him the promise of the throne of Israel, a promise already fulfilled, was still alive, and the king knew that he could tell him whether the child would be spared or die. It could well be that Jeroboam suspected that his son's sickness came from the Lord, so he wanted to learn His mind on the matter. It would be difficult to ask the man he had despised for years and whose words he had ignored. Therefore he adopted the stratagem described and sent his wife disguised as a peasant and taking with her a present in keeping with one in poor circumstances.

He should have realised that a prophet able by the Lord to tell the future, could also, by Him, see through a disguise. Paying a prophet for his service seems to have been a custom in Israel. Even Saul was pleased to have a quarter shekel of silver to give to Samuel for his directions (1 Sam 9.8). In this case bread and honey were of little value and were intended to confirm to the prophet that she was an ordinary Israelite. Like Eli before him, the prophet had lost his sight, so neither her appearance nor her gift would mean much to him.

Before she had time to present herself as one of the common people she was addressed as the "wife of Jeroboam". Ostensibly, she had been sent to the prophet, but, in truth, the prophet had been sent to her with solemn news. The word she received must have pierced her heart, and turned her distress into despair. The words of the prophet recalled the earlier message he had brought to Jeroboam when he first met him and told him of his kingship over ten tribes (11.30-31). Unlike David, who remained faithful, he had turned his back on God, and had wholeheartedly devoted himself to idolatry. He may have tried to convince himself that the calves he had made were not idols, but the Lord viewed them as such. The prediction concerning the death of his family and the fate of their corpses would be especially distressing. Ingrained in every Israelite was a high regard for the dead bodies of those they loved. The very bones of the dead were treated with respect, as seen in the way those of Saul and Jonathan were dealt with (2 Sam 21.12-14).

The final words of the prophet confirmed her fears by announcing that her son would die before she reached the palace. He alone of the family would be granted a proper burial, and this because there was found in him "some good thing toward the Lord God of Israel".

That anyone reared in the house of Jeroboam, whose zeal for idols knew no limits, should have respect for the Lord is remarkable. Nevertheless, it could well be that Abijah was unlike his father and disagreed with his idol worship. If this was the case, he was a shining star in a dark sky.

So Jeroboam's family was to be removed, and that by a king of Israel. What many in Israel thought was a stable kingdom, and one which would continue for many years, was in fact like a reed in water which the wind could blow away. Not only would the house of Jeroboam be wiped out, but the people he ruled, and who had, like himself, provoked the God of Israel, would also be carried away beyond the river Euphrates.

That Ahijah was a true prophet was quickly confirmed by the death of Abijah exactly as foretold.

With this sad event the historian brings to an end the story of Jeroboam. How he died and where he was buried is not said, but a simple reference to where further information regarding him can be obtained is given. His twenty-two years of rule were dark days for the ten tribes. He led them into gross idolatry, and his name will always be remembered as the king who sinned himself and made Israel to sin. Just as David set the standard for all the kings who reigned in Judah, so, sadly, was Jeroboam for Israel. Although he lost Abijah through sickness, he had another son, Nadab, who reigned after him. Thus his house was not immediately cut off.

Verses 21-31
The reign of Rehoboam

The history now returns to Judah under Rehoboam. It too, is a story of departure from God and of evildoing by those who had in their territory the divine centre and all that should have preserved them in the fear of God. Rehoboam, though a grandson of David, showed little regard for the God of his fathers. The fact that twice in this short passage the name of his mother is mentioned may suggest that she had an influence on him for evil. She, being an Ammonite, would have little conscience about immorality or idolatry. The privilege of the southern kingdom in retaining the Temple, the priests and the Levites increased its responsibility and made the multiplying of high places for the worship of idols utterly inexcusable.

Where false gods are worshipped, there will be low moral standards. It is not surprising then that the evils for which the Canaanites were expelled from the land again raised their ugly heads. Among these evils "there were also sodomites in the land" (v.24). The sin that brought down fire and brimstone on the cities of the plain was again provoking God. When good kings reigned in Judah they destroyed these sodomites and cleaned up the land (15.12; 22.46). The modern homosexual, or sodomite, may be tolerated by society and in some cases excused for what some consider to be a natural tendency, but

God has not changed His thoughts about this evil and will judge all who are guilty of it.

If God used Israel to cast out the original inhabitants of Canaan because of their idolatry and immorality, it follows that, if Israel practised the same sins, a similar destruction would befall them. Thus, while Israel kept right with the Lord, no enemy could penetrate, but, with departure, invasions by surrounding nations were the order of the day. So Shishak stripped the Temple of its treasures and carried down to Egypt those precious things David had stored up and given to the Lord. When the children of Israel left Egypt its treasures were brought out with them. Now this was reversed and the wealth of Israel was taken and used to decorate the temples of that idolatrous nation. If Egypt is taken as a picture of the world in its ungodliness it can be learned from this passage that the spirit of the world entering among God's people robs an assembly (the house of God) of its spiritual treasures.

When the real thing has gone, the danger is that men are likely to be satisfied with substitutes. So Rehoboam replaced gold shields with copper.

When he walked from his palace to the Temple, officers bearing the shields led the way. The shields were then returned to their place in the palace. It is obvious that despite any idolatry introduced by Rehoboam he maintained his attendance at the Temple. By so doing he may have imagined he was still true to the God of Israel.

Although 1 Kings does not give details of the wars between the northern and southern kingdoms, it does note that these took place throughout the reigns of Rehoboam and Jeroboam. When the former died he was buried in the city of David. He was honoured in his last resting-place in spite of his failings and the state of the land. He was succeeded by his son Abijam (called Abijah in 2 Chronicles). According to 2 Chronicles 11.21 Rehoboam had eighteen wives, but the one he loved most was Maacah the daughter of Absalom. Although he had older sons than Abijam, yet, because he was the oldest of her sons, he appointed him to be prince and heir to the throne. Abijam reigned for only seventeen years, and, if he was forty-one when anointed, he died at the age of fifty-eight.

Notes

2 Jeroboam's wife was not the first to "disguise" (SHANA - 8138) herself, for Tamar had done it previously (Gen 38.14). David had "changed his behaviour" (1 Sam 21.13). The wise woman of Tekoah likewise feigned to be another (2 Sam 14.2).

3 The "cracknels" (NIQQUD - 5350) were probably "spotted cakes" of little value. The word is used of the "mouldy" bread the Gibeonites brought to Joshua (Josh 9.5).

9 The expression "cast me behind thy back" occurs also in Ezekiel 23.35, where idolatry is likewise involved.

14 The words "but what? even now" have caused difficulty. The possible meaning is that the house of Jeroboam will be cut off in the future, but "what of that", when even "now", through the death of Abijam, the cutting off has begun. Thus the death of the child was a token that the entire house would be destroyed.

15 The "groves" (ASHERA - 842) were wooden poles or trunks of trees regarded as symbols of the goddess Asherah. These were erected beside the altars of Baal. Later, women wove hangings for a grove in the Temple but Josiah burnt it (2 Kings 23.6,7). These objects of worship were revived from the idolatry of the original Canaanites.

17 Jeroboam may have changed his place of residence from Shechem to Tirzah because the former was between two hills and, unlike Jerusalem, had no natural fortifications.

21 Because Rehoboam is referred to as young, and his contemporaries as young men, some have questioned whether forty-one was his true age and would change it to twenty-one. There is, however, no textual evidence for such a change. (see 12 and 2 Chr 13.7).

30 Information about the wars between Israel and Judah is given in more detail 2 Chronicles.

CHAPTER 15, Verses 1-8

The reign of Abijam

As noted above, Rehoboam did not put the eldest of his twenty-eight sons upon the throne but rather he chose Abijam, the first-born son of his favourite wife, Maachah (2 Chr 11.21,22). Apparently she was a granddaughter of Absalom and a woman who had influence in the kingdom even after the death of her son (2 Chr 15.16). The brief reign of three years afforded to this king were stained with evils copied from the practices of his father. He only became king because of his link with David yet he had no regard for David's Lord, nor for His commandments. There may have been some excuse for the kings of Israel to disregard the faithfulness of David but the kings of Judah, who were reigning because of their relationship with him, were surely under an obligation to follow in his footsteps. Alas, most of them failed miserably to do so.

Though the Lord forbad Rehoboam to fight against Jeroboam, this did not end the strife between the two kingdoms. Abijam continued the struggle, and according to 2 Chronicles 13.19 he did so with a good measure of success for he enlarged the borders of Judah by taking several cities from Jeroboam. He viewed his kingdom as being faithful to the true religion of David and therefore worthy of divine help. Here, however, the war is between Rehoboam and Jeroboam and the deeds of Abijam are viewed as continuing the aims of his father. In Kings, very little is said about him. His age is not given either at the time of his accession or at the time of his death.

Verses 9-24
The reign of Asa

Jeroboam lived to see at least four monarchs reign in Jerusalem. The last of these was Asa who reigned forty-one years and so exceeded the reigns of both David and Solomon. The historian gives the name of his grandmother, a granddaughter of Absalom, and not the name of his mother perhaps because of her sin as described in v.13. He was one of the good kings of Judah, especially in his earlier days. Conditions in the kingdom had deteriorated during the reign of the previous kings so there was much to do by way of clearing away the evil that had developed. Idolatry had almost swamped the land and with it moral corruption had become rampant. Sodomy had to be dealt with and according to 2 Chronicles 15.8, the very altar of burnt-offering had to be renewed.

He had also to deal with the sin of his mother who was queen. She had an idol made for the goddess Ashtoreth. Idolatry of the worst kind had, therefore, penetrated even the royal household. She was removed from her position and her idol was burnt at the brook Kidron. Through this he proved to the nation that he was not partial in his dealings with idolatry. However, a defect remained in that the worship of the Lord was not confined to the divine centre, but "high places" for worship were frequented. These were tolerated by some good kings and must be distinguished from the "high places" of idolaters.

Asa copied the example of David in that he enriched the treasures of the house of God by storing there the dedicated things he had obtained through battle. The wars must have come after he had reigned for a time, for he had at the beginning ten years of peace. Later, according to 2 Chronicles 14 he was attacked by an unusually large army led by Zerah king of Ethiopia. The Lord delivered him on that occasion. However, a greater test came to him when Baasha king of Israel came up against Judah, and built a fort at Ramah in Benjamin. This actually established a foothold in the southern kingdom. It is not certain why Asa was so terrified at this move. Even his father, who was much weaker than he, was more than enough to repel an offensive from Israel. It may have been that the war against Zerah left his army depleted even though victorious.

The fort at Ramah may have been intended by the northern king, Baasha, as a means of preventing those of his citizens who still wished to do so from travelling to Jerusalem for the various feasts.

It is surprising to learn that the very man who put treasures into the Temple became the one who stripped it of its wealth and sent it to Ben-hadad. Of course it was only a fraction of its value when it was first raided in the time of Rehoboam. The purpose was to obtain the help of this foreign king in defeating Baasha. The silver and gold were a bribe to make the Syrian king break his allegiance with Baasha and become confederate with Asa. By attacking the northern part of the land he was able to draw away the power concentrated on Ramah, because the king of Israel, of necessity, had to defend his own territory.

The scheme worked and Asa was then able to take the material assembled to build Ramah and use it to build two cities, Geba of Benjamin, and Mizpah. He no doubt judged that his plan had proved to be wise, but the prophet Hanani was sent to disillusion him (2 Chr 16) and to rebuke him for relying upon the king of Syria instead of the Lord who had earlier delivered him from the Ethiopians.

The end of Asa was not as good as his beginning. In his old age he seemed to have lost confidence in the Lord, not only in the major matters of his kingdom, but also in his own physical weakness. The disease in his feet may have been gout, but whatever it was, it was from the Lord and sent by Him to bring about the restoration of his soul. When his death took place he was buried in the city of David, and, according to 2 Chronicles 16.14, in his own tomb with a bed of spices. That he was highly esteemed by his people was shown by the very great burning associated with his death.

There are lessons to be learned from the story of this good king. One to note is that when men feared the Lord they needed to fear no foe. Since the reign of Solomon it was rare for any king to have ten years free from war (2 Chr 14.1). This was due to Asa walking in the ways of David and to his keeping God's commandments.

A further important feature arising from this history is that saints are more likely to trust God to defeat their worldly enemies than they are to trust Him when opposed by their brethren.

Lastly, it must always be remembered that because a course of action succeeds does not prove it to be right in the eyes of the Lord.

CHAPTERS 15.25-22.40

THE KINGS OF ISRAEL

The historian, having covered the kings of Judah until the death of Asa, then traces the history of the kings of Israel until chapter 22.40 when he again returns to the southern kingdom by taking up the story of Jehoshaphat. In these intervening chapters he deals with five kings, all of whom did evil in the sight of the Lord. This history is not given in 2 Chronicles, for only when the northern kings had dealings with the kings of Judah are they mentioned by the Chronicler. In spite of these evil rulers God was still interested in His people and used His prophets to rebuke them.

Verses 25-26
Nadab reigns over Israel

The historian goes back about 40 years from the death of Asa to the time of Nadab king of Israel. He was a son of Jeroboam, but his reign lasted for only two years. He copied his father's evils and "made Israel to sin". He was the only son of Jeroboam to reach the throne. His reign was short. The promise made to his father that his seed would continue on the throne of Israel was nullified by the idolatry he introduced. Had he and his sons been true to the Lord their place would have been assured, but they threw away every prospect and plunged deeper into idolatry to their own ruin.

CHAPTER 15.27-16.7
Baasha takes the throne of Israel

Baasha, from the unimportant tribe of Issachar, now comes to the throne having plotted against Nadab and killed him at Gibbethon in Dan. Though his father's name was Ahijah he should not be confused with the prophet of 11.29 who was an Ephraimite. That he was "exalted...out of the dust" (16.2) may suggest that he came from a very humble background. A similar phrase is used of Jeroboam, (14.7).

Evidently there had been a period of Philistine resurgence toward the end of Jeroboam's reign when they had captured Gibbethon. Nadab had mustered an army to recapture it. During the siege Baasha killed him. How Baasha came to prominence is not explained but the success of his conspiracy implies that he had many supporters. Though probably unaware that he was fulfilling the decree of God, he was used to remove the house of Jeroboam. He completely eradicated the family of Jeroboam as prophesied by Ahijah (14.10-14). Usually only the males were killed at such times but in this case the entire family was wiped out.

It is significant that no matter who took the throne of Israel there was no change in the religious sphere. They all followed the steps of Jeroboam by practising the idolatry he had introduced.

Baasha was left without excuse as a result of the visit of Jehu the prophet. The Lord had exalted Baasha yet he had provoked Him. His house, too, would be cut off with the added dishonour that those killed would not be buried but eaten either by dogs or vultures. So he died and was buried in Tirzah which had become capital of Israel. It remained so until the days of Omri who built Samaria as the new capital.

Verses 8-10
The reign of Elah

Just as Jeroboam had a son who reigned for two years so Baasha had a son, Elah, who also reigned for only two years. Nothing is said about his character or deeds. It can only be assumed that he was a follower of his father. He had chariots and had appointed Zimri to be over half of these. Like many other examples where experience of military power created a thirst for royal power, this captain turned traitor, took advantage of the king's indulgence, and slew him. The record of his drinking bout at the time of his death suggests that Elah had more interest in gratifying his own appetites than in ruling the nation.

Verses 11-20
The reign of Zimri

The family of Baasha suffered the same fate as the family of Jeroboam. As soon as Zimri began to reign he slew all the males, not only of Baasha's immediate family, but also of all his entire kin. This slaughter fulfilled the prophecy of Jehu (v.3). Of all the kings of Israel, the reign of Zimri was the shortest for it lasted only seven days. He had failed to win the hearts of the people. As soon as they heard the news of the mutiny they immediately made Omri king. For a few days Israel had two kings, one in Tirzah the capital and the other at Gibbethon. Already the latter had been mentioned as the scene of the killing of Nadab (15.27). Apparently it was still a place of warfare and had not as yet been taken from the Philistines.

The usurpation of the throne by Zimri was considered by the army to be more important than the besieging of Gibbethon, so they went to attack Tirzah with the object of ending the reign of Zimri. With the city surrounded he chose suicide rather than be captured. No doubt his motive in destroying the house of Baasha was to secure the throne for himself and his posterity. His high hopes were quickly dashed, for he had hardly seized the crown before he was consumed in the flames he himself had lit. His sudden destruction came because he, like all kings of Israel, walked in the evil ways of Jeroboam.

Verses 21-28
Omri reigns in Israel

Even though Omri had been made king he had a rival. Tibni the son of Ginath had secured the support of half of the people for his bid for the crown. However, Omri proved to be the stronger, and, with the death of Tibni, became the sole ruler in Israel. For a period of about three to four years there was little stability as regards the throne of Israel, but, with Omri in the ascendant matters were more settled. He reigned twelve years (including the three to four year struggle with Tibni) and his dynasty continued for three generations and more than forty years.

During his reign great changes were made. He bought Samaria where he built the new capital and transferred his palace to it from Tirzah. What Samaria was like when he bought it is not described. However the price he paid, two talents of silver, was not high. Just as David had made the hill of Zion and Jerusalem his centre of operations, so Omri chose the high hill of Samaria as a natural fort and one likely to withstand any attack that might be made upon it. The Word of God has nothing good to say about him or any of his sons for he even exceeded in wickedness all the kings of Israel who had preceded him. The fact that there is no mention of his father or mother may suggest that he was not a true Israelite. Be that as it may, it is clear that he followed the behaviour of Jeroboam "who made Israel to sin". In spite of his wickedness, when he died his son, Ahab, reigned in his stead.

Verse 29-22.40
Ahab's lengthy reign

During the stable reign of Asa no less than seven different kings sat on the throne of Israel. The last of these, Ahab, occupied the period until almost the end of 1 Kings. Although he was the worst of the rulers of Israel his reign was comparatively long. For twenty-two years he ruled in Samaria and went further into idolatry than the kings before him. Foremost of his evils was the choice of a Zidonian, Jezebel, for his wife. She, being a worshipper of Baal, soon influenced him to introduce this form of worship into Israel. He built a temple for this idol and had an altar beside it on which to offer sacrifices. These together with an Asherah pole, or wooden idol (grove), completely turned the kingdom to heathen worship. Influenced by Jezebel, Ahab went much further than Jeroboam, for the golden calves were considered to be in some way representatives of Jehovah. Baal worship, however, was the introduction of a rival god and one for whom a magnificent temple with a gold tower was built at Tyre. Ahab built an imitation of this in Samaria (16.32) and any acknowledgement of the God of Israel vanished with the development of the new religion.

When idolatry takes over the fear of God no longer prevails, so it is not surprising that it was at this time Jericho was rebuilt. Jericho was originally allotted to Benjamin but was on the border and became part of the northern kingdom. The motive for rebuilding it may have been to have a fort near to the passage across Jordan. It seems probable that most Israelites no longer took seriously the curse predicted on the man who dared rebuild it (Josh 6.26). Disregarding the warning, and probably concluding that it was long out of date, Hiel proceeded to build the city. To his sorrow he learned that God's threats are not false alarms.

Israel may have turned away from God and viewed lightly the evil of idolatry, but He was still watching over His land and continued to prove that He had not given up dealings with it.

Notes
Chapter 15

2 "Maachah" (also called Michaiah - 2 Chr 13.2) was the

granddaughter of Absalom, though called "daughter". This is not unusual in Scripture. Her father was Uriel, who must have married Tamar the only daughter of Absalom.

5 The one blot in the record of David not erased by the passage of time was the murder of Uriah (2 Sam 11).

9 As Abijam began to reign in the eighteenth year of Jeroboam, and Asa began to reign in the twentieth year, he could not have reigned the full three years, but two years and some months (v. 1). However in this mode of reckoning a part year was regarded as a whole year.

13 Maachah may have been Queen for a time as a result of the death of Asa's mother.

The word "idol" (MIPLESET - 4656) used here is not the same as is used for the idols in v.12, (GILLUL - 1544). There it is a filthy thing and is a favourite term for idols in Ezekiel where it occurs almost forty times. Here the word refers to an image which creates fear.

Chapter 16

13 The term "vanities" (HEBEL - 1892) first used in Deuteronomy 32.21, may, when plural, refer to idols (Jonah 2.8).

THE DAYS OF ELIJAH

Introduction

Though the history of the kings of Israel continues, an entirely new feature of the story commences at ch.17. Hitherto the deeds of the kings were the prominent theme and the prophets were only introduced as and when necessary. From now to the end of the book, and indeed well into 2 Kings, the main theme is not the kings, but the prophets.

The ministry of Elijah and Elisha covers a period of some eighty years. During the first twenty of these the former dominated the scene and played a leading role in the affairs of the nation. He is rightly called the Reformer of Israel and though he was unable to accomplish all that he longed for, he did see the day when the people acknowledged that "the Lord, He is the God" (18.39).

Already attention has been drawn to the absence of prophetic ministry during the days of Solomon. From his death until this chapter prophets appear on the scene from time-to-time to bring God's message to king and people. A broad survey of the OT allows the conclusion to be reached that there is a close link between departure from God and the sending of His prophets.

The prophetic books, beginning with Isaiah and continuing to Malachi, are mainly directed toward the recovery of those who had departed from the Lord. In most cases it would appear that those in close touch with the Lord heard directly from Him, whereas those who were at a distance from Him heard His voice through the prophets.

CHAPTER 17, Verses 1-16
Elijah calls for a famine, and hides

Elijah appears on the scene as suddenly as he departs from it. He abruptly emerges without introduction or pedigree. While his birth-place was possibly Tishbi in Galilee, he is here found living in Gilead which was east of Jordan. Thus he was far from the centres of power. The kings of Israel ruled from Samaria and Judah was ruled from Jerusalem.

Gilead may have been rich in spices and balm, but it was desolate and barren as regards the worship of the God of Israel. The tribes occupying it had turned to idolatry and later were the first to go into captivity. However Elijah's parents must have had some knowledge of the Lord for the name they gave their son means "My God is the Lord". The words "before whom I stand" in v.1 indicate that he considered himself a servant ready to do his master's bidding.

Ahab must have been startled to be approached by this man dressed in a garment of hair with a leather girdle (2 Kings 1.8). He would be further amazed to hear him speak with striking authority as though he were an angel of the Lord.

That a mere man could claim to control the weather and as it were have the keys of heaven to shut it up or open it at his will was the boldest claim ever heard in the royal court.

Canaan was totally dependant upon the Lord to grant rain in due season. By including the dew as well as the rain the prophet's threat was given added weight. A heavy dew could give some relief, if not actually make rain unnecessary, as seeems to be the case before the Flood (Gen 2.5-6).

No doubt Elijah prayed that it might not rain (Jas 5.17) because he had learned from Deuteronomy (11.17) that withholding rain was the Lord's way of chastising His people. This meant that if they turned from Him and worshipped idols, He had the means at hand to arrest their folly and to show to them His displeasure. Elijah, who stood before Him, was fully in the current of His will when he made intercession regarding the rain. The serious feature of this threat was that the drought would continue for a long period. James states that it continued three years and six months, but no time limit was set when the announcement was first made. The probable reason for this was that the time would be determined by the attitude of the people. If they had repented when they first heard the message there would have been no need for the chastisement to continue.

After making this alarming statement to Ahab, the safety of the prophet was of great importance, and the One before whom he stood immediately gave him the message to go to the brook Cherith and hide. By staying there he secured his own safety and made contact with him by the people impossible. There would be no relief from the drought until he appeared again.

Where exactly this brook was situated is not certain, nor can the word "before" settle which side of Jordan it was on. However, the fact that he was sent eastwards suggests that he was returning in the direction Gilead.

The Lord not only told him where to go but also assured him that food and drink would be provided. Despite the drought, the brook would be sustained for a time and ravens would carry bread and flesh to him and not eat it themselves, and do so morning and evening.

This miracle shows that God can control the appetite of His creatures. The ravens, being carnivorous birds, would have relished the meat yet they did not devour it. They laid both bread and meat on the table for God's servant to enjoy.

One wonders where this food could have been obtained. Perhaps it came from the king's palace where the surplus supplies were possibly left outside. God taught His servant that the unclean birds had more care for him than his own people. Later he enjoyed the hospitality of a Gentile woman.

Like Moses who similarly fled from an angry king and was sustained by the priest of Midian so Elijah was supplied by those directed by the One whom he served. The Lord Jesus also, one greater than either prophet, had His needs supplied by Gentiles from the East when they presented Him with gifts at the time when He and His parents were likewise fleeing from an angry king.

Elijah, like many of God's servants, was not allowed to settle permanently, free from anxiety. The time came when the brook dried up due to the absence of rain. He had been sent to it by the Lord and had proved the faithfulness of the promise made to him. He was not left destitute nor to his own devices. The Lord had observed from above and once more gave directions.

Again the means used to meet his need may have seemed surprising. It was a Gentile widow who would spread a table for him. Given her address he immediately left the dried up brook and proceeded to Zarephath where she lived. As he approached the city the first to meet him was the woman gathering fire-wood with the end in mind of baking a cake of bread with the last of her store of meal.

The God who directed the ravens to the brook had again shown His servant that He could direct the steps of the widow. Elijah's supplies had dried up and the widow's were about to reach the same point. The two were almost alike in their needs. It may not have been a great surprise to the widow to be asked for a drink of water but to be called back and also asked for bread provoked her to recount her distress. If she were to do as he had asked then the prophet would be kept living at the cost of two early deaths. Instead of dropping his demand he re-stated it, but with a most assuring promise of a continuing supply.

It might be thought that asking for his own cake first was a selfish request, but he was the Lord's representative and thus was asking for her to give the Lord His portion and then her needs would be fully met. The words of the Lord in Mal 3.10 are in a similar vein: "Bring ye all the tithes into the storehouse...and prove me...if I will not open you the windows of heaven, and pour you out a blessing...".

When she was first approached she must have detected he was an Israelite, for she spoke to him about the Lord his God (v.12), and her actions thereafter demonstrated her confidence in the words of his God. Could it be that she had heard why the drought had come and so concluded that the Lord who had sent it could do whatever He promised?

For possibly a year the three were sustained by the scant supply. It would appear that the amount of meal did not multiply to fill the barrel, nor was there any great accumulation of oil. The meal and oil never diminished, but the supply was only for the widow, her son and the prophet. She had no surplus to sell or give away. Like the manna in the wilderness, which was supplied without variation during the journeys of the Israelites, so the supplies here were not changed.

These verses contain important lessons. First is that though God's people turn away from Him yet He makes every effort to restore them to Himself. King and people turned to Baal and deserved to be given up to their evil ways, but not so. God raised up His faithful servant and through him set in motion the means of their recovery.

It should also be noted that Elijah, who called for the drought, had himself also to bear the consequences of his own prophecy. God makes His servants feel the weight of their own ministry. Even though his needs were met Elijah had no luxuries. Only the bare necessities were provided for him. Like every servant of God his patience was tried and many days passed without the slightest sign that the looked for repentance had been produced.

One must also note the simple fact that the means used for the support of God's servants are often unexpected. Here they were unclean birds and a Gentile widow.

There is a temptation to think that when the Lord guides to a particular place it will never be changed. The dried up brook shows that there can be no settling down to think that all will continue as it has in the past.

God could have kept the brook flowing just as easily as He kept the meal in the barrel but He often stirs the nests of his servants and keeps them in constant dependence upon Himself. Just when it might be thought that all is settled and firm, He can disturb the situation and not allow men to become "settled on their lees" (Zeph 1.12).

These verses also show the importance of being able to live with others and share their circumstances. While at the brook Elijah was probably alone and so could do as he pleased. In the widow's home he had no such freedom nor was he the only one to be considered. It would not be easy for him to keep calm and happy in such trying conditions. Often God's servants, especially those on the mission field, have very unpleasant conditions to endure, which can test tempers. Being able to adapt to the portion allotted by God requires His grace, for human nature does not react well to constant strain.

Verses 17-24
The death and resurrection of the widow's son

Already notice has been drawn to the fact that God disturbed the rest of Elijah by the drying up of the brook. Another example of His strange workings is now given. The widow who befriended the prophet had but one precious treasure in this world, her only son.

The story is related here not only of the boy's sickness but also of his death. Earlier she had feared the death of herself and her son but it might not have occurred to her that she might be spared and her son taken. His death was not due to lack of food but rather a fatal sickness. As might be expected, she turned to the prophet and sought from him an explanation of the disaster. The first thought to strike her was that this judgment had fallen upon her because of sin in her life. The presence of a man of God under her roof caused her to think that he, as God's representative, had in some way contributed to the child's death. Elijah did not attempt to answer her question, but took the boy out of her arms, carried him upstairs to his bedroom, prayed to God, and stretched himself upon him. While doing so he continued crying to the Lord for His help to restore the lad to life. His prayer was heard, the soul of the boy returned (proving he had not been merely in a swoon but had truly been dead) and he was given back to his mother. Whatever doubts she may have had regarding Elijah and His God were swept away. This second miracle convinced her that the prophet was a man of God. What at its onset was a calamity turned out to be a blessing, for it strengthened her confidence in the God of Israel.

Here it is shown that the Lord allowed a Gentile to experience what the founder of the nation of Israel experienced. Just as Abraham had his son restored from the point of death and his faith strengthened, so this widow lost her son and had him returned to her again. A greater than Elijah also raised the only son of a widow and dried the tears of a broken-hearted mother (Lk 7.11-15).

This first case of actual resurrection in Scripture may have a typical significance. The revival of the nations, and especially the nation of Israel, is often compared to the raising of the dead. The coming of Elijah meant deliverance for the woman and her son from death through the famine. He restored her son from death and this was followed by the restoration of the nation (ch.18). The coming of Elijah in the future will signal the coming of Christ and this will be "life from the dead" (Rom 11.15).

The rejection of Christ, the true Prophet, by Israel has resulted in blessing amongst the Gentiles. However, this is not the final state of things for later the restored nation will be the channel of blessing to the world (Rom 11).

The ways of God with the faithful are often puzzling. In the case of the widow who had befriended the prophet one might have expected that such a soul would be free from sorrow. That those closest to God are the most likely to be in trouble seems to be most unreasonable. Despite this, a glance through the Scriptures will confirm the fact that those who walk with Him quite often find the road far from smooth. A consideration of Abraham with the famines he endured, the barrenness of his wife and the offering of his only son makes clear that life was not easy for him. Likewise, if the evil days which befell Jacob are noted, the same conclusion will be reached that contact with God is no guarantee that life will be free of trouble. Indeed it is likely to be the reverse.

The woman felt that the presence of Elijah was causing God to deal with her sin, and that this was the reason for her son's death. Like most, when calamity strikes, she was concerned with the reason for it. Her fears were groundless, for the real purpose of the sad event was to lead her into a deeper knowledge of the Lord.

Notes

1 "of the inhabitants" (TOSHAB - 8453) is normally translated "sojourners" as in Genesis 23.4, and 1 Chronicles 29.15.

9 Zarephath lay between Tyre and Zidon and close to the shore of

the Mediterranean Sea. It was in enemy territory, and was the birthplace of Jezebel. God preserved His servant there as well as providing him with food. Often God's most faithful servants found themselves in danger zones. Moses in Egypt, Daniel in Babylon, Paul in Rome and here Elijah in Zarephath are examples. Even though there were widows in Israel, yet none of these had the honour of entertaining the prophet (Lk 4.25-26).

10 In the East, to ask a drink was not only a normal request, but often a polite way of approach. The servant of Abraham (Gen 24.17), and the Lord (Jn 4.7) introduced themselves in a similar way.

17 The widow is called "mistress" (BAALA - 1172), a term only used of two others (1 Sam 28.7; Nah 3.4). It occurs quite often in the masculine form.

18 Here Elijah is called "man of God" for the first time.

19 The word "loft" (ALIYA - 5944) is translated "chamber" in v.23, and "parlour" four times in Judges 3.20-25.

21 Elijah "stretched" (MADED - 4058) or "measured" himself upon the child. The exercise is more clearly described in 2 Kings 4.34.

CHAPTER 18, Verses 1-15
Elijah meets Obadiah

This chapter records the greatest achievement in the ministry of Elijah, and shows that the drought he was instrumental in bringing about resulted in a restoration of the honouring of the God of Israel. While it is too much to claim that the nation was restored fully to the Lord, at least the worship of Baal was dealt a severe blow.

After three years, most, if not all of which were spent with the widow and her son, Elijah was directed by the word of the Lord to go and meet Ahab. This was by no means an easy encounter for the prophet well knew that he was being blamed for the hardship being suffered by the king and the people. Fodder for Ahab's horses had all but disappeared. Provision for them had to be found soon or else they would have to be put down. Thus there is described the extensive search by Obadiah and the king, each setting off in a different direction.

In the execution of this task, Obadiah was met by Elijah whom he greeted with the utmost respect, not only did he fall to the ground, but while he did so, he cried out, "Is it thou, my lord Elijah?" (v.7, RV). Evidently he had no difficulty in recognising the prophet, possibly helped by his distinctive garments. However, when given the charge to tell Ahab that Elijah was here he was completely terrified. If the prophet disappeared, as he seemed to have done before, then the messenger would suffer death for bringing a false report. Obviously Elijah had the secret of escaping arrest. Whether he had been at times transported by the Spirit from one place to another, or whether he knew how to steal away without being detected, is not certain. It may only refer to his time at Cherith and Zarephath. One thing was clear, the efforts of the king to find him had been futile in spite of his diligence.

Obadiah was exceedingly anxious to impress on the prophet the risk he (Elijah) was asking him to take. Putting him in jeopardy might have been reasonable if had he been a worshipper of Baal, or a supporter of the persecution of the Lord's prophets. But to do so to a man who had preserved the lives of a hundred prophets of the Lord by hiding them in a cave and supplying them with food was most unfair.

However, when the prophet assured him, by speaking in the name of the Lord Almighty, that he would see Ahab that day, he lost his fear.

The meeting of Elijah and Obadiah was of much greater significance than might at first appear. The former had not met an Israelite with a kindred spirit for the three and a half years he had been in exile. It is probable that he was totally unaware that the Lord had at least one who served Him in the court of Ahab and his wicked wife. Like Joseph of Arimathaea, Obadiah was a secret disciple, yet was fulfilling the purpose for which he was appointed. He was not a new convert, but one who had worshipped the Lord from early life. How he rose so high in a time when wickedness was the order of the day is difficult to understand. However quite often God-fearing men are valued by those in authority, not because they like their beliefs, but because they can trust them to an extent they can not do with others.

Verses 16-40
Elijah meets Ahab, and the events on Mount Carmel

Elijah having appeared and wishing to meet the king, the two soon met face to face. The attitude of Ahab was very different to that of Obadiah. Seldom have any two men talked together whose hearts were further apart. Boiling up in the heart of Ahab was bitter rage toward the man he looked upon as the one to be blamed for bringing the nation into deep distress. As for Elijah, he likewise had no love for the king who had led the nation into gross idolatry. Each man blamed the other for being the one who "troubled" Israel. In a sense both were "troublers". Elijah had brought the nation to its knees with the famine but Ahab's idolatry was the root cause of it. The courage of the prophet on this occasion was outstanding. He knew that the king had sought to kill him from the time he had shut up the heavens. Obadiah had already made plain to Elijah that no effort had been spared by the king in his search for the "troubler", and, had he succeeded in finding him, would have fulfilled his intention to kill him. Since on this occasion, the Lord had sent him to the king Elijah could depend upon divine preservation.

In a similar way when all Egypt trembled in the presence of the despot Pharaoh, Moses threatened him with the plagues, yet showed no sign of fear. Thus men in all ages who move in obedience to the Lord are more than a match for the greatest monarchs on earth.

The prophet's demand for the call of the nation to Mount Carmel was intended to settle whether Baal or the Lord was the true God. For years the people had been "halting between two opinions"; at times they would give all the glory to Baal, while at other times they gave it to the Lord. However not all were "halting", for Jezebel and her priests were fully persuaded that their idols were the true gods. Likewise, Obadiah and those like him were in no doubt that the Lord was the only God, but the mass of the people were undecided. When Ahab called the nation together the idolaters were well represented. Four hundred and fifty prophets of Baal and four hundred prophets of Asherah, the female idol, together with a great crowd of the people led by these deceivers, were gathered on the Mount. Against this great crowd was Elijah who felt he was alone for no one dared stand by his side. Like Paul, when making his defence at Rome with none save the Lord standing with him (2 Tim 4.16,17), the man of God was conscious of the Lord's presence. Although it may not have been apparent, he had might on his side.

Why Carmel was selected as the venue of this important meeting is not clear. However being near to the sea it was a suitable place where the barrels of water later used to drench the altar could be found.

The whole drama was initiated by Elijah. He decided the test, which was accepted by the king; the "God that answereth by fire, let him be God". No doubt "fire" was to be the deciding factor since, from the beginning of Scripture, this was the way in which God showed that He had accepted an offering. The examples, among others, of

Abraham (Gen 15), Moses (Lev 9), David (1 Chr 21), and Solomon (2 Chr 7) demonstrate this.

All was put in order for sacrifice and the worshippers of Baal were given the first opportunity to demonstrate the power of their god. In fairness to them, it must be admitted that they did believe their god would answer by sending down fire upon the sacrifice. Their cries were accompanied with the usual religious dancing, as was the case when the golden calf was surrounded by Israelites (Ex 32.6). To their amazement and bitter disappointment no response from Baal was forthcoming. One notes Elijahs taunts. These must have provoked them to intensified efforts. So frantic did they become that they slashed themselves with knives till their blood poured out. How unlike the God of Israel was their god, for he was not only deaf, but was neither omnipresent, omniscient, nor omnipotent. Elijah gave them ample time. He waited patiently until the time of the evening sacrifice before giving proof that his God was all that theirs failed to be.

Close by the disgraceful scene of the idolatrous display were the remains of an altar which had been used for sacrificing to the Lord. Indeed, it could have been that this relic of former true worship had some bearing on the choice of this Mount at this time. Selecting twelve stones from this ruin Elijah built an altar. In so doing he was demonstrating that he believed in the unity of the divided nation. Each stone represented a tribe. Round the altar he dug the trench for water. When the slain bull was placed on the wood and all was ready for burning, the prophet called on them to pour water upon it, not once, but three times, so that, not only was the sacrifice drenched, but the trench around the altar was also filled with water. In this action the prophet was proving to the sceptical people that his God could not only send fire, but when sent, it could consume the sacrifice despite the water.

It might have been expected that when all was set and ready the fire would have fallen immediately upon the altar, but this was not so. Not until Elijah stepped forward, prayed to the God of the nation's fathers, and pleaded earnestly with Him by repeating, "Hear me", did the fire descend. In his prayer he discloses why all that he had asked to be done that day was done as it was, for in everything he had been directed by the Lord.

Although he was confident that the fire would descend, yet he would let the people see that his God could hear, and that it was not the prophets own power which produced the wonderful sight.

When the fire did come it was far from ordinary. It not only consumed the wood, the sacrifice, and the stones, but dried up the water as well. With such a proof of divine power, the people could not remain in further doubt, and had to exclaim, "The Lord, He is the God". These words were like music in the ears of the prophet. They were evidence that the reform he had yearned to see had at length taken place. Not only had he been honoured in the presence of the king and people, but he no doubt felt that a death blow had been struck to the whole fabric of idolatry.

Now that the falsehood of Baal had been shown it followed that his prophets were also false. These had been instrumental in turning Israel from the Lord, so Elijah ordered them to be taken prisoner and brought down to the brook Kishon, where they were summarily executed. His authority to do this is found in Deuteronomy 17. Thus the brook, which may have supplied the water, now received the blood of these wicked servants of Satan.

At the destruction of the golden calf Moses had acted in a similar way for at that time about 3,000 of the people fell (Ex 32.28). According to v.4, Jezebel, who had fed the prophets of Baal (v.19), had cut off the prophets of the Lord, so, in the destruction of the evil prophets, there was a reaping of what had been sown. False worship is often associated with folly. In v.28 the prophets of Baal "cut themselves...with knives and lancets".

A review of these verses reveals a common error. Sinners often blame the means God may use to judge them rather than recognising the reason for the judgment. The Israelites blamed Moses and Aaron for the trials in the wilderness (Ex 16.2). Thus when Korah and his followers were judged, they blamed the two leaders, for they said to them, "Ye have killed the people of the Lord" (Num 16.41). Those who know God are entirely different, for when calamity overtakes them they are ready to acknowledge their sin and failure. They see beyond the instruments He may have used to chasten them. Their attitude is governed by the fact that they realize that "no evil dart can hit, unless the God of love sees fit".

Exposing the emptiness and uselessness of idols was a feature of the ministry of the prophets of the Lord. Whether Isaiah, Jeremiah, Elijah or others less prominent they all alike exposed the folly of worshippers who bowed down to such worthless objects. Perhaps in our day there should be, more often than there is, an exposure of the emptiness of the world and its so-called treasures.

"Little children, keep yourselves from idols" (1 Jn 5.21) is a needful injunction.

Standing alone in a crisis is not only difficult but all but impossible without the help of the Lord. Elijah not only stood before the Lord, the Lord stood with him otherwise the mass of opposition would have overwhelmed him. What can be done with His help is beyond human expectation. The weakness of men, when they are left to themselves, is no less surprising.

The altar of twelve stones speaks loudly. It shows that true revival brings God's people back to first principles. Elijah, though practically unknown in Judah, did not exclude any of the separated tribes. Likewise, in spite of divisions that may arise amongst saints, there must be no forgetting the oneness of the body of Christ.

God may not answer His faithful people by fire in this age. Nevertheless He does make known His presence when they gather together and He accepts the worship of their hearts. When the gift of prophecy was in exercise in the church at Corinth a visitor would go out and say, "God is in you of a truth" (1 Cor 14.25). There should always be concern that His presence is known when His people are gathered together.

Verses 41-46
The rain is promised

The king had gone down with the masses to the river Kishon and was in touch with Elijah. In such a day of intense excitement it is possible that he had no thought of eating. He must have been bewildered at the dramatic change of his subjects from being worshippers of Baal to being worshippers of the Lord. Instead of the king ordering the prophet, it was the prophet ordering the king and telling him to go up from the river and to eat and drink. The greatest concern of his mind was the absence of rain. Now he was assured that an abundance of it was on the way. He could not only have a meal, but he could enjoy it, having had this burden lifted from him.

Again it might have been assumed that the rain would be granted immediately upon the word of the prophet, but this was not so. On the top of Carmel he was bowed in earnest prayer that the long awaited showers might fall. Just as he had prayed for the fire (vv. 36,37) here we see him earnestly praying for what was sure to come but had not yet appeared. Unlike his earlier petition, which was granted almost immediately, this one was delayed. After each prayer a servant was sent to see if there were any signs of dark clouds in the sky and at the eighth observation a small cloud appeared.

This was the token that convinced him that the floods were coming. If Ahab was to reach his house at Jezreel he had no time to lose. He had to yoke his horses and descend as swiftly as he could, otherwise the flooded highways would have made the journey impossible. The king, who was told to "go up" in v.41, is now told to "go down". In both cases he is treated as though he were the servant of Elijah, into whose hands the Lord had committed the entire operation. At the end of a day of momentous events there was unexpected behaviour by Elijah. Instead of the prophet retiring to some shelter for a rest, especially after such a strenuous time, he girded up his loins and became a forerunner of the king. No matter how fast the chariot horses galloped along the road to Jezreel the prophet kept ahead. This he could not have done in his own strength. Having spent much of the day on Carmel, building a stone altar, going to Kishon and slaying the prophets of Baal, climbing the mountain to pray, and probably having nothing to eat, Elijah must have been weary. But "the hand of the Lord" was upon him. By His enabling the feat was accomplished. The distance was about 14 miles (22.5km) and so was not a short sprint but a fairly long journey. Wisely, and no doubt guided by the Lord, he did not venture into the city. Had he done so Jezebel would have attempted his destruction.

Looking back over these verses there is clear evidence that, although Elijah was involved in critical matters, yet in thinking of the king's physical needs he showed proper compassion. The Lord Himself is a great example of this. When He saw the hungry thousands He said to the disciples, "Give ye them to eat" (Mt 14.16), and later said to His disciples, "Children, have ye any meat?" (Jn 21.5).

The delay in sending the rain shows that God's ways of answering prayer are not stereotyped. There are times when the answer comes almost at the time of asking, and there are other occasions when some delay is encountered before the answer is received. Those who wait upon God are often thankful for even the smallest evidence of approaching blessing. The small cloud was not going to descend in a deluge, but it was the harbinger of greater things. Men should not only pray, but should look out for answers, and be spiritual enough to know how to value the least evidence of coming blessing.

Notes

17 The word "troubleth" (AKAR - 5916) is used of Jacob's sons (Gen 34.30), and especially of Achan, "the troubler of Israel" (Josh 6.18; 7.25; 1 Chr 2.7).

21 The word "halt" (PASACH - 6452) is derived from the idea of "lameness", and here implies that they were hesitating between Baal and the Lord. Compare "leaped" (v.26), which is the same Hebrew word but implies a type of pagan ritual dance.

30 He "repaired" (RAPA - 7495) the altar or "healed" it.

32 This is the first occurrence of "trench" (TeALA - 8585). It is translated "conduit" in 2 Kings 18.17 and 20.20.

CHAPTER 19, Verses 1-18
Elijah flees to Horeb

Having reached the peak of his work of reformation on Mount Carmel, Elijah, like most servants of God, descends to lower ground and shows some of the weaknesses of fallen man. When God in a singular way grants any of His servants a special revelation of Himself, often He allows them to feel their own weakness, yet, while doing so, upholds them by His grace. Paul revealed how this principle worked in his life (2 Cor 12). Those who have experienced blessing, even in small measure, can testify that it was often followed by unusual trials. The hero of ch.18, who stood up to Ahab with undaunted courage, who did not shudder at the united voices of the hundreds of prophets of Baal, is terrified at hearing of the threat of the wicked woman Jezebel. Even though he asked the Lord to take away his life (v.4), he did not want her to be the means of doing so.

Jezebel was not on Carmel to witness the descending fire, nor did she stand at the river Kishon and see the blood of her servile prophets flow into its waters, but she had reported to her by the king a detailed account of what had transpired. She was not impressed with the report, nor did she seriously consider that the descent of the fire had proved the God of Israel to be the only true God. The rage which filled her and which she expressed left Ahab speechless. Her words were fierce and threatening. Indeed her entire attitude betrayed her defiance and her disregard for the astonishing demonstration of His power that God had given to the nation. Her only thought was to kill Elijah, and do it almost immediately. Her oath implies that the severest dealings of the gods would come upon her if the threat she was making were not carried out. It was as well for her that they were not gods at all, otherwise she would have suffered from them for her failure!

It was beyond her power to carry out her threat without the consent of Ahab. He might not have been willing to agree with her plan. Nonetheless, courageous as Elijah was, her threat drove fear into his heart and he decided to flee. "The fear of man bringeth a snare" (Prov 29.25), but, in this case, the fear of a woman brought terror to the heart of one of the most courageous men in Israel.

In order to escape the threat Elijah left the northern kingdom and went over to Beersheba in Judah, which was at this time ruled by Jehoshaphat. He must have thought that in a different jurisdiction he would be safe. This is also suggested by the fact that he left there his servant who had accompanied him, and who, some think, may have been the widow's son whom he raised from the dead. So distressed had he become that he wished to be alone and, as the passage relates, travelled a day's journey into the wilderness where he sat down to rest under a broom bush. He had become not only weary with his journey, but also tired of life. Hence his plaintive cry, "Take away my life". This desire to die is in sharp contrast to his fleeing from the death threat of Jezebel, for, if he were tired of life, she would have been only too willing and ready to bring it to an end.

It might be asked what brought about such despondency and changed the prophet's mind from one who sought to be spared to one who desired to die. It has been suggested that when he fled he was more anxious to return to solitude than to escape execution. However perhaps the real reason for the change was that he was disappointed that what seemed to be true revival by the nation was only a momentary arresting of its slide into idolatry. As long as Jezebel was a ruling force in Samaria the prophet could see no hope of the people escaping her evil influence. What at first appeared to be a wonderful conversion to the true God, was, after all, only a passing flash like that of a falling meteor. On Carmel he may have thought that he had succeeded where his fathers had failed, but he had to learn the humiliating lesson that he was no better than they.

"It is enough" are words which imply that he judged his work to be at an end and that he wanted to be no longer in the struggle. However, he later learned that other service was ahead of him. The Lord had put into his hand the key to open and shut the heavens, but he had not given him the keys of death nor the right to decide when his work was done. His prayer is in contrast to that of Simeon, who also wished to depart this life (Lk 2.25-32), and to the triumphant words of Paul "I am now ready to be offered" (2 Tim 4.6). The strange feature of Elijah's case is that, though he wished to die, he went to heaven without dying.

He was not the only prophet who wanted to die. Jonah, outside the city of Nineveh, realizing that what he had prophesied had not come to pass, also said, "It is better for me to die than to live" (Jonah 4.8).

It is not surprising that after all his travels and depression Elijah fell asleep under the shelter of the bush. However, although travelling on a course without direct guidance from God and with his spirit somewhat depressed, he was not without divine attention. The angelic provision of food and water in the desert were necessary for him to be able to travel to Horeb. Earlier he had experienced the Lord's hand in supplying his need at the brook. He had eaten of the meal and oil in the widow's barrel. However this time, he was again not only miraculously fed, but within him a further miracle was involved in that the strength derived from these meals lasted for forty days. This was also the period Moses was on Sinai without food, and the time spent by the Lord in the wilderness. It was just as easy for God to extend the nourishment from these two meals as it was for Him to maintain the meal and oil in the widow's house.

In reaching Horeb, it would appear that Elijah was attempting to retrace the steps of the Israelites when they journeyed from Horeb through the wilderness to the Jordan. The 200 mile (over 300km) journey, would not normally take 40 days. He may have travelled slowly because he had no direct instruction as to his movements, or he may have visited some of the places where the nation had camped on its journey. If so this would have diverted him from the direct route.

He must have had a deep desire to visit the holy mount where the Law was given to Moses and to recapture in his mind something of the wonder of that scene. This sacred spot is called here "the mount of God". The cave in which he rested for the first night has been suggested to be the very cave in which Moses hid himself when the Lord appeared to him (Ex 33.22).

Although a lonely man in a cave, he was not out of touch with heaven, for the "word of the Lord" sounded in his ears again. In response to the enquiry as to why he was in Horeb, he gives the very pessimistic reply recorded. Instead of rebuking him for his limited grasp of the situation the Lord told him that He would pass by. The same glorious person who had appeared to Moses was now going to be seen by this depressed prophet. Just as at the giving of the Law when there were physical phenomena which were alarming to the people, so on this occasion there was the great storm, the earthquake and the fire. But in none of these did the Lord appear. They were all associated with judgment and revealed only one side of God's character. The whisper was the signal to the prophet that the promised visit by the Lord had come and that, by appearing in this distinctive way, gentleness would characterize this very different message. Elijah, afraid to look upon God, covered his face. The question and the answer were the same as on the former occasion, but this time were accompanied by the detailed outline of the appointments he was to make. All the chief actors on the stage were to be changed. While Elijah was told to execute these commands, it transpired that only one of them was carried out by him personally, namely the anointing of Elisha. The other two were the work of this new prophet who took his place.

In this programme of events one of his problems was solved. To him, and to the faithful in all ages, the sparing of the wicked and the slaughter of the righteous has always been a puzzle. Here he is shown that the judgment of the wicked, though delayed for a time, is nonetheless certain. The final statement of the Lord must have surprised him most of all, for although he had claimed that he alone was left, and threatened with death, he is told of the 7,000 in Israel who had not been worshippers of Baal. Thus the Lord corrected both of his wrong thoughts.

There is instruction in these verses for God's servants which bears close examination. To begin with, Ahab is a clear example of weak rule and the consequences it brings. While he claimed to rule Israel, the real authority was in the hands of his wife. Even though Elijah had convinced him as to the true God, this did not alter the kingdom, for Ahab was powerless to act without her consent. It is a sad day when men are in professed authority in any sphere but are mere puppets of their spouses. He may not have been as fanatical about Baal as she was, but whatever his convictions, these did not effectively matter.

Again, it should be noted that fear plays an even more important role in the lives of God's servants than might be thought. After all that Elijah had experienced from the hand of the Lord, especially on Mount Camel, one would think he could have faced the greatest danger without a quiver, yet the threat made by a woman was enough to make him flee for his life. Peter could smite the servant of the priest and cut off his ear, yet in a matter of hours he denied the Lord when confronted by a door-maid. "Let him that thinketh he standeth take heed lest he fall" (1 Cor 10.12).

Another feature of this story is that though the prophet had become discouraged and downcast, the Lord had compassion upon him and did not directly rebuke him for his unwarranted state. It is well that He still deals graciously with His servants, especially when their failings are known to themselves and Him alone. What men are in public, they ought to be in private, but sometimes, as in the case of Elijah, they are not consistent. He was a different man under the tree from the one who stood on Carmel.

Although the prophet felt his work was done, yet the Lord was not finished with him. When success is the result of service then there is every encouragement to continue in it, but when apparent failure is stamped upon it then the temptation to retire early arises. God can uphold His servants until their work is done, and none of them should judge a set-back to be the signal to them that He has finished using them.

One other lesson in these verses is that the greatest of servants can be replaced, and those who take their place may, as in this case, far surpass, in some respects, the one taken away. No man, be he ever so useful, is indispensable. God is always fitting men for his work and can bring them forward when they are needed.

Verses 19-21
The call of Elisha

Although the anointing of the prophet was the last of the three responsibilities put upon Elijah, it was the first to be carried out. He travelled from Horeb to the Jordan valley, and, as in previous cases, he was quick to find the person he sought. The deluge of rain after the time of drought would have encouraged many to cultivate the land and replenish the grain which must have been all but exhausted. Twelve yoke of oxen ploughing in the one field was doubtless an arresting sight. Being in the Jordan valley meant that this farm was in the most fertile part of Israel. As far back as the days of Lot these well-watered plains were renowned for their fertility. Shaphat was a wealthy farmer, so his son Elisha, though ploughing last in the row of ploughmen, was by no means in poor circumstances. Whether Elijah knew the young man before this is not said, but when he was told to anoint him he raised no question as to how he would identify him.

This may suggest that the two men knew each other before this time.

Except for the prophecy that Christ will be the anointed prophet (Is 61.1), there is no other reference to this ceremony occurring in the experience of prophets until Elisha. Whether anointing implied pouring oil upon his head, or simply the casting of Elijah's coat upon him, is not made clear, but the latter idea seems the more probable. It symbolized that he was to become Elijah's adopted son, that he was to wear the character of his master, that he was to fill his position, and that he would be empowered by the Spirit to do miraculous works. His ministry would be characterised by grace and thus was in keeping with the "still small voice".

Just as Aaron was stripped of his garments and these were put upon Eleazar (Num 20.26), thus transferring the high priesthood from father to son, so here the prophetic office was transferred from Elijah to Elisha. The difference, however, was that Aaron died at that time, whereas Elijah continued for a period with Elisha acting as his companion and servant and the one who "poured water on his hands" (2 Kings 3.11).

It would appear that when Elijah had performed his symbolic act he attempted to leave the field. Elisha had to run after him to ask for time to say good-bye to his parents. His request was granted, for nothing had been done to him which would have made this out of place. However, there was to be no thought of remaining at home. The proof of his willingness to follow his master was demonstrated when he burned the plough and boiled the flesh of the oxen to provide a banquet for his family and friends. Like the fishermen who left their nets to follow Christ, and like Matthew the publican who made a feast as he became an apostle, so the young prophet left all that he treasured and began his life of service. In 2 Samuel 24.22 David used the threshing implements and the oxen to offer a sacrifice to God, showing that the threshing floor would no longer be used for its original purpose. Similarly, Elisha would no longer have any use for his plough and yoke of oxen. To him it was no light matter, for it entailed leaving forever his earthly prospects and stepping into the unknown.

From this time Elijah had a faithful companion. His life of isolation and loneliness was at an end. This was no small comfort to the aged prophet and at the same time it was a great privilege for the young man to be allowed to learn from the experiences of one of the few men in that age who knew God and had proved His power.

The call of Elisha shows that God is sovereign in His choice and that he can take men from the ordinary walks of life to do great things for Him. However, those He chooses are not idlers or lazy, but rather men who are diligent in all that they do, both sacred and secular. Though Elisha was the son of the land owner, yet he was not driving the first yoke of oxen. He was humble enough to follow his father's servants.

It is probable that, whatever he may have known about Elijah, it never dawned upon the young man that the day would come when he would be wearing Elijah's mantle. What God's purposes are for any young convert may far exceed his or her expectations, but, in fellowship with God, believers ought to hold themselves ready for any service He may call them to do.

In burning the plough and slaying the oxen he had demonstrated that his call to service, like all such calls, was no temporary appointment but a life-long work. From henceforth, his needs would be met by the Lord who had called him, and should this at any time need a miracle, then this would be performed.

Notes

3 "When he saw" is given in many versions as "he was afraid". The fact that he "went for his life" implies that he was fearful.

4 The juniper tree, a type of broom, is said to grow to a height of several feet, and to be often used by travellers as shelter. Elijah sitting under the juniper tree could be compared with the man of God under an oak tree (13.14).

6 "Baked on the coals" (RESHEP - 7529) is used only here in the OT, but compare "a live coal" in Isaiah 6.6.

10 "I have been very jealous" (QANA - 7065) is literally "being jealous I have been jealous". As often in the OT, a word is repeated for the sake of emphasis. Compare "perfect peace" - literally "peace peace" in Isaiah 26.3.

18 These 7,000, who had not bowed to Baal, are viewed by Paul as typical of the remnant of Israel now being saved, while the mass of the nation rejects Christ (Rom 11.3,4).

The kissing of idols was a token of devotion to them. Compare Elisha kissing his parents (v.20).

19 Elijah did not part with his mantle when he cast it upon Elisha. He still had it at Jordan, when he was taken up to heaven(2 Kings 2).

There is no mention of miracles of judgment being performed by Elisha. The slaying of the boys, strictly speaking, was not a miracle (2 Kings 2.24).

CHAPTER 20, Verses 1-47

AHAB'S VICTORIES OVER SYRIA

CHAPTER 20, Verses 1-12
Samaria besieged

The historian breaks off the story of Elijah and describes briefly the successes of Ahab toward the end of his reign. In these victories the prophet plays no part although other un-named prophets appear in the story. Thus the king was not without communication from God. He was not scarce of prophets in Israel nor was He confined to Elijah as His mouthpiece. Whatever may have been lacking in the results of the wonderful display of divine power on mount Carmel, one thing this chapter makes plain is that Ahab now has respect for the word of God, and equally clear is the fact that Baal plays no part in these campaigns. This seems to prove that Jezebel's influence on the kingdom was not as strong as Elijah feared. She is not once mentioned in this chapter. The defeat of Baal and the slaughter of its priests had brought some good to the nation.

Since the reign of Omri, Samaria had been the capital of Israel and the seat of its kings. Although fortified, it was not a city with the strength of Jerusalem and was not considered impregnable. Ben-hadad had his heart set on the treasures of Israel, and, helped by no less than thirty-two other kings, he made an attempt to capture the city, and to plunder its wealth. These kings were probably merely heads of small provinces or cities and not rulers over large territories. They may also give a faint picture of the hosts of the kings of the North in Daniel 11.40-41.

After surrounding the city Ben-hadad sent his messengers to Ahab demanding his surrender. He was claiming possession of Samaria before the battle had begun and was so sure of victory that he assumed the result. Like Pharaoh before him, he failed to reckon on the God of Israel, for he too thought that he could easily bring back into slavery those whom he had released a few hours earlier (Ex 14). What is equally clear is that Ahab also had no belief in the power of God to defend, so both were wrong.

The terms of the message were arrogant and alarming, yet the answer given via the messengers was one of meek submission. When it was received by Ben-hadad he was convinced that no resistance would be made to his sacking of the city, so he sent a second message with increased claims and threatened to execute his attack on the following day. The first demand was so excessive that no submission to it should have been considered, but Ahab was prepared to go to its full length. However this second and stronger ultimatum went beyond what he was prepared to do and so he called the conference of the elders. The united decision was that the invader should be resisted. Nothing would satisfy Ahab but the sacking of the city. His proverbial reply, "Let not him that girdeth on his harness boast himself as he that putteth it off" (v.11), was to warn the invader that it is the end of the battle which really counts. Like the popular saying about counting chickens before they are hatched, it was a caution that Ben-hadad was boasting too soon. The fact that he was carousing with his fellow kings showed his confidence in his army to do as he had threatened.

There is always the temptation to think that if the claims of enemies are conceded this will end their demands. Here is another proof of the fact, that yielding only encourages greater demands. "Resist the devil, and he will flee from you"(Jas 4.7), are words of great importance as well as words of wise counsel.

This siege also shows that God allows grave situations to arise so that He might bring to light those who are true to Him. Often good men are not recognised and their qualities only become apparent when difficulty arises. The need of the time brings them into the light.

Verses 13-22
A prophet assures Ahab of victory

Like other prophets in this history, the one who came to Ahab at this critical time is not named. He must have been one of those who had escaped from Jezebel's slaughter, and possibly one who was familiar with Obadiah. The fact that he would approach the king, and that his message was appreciated, indicates that the time of fear for the prophets of the Lord was now passed and that the nation was again turning to the God of its fathers.

He came to the king and poured into his ear a word from the Lord.

It was full of promise, and, when fulfilled, it would show once again the power of Israel's God. That such an unworthy man should be granted divine help is perhaps surprising. However it is evident throughout this book that every possible effort was made to keep the northern kingdom from becoming totally idolatrous and from losing the knowledge of the Lord which still lingered in the souls of a faithful remnant.

When Ahab was promised victory he was anxious to learn how this would be achieved, so the prophet, as though he was an experienced general, gave him his orders. The 232 young servants of the provincial governors, an elite bodyguard, were to be the vanguard, the king himself was to take charge, and the 7,000 standing army was to follow the servants and play its part in the battle. The situation is a reminder of Gideon and his army. In number the defenders were so few and the attackers so numerous that, humanly speaking, victory seemed impossible. When the Lord is involved in warfare He delights to prove that He can save by many, or by few. Whether it be Pharaoh at the Red Sea, or Gideon, or David and the giant, or many other instances, only His power could have secured the victory. It is encouraging to see that, in spite of Israel's rebellion from Him, and in spite of the wicked queen still by the side of the king, the same Lord who had helped in former times was still willing to show His strength to His people and give them this undeserved deliverance.

Not only were the defenders assured of victory, they were not to wait until the enemy attacked them but were directed to be first to engage in the conflict. When the young men appeared before the Syrians, Ben-hadad's men assumed they were coming out to surrender the city, but the drunken king gave orders that, whatever their errand, they were to be "taken alive". The drunken king considered the approaching princes as potential prisoners, and so helpless as to be easily surrounded by his troops.

The unexpected happened, however, for the vanguard slew every man who came before them, the army followed, and the Syrians panicked and fled for their lives. Even their king barely escaped. Only by riding on one of the spare horses did he manage to survive. Instead of Samaria being ransacked and its dust taken by the invaders, great numbers of the Syrians were slain, their chariots and horses destroyed, and their king's boasted claim dashed to the ground.

This amazing victory was intended to add another proof to Ahab that the Lord is the only true God. The proof already granted at Carmel, when the Lord answered by fire, did not reach out beyond the nation, but this demonstration of divine power was granted, not only to Ahab and the people, but to the northern group of united nations under the command of Ben-hadad. No wonder that, as is shown later, he knew that the victory was due to the help of the God of Israel.

Verses 23-34
A second victory over Syria is granted to Ahab

Even though shamefully defeated and humiliated at the first attack on Samaria, yet the Syrians were prepared to try again. This did not come as a surprise to Ahab for the prophet of the Lord had warned him of it soon after the first battle was over (v.22). Even though Benhadad's army had not been successful on the first occasion it was far from extinction. His officials advised him to make a second attack. Like all heathen kings and generals in those days the outcome of wars was always traced to the gods. Their counsellors had concluded that the God of Israel was God of the hills only and had little or no power in the plains. He did not allow His people to have chariots, but, being infantry soldiers, they could fight on the hilly terrain which characterised Samaria as well as in the valleys, and thus were able to wage war in areas where chariots could not operate. The Syrians failed to grasp that the God of Israel had universal power and could defeat His enemies as easily in the plain as on the hill top.

The second attack was planned with great care. The kings who led the earlier assault were to be replaced by other captains, but the army at their command was not to be reduced in either men or chariots. Obviously the kings were considered as the cause of the earlier defeat and it was hoped that the same army, under different leaders, and fighting on the level ground, would gain the victory. As soon as the winter was passed and the spring time came, Ben-hadad mustered his huge army and again attempted to subdue Israel, but this time he chose Aphek in the plain of Jezreel for his battleground. The Israelite army went to meet him, but, in comparison with the hosts of Syria which filled the countryside, it appeared to be like two small flocks of goats.

When confronted with such a perilous situation, a word from the Lord must have been more than welcome. In wonderful grace this was sent to assure the king that he would be victorious in this second engagement, as he had been in the first. It seems strange that seven days were spent before the two armies engaged in conflict. Possibly the invaders were consulting their gods and seeking from them some signal as to the best time to begin the attack. The number of the Syrians slain by the Israelites in one day was 100,000. The enemy's loss was colossal. To add to this there was the further calamity which came about through the wall of Aphek falling and killing an additional 27,000. The city in which they sheltered, and where they imagined they would be safe from harm, proved to be a false refuge. The Lord demonstrated that He could use the stones of the city to destroy His enemies as well as employing soldiers with their swords.

Saints might be led to think that when they have been tempted by spiritual enemies and the Lord has granted them victory, all danger is past. This passage shows that further attacks can be expected. They cannot afford to be off their guard, nor can they be complacent as though no further help from the Lord will be needed. Satan and his hosts take no holidays and will try every device to overcome the children of God. Perhaps by increasing the pressure, or by changing their manner of approach. The words of Jehoshaphat should always be kept in mind: "We have no might against this great company that cometh against us" (2 Chr 20.12). Like him, those tested can turn their eyes to the Lord. Only He can grant deliverance, and it is foolish to lean upon the arm of flesh.

After two victories, which were due alone to the Lord's help, it could rightly be expected that Ahab would never again doubt His unrivalled power, and that he would walk humbly before Him and have complete confidence in His prophets. Later it is seen that there was no such reformation in his heart, but, like so many in the world, although he valued the deliverances granted, these did not change his way of life, nor did they turn him into a devout worshipper of the God of his fathers. "Let favour be showed to the wicked, yet will he not learn righteousness" (Is 26.10), was, alas, all too true in his case.

God desires to reproduce His character in His people, so it is no surprise that throughout the neighbouring nations the news that Israel was a merciful people would have been familiar to them. Ben-hadad, realizing that he could not escape even by hiding in the city, must have been only too willing to listen to his servants as they told him of this special feature of the Israelites. Hopes of being spared then arose and, without delay, he proceeded to appeal for this mercy. His men, dressed in mourning attire, and with ropes on their heads to demonstrate that they were captives, came to the king of Israel and presented to him their plea: "Thy servant Ben-hadad saith, I pray thee, let me live" (v.32). Ahab's reply was amazing, for, after learning that he was still alive, he called him "my brother". This may not have implied that there was any relationship expressed, but rather that both were kings. Hiram used this form of speech when speaking to Solomon (9.13). Nevertheless, the servants were anxious that what they were hearing from Ahab was indeed the sincere expression of his mind. Whatever gave them the assurance they desired, they received it as a good omen and repeated the king's words for him to assent to them and show his sincerity. They then called Ben-hadad from his hiding place and brought him to Ahab, who invited him to sit with him in his chariot. This was a seat of honour for Israel's sworn enemy and one which revealed the shallowness of Ahab. No doubt he was drunk with the wine of victory but this did not excuse him for acting so unreasonably with such a tyrant. In this part of the story there is no mention of the prophets being consulted for their advice. He acted as he thought fit, and that without divine sanction.

Ben-hadad succeeded not only in having his life spared, but in making a covenant with his brother king. It is strange that the terms of the covenant were dictated by the defeated king and not by the victor. Scripture is silent as to the wars in which the cities of Israel referred to had been captured by the Syrians, but it is obvious that over the years parts of the land had been overrun. Not only were these returned, but the city of Damascus was to be opened for the Israelites to trade in it. This seems to be the idea in the phrase, "thou shalt make streets for thee in Damascus".

At the end of the first battle, Ben-hadad rode on a horse, but at the end of this one he is seated in the chariot of the King of Israel. Thus a man appointed to death returned to his palace with an agreement between him and his conqueror, which must have been as surprising to him as it was unjust in the sight of God.

Verses 35-43
A disguised prophet sentences Ahab

As one ought to expect, the foolish act of Ahab had repercussions amongst the prophets. Though they were ignored by Ahab they were still receiving communications from the Lord. One was now commissioned by God to rebuke the king and to approach him wounded. He asked one of his fellows to strike the blow, but he refused. Because he disobeyed the word of the Lord, he forfeited his life. This recalls to mind the fate of the man of God described in 13.21-26. In both cases the disobedience seems almost excusable, the prophet appears to be dealt with severely and is punished immediately, while the king escapes. A lion is used in the slaughter of both. However strange these events may appear, they teach the solemn lesson that those who were privileged to be among the prophets of the Lord were expected to obey His word even when it was, to their own minds, unreasonable. Disobedient kings might be spared for a time, but no such clemency was afforded the prophets.

A second request by the son of the prophets to be smitten was more successful. With his bleeding wounds bandaged he waited until the king was passing and then told his parabolic story. He proceeded to tell how, being busy in other matters, a prisoner entrusted to him was forgotten and managed to escape. The king passed judgment on the case without delay and confirmed that the penalty fixed must be paid. This was the answer the son of the prophets expected. In this verdict the king had passed sentence upon his own head. The headband which had camouflaged the prophet was then removed and immediately he was identified by the king. The application of the acted parable was then pressed home and the Lord's message to the king clearly expressed. He had allowed to escape a prisoner appointed to death. He would pay the penalty for doing so by forfeiting his own life. Little wonder that he returned home with a heavy heart. What was the greatest victory of his reign, became, through his own folly, the greatest disaster.

This story of the son of the prophets is a reminder of the similar case in the life of David 2 Sam 12). Nathan told the story of the poor man's lamb which the rich man took for his own selfish purpose. David pronounced his judgment of the case, as did Ahab, and in doing so, passed sentence upon himself.

The importance of ascertaining the Lord's will, not only in times of distress, but especially after deliverance has been granted, cannot be too strongly emphasised. Strange as it may appear, quite often there is more submission to Him in times of trouble than when success is granted. Not a few have vowed to live changed lives if He would raise them up from illness, but, alas, when healed and back to normal health the promises were soon forgotten. In dealing with spiritual enemies it must always be remembered that deliverance from them is by God alone. When victory has been granted there is still the danger of tolerating that which God has devoted to destruction. This evil is illustrated in Israel sparing the nations of Canaan and making agreements with them. The case of the Gibeonites with whom Joshua made a covenant is of interest here. Their approach was not unlike the approach of the Syrians to Ahab (Josh 9).

Notes

1 This chapter is transposed to follow ch. 21 in the LXX, possibly with a view to bringing the actions of Elijah together.

11 There is a very special warning against "boasting" (HALAL - 1984) in Jeremiah 9.23 where the word occurs three times, is translated "glory", and refers to pride in the things of man. The One in whom men ought to boast is the Lord (Jer 9.24).

18 "Take them alive" The drunken king considered the approaching princes as potential prisoners, and so helpless as to be easily surrounded by his troops.

20 Ben-hadad apparently escaped on a chariot horse (SUS - 5483) and not on a riding horse with the horsemen (PARASH - 6571).

26 The "Aphek" mentioned here must be the city in the plain of Jezreel not the one in the hill country at the east of the sea of Galilee. The plain, where the Syrians expected their strength would prevail, became a death-trap to them. The city, instead of sheltering them, became their graveyard.

27 "present" (KUL - 3557), translated "victualled" in the RV, means to sustain with food. See 4.7; 17.4, 9; 18.4.

42 "Appointed to utter destruction" (CHEREM - 2764) means that which is devoted, either in a good sense as in Leviticus 27.21, 28,29, or to destruction as was the city of Jericho (Josh 7.17,18).

AHAB AND NABOTH'S VINEYARD

CHAPTER 21, Verses 1-4
Ahab attempts to buy Naboth's vineyard

After the story of Ahab and the Syrians, which is parenthetic in character, this chapter returns to an event which once again involves the prophet Elijah.

When the victories over Syria granted to Ahab by God are considered, it might be expected that some reformation would be seen in his character and that there would be some evidence of the fear of the Lord in his behaviour. No such improvement came about. In the coveting of Naboth's vineyard, and in the way he later obtained it, he is seen in his true light. The wickedness of both he and his wife Jezebel, reached its height in this incident

During the lull in the fighting between Israel and Syria which lasted for some three years (22.1), Ahab had opportunity to enjoy his palace and its surroundings at Jezreel. No doubt he chose this site for his additional palace because it had been famous in the past and because it gave him a splendid view of the valley of Jordan. It may have been his summer residence. His official residence was in Samaria (20), about 25 miles (40km) away, from which he had to go down to the vineyard (v.16). Close by the palace in Jezreel was this choice vineyard which belonged to Naboth. This he coveted for himself, even though he probably had other vineyards and gardens. Not that he wanted it as a vineyard, but rather to convert it into a garden of herbs. Its proximity to the palace would make it a convenient place to grow herbs for the royal kitchens and these would be readily at hand for his servants to use as required. To the mind of Ahab the offer he made to Naboth was both reasonable and fair. The vineyard to be granted in exchange was even better than the one to be surrendered, so, in the transaction, Naboth, by parting with his property would be advantaged and not in any way be a loser. If the offered vineyard was not acceptable, the king proposed to buy the one desired at the full price in silver. This desire for a garden was in keeping with Ahab's other projects, for he had an ivory house, and had built several cities (22.39).

The response of Naboth to the king's offer must have been as surprising as it was disappointing; "The Lord forbid it me, that I should give the inheritance of my fathers unto thee". The requested piece of land was part of the inheritance of his fathers and he was the present custodian of what had been handed down to him by them. Not only so, but to sell it would be disobeying the commandment of the Lord. At least two features of the character of Naboth become evident in this reply. The first, that he feared the Lord, so he had not turned to Baal, and the second that he was acquainted with the Law of Moses (Lev 25.27-28; Num 36.7-9).

Although Ahab had greatly desired the vineyard, yet, because of the religious grounds of the owner's refusal, he did not pursue the deal further. However he returned home "heavy and displeased" as he had done after the prophet's words in 20.43. On this occasion he was even more upset for he went to bed and refused to eat. Like a spoiled child who sulks when not given the toy it wants, so he demonstrated his sullenness by turning his face away from all around him.

Circumstances play an important role in life. It may have been thought a benefit to have a vineyard so near to the king's palace and to be allowed to operate in such a picturesque site. However, for Naboth, what seemed to be an advantage proved to be a disaster. The unexpected changes which upset the lives of men are often not of their own making, but come to them whether they anticipate them or not. In many cases a visit by the king would be a great honour, but this visit to Naboth's house by Ahab was the beginning of his sorrows.

Things that at first seem to be an advantage can prove in the course of time to be ruinous. Even in the spiritual realm it can happen that those in authority covet what belongs to others. God in his sovereignty distributes to his servants their respective responsibilities and fits them to perform these by the help of His Spirit. For anyone in a position of responsibility to deny opportunity and so rob them of the joy they should experience in fulfilling them, would be a serious wrong. Even to offer them an alternative duty would not justify such conduct.

Verses 5-16

Jezebel obtains the vineyard for Ahab

Naturally Jezebel inquired why Ahab was so depressed. He related the story of Naboth and the refusal of the vineyard. He did not divulge the reasons for that refusal. Her immediate response was to ask him to recognize that he was king, and, as such, no subject in his kingdom should dare to refuse him anything. She went further and stated that she would obtain for him the vineyard.

Jezebel quickly perceived that all that was needed was the death of Naboth and his sons and then the king could take possession of the vineyard. Only an exceptionally wicked mind would have devised in such a short time the murder of an entire family. Her plan was outlined in the official letter stamped with the king's seal, thus bearing the hallmark of his authority. Two false witnesses were to come to the feast that had been called and testify that Naboth had cursed God and the king. Even the best men in the city were so terrified of Ahab and Jezebel that they meekly submitted to these demands. With this united witness, and no defence offered, the verdict of guilty was passed. The penalty for such blasphemy was death by stoning. Naboth was duly executed. It is shown in 2 Kings 9.26 that his sons were also slain, for they too could have claimed the inheritance of their father.

Thus the coveted vineyard was without an owner and could be claimed by the king. When a city was destroyed for turning to idolatry the spoils were destroyed and regarded as being devoted to God. Thus, though the Law gave no authority for the state to claim the property of one who blasphemed the king, this principle may have been an excuse for a traitor's possessions to become the property of the crown. In this there is another example of the triumph of evil and the suffering of the innocent. Indeed in some respect it is reminiscent of Christ Himself, for he was cast out of His Father's vineyard and slain, so that it could be possessed by the husbandmen (Mt 21.39). He too was charged with blasphemy and opposed by false witnesses; He too was slain outside the city; and, just as the house of Ahab suffered for its treatment of Naboth, so the Jews and their city suffered for their murder of Christ some forty years later.

Jezebel's letter can be compared to the letter sent by David to Joab (2 Sam 11.14); that sent by Jehu (2 Kings 10.6); those sent by Haman to the Jews (Est 3.13); that sent by Rabshakeh to Hezekiah (Is 37.14); and those Saul was carrying to Damascus (Acts 9.2), all of which were, for practical purposes, death warrants.

Throughout the history of the Church faithful men and women have suffered for the truth which was their spiritual inheritance. These martyrs in a special sense paid dearly for their witness, but like Naboth they would not sell what was dearer to them than life itself. The temptation at this present time is to let go the precious truths found in the Word of God including those long neglected. Such truths as the new birth, the priesthood of all believers, the simple remembrance supper, the freedom to exercise spiritual gifts when the saints gather, the coming of the Lord for His own and other precious doctrines were practically unknown for centuries. Some of these were claimed to be only for a special class and others were so corrupted as to become unrecognizable. The injunction, "Buy the truth, and sell it not" (Prov 23.23), is an instruction to be heeded in all ages.

Verses 17-29
Ahab is confronted by Elijah

As soon as news reached the palace that Naboth was dead Jezebel urged the king to go and take possession of the vineyard. He went down, possibly from Samaria, to Jezereel and fulfilled her request.

He must have been thrilled that what had been formerly denied him and had given him such grief was now in his hand. However, just when he had seized his prize, he was met by Elijah. This was no accidental meeting, for before the prophet had reached the scene a message from the Lord had been given to him in which the entire transaction regarding the vineyard was revealed. The Lord had witnessed the murder of His faithful servant and the seizing of his property. The seed of murder which the king had sown must be reaped by him, so the place where the blood of Naboth was shed would be stained by his blood. Ahab's response to the prophet was, "Hast thou found me, O mine enemy?". Earlier he had blamed him for being the troubler of Israel (18.17), but on this occasion he felt the pangs of the personal charge levied against him. The prophet continued to expand what he had introduced and declared to him what would befall him and all his posterity. The sentence was heavy, for not one of his family would be left to inherit either the throne or the royal estate. This would make his house like that of Jeroboam and Baasha, both well known examples of those whose links with the throne were cut off for ever. Added to this devastating message was one concerning Jezebel. She, too, would die a violent death and she would never have a burial. Indeed, all belonging to that wicked family circle would have a similar end, for none of them would be buried. The vineyard was an expensive possession for it cost Ahab his life and his posterity.

In a short parenthesis, the historian breaks off to give a summary of the extreme wickedness of Ahab. He singles him out as the greatest of all evil doers and one who was a slave to sin. He was an idolater as corrupt as the Amorites who had been driven out of the land by the Israelites. His partner, Jezebel, was always pressing him to do evil, and he responded freely to her wicked demands. Instead of doing what he knew to be right in the sight of the Lord he allowed her to dictate how he should act in almost every circumstance.

Jezebel demonstrates the evil principle of idolatry. Wherever it exists cruelty and corruption are sure to be present. It is impossible to worship a false god and not be influenced by so doing. Men undoubtedly become like the objects they venerate.

The message of Elijah had some effect on Ahab. He humbled himself and put on mourning apparel. He had lain down in sullenness in v.4, but now he lies down in sorrow. Although he could not undo his evil deeds nor re-live the life that was soon to end, he did demonstrate a measure of repentance. The Lord, in His grace, took notice of this and gave the message that the threatened disasters would be deferred until the days of his sons. This is another example of God's respect for repentance. If ever a man deserved immediate execution it was Ahab, yet he was spared to use his ill-gotten vineyard for a short while.

The saying is often repeated, "It is never too late to mend". However it needs to be realized that there are deeds done which are known to be wrong and which can never be undone no matter how much they are repented of. Better to do what is right, even though it may at times be costly to do so.

Notes

4 "heavy" (SAR - 5620) means peevish or sullen, and is used only in connection with Ahab (20.43; here and at v.5). "Displeased" (ZAEP - 2198) means angry and fretful. It, too, is only used of Ahab (here and at 20.43)

10 "Sons (or children) of Belial" are first mentioned in Deuteronomy 13.13 where their crime is idolatry. They were wicked, ungodly, worthless, and always opposed to what was right.

CHAPTER 22, Verses 1-39

JEHOSHAPHAT AND AHAB JOIN AGAINST SYRIA

CHAPTER 22, Verses 1-4
Ahab's resolve to re-capture Ramoth-gilead

The three years of peace mentioned here were the years after the defeat of Syria recorded in ch.20. It was during this time that the episode of Naboth's vineyard took place. The fact that here there is a resolve to re-capture Ramoth-gilead shows clearly that Ben-hadad had not kept his promise to Ahab (20.34). Perhaps he concluded from the lenient way in which he was treated that he need not be too particular in fulfilling his vow. The king of Israel however could never rest so long as part of Israel's territory was in the hands of the Syrians.

Unlike much that has been considered in former chapters, this episode is also recorded in 2 Chronicles 18 where extra information is given. What is striking, and indeed surprising, is the fact that the king of Judah and the king of Israel are for the first time on friendly terms. Prior to this the two were totally opposed. If a lull in the fighting between them did occur it was no more than toleration of each other. There is no secret as to what had brought about the change. It was simply the result of Jehoram, the son of Jehoshaphat, marrying Athaliah, the daughter of Ahab (2 Kings 8.18,27). What neither sword nor chariot could do was brought about through this domestic affinity. A God-fearing king of Judah should have had nothing in common with a man like Ahab. However natural relationships can prove very strong.

According to the account in 2 Chronicles, the visit of Jehoshaphat to Ahab was an official one, and accompanied with ceremony and social entertainment. However, the major purpose behind the meeting was the re-capturing of Ramoth-gilead which had probably been taken from Omri by Ben-hadad's father. Ahab presumably felt that the combined forces of the two kingdoms would be more than a match for the Syrians and that soon the disputed city would once again be in the hands of its rightful owners. Since he had already defeated the Syrians with his own army he naturally concluded that, with the king of Judah on his side, it would be a simple matter to rout them completely.

Verses 5-28
The prophets are summoned

For reasons not given, Elijah was not involved in giving counsel regarding this campaign. Nevertheless, God's messenger, Micaiah, was available, and proved to be a faithful witness. Jehoshaphat knew enough of the fear of God to be aware of the importance of having His guidance when waging war. Because of this, he mentioned to Ahab the matter of inquiring through the word of the Lord what the outcome would be if an attempt were made to recover Ramoth-gilead. In response to his request no less than four hundred prophets were assembled. These were prophets of Baal, even though they claimed to speak as prophets of the Lord. Their leader said "Thus saith the Lord" (v.11). Whatever their profession they were false men. With one voice they all assured the kings that they would be successful in their attack. However, Jehoshaphat asked for a "prophet of the Lord (Jehovah)" to be called so as to be absolutely sure that all would be well. The fact that he sought such help implies that he was not satisfied with the unanimous words of the prophets who had already spoken. Ahab knew Micaiah, but would not call him because he had been so faithful in the past in foretelling the evils which were approaching the king as a result of his wrong-doings. With reluctance Micaiah was eventually summoned to appear at the gate of the city. Before he was allowed to speak, Zedekiah, who appears to have been chief of the false prophets, gave to the kings a symbolic demonstration of the power they possessed. It was quite normal for prophets to demonstrate their words in this fashion. Both Jeremiah (Jer 27 & 28) and Ezekiel (Ezek 4 & 12) were told to act as well as speak. For his part, Zedekiah did this by wearing on his head two iron horns and proclaiming that with these the power of Syria would be exterminated. He was supported, as could be expected, by his fellow prophets, and the entire procedure was meant to convince the kings that their ambition would be realized. Even the messenger who brought Micaiah sought to prejudice him in his judgment, for he told him of the united verdict of all the other prophets and prayed him to acquiesce with it.

Such pressure was rejected. The prophet made clear that he was appearing at court to tell what Jehovah would say to him.

When the question was put to him by Ahab, "Shall we go against Ramoth-gilead to battle?", his reply was, "Go, and prosper". Evidently the tone of the question implied that the king was not genuine and the answer likewise sounded equally insincere. When the question was again put with sincerity, the answer was correspondingly a true one. Its parabolic language conveyed to the king his fate and left him in no doubt that if he ventured into battle it would cost him his life. These tidings were a confirmation of the fact that this prophet was always predicting evil of the king. However he should not have blamed the prophet, for the Lord was against him. The messenger should not have been blamed for the message he carried.

Having answered the question and noted the response, the prophet proceeded to tell in great detail how he learned the result of the battle through the vision he describes. In this mysterious passage there is a parallel to the book of Job, where a similar conference was convened. While neither passage accuses the Lord of doing evil, both show that He can allow evil spirits to accomplish His will. They can go only as far as He permits and, of course, He has power to withstand them when they try to venture beyond His purpose. Ezekiel 14.9 states, "If the prophet be deceived when he hath spoken a thing, I the Lord have deceived that prophet". In all such cases the principle is the same, for the Lord often punishes sin by allowing the sinner to reap what he has sown. Ahab wanted to believe that he would be victorious, so God allowed him to hear what appealed to his heart. A like principle will obtain in the future when the "strong delusion", which will be sent by God, will result in the doom of the worshippers of the Antichrist (2 Thess 2.11-12). The courageous prophet was smitten by Zedekiah for speaking the truth. He too was told of the time when he would be so frightened for his life that he would be seeking a hiding place. It is not said whether his terror would arise from the anger of Jezebel, who would blame him for encouraging the king to the battle that caused his death, or whether he would fear that the victorious Syrians would pursue him. Whatever the cause of his panic, it would prove him to be a coward despite his present show of bravado in daring to strike the prophet of the Lord.

When the interview was over Micaiah was to be imprisoned and harshly treated until the king returned from battle. The prophet's confidence is seen in his statement that if what he had predicted did not take place then he was not the Lord's messenger. This echoed throughout the land.

It has been concluded from the words, "carry him back" (v.26) that he was already in prison before he was summoned to appear before the king. But all that is said here is that the conditions into which he was going were much more severe than those he had left. He was to be given a diet that would merely keep him alive. Apparently one of the king's sons was a joint keeper of the prison, therefore there was no hope of leniency being shown him. However harsh his treatment, he was more safe in the prison than the king was on the battlefield. Perhaps the saddest element in the story is that Jehosaphat sat on his throne and heard the sentence being passed, yet never spoke a word on behalf of the prisoner. He was the man who had asked for a prophet of the Lord to be called; thus Micaiah was brought into the difficult situation on his account. For a good king to be silent at that time was to his shame. This suggests that when one steps out of the path of the will of God that person is liable to be brought into embarrassing circumstances where their weakness becomes evident.

This interesting passage gives an insight into the spiritual background to the actions of men on earth. It reveals that even when evil spirits are united in their deceptive work they are overruled by the Lord who can thereby fulfil His purposes. Perhaps believers are slow to believe that often there is more unity among Satan's agents than there is among the true servants of the Lord. Quite often the wicked can sink their differences when a common object is involved. Pilate and Herod united in the condemnation of Christ. Likewise the Jews, who hated the Roman yoke, claimed to be friends of Caesar in order to have Christ crucified.

The unreasonableness of worldly men illustrated here ought also to be considered. Poor Micaiah was treated as though he was putting down the king when in fact he was simply the messenger carrying the Lord's message. It is like blaming the postman for the content of the letters he carries. Those who speak for God must be prepared to share the opposition which is directed against Him and at times be treated as though they were personally responsible for His judgments.

Jehoshaphat's actions at this time also show that, when involved in the unequal yoke, even the most mature believer can stoop to levels he never thought he would reach. It is all but impossible to take sides with God when having friendship with the world. Jehoshaphat did not raise Ahab to his level, but rather was himself brought down to the level of the ungodly.

Verses 29-40
The battle of Ramoth-gilead and the death of Ahab

In spite of the warnings of Micaiah the two kings proceeded to attack Ramoth-gilead. While not accepting the prophet's words, there was in the heart of Ahab some fear that he might be right. For this reason he dressed as an ordinary soldier to avoid being made a special target. He knew that his royal robes and special chariot would have made him conspicuous among the host. He offered no such camouflage to Jehoshaphat. Unknown to either king was the instruction of the king of Syria that his army should ignore the common soldiers of the Israelite army and concentrate their efforts in slaying Ahab. When the battle began the captains of the Syrians thought, when at some distance they saw Jehoshaphat, that they had found their desired target, so they closed in upon him. However, to their surprise, when he cried out, possibly for help from the Lord or from his men, they discovered that he was not Ahab. The Syrians then withdrew from him.

At the same time one of their soldiers fired his arrow and, without realizing whom he was striking, delivered a fatal wound to the king of Israel. Possibly he thought he was hitting an ordinary soldier. Doubtless the Lord overruled his hand and fulfilled His word through his prophet. Although Ahab was propped up in his chariot until the evening, he bled to death from the injury received through the joints of his armour. With such a disastrous outcome to the day's fighting the armies returned to base and gave up the contest.

The blood from the king's chariot was washed at the pool of Samaria and the dogs licked his blood. The water, normally used by the harlots of the city for their bathing, was, on this occasion, used to wash royal blood. It might be thought that the prophecy concerning his blood being licked at Jezreel (ch. 21.19) was not fulfilled. But it must be remembered that this threat was modified, so that the judgment initially pronounced against him would befall his sons (v. 29). This was fulfilled at the hand of Jehu in 2 Kings 9.26. Ahab's body, however, was given an honourable burial in the city. Thus ended the life of one of the most evil kings of Israel.

The historian adds a brief note to show that there was another book in which more about Ahab's doings, his house decorated with ivory, and the cities which he built was written. This is a reminder that the inspired writer of Kings has chosen episodes that illustrate lasting spiritual lessons.

What happened to Micaiah after his warnings were proved to be true is not recorded. The fact that he was imprisoned where the king's son was in charge suggests that his treatment would be anything but favourable.

Verses 41-50
The reign of Jehoshaphat

The history of Jehoshaphat is briefly told in 1 Kings, but is given more elaborately in 2 Chronicles 17ff. Here there is a summary of his life and the mention of his mother's name, "Azubah the daughter of Shilhi". Nothing further of her is given in Scripture. He was set a good example by his father Asa and this he followed in the main. However, he had not removed the places where the people worshipped the Lord away from the Temple at Jerusalem. The high places of Baal were different, for these were centres of idolatry, and the good kings of Judah destroyed them.

Another evil existed in the land, that of sodomy. This evil brought down the fire of God on the cities of the plain and had already been attacked by his father. He had the right and responsibility to continue to try to eradicate it.

As already noted, the marriage of his son to Ahab's daughter meant that there were no more wars between Judah and Israel. Since the neighbouring nation of Edom had no king this meant that the way was clear for Jehoshaphat to proceed through its territory to the coast of the Red Sea at Ezion-Geber where he could build ships, a venture which otherwise might not have been possible. He thought to imitate Solomon in going to Ophir for gold, but his ships were broken in the harbour where they were built. In 2 Chronicles 20.36, 37 we learn that this adventure failed because the ships were a united venture between him and Ahaziah king of Israel. God was grieved at this, yet another unequal yoke, and smashed the vessels. A second attempt was made by Ahaziah to fulfil his ambition, but on this occasion Jehoshaphat refused to join him.

After twenty-five years on the throne Jehoshaphat died and was buried in the royal tombs in Jerusalem, and his son, Jehoram, reigned in his stead. In many ways Jehoshaphat followed the pattern of Solomon, except that he was preserved from any links with idolatry, unless such a connection is implied in his close association with the kings of Israel. The one great blot in his otherwise good reign arose from the marriage of his son to Ahab's daughter. This family bond led him into failure, and is a reminder of the fact that many, through family ties, have been brought into relationships which have blotted their testimony. Modern thinking might endorse his action in joining with Ahab and declare it to be a wonderful achievement in that it brought together the two parts of the long-divided nation. However, that which human reasoning views with approval is not so seen by God. Much that passes for unity in Christendom is only the yoking together of things contrary to the teaching of the Word of God. When that is the case, for believers to join in would simply involve them in an unequal yoke.

Verses 51-53
The reign of Ahaziah
The closing three verses of 1 Kings give a short summary of the brief reign of Ahaziah. It could hardly be expected that an evil woman like Jezebel would rear a good son. It is therefore no surprise that his history confirms that he too was evil. Though only two years on the throne of Israel, he reigned long enough to reveal the wickedness of his heart. Like most of the kings of Israel, he took his pattern from Jeroboam, the man who made Israel to sin. His father and mother, who had trodden the same path, left him their evil example, which he followed as closely as possible.

As pointed out in the introduction, the break between the two books of Kings is not in a particularly appropriate place. It divides the reign of Ahaziah, and also the life of Elijah. To keep the original history in one book would have been preferable.

Notes
3 Ramoth-gilead was a city of refuge, so was of special interest to the kings. "We be still" (CHASHA - 2814) means "we keep quiet", or "We hold our peace".

5 When Jehoshaphat speaks of the "Lord" he calls Him "Jehovah", but when the prophets of Baal speak in v. 6 they call Him "Adonai". Later (vv.11,12), they also use "Jehovah", no doubt to please the king.

9 The officer called was a "eunuch" (SARIS - 5631). This shows that heathen practices had penetrated the court of Ahab.

10 The "void place" (GOREN - 1637) was a "threshing floor" – usually an elevated place where the blowing of the wind would not be impeded.

27 The bread and water of "affliction" or "oppression" (LACHATS - 3906) was the food of slaves in bondage (Ex 3.9; Is 30.20).

30 Three kings "disguised" (CHAPAS - 2664) themselves; Saul (1 Sam 28.8), Ahab, and Josiah (2 Chr 35.22).

34 At a "venture" (TOM - 8537), literally means "in his simplicity" or "in integrity" (Gen 20.5; 2 Sam 15.11).

II KINGS

CHAPTERS 1.1 - 2.11

THE CLOSING DAYS OF ELIJAH

As noted in the Introduction there is no special reason for the division to be at this point. The history of Ahaziah and Elijah continues without any break or interruption.

CHAPTER 1, Verses 1-18
The fall and death of Ahaziah

The brief statement about Moab which opens this chapter indicates the circumstances prevailing at the time when Ahaziah fell. Apparently the death of Ahab and Ahaziah's illness were deemed by the Moabites to be an opportunity for them to cast off the yoke of Israel. From the days of David (2 Sam 8.2) the tribute paid to Israel by the Moabites was extensive. As will be seen in ch.3.4, both sheep and wool in large quantities had to be contributed annually to Israel. What is surprising about this is that the northern kingdom should continue to have sway over a people whose territory was actually south of Judah, and thus a long way from Samaria.

The lesson which can readily be learned is that when rule is weak, then the door for rebellion is opened. Apparently as long as Ahab was on the throne Moab was afraid to attempt any resistance, so the tribute was paid.

When reading this account of Ahaziah's fall through the lattice, it should be remembered that there was no glass in his day. The normal window at that time was made of lattice work. Evidently he fell through one of these apertures and seriously injured himself. His great fear was that his injuries might be fatal. His devotion to idols was seen when he sent messengers to Baalzebub the god of Ekron, to learn whether, or not, he would recover. However, these messengers were halted on their journey by Elijah. He had earlier received a message from the angel of the Lord, that the fall was fatal. This is another occasion when God intervened to prove to the northern kingdom that

He was the only true God, and that the drift toward idolatry amongst the ten tribes and their kings was the greatest of folly. These messengers must have felt embarrassed when they stood before the king and delivered the news. The fact that they accepted the words of Elijah at face value, shows that they believed them to be a reliable prophecy. Faced with this death sentence, the question naturally arose in the king's mind as to the identity of the man who had dared to make such a statement. This problem was soon solved. Once the messengers described the man as one "wearing a hairy garment and girded with a leather girdle", he realized immediately that this could be no other than Elijah the Tishbite.

In spite of Ahaziah's physical weakness and that he was near to death, he sent to Elijah, not two servants, but a captain with fifty soldiers with the demand that he come down to him. This attempt to arrest the prophet is another example of the messenger being blamed for the message carried. Had the king been seeking help from the prophet he would have commissioned some of his noble servants to go and plead with him to come down. The fact that an army was sent, showed that revenge was in his heart. Like Jezebel his mother he dared to take the life of the man who had spoken God's message.

Whatever fear may have been in Elijah's heart when he saw the approaching soldiers, this was quickly dispelled. The fire from the Lord defended His servant and consumed the approaching soldiers. As already noted, fire was important in the life of the prophet. It is referred to in the case of the widow gathering the sticks (1 Kings 17), the scene at Carmel (1 Kings 18), the hot coals baking the bread (1 Kings 19), the fire on the mountain (1 Kings l9), two fires here and the chariot of fire (2 Kings 2.11). It can be seen why he is sometimes called "the prophet of fire". By way of contrast when the Lord was rejected by the Samaritans and two of His disciples thought that He should, like Elijah, call down fire from heaven (Lk 9.54) they were rebuked. Their spirits were out of harmony with the Lord's mission of mercy.

Notwithstanding the tragedy which had befallen the first soldiers the king was foolish enough to send a second troop with the same intention, but with the additional order that the prophet come down "quickly". These soldiers suffered the same fate as their colleagues. The third batch of soldiers sent approached him in a very different spirit. Their captain bowed down in reverence before the Lord's representative and pleaded for his life and the lives of his men. With the assurance from the angel of the Lord that it was safe for him to go he went and met the king face to face. When the prophet was beside the king's bed he was bold enough simply to repeat the message which he had sent with the messengers. There may be in the words a hint that if the king had sought the Lord, and not the god of Ekron, he would have recovered from his injuries. That this is the case is strengthened by comparing the incident with that which befell Hezekiah (ch.19), who was given a similar message. When he turned to the Lord in repentance he was granted an extension to his life of fifteen years.

Many have been cut down without a moment to think. This king though given space to repent, failed to do so. Without the historian telling what befell Elijah after he left the king, the story continues to state that the prophet's words proved true, for the king died. His accidental fall through the lattice had been just as effective in bringing about his end as the accidental shot from the bow of the Syrian soldier that brought about the death of his father, Ahab. He may have been the only king of Israel who died as the result of an accident in the palace.

He was succeeded on the throne by his brother, Jehoram, because he himself had no son. Azariah's reign was short lasting only two years (1 Kings 22.51). It so happened at this time, that both the king of Israel and the king of Judah bore the same name. This may suggest that there was a close relationship between Jehoshaphat and Ahab, since each called a son "Jehoram".

Notes

8 A "hairy man" (BAHGAL - 1167) means an "owner of hair". While generally taken to refer to the garment he wore it has also been claimed to mean having long hair (in contrast to bald Elijah). Compare "the hairy garment to deceive" (Zec 13.4 R.V.).

CHAPTER 2, Verses 1-11
The rapture of Elijah

From the time that Elisha was called (1 Kings 19), little is said about his relationship with Elijah. That he was his servant for a time and that he poured water on his hands is made clear, but there is no mention of them being together throughout his many experiences. However in this passage the two are closely linked together and could not be parted until the whirlwind swept Elijah away.

Before leaving earth Elijah, in company with Elisha visited the sons of the prophets in the various centres where they were located. He wished to give them an opportunity to say farewell to him before he left them. They would not be likely to rise to the height of fame of Elijah but they had the solemn responsibility to continue as representatives of the Lord, whom he had so faithfully served.

His first call was at Gilgal, not the Gilgal near Jordan, but the village of this name, in the tribe of Ephraim, and near Shiloh (Deut 11.30). From this elevated spot he could survey the land of his labours and call to mind the past. Here he asked Elisha to remain, and thus allow himself to move on alone, but on no account would the younger prophet accede to his request. The two proceeded to Beth-el where they were met by the sons of the prophets. It is amazing that the very centre where Jeroboam had established a high place for one of his gold calves, had in it a school of the prophets of the Lord. These sons of the prophets were fully aware of what was about to happen. It had been revealed to them that Elijah was about to be taken away. They were told to keep quiet about this matter, possibly with the end in view that there would be as little stir as possible at the time of his departure. The next place of call was Jericho where again the sons of the prophets reminded Elisha that he was about to lose his master. To them he gave the same instruction as before. They too, were to hold their peace.

The last leg of the long journey was to the river Jordan. Its banks had witnessed many strange happenings, but what was about to take place eclipsed them all. No less than fifty prophets gathered on the nearby heights to watch and see what took place. As Jordan was reached, and appeared to be a barrier in the way of their progress, Elijah took off his mantle, wrapped it into a roll and smote the waters as though he were using a rod. They immediately were parted and the two prophets walked on the dry bed of the river. In this there was a repeat of that which Moses did at the Red Sea. It shows that Elijah had much in common with that first great prophet in Israel. Just as the Sea was parted, and later Jordan was parted for Joshua so here for the second time the river had yielded to divine power. After this miracle Elijah offered to do for Elisha whatever he wanted. Without hesitation Elisha made his request that there be granted to him a double portion of the spirit which had been so effective in Elijah's own ministry. Like the first-born in Israel he wanted a worthy portion of his father's inheritance (Deut 21.17). In a sense it was not in the hand of Elijah to pass on his spiritual power to his successor. However he had faith that God would grant this request on the one condition that Elisha saw his translation to heaven. While the two men were conversing there suddenly appeared the chariot of fire drawn by horses of fire. This was accompanied by the whirlwind that swept away Elijah. The two prophets were then permanently separated. It is fitting that the "chariot of Israel" (v.12) (see footnote) should be transported to heaven like a conqueror triumphantly celebrating his victory. Equally fitting was the fact that both the chariot and its horses were a flaming fire. He had been the great defender of Israel, and as has been pointed out was specially associated with "fires". Often he had been caught away and landed in somewhere else on earth, but on this occasion he was transported never to be on earth again until he appeared on the Mount of Transfiguration.

In considering the history of Elijah it is important to note that he had many similar experiences to the great Lawgiver. It was not his to introduce new ideas rather his work was that of a reformer. Just as Moses was a prophet who was sent to wage war against the idolatry of Egypt, so Elijah was a prophet who opposed idolatry in Israel. Both men spent much time away from his own people. Moses, like Elijah, was associated with miraculous fire. The burning bush (Ex 3); the fire which ran along the ground (Ex 9), the pillar of fire (Ex 13); the fire on mount Sinai (Ex 19); the fire from before the Lord which burned the sacrifices (Lev 9); the same fire which burned Nadab and Abihu (Lev 10): and the fire which consumed Korah and his company (Num 16) refer to some of these.

Moses and Israel were sustained by bread from heaven, and Elijah was sustained by the extension of the meal and oil. Moses prayed and his sister was delivered from death, Elijah prayed and a boy was raised from the dead. Neither man feared the wicked kings whom he confronted. Waters were divided by both in much the same way. Moses was forty days without food on Sinai, and Elijah was forty days on the same mount without food. There came a time when each asked to die, for Moses said "kill me", and Elijah said "take away my life". Before each of them departed he appointed a successor. Joshua took the place of Moses, and Elisha took the place of Elijah. They both had an unusual end to their lives. Neither showed any sign of natural weakness, nor had any death-bed experience. The last two names in the OT are Moses and Elijah, and in the closing book of the NT, two witnesses are described who will repeat miracles similar to those performed by them (Rev 11)

The spiritual instruction suggested by these two men on their last journey together is indeed precious. One fact that becomes clear in this story is that God always makes provision for the continuation of his testimony. Whether Joshua, the Apostles, Timothy, or, in this case, Elisha be considered He has His man or men ready to fill the gaps that are left when His choice servants are taken away. A further encouraging lesson is that the Spirit's power remains after those who have been the instruments of its working are removed. Equally important is the fact, that though the successors carried on the work of their departed leaders, they were distinct men, and not mere repeats. Joshua was very different from Moses, Elisha was very different from Elijah, and Timothy was also different from Paul. None of the successors of these great leaders lost their own identity.

There are three great ascensions to heaven described in Scripture, Enoch, Elijah and the Lord. While there is no record of a witness to Enoch it is possible that the account of his ascent was handed down from eyewitnesses through the days of Noah and on to Moses. Witnesses certainly saw both Elijah and Christ ascend. At the Lord's return for His saints (1 Thess 4), something similar will occur, There will be a great ascension of all the saints that will include the "dead in Christ" who will rise and join with the living and so meet Him in the air. No doubt after the Church has been taken the faithful remnant in Israel will experience the Spirit's power and will gather the subjects of the earthly kingdom which will be introduced when Christ returns once more to the Earth.

The Lord promised the disciples that when He left them, they would perform greater miracles than He did. This does not mean that they would be greater in quality, but rather that they would be greater in extent and number. Similarly Elisha also performed miracles greater in number than Elijah.

It should also be noted that just as Elisha had to keep his eye on his ascending master, in order to experience the double portion of his power, so the secret of the power of the saints today lies in keeping the eye of faith on the ascended Christ. The daunting task facing Elisha might well have driven him to despair. With the assurance of a double portion of the power of Elijah he could face the future with absolute confidence. It is of utmost importance that a consciousness of the need for the power of the Spirit, whether in preserving from the desires of the flesh, or in enabling service for the Lord should always be present in the hearts of the saints.

CHAPTER 2.12 - CHAPTER 13.21

THE LIFE AND TIMES OF ELISHA

Verses 12-18

The spirit of Elijah rests upon Elisha

These chapters, while continuing to give the history of both North and South of the nation, are marked by a continuous record of the work of the prophet Elisha. Much of this material is not included in Chronicles and the history of the kings in some cases is given a secondary place to that of the prophet. His work, like that of his predecessor was mainly in the northern kingdom. This shows the interest God had in that part of the nation which had turned away from the true centre, and had to a great extent been plagued with various forms of idolatry. When at length it was swept into captivity the cause was not God's failure to provide true witnesses, but the failure of the people to pay heed to the faithful ministry of His servants.

It is all but impossible to enter into the feelings of Elisha when he discovered he was bereft of his spiritual father. A few years had passed from the day Elijah threw his mantle across his shoulders and took it back again. It lay at his feet and became his own. Before he lifted it he rent his own clothes from top to bottom. This action was, no doubt, an outward symbol of his rent heart. Filled with grief and conscious of the heavy responsibilities which now devolved upon him, he felt compelled to put to the test whether he had indeed become heir to the spirit of Elijah. Without delay he proceeded to the lip of Jordan, and with the rolled up mantle smote its waters. His cry, "Where is the Lord God of Elijah?", did not indicate that he had no confidence in God, but rather that he desired proof that the One who had wrought so mightily for his master would also work for him. The divided waters dispelled all his doubts and fears. It must not be thought that there was any magic in the coat. Rather it was the symbol of Elisha's relationship with Elijah used by God to display His power. Just as God had used the rod in the hand of Moses to perform miracles in Egypt, so He used the mantle on this occasion.

The sons of the prophets who had been watching events from the west side of Jordan immediately recognized by the dividing of the waters that the spirit of Elijah was now resting upon Elisha. In response they bowed down before him in humble respect. As God's new representative he was counted worthy of their highest esteem. They would turn to him in every future crisis.

The sons of the prophets were slow to believe, as Elisha did, that their great leader had parted from them permanently. They imagined he had been snatched away and deposited in some lonely glen, or somewhere along the banks of the river. They were not looking for his dead body that they might give it an honourable burial, but rather that they might find him alive and well. All the assurance Elisha gave them regarding this was not accepted. The strongest of them went and searched, but they had to return without finding the slightest trace of Elijah.

Verses 19-22
Elisha heals the spring at Jericho

The prophet, having crossed the Jordan, remained in Jericho until the searchers had returned. While there his attention was called to the greatest need of the city. Even though it was situated in a delightful site and was called "the city of palm trees" (Judges 3.13), yet it lacked the one essential, a good supply of wholesome water. The trouble was not that there was no supply, but the quality of the water in the only well near the city, was bad. What was even worse the land dependent upon it had become unproductive. This great problem opened the way for Elisha to show once again that "man's extremities are God's opportunities". The power of the Lord working through him soon solved the problem. The fact that the men of the city sought the help of the prophet demonstrated their confidence in him. They then believed he had no less power than his master who had been so suddenly taken away. In most of Elisha's miracles he used some instrument. In this case he called for a new dish, or basin, together with some salt. These items may not themselves have purified the water and may have been only symbols to demonstrate what was needed. The new cruse had never been contaminated. The salt in it spoke of that which preserves from corruption. The prophet made clear that neither he, nor the material he used, healed the water, but the Lord Himself had done it. From that day onward, the fountain supplied the need of the city and the surrounding area with a plentiful source of good spring water. This not only improved the health of the people, but also made the land fertile.

Those who view Elisha's ministry as typical of the Lord working through His Spirit in the present age, can readily see in this miracle an illustration of the effects of the new covenant, or the Gospel, in the world. To them the world has much that is counted pleasant, but its natural resources have left it barren and fruitless. The Gospel, like the salt, has been used by the Lord to change many from spiritual sterility to become fruitful plants in His garden.

Verses 23-25
Elisha curses the youths of Bethel
Elisha retraced the path which he and Elijah had trodden on their way to Jordan and arrived at Bethel. Unlike the people of Jericho, the youths of the city had no respect for him, but mocked and taunted him, crying "Go up thou bald head". The implication of their words was that he should go up and join his master. This made clear that he was not welcome in their city. They did not respect anyone who had links with Elijah. He turned towards them and cursed them in the name of the Lord. He regarded their jeering as an insult to the Lord whom he represented.

It might be wondered why little children (as is suggested by the wording of the AV) should speak as they did, but it could well be that they were but echoing what they had heard their parents say in their homes. While the use of the word "little" in v.23 seems to emphasise that they were children rather than youths the other terms used of them were used of those of responsible age.

God defended His honour. Once again He showed His control over the wild beasts as the two she bears came out of the wood and mauled forty two of the mockers. Earlier it is recorded that lions executed those who were disobedient (1 Kings 13.24; 20.36).

Almost all the miracles of Elisha were works of mercy, but this is different. Likewise the miracles of the Apostles in the book of Acts were deeds of mercy, yet, even there an exception is seen, for Peter, who had healed the lame man (ch.2) pronounced the death-sentence on Ananias and Sapphira (ch.5), Although this is the day of grace it must not be assumed that evil doers are not punished. Not a few, who have rejected the Gospel and abused the servants of God who preached to them have filled early graves.

Another lesson these verses teach is that the evils of idolaters are reproduced in their offspring. These children were surely the mouthpieces of their parents and were repeating the language which they heard from them.

Elisha left Beth-el and travelled to Carmel, where no doubt he would have time to reflect and be free from the bustle of city life. The memories of the victory of his master on its slopes must have been an encouragement to him. In a sense, he was treading on holy ground, for there he could view the spot where the fire of God consumed the sacrifice and the altar (1 Kings 18),

Notes

9 The "double portion" was literally "two mouths", it is translated as here in Deut 21.17 only, but see "two parts" Zec 13.8.

11 The chariot and horses of fire which appeared as the whirlwind swept away Elijah, were symbolic of divine power and majesty. They could be compared with the "cloud" which was present when Christ was carried up into heaven (Acts 1).

19 The word "naught" (RAG - 7451) is the common word for "evil". The word "barren" (SHAHCHOH - 7921) implies that crops were grown, but none of them came to full growth. It is used of vines casting their fruit before the time (Mal 3.11)

23 The "children" (NAHGAR - 5288) and the "children" (YEHLED - 3206) v.24 were most likely "lads", or "youths", as these words are translated elsewhere. They "mocked" (KAHLAS - 7046) "scorned" (Ez 16.31) or "scoffed" (Hab 1.10) at the prophet.

24 This is the only occasion in Scripture where bears succeeded in taking human life. David slew the bear, which attempted to take his sheep (1 Sam 17.36,37).

CHAPTER 3, Verses 1-27
Jehoram and Jehoshaphat attack Moab

The opening verses of this chapter might lead the reader to think that the historian had left reporting on Elisha, and had returned to the history of the kings. However before the middle of this chapter is reached he tells of another outstanding miracle by the prophet.

Already there has been mention of the reign of Jehoram and of the rebellion of the Moabites (Ch.1). Here his reign is said to begin in the eighteenth year of Jehoshaphat, whereas in ch.1 it is said to begin on the second year of Jehoram, king of Judah. Jehoram of Judah may have reigned as co-regent with his father for several years. Jehoram of Israel's reign lasted twelve years and so was much shorter than that of Ahab his father, but not so short as that of Ahaziah his brother. Like all the kings of Israel he was an idolater. For reasons not given he differed from his father in that he refused to worship the image of Baal which his father had made. Evidently, the calf worship had still the name of the Lord linked with it, so it was reckoned by many in Israel as not fully fledged idolatry. The grand statue of Baal which Ahab had made was of special significance, and must have been given a distinguished position so that all who entered the city might be impressed by it. For Jehoram to remove this grand masterpiece of idolatry was indeed a formidable task. This was especially so since his mother was a devoted worshipper of Baal. Perhaps he imagined that by doing so he would obtain the help of the Lord. At the same time he desired to retain his popularity with the nation by continuing to worship the golden calves. There are still those who think that if they reject certain extreme evils their holding on to others, apparently less heinous, will be overlooked by God. The day came when the prophet let him know, in the strongest terms, that this vain idea did not in any way find acceptance with the God of Israel.

The rebellion of the Moabites is now dealt with in detail, and the story of their defeat is developed. The description Mesha, king of Moab, as a "sheepmaster" suggests that he specialized in this with some success. The supply to the king of Israel of so many lambs, rams, and wool, must have damaged greatly the economy of Moab.

Although the tribute had been withheld since the death of Ahab no attempt had been made to have it reinstated. The reason for this tolerance was that with the threat of Syria, and other problems, Ahaziah was not free to engage in any additional conflict to establish his claims. However, Jehoram, his brother, judged, at the beginning of his reign, that the time was ripe for an attack to be made on Moab, and with its success to restore once again the supremacy of Israel.

The relationship with Jehoshaphat, developed by Ahab, continued with Jehoram. Thus when the attack was planned against Moab, the king of Judah was called upon to help. The combined forces advanced on Moab in a circuitous manner. Instead of facing Moab directly, they went via Edom and near the Dead Sea. The Edomites at this time were subject to Judah and so would not have attempted to prevent the armies going through their territory (1 Kings 22.47). How unlike this is to the occasion Israel sought permission to pass through Edom, but were halted (Num 20.21). The plan at this time was to invade Moab from the south. Moab may have had strong defences on its northern border, so these were shunned, and the longer, but less difficult, approach was deemed the best. Furthermore, the Moabites would have less expectation of an attack from the south and so were likely to be unprepared. However, an unexpected difficulty arose, namely, lack of water. The thirst of both the soldiers and of the animals which accompanied them was so great, that death stared them all in the face. Little wonder that despair filled the heart of Jehoram. He concluded that the Lord was delivering him and his army, together with his two fellow kings and their armies, into the hand of Moab. The presence of Jehoshaphat, who had some knowledge of the Lord, saved the situation. He asked for a prophet of the Lord. In the providence of God, or by His guidance, Elisha was near at hand at this time, and so could be consulted almost immediately. Unlike former times when prophets were summoned to come to the kings, on this occasion the three monarchs went down to the prophet and humbly asked for his help.

The visit of three kings to the prophet must have been an unusual sight. They were there because of need, and at the same time to be taught the greatness of the power of Jehovah. Instead of Elisha bowing in the presence of these great personages he turned to the king of Israel and let him know that he had nothing in common with him. Then he directed him to the false prophets, who were so valued by him and his parents. Without any defence of these, the king of Israel poured out his distress which was that, "the Lord had called these three kings together to deliver them into the hand of Moab". Apart from the presence of Jehoshaphat, no help from the prophet, nor from the Lord, whom he represented, would have been granted. What Jehoram feared would indeed have been their fate.

It is amazing that Jehoshaphat, who had been earlier rebuked for being an ally of Ahab, would again be involved in an unequal yoke with a king of Israel. Here, as on the former occasion, he almost lost his life. These failings, only mentioned in Kings, read so differently from much which is said of him in 2 Chronicles that we can scarcely imagine such weaknesses would surface in one, who otherwise, was a good king. In this there is a solemn reminder that virtues do not exempt from failure.

While listening to the soothing strains of the harp, the hand of the Lord came upon Elijah and he was enabled to give direction as to how the serious situation could be remedied. Thus the trenches were dug so that the water would be retained. This water would not fall in their presence as rain, but flow into the trenches from the mountains of Edom, upon which it had previously fallen. This meant that the Moabites would not know of it. The promise he gave at this time to the three kings went far beyond telling them of the supply of water. It extended to their assured and complete victory over Moab.

Although the water was sorely needed it did not come until the following morning at the time of the offering up of the daily sacrifice. Whether this refers to the sacrifice at the Temple in Jerusalem, or whether in the camp there was formal morning worship, is not certain but one thing is clear, that only the Lord to whom the sacrifice was offered, could have sent the abundant supply of water. It is important to link this deliverance with Elijah's experience on Carmel (1 Kings 18). There the fire came down at the time of the evening sacrifice (v.36) and was followed by a downpour of rain. Ahab was taught by Elijah that God was the source both of fire and water, and that He granted both at His servant's request; likewise in this passage Ahab's son, Jehoram, was also shown that the Lord could again supply water, and do so, in response to the newly appointed prophet, Elisha. The man, who had been a servant who "poured water on the hands of Elijah", proved to these three kings that he was indeed the prophet of the Lord and the one through whom He was prepared to speak and to do miracles.

Once the crisis of the drought was over, the three kings and their armies proceeded. The Moabites made a desperate attempt to ward off the attack, and mustered every man who could bear arms to join the defence of their country. The water which had relieved the distressed invaders was so copious that the entire valley was flooded. The shining of the morning sun on this mass of water caused the defenders to think that they were looking on a sea of blood. They concluded that the kings had fallen out amongst themselves, and that the armies had slain one another. This was a logical assumption for the mixed alliance of Israel, Judah and Edom must have appeared to the Moabites as a band that could readily disintegrate. This wishful thinking cost them dearly. They went out to collect the spoil, and discovered they had been deluded by an optical illusion. The invaders, not only halted the Moabites, but put them to flight. Thus they fulfilled the prophecy of Elisha by destroying the cities, and spoiling the land. It is noticeable that no reference is made to the taking of the spoils of these cities, so destruction, not possession, was the main objective of the campaign.

Though all the cities approached had been destroyed by Israel, yet the stronghold, and possibly the most important of them, Kir-haraseth, was not so treated. Whether it was too strong, or whether it was better defended is difficult to decide, Instead of demolishing its walls the invaders used their skill in slinging stones at the defenders. These missiles proved very effective. The king of Moab perceived that he could not hold out against the pressure, so he made one gallant attempt to escape. He ventured to go to that part of the army confronting him, which he judged to be the most favourable, namely the Edomites. He knew that quite often they and Israel had fought against each other. However, he failed in his attempt, so in desperation resorted to the most heinous form of idolatry the offering of a human sacrifice, his son and heir. In this barbarous act he demonstrated human depravity at its lowest ebb. For reasons not stated it had the effect of making Israel call off the siege. The statement "There was great indignation against Israel" is one which can be viewed in two different ways. If we take it to refer to God's wrath, as it does in most other places where it occurs, then the inference of the passage is that God was angry with Israel for driving the king of Moab to such an extremity as to cause him to burn his son. If the "indignation" is viewed as that of the reaction of the Moabites this leads to the difficulty in knowing how this brought about the end of the invasion. It has been suggested that the offering was so detestable to the religious and refined minds of the Israelite army that it turned away in disgust. Had God's indignation been spent upon the offending king of Moab this could be understood. That it should be against Israel, at this time was fulfilling the words of Elisha, presents a difficulty. However, it could be that the invaders went beyond what was intended by God and that He intervened to halt the siege. Whatever the truth of the matter, the armies returned to their own territory without accomplishing the subjugation of Moab, and the restoration of the tribute formerly paid.

Again it can be argued that the word of Elisha did not promise complete victory. Certainly there is no evidence that God's intervention on behalf of Israel caused Jehoram to give Him glory. Accordingly it may be that the Lord having brought them to the point of victory now turned against the nation for its continued hardness of heart. There may be the suspicion that Jehoram and the Edomites still harboured idolatry in their hearts towards the gods of Moab.

Just as Ahab's victory over Ben-hadad failed to accomplish what was at first intended (1 Kings 20), so this victory also failed to have the desired outcome. The destruction of the cities of Moab, and of its fields brought no profit to Israel, nor did either of the two kings return home satisfied that his venture had been worth while. Such victories are a reminder of the solemn fact that a battle can be won, yet the war can be lost. If victories were to be measured by their ultimate result there might be less boasting about them. Quite often they prove very disappointing.

Notes

2 "The image" (MATZTZEHVUH - 4676) is likely to have been a stone pillar. Jacob was the first to set up such a pillar (Gen 28). There was nothing idolatrous about his stone. Israel was later forbidden to set up any statues or pillars (Deut 16.22), Those already erected by the Canaanites were to be broken down (Deut 7.5; 12.3).

4 Mesha was a "sheepmaster" (NOHKEHD - 5349) or "herdman" (Amos 1.1) the only other place where the word is used. Some readings imply that it was only the wool of these sheep that was given, but the mention of "lambs" as well as "rams" strengthens the commonly accepted idea that the animals themselves were given.

16 Even though the armies were almost exhausted from the lack of water, yet they had to begin the heavy task of digging trenches. While they did not labour to bring the water, this did not mean that they had not to make preparation for receiving it. Often God is prepared to pour out His blessings, but much exercise is needed to prepare hearts to receive them.

The word "ditches" (GOHU - 1356) occurs four times, (1 Kings 6.9; Isa 10.31; Jer 14.3). The "vault-beams" of the Temple roof, the "pits", and the "trenches" were all "cut out" which is the basic meaning of the word.

CHAPTER 4, Verses 1-7
The widow's debt paid

From the commencement of this chapter until ch.6.7 the historian leaves the scenes of battle and concentrates on the private miracles of mercy performed by the prophet Elisha. He shows how the needs of Israel were met, and in ch.5 he shows that an unworthy Gentile also had his need met. In the sovereignty of God the fame of the prophet was enhanced by the dire circumstances of the hour. In spite of all the idolatry in the northern kingdom he maintained his witness and let the people know that he served the only true God.

Like his master Elijah, Elisha had a tender heart for widows in their distress. In this case the widow was in great straits. She had not only lost her husband, but was threatened also with the loss of her two sons. Evidently when anyone in Israel was unable to pay a debt he had to sell himself to his creditor and become a bondslave. This bondage would, of course, only last until the year of jubilee, and then he would return to freedom. Even so the poor widow might not live until then. With this possibility in mind, the stark reality of her plight would not be relieved, even by such a hope. Her extremity did not arise as a judgment for her husband's sins, for he was one of the sons of the prophets, and one who feared God. If she knew the words of David, "I have been young, and now am old; yet have I not seen the righteous forsaken, nor his seed begging bread" (Ps 37.25), she must have been perplexed by her circumstances. Her only hope was Elisha and to him she poured out her tale of woe.

Like most, if not all of Elisha's miracles, he asked for something to be used in performing them. In this case he employed the "pot of oil" which was the only item left in the widow's house. This oil may have been for anointing. The word usually means "olive oil", which had many uses. The container or, "pot" ("little" NIV) which held it was very small, Nevertheless it held the key to her deliverance. When the pots were gathered from her neighbours she was told to shut the door, and commence pouring out the oil into the empty vessels. Only she and her two sons witnessed the miracle. They must have been amazed that as long as there was an empty vessel the oil continued to flow. When these were all filled it stopped. While there was no limit to the supply, there was no oil wasted, nor spilled on the ground. Selling the oil as instructed by Elisha would not only enable her to pay her debt, but would give her a surplus on which she and her sons could live, Like the widow of Zarephath, who had a "little oil in a cruse" which never failed (1 Kings 17.16), she proved the sufficiency of God to meet her every need.

There are a number of practical lessons in this short story which ought to be considered. One is, that conditions in the land at that time were such that God was grieved with His people. Those who spoke against the evils were sure to suffer privations. This servant of the Lord had died and left his widow desolate, He must have been taken away in relative youth "sons" or "children" were still at home with their mother. Their subsequent experience was not uncommon in that troubles often come in pairs, or even trebles. Here death was followed by debt, and close on the heels of these two trials followed the threat of bondage. The people of God in this present day do not turn to a prophet in times of distress, but to the Lord on the throne. He will never leave, or forsake.

Again, it is worthy of note that the supply was never exhausted, but the empty receptacles to hold it were limited. Similarly, spiritual blessings are abundant, but often conditions to receive them are not as they ought to be.

There is a loose parallel with the experience of the apostles in Acts 1. They had been bereaved of their Master and Lord; they were in debt in the sense that they had a responsibility to preach the Gospel; they had an outpouring, not of oil, but of the Holy Spirit; and after they received the supply were able to preach. Paul also was very conscious of his responsibility to pay his debt to "both Greeks and the Barbarians" (Rom 1.14). There is still a responsibility to pay the debt owed by spreading the grand message. Failure in this responsibility could have a similar outcome to that feared by the widow, namely that the next generation would have to bear the consequences of their parents' default.

The difficulty today is in finding "empty vessels", or what they represent, needy sinners who will gladly receive the message. Obviously Peter had no such problem when he preached on the day of Pentecost, for he saw some three thousand saved at that time. How different was Paul's experience at Areopagus. The vessels there were too full of philosophy to respond to his message (Acts 17.22-33)!

Verses 8-37
The woman of Shunem

In the course of Elisha's extensive travels through the northern kingdom he had occasion to pass through Shunem on his way to and from Mount Carmel. This village lay at the foot of Little Hermon in the territory of Issachar. In this unimportant place a very important woman resided. She is called "a great woman". These words imply, not only that she was wealthy, but also that she was of considerable influence in her area. Her home was a resting place for the prophet and a place where he was constrained to enter and partake of her hospitality.

After several passing visits she became convinced that he was a holy man and one worthy of even better service. This led her to converse with her husband about building for him a little private apartment which he could enter at will, and where he could enjoy rest and refreshment. This structure was evidently built with stone or brick and was more than a temporary shelter. In it were put the essentials which a traveller would require. He would need a place to rest his weary body, so she provided a "bed"; he would require to eat, so she provided a "table"; he would be given to meditation, so she provided a "stool", or "chair"; and he would be in the chamber at night, so she provided him with a "lampstand".

On an occasion when this provision was being enjoyed by the prophet and his servant he decided that the lady should be compensated for her attention and care. A wealthy woman would be unlikely to accept money, so he decided to ask what he could do for her. Because of the deliverance he had wrought for the king and captain, recorded in ch.3, he had influence in the court and could procure for her any favours she might desire to have from that quarter. However, she refused this offer, for she was content to dwell amongst her own people, and accept the circumstances as they were. Gehazi, Elisha's servant, could see clearly there was one major shortcoming in her home – she had no son. The stigma of barrenness had been her lot, and the fact that both her husband and herself were advanced in years meant that any hope they ever had of having an heir had completely vanished. Here was the one miracle that would compensate for all her trouble and care. When she was called, she was told that the following year she would embrace a son. The news was too absurd for her to believe, so she could only imagine that she was being deceived with a false promise. In spite of her unbelief, she did bear a son at the time promised. Although living many centuries after the father of the nation, she and her husband had a repeat of the experience of Abraham and Sarah. They had entertained three men, one of whom was the Lord; they had been promised a son; Sarah laughed with unbelief. In spite of this, she bore a son (Gen 18). No doubt the promise given to the great woman and her husband was meant to prove in that dark day that the God of Abraham had not changed but was still the same. Nothing was too hard for Him to do. It should be noted that here the woman is prominent, whereas in Genesis the man is in the foreground.

Several years passed, which allowed the Shunammite woman and her husband to enjoy the honour and company of a son in the home. Now the time of harvest came round once more. The lad went out to the field with his father and the reapers. Like most boys in the country, work in the fields had an attraction for him. Even though he was too young to give help, he could at least play among the sheaves, and even rest himself in them if he became weary. However, the morning sun was too much for him to bear, for apparently he fell victim to sunstroke. In his faint condition his father ordered one of the young men to bring him home to his mother. Obviously the father did not think the problem was serious, for he did not carry him home himself. In spite of his mother's kind attention he died at noon, so in a few hours, her greatest treasure on earth was taken from her. No sooner had the tragedy happened than thoughts of the prophet came into her mind. He had been instrumental in procuring the birth of the child. She immediately set out in haste to make her way to where he dwelt at this time. Not however until she had laid the dead son on the bed in the prophet's little chamber. Some sixteen miles lay between her and mount Carmel, where the prophet was at that time. Riding on a she ass she made the journey as fast as was then possible. The prophet recognized her, even at a distance and immediately suspected there was something wrong with either herself, or some of the family. He therefore sent Gehazi to ascertain from her what was the matter, but she refused to divulge to the servant her distress, but instead went direct to the prophet with her sorrow. In her anguish she ventured to lay hold of his feet, an action which Gehazi considered to be unbecoming, but one which was understood by Elisha. He perceived that she was in deep sorrow, and that because of this, his help was sought. Without saying anything about her son's death, she reminded the prophet that she had asked for a son. By her ambiguous statement he concluded that her son was dead, and that he would have to go to where the child's body lay. Possibly with the end in view of comforting her, he sent his servant with his rod, and told him to put it on the dead boy's face. Whatever was the motive for this mission to the child, it was not expected by the mother to be the answer to her trouble. She insisted that the prophet return with her to the home where the dead boy had been left. When Gehazi came to the child he did as he had been commanded, but there was no response. He had to return to his master and tell him the child was not awakened. At length the prophet reached the home and entered the familiar chamber. On his bed lay the still form of what was once a lively child. He closed the door and began to pray to the Lord that the lad might live again. In addition to his prayer, he prostrated himself upon the still body of the child, and remained there until the heat of his body penetrated into the cold body of death. Even then there was no response. After he walked about in the room, and repeated his former exercise, the child sneezed seven times, and opened his eyes.. The mother must have waited for the outcome with great anxiety, and with no small strain upon her faith, The message of Gehazi, "take up thy son", must have been the sweetest she had ever heard, In deep appreciation of Elisha's help she bowed before him in humble gratitude. In this miracle Elisha was repeating what his master had done in raising a boy to life (1 Kings 17.21), but here, the process was either slower than in the former case, or else the details of the prophet's efforts are more fully given.

Already the connection between the birth of this child with the birth of Isaac in Genesis has been considered. Now a further connection between the two comes into view, for just as Abraham saw Isaac as good as dead on the altar, so the woman here saw her son dead on her knee. The deliverance of Isaac was like a resurrection. In the former case the mother seems to be kept in the dark as to the fate of her son, and in this case the father seems to be oblivious of what had befallen his son. Both Abraham and this woman had their faith tested to its limit, yet both held on to God and believed in His resurrection power.

The staff carried by Gehazi has often been likened to the Law. The law could never give life, nor could it give any assistance to dead sinners. Had the staff been successful there would have been no need for Elisha to go to the dead boy. Equally if the Law could have saved, there would have been no need for Christ to come to earth and die. A staff may be useful to the living, but it serves no purpose for the dead.

In this raising of the child therefore there is a striking type of the life-giving Lord Himself, for just as Elisha came to where the dead child was, so He came to where sinners were dead in their sins. Just as the prophet entered into death and humbled himself to the smallest size to do so, so Christ humbled Himself to enter into death. The outstretched hands of the prophet on the hands of the child, are a reminder of His outstretched hands on the Cross. The shut door on the prophet, meant that none were present when he was stooped in death. Likewise there were experiences of Christ in His death not seen by those who looked upon him on the tree. When Christ rose from the dead He was held by the feet and worshipped (Matt 28.9), and when the prophet rose out of "death", he too was held by the feet by the child's mother who bowed in gratitude before him.

The experiences of Abraham and this woman illustrate that God at times takes from His own what they cherish most. Even those special blessings which he has graciously bestowed may be removed. It should teach that He is more precious than all the blessings He grants. Tests of faith are indeed painful at the time, but when deliverance comes they prove God's faithfulness and strengthen confidence in Him.

Verses 38-41
Death in the pot

The chapter has shown how Elisha was able to relieve the debtor, to make the barren fruitful, and to raise the dead. In these next verses he turned poisoned pottage into wholesome food. The scene was at Gilgal where earlier he had been in company with Elijah (ch 2.1), and where there was a school of prophets. Most likely Elisha visited these centres from time to time, and while there instructed the sons of the prophets in the ways of God. Seeing these men were opposed by the great system of idolatry which was under the wing of Jezebel, it is not surprising that many difficulties arose in their lives. This meant that they were often in straits as regards finding sustenance. On this occasion Elisha ordered the men to put on the great pot, and make some thick soup, or vegetable broth. With the dearth in the land at that time, there was a scarcity of vegetables. When one of the sons went out, all he found was a wild vine. The gourds from this were collected into his lap, and later sliced into the pot as vegetables. He was totally unaware of the danger from poisoning that these gourds brought to himself and his fellows. However, upon tasting this soup the discovery was made that it was deadly and totally inedible. The cry rang out, "O man of God, there is death in the pot". As on former occasions of need, this was another golden opportunity for Elisha to act. As he had asked for salt to heal the bitter waters (ch 2.20), so here he asked for meal. When it was cast into the pot, the soup was no longer harmful.

Like former miracles this one brings important lessons. One of these is that there can be poison in spiritual food just as in physical. Many might not be aware of it. These wild gourds seemed to the gatherer to be ideal for the purpose, but he was ignorant of their poisonous character. Many have gathered ideas which to them looked good, but those who had spiritual discernment were able to taste the deadly poison in them. Timothy was always to be careful that he kept to wholesome doctrine (1 Tim 6.3), and to avoid profane and vain babblings (1 Tim 6.20). The meal put into the pot was really "killed grain" and this is a reminder, not only of the fine and even character of Christ, but also of His death. It must always be remembered that no whole grain was ever offered to God in any of the offerings. Even the green ears of corn were roasted by the fire, so their life was ended. The ministry of Christ is often the antidote to evil teaching, which if imbibed, would ruin the saints. Paul counteracted the "philosophy and vain deceit" which threatened the church at Colosse by exalting Christ in his letter to it (Col 1.12-19).

Verses 42-44
A hundred men fed with little bread

Already Elisha had healed waters and soup. A miracle of a different kind is now recorded, one also dealing with food. On this occasion he increased the bread, so that what would have merely sufficed for twenty men fed a hundred. Gathered with Elisha were a hundred men; in all likelihood they formed a school of prophets. They were dependent upon those faithful to God to provide them with the necessities of life. In a special way, during a time of drought, their needs would be pressing. In spite of the difficulties of the time, a man from Baal-shalisha, moved with compassion, brought to the prophet twenty loaves made from the first-ripe barley, and also some fresh ears of corn in a sack, This would suggest that Passover time was just passed, and that the first-fruits had been reaped. Instead of bringing these to the priests at the Temple, this man considered Elijah, the man of God, to be God's representative, and the one worthy to receive the portion due to God Himself. Obviously this kind donor had no respect for Baal, or the priests of Baal. Otherwise, he would have offered the first-fruits to them. There was nothing wrong with the gift brought, but the difficulty arose because the supply was insufficient to meet the needs of the number present. The embarrassed servant exclaimed, "What, should I set this before a hundred men?" The prophet, who had a private intimation from the Lord as to the outcome, told the servant to go ahead and serve up the meal. It would not only suffice to satisfy the hungry men, but there would be some left over. The promise proved true, for they ate the bread, with the ears of corn, and left some over. In previous miracles the needs of others were met, but in this case the prophet himself, like Elijah before him, has his own needs, as well as those of his school, met at the same time.

In this miracle there is a similarity to the feeding of the thousands by the Lord, recorded in the Gospels. In both cases there was surprise that the little possessed could be multiplied to feed the large number present. On both occasions, there was some left after all were fed. Neither the man from Baal-shalisha, nor the lad with the loaves and fishes, had any idea that what they gave up would, by the Lord's power, be sufficient to meet the need. Perhaps men are slow to learn that what may seem small in their eyes, can become great if put into God's hands. Many a servant of the Lord has passed on a word which he considered to be of little worth, and the Lord has so developed it in the minds of those to whom it was ministered, that to them, it became indeed a feast, Both the loaves, and the ears of corn were fresh and the fruit of newly harvested fields. In this there is taught that something fresh ministered from the Word of God, is often relished in the minds of those who hear it.

Notes

13 The word "careful" (GHAHRAD - 2729) is translated elsewhere "tremble" or "afraid". Here the fear must have been that reverential fear that she felt in the presence of the holy man of God.

26 When she said it was "well" (SHAHLOHM - 7965) "peace", she was merely using the normal word of greeting, and was not implying that there was nothing wrong with the child.

29 It may have been that Elisha thought that his staff would be as effective in raising the lad, as Elijah's mantle in his hand was effective in opening Jordan. Whatever spiritual power he possessed, it was not transmitted to the instruments he used.

39 The "gourds" (PAKKOOGOHTH - 6498) which the son of the prophets gathered were either the colocynth, or the squirting cucumber. The former bears gourds about the size of a large orange, but those borne by the latter are much smaller. Only in time of drought would anyone think of using either of these gourds, so this may explain why the gatherer was unaware of their poisonous nature.

42 Baal-shalisha was a village some seven miles north of Bethel and about twenty miles from Gilgal, where the prophet was at this time. The "full ears of corn" (KARMEL - 3759) were the "fruit of the field", and the word used for mount Carmel. The word "husks" (TZIKLOHN - 6861) used only here, comes from a root meaning to "wind', and may mean a "sack" tied at the mouth RV, or even a garment tied up in this way.

CHAPTER 5, Verses 1-14
Naaman the leper healed

In the previous chapters God was making His name known through Elisha in the land of Israel. As long as the worship of Baal and the influence of Jezebel covered the northern kingdom it was vital that in it a testimony be raised to Jehovah. This ensured that all who sought Him had direct evidence which proved to them that He alone was the true God. In this chapter, the prophet's fame was extended to the Gentile world. It reached a nation which was often an enemy of Israel. That the king of Syria sent a letter to the king of Israel and that Naaman was allowed free passage suggests at least a temporary period of truce. The response to the letter, that an occasion for fault was being sought, adds support to this view. The outcome was that a notable person in the ranks of Syria became a worshipper of the God of Israel. This is one of the passages in Scripture which demonstrates the sovereignty of God, and His grace. If ever there was an example of one deserving the judgment of God yet shown unmerited favour, surely Naaman was that one. It is easy to understand blessing flowing out to Gentiles such as Rahab and Ruth, both of whom favoured Israel. However, that a cruel oppressor and captor of Israelite children for slaves should be favoured by God, or by His servant, is something which exceeds the limits of human kindness.

In 1 Kings 20.31 there is evidence that the Syrians already knew the kings of Israel to be merciful. Through the experience of their captain they were taught that the God of these kings was also merciful. Elisha is here an example of the truth that people become like the gods they worship. Those who serve idols become like Satan himself, who is the unseen object behind idolatry.

In the opening verses of this chapter attention is directed to the court of the king of Syria. Apparently Ben-hadad in his latter days had appointed Naaman to the top post of captain of the Syrian army. Although a truce had been made with Israel after the defeat of Ben-hadad (1 Kings 20.34), this did not last, for the bands of the Syrians made constant raids into the cities of Israel. Naaman was in charge of these attacks, and by the help of the Lord, Who was grieved with the evils of His people, he was successful. He was not only a general, but had proved himself to be a man of courage, and so was highly esteemed by the king. To his own grief, and to the distress of his master, he was smitten with leprosy. He had power to conquer and oppress the people of surrounding nations, but in this disease he was faced by a more formidable foe. However, a flash of light crossed his dark sky. The little maid captured from Israel intimated to his wife that if he would go to the prophet in Israel, his disease would be healed. The insignificant girl God used on this occasion has often been noted with surprise. Although she had never heard of Elisha healing a leper, nor had she any proof that he would consider Naaman a suitable subject for his attention, yet with childlike confidence she put forth her conviction without reservation.

Upon hearing this welcome news Naaman went to the king and reported to him what he had just heard. The response was as might be expected. The king was as anxious, as he was himself, that he be healed. To make sure that there would be no obstacle a letter was given to him to be presented to the king of Israel upon his arrival at Samaria. Both the captain and the king of Syria concluded that a prophet with such powers as they were told he had, would be at the command of the king who would have authority to direct him in his healing operations. They were entirely wrong; Elisha took his orders from the God of Israel, and not from an earthly monarch.

Like most in the world, Naaman judged that if he was going to have such a miraculous cure, he would have to pay heavily for it. He took with him many thousands of pounds worth of silver and gold, together with ten changes of clothing. As Scripture says "All that a man hath will he give for his life" (Job 2.4). The king of Israel read the letter with dismay, for everyone in Israel knew that this healing could only be accomplished by God. Immediately the king concluded that something more sinister was afoot. To him it read like a demand for him to do the impossible, and if he failed to do it, then this would be used as an excuse for the Syrians to attack Israel. With all this before him and fearing the worst, he rent his clothes in deep distress.

News of the king's action reached the prophet, who in turn, sent him word saying "Let him come now to me, and he shall know that there is a prophet in Israel". In response to this message, Naaman and his retinue made their way to the prophet's house, and stopped outside his door. Never before had Elisha seen such a cavalcade approach his humble abode. However, he was not perturbed, for to him it was only a poor leper seeking to be healed. To the surprise of Naaman and probably of his servants, there was no official welcome by the prophet. He did not come out to see his visitor, nor did he make any physical intervention. A simple message was all the response granted. "Go and wash in Jordan seven times, and thy flesh shall come again to thee". If ever a man was disappointed and nonplussed, it was the captain. Never in all his career had he been treated with such disrespect. Little wonder his temper was stirred, and in his anger he spoke his thoughts aloud. He had imagined a course of action the prophet should perform to accomplish the healing. Possibly he had heard of, or had seen some of the false prophets attempt to perform miracles, and thought a similar practice would be associated with the prophet of the Lord. An additional problem was involved in the message. It meant that he would have to travel some twenty-five miles to the Jordan where he was to wash. In his campaigns he probably had seen this river, and its waters did not appeal to him as having any superior quality about them. Compared with the rivers which flowed through Damascus, it was indeed inferior. He reckoned that if river-water would cleanse, why not use the best obtainable.

If Naaman lacked wisdom, he was favoured with sensible servants. Just as the little maid gave him his first good advice, so here the servants came to his rescue. Otherwise he would have returned home none the better of his journey. They reasoned with him to do what he had been told. Because it was not difficult to do, it was on that account humiliating for him to accept. At length he took their counsel, and obeyed the word of the prophet by dipping the seven times in Jordan. True to the promise, he was made perfectly whole, and was later able to say "Now I know that there is no God in all the earth, but in Israel". This testimony indicates that he had his soul healed as well as his body. The purpose of God in the whole operation was that His name would be honoured in Syria, and this, in the very place where it had been despised for many years.

Although the banks of Jordan were much nearer his home than Samaria, yet Naaman was so grateful to have his plague cured that he took the journey back and stood a second time at the prophet's door. His request that Elisha accept a reward was refused in the strongest possible terms. Even when pressed to yield he still remained firm in his refusal. When Naaman saw that he could not change the prophet's mind on the matter of the present he proceeded to ask for "two mules' burden of earth" This earth was apparently to build an altar in Syria, and to offer on it sacrifices to the God of Israel. What had happened in Jordan left him convinced in his soul that the Lord alone was worthy to receive his worship. However, a problem rose in his mind. The king was a worshipper of Rimmon, and probably, due to his age, he would be accompanied by his chief officer, when he went into the house of Rimmon. The two would bow before the idol. In this part of his duty he had a conscience that by thus bowing, he was doing wrong, for it implied that he was no less an idolater than the king. He requested pardon for such inconsistency. There could have been in his mind that the prophet who could cure leprosy could just as easily inflict punishment for wrongdoing. The prophet understood his difficulty and sent him away in peace.

The story in these verses is full of lessons. In a special way it suits the present age, for just as blessing went beyond Israel in the healing of Naaman, so blessing is now spread among the Gentiles. The Lord Himself made reference to this man, and showed that though there were many lepers in Israel, yet none of them was healed, but this Syrian (Lk 4.27). Since leprosy is a type of sin in its uncleanness, Naaman is typical of the whole human race, for all are spiritual lepers, being sinners by birth. Just as there was only one on earth who could cleanse him, so those who feel their need of cleansing, have only One, the Lord Himself, to whom they can go for forgiveness.

In this case there is an example of human pride, for though a leper has nothing to be proud of, since he is dying on his feet, yet Naaman felt insulted both by the way the prophet treated him, and also by the way he was directed for cleansing. His haughty spirit was shown by his rage. Perhaps the last thing a sinner will give up in order to be saved is his pride. The very simplicity of salvation becomes to him a stumbling-block. There were few in Syria who could lead an army to victory, as did the general, but when it came to his cleansing, even a little child could have done as he was told to do.

Learning to accept salvation as a free gift is not easy for mankind. Most think they will have to pay for it in some way. Some hands are too full of "good works", and "self-righteousness", to accept, as a beggar would a coin, the greatest of all blessings. While all who are saved are deeply thankful for the mercy experienced, yet not one of them can boast. Neither before, nor after conversion, can anyone claim to have paid the price of his redemption.

The sovereignty of God is evident in the story. When Naaman was taking captive the little maid, he never thought he was playing a role in a grand scheme that would result in his conversion to the Lord. It was no small trial for a little girl to be wrenched from her people and to find herself in the house of strangers, who had a different language, and a different culture. Yet she was not there in vain, but to be used as an instrument in the plan of God. Like Joseph in Potiphar's house, and later in prison, who was God's representative in Egypt, she was God's ambassador, in the right place, and at the right time. In this it can be learned that apparent misfortunes are often allowed for the glory of God, even though at the time, those involved may be unaware of the purpose behind them. It is one thing to sing "Ill that God blesses is our good", but when the "ill" comes it may not always be easy to detect the "good" that can accrue from it. From the spark of light in the dark home of a heathen general there was developed a flame that spread abroad in Syria. Can any fully appreciate the joy that must have filled the heart of the little maid when she discovered that her master worshipped the same Lord as herself?

In the act of Naaman dipping, and washing in Jordan, we have a picture of regeneration, for his flesh became as the "flesh of a little child". As it were, he was born again. The reason he was sent to this particular river was that it represents "death and judgment". In a sense, he had to demonstrate in a perfect way (for it had to be seven times) that he deserved to die, and that he was deserving of judgment. Again his experience at Jordan illustrates what believers demonstrate at their baptism. Death, burial and resurrection with Christ are figuratively indicated by immersion in and raising from the water. Just as Naaman was told to wash in Jordan and his uncleanness would be taken away, so Paul was told to be baptized, and wash away his sins (Acts 22.16) In neither case did the water effect the removal. The outward action illustrated what was occurring, or what had occurred inwardly.

In the matter of bowing to Rimmon we learn that believers in their employment have to obey their masters. This at times may mean they are asked to do what for them is not in keeping with their convictions. For example, they may be compelled to wear uniform which may not become their sex, but this should be tolerated, and they should not be blamed for it, for they only wear this when necessary. In a similar way there are sisters who have been grieved when they had to have their hair shaved for a brain operation. In cases like this it is well to say to such "go in peace", God knows the heart and conscience, and He values the sincerity of His own. If Naaman, after his cleansing, had deliberately gone to worship in the house of Rimmon, then all he said to Elisha would have been empty profession. Likewise, if those who profess salvation return to their old ways they are likened to a sow washed, returning to the mire (2 Pet 2.22)

On the other hand in the case of Daniel and his fellows there is an example of standing firm when asked to do something that is offensive to the mind of God (Dan 1.8). The balance between the attitudes of Naaman and Daniel is a matter for the individual conscience.

Verses 15-27
Gehazi smitten with leprosy

This chapter in 2 Kings is really the story of two lepers, one of whom was cleansed, and another who would never be cleansed. The latter would remain a leper to the end of his days. One was an unworthy Gentile, the other a privileged Israelite, One was a stranger to the prophet Elisha, the other was his long-time servant. One became an encouragement to all who are afar off, the other a warning to those who are near.

It grieved the covetous Gehazi to see Naaman return home with the valuable items he had brought to pay for his cure. He could not understand why his master had let such a wealthy man off so lightly, and why such a favour should be granted, without any recompense to the giver. After running at great speed, he overtook Naaman, who, recognizing him, alighted from his chariot, and greeted him. In order to extract the coveted wealth from him, he asked for it in his master's name. The story he told was all lies but was sufficiently plausible to bring about the desired result. In the end Gehazi obtained two talents of silver, even though he asked for only one, and to these were added the two garments which he requested. All these were carried by the servants of Naaman, to the house of Gehazi, where they were hidden.

Without the slightest sign of embarrassment he boldly entered into the presence of his master, and when asked where he had been, he told another lie. He did not deceive Elisha. All that he had done had been revealed by the Lord to the prophet, who could tell him the facts as though he had been present when they occurred. After asking one solemn question, the prophet pronounced the heavy sentence upon him which involved, not only himself, but his posterity. He obtained some of Naaman's wealth, but along with it he was given his leprosy. He was allowed to keep the riches, but they would be of little benefit to him, seeing he had no health to enjoy them.

There are principles taught in this passage which are most important for all to accept. One is that severe punishment is meted out to those who are privileged to be enlightened, and who sin. God can have mercy on the ignorant, even on the vilest of them, but He cannot tolerate those who sin wilfully after they have received the knowledge of the truth. Gehazi knew well that what he was doing and what he was saying were both wrong. When he received the silver and the garments he did not bring them to Elisha for whom he had requested them. For this evil he was smitten with the leprosy, which left him as white as snow, and cut him off from the very house where he had hidden them.

A second principle which can be learned is that covetousness is the root cause of the downfall of man. Whether in the case of the Fall in the Garden (Gen 3), or of Achan and the accursed thing (Josh 7), or of Judas and the thirty pieces of silver (Matt 27), or of Gehazi in this passage, it is evident that behind each was the lustful desire to obtain what was not lawful for him to possess. The seed of this evil is in every breast, and great care must be taken to prevent it from bearing fruit.

The importance of the servant having the same spirit as his master is also illustrated here. Had Gehazi viewed things as did Elisha the idea of obtaining the goods from Naaman would never have entered his head. The Lord constantly stressed to His disciples the importance of their thoughts being in harmony with His. Paul enjoined the same principle when he wrote, "Let this mind be in you, which was also in Christ Jesus" (Phil 2).

There will come a time when the nation of Israel will accept gifts from Gentiles (Ps 45.10-12), but in the days of Elisha, the conditions in Israel were not as they will be then. In his time, only a remnant testimony was left in the land. The majority were worshippers of the gold calves, or of Baal. Thus Gehazi's receiving of the money and garments was entirely out of keeping with the time, so he was asked by the prophet, "Is this the time to receive money etc?" The believer in this age must be diligent to live in keeping with the day in which he lives, The Galatian saints allowed their clock to run slow, for they were going back to the Law (Gal 3). The Corinthian saints allowed their clock to go fast, for they were reigning before the time (1 Cor 4). In this present dispensation, God is acting in grace toward man, Christ is still rejected, and His people are strangers and pilgrims on the earth.

Another solemn fact which this story illustrates is that long experience is not a safeguard from evil. Had this fall occurred when Gehazi had just joined Elisha there might be little surprise, but that it should happen after years of witnessing the power of God working through his master, is astounding. Many imagine that if only they were spared and granted more experience then they would sin no more. Alas many have gone on well for years, yet when temptation came to them in their latter years, they were overcome. Until in heaven, the prayer of the Psalmist, "Preserve me, O God" (Ps 16) should be always on the lips of the saints.

Notes

There is a body of opinion that holds that the accounts of the deeds of Elisha are not in chronological order. It is suggested that this chapter brings together his miracles and that the cleansing of Naaman took place much later. This would provide an explanation for Gehazi's appearance in ch 8 without the slightest hint that he was a leper. A contrary view is that he was pardoned by the prophet and cleansed. However there is no textual basis for this.

3 "would God" is an interjection translated "O that" (Ps 119.5) in the only other passage where it occurs. There is no reference to "God" in the original.

7 The words of the king imply that only God could cure leprosy, because to do so, was like bringing a dead person to life. The word translated "seeketh a quarrel" or "an occasion" (AHNAH - 579) is found elsewhere only in Ex 21.13; Ps 91.10; and Prov 12.21.

12 The two rivers mentioned both flow through Damascus. Abana, now Barada, is the more important and is considered to be one of the attractions of that city. Pharpar, was probably a tributary of the Abana, and is not easily identified.

18 "Rimmon" (a pomegranate), was the "god of storms", and one of several gods worshipped by the Syrians. He was equal to, or may have been identical to, the god Hadad. The two are combined in the name "Hadad-Rimmon" (Zec 12.11).

25 Gehazi stood before his master without realizing that all he had been saying and doing was known as clearly as if the prophet had been with him when he was asking for, and taking, the presents. Elisha himself refused because he "stood before the Lord" (v.16), so if Gehazi had realised that he was standing before his master, at the time when he thought of following Naaman, he never would not have ventured on his covetous errand.

CHAPTER 6, Verses 1-7
An Axe head is made to swim

Elisha usually lived in Samaria but he did travel to the various centres where there was a school of prophets. At this time he was with one such group, possibly at Jericho. In spite of all the adverse circumstances of that day, the numbers in the school had outgrown their accommodation. The sons of the prophets decided to expand their centre, and to change its site to the banks of Jordan. They were wise enough to consult their master, and seek his consent for the project. He agreed with their suggestion, and wished them God's blessing, but this did not satisfy them, for they wanted him to accompany them in the task, and possibly supervise the work. To this also he consented, so the entire band proceeded to the banks of Jordan where there were many trees that could be taken without seeking permission from any owner. The responsibility of each young man was to fell his tree, shape it into a beam, and carry it to the chosen site. All the work was shared, and the project was to be an example of harmonious action being to the benefit of all involved.

Just when the work was progressing as expected, one of the hewers had a serious mishap. The axe he was using lost its head, and what was worse, it fell into the river where it disappeared out of sight. Had the user been the owner, it would have been bad enough, but the axe was one which had been borrowed, or begged for use on this occasion. This young man would have felt most embarrassed if he had to return to the owner and tell him he had lost his axe head. In his distress he turned to the prophet and cried out, "Alas, master! for it was borrowed". After the place where it fell into the river was indicated, the prophet cut down a stick, cast it into the river, and the axe head returned to the surface. All that the young man had to do to retrieve his lost iron was to reach out his hand and take it.

This brief story brings, to mind some obvious lessons. It is encouraging to learn that the school of prophets had outgrown its accommodation. This story illustrates that in the expansion of the work of God, it is vital that all work together. The importance of having the Lord's presence is suggested by the workers having the prophet with them. As regards the "axe head", it suggests that the power to work for God, on this occasion to hew the trees, is no less borrowed than the axe was. Just as it was lost, so too through slackness, can power be lost. Peter used the axe in Acts 2 when he cut to the heart the assembled Jews, but he, like the man in this story, was using the power of the Spirit, and not that which belonged to himself. The stick cut down, and going down to where the iron lay, and both coming up again, is a type of death and resurrection. The labour entailed in cutting down trees and carrying the heavy beams to the site teaches that there are heavy burdens to be carried if the work of God is to be expanded.

Verses 8-23
The army of Syrians overcome by Elisha

In this section the historian returns to the wars with Syria, and shows the debt the nation of Israel owed to Elisha. Although Ben-hadad had been spared by Ahab, yet he soon forgot his agreement, and persisted in his attacks on the northern kingdom of Israel. On this occasion, his plan was to launch an unexpected raid and so win an easy victory over the surprised Israelite army. However, no matter where he ventured, he discovered that the King of Israel was fully prepared for his coming. He could understand this happening once, but that it occurred every time made him suspicious that one of his officers was giving away the secrets of his strategy. One of his men, however, informed him of the real reason for his problem. The prophet Elisha was telling the king of Israel all Ben-hadad's secrets, and doing so as clearly as if he were sitting listening to him in his bed-chamber. The first thought in the Syrian king's head was to capture the prophet, and possibly kill him. When he discovered that Elisha was at Dothan, he proceeded to attack it during the night, and did so with a strong force of chariots and horses. When a servant of the man of God arose in the morning, he saw that the city was surrounded, and cried out, "Alas, my master!". These were the usually employed words when an appeal to the prophet was being made in a time of trouble. Whenever this cry of distress was heard, then miracles began to occur. The first of these was in answer to the prophet's prayer, and involved the opening of the eyes of the distressed young man to see the host of the Lord at the disposal of His surrounded servant. The second miracle was also in answer to the prophet's prayer, but was in sharp contrast to the former one. It entailed the dulling of the sight of the attacking army. When they entered where the prophet was in the city, he told them they had landed in the wrong place, so he offered to direct them to the man whom they sought, but brought them to the capital of the nation, even into Samaria. When in this city, they had their eyes opened, and discovered that they had not only met the man they sought, but had been trapped into the heart of their enemy's citadel. They were therefore at the mercy of the king of Israel, who asked Elisha, should he smite them. Instead, he was instructed to set food before them. He not only gave them bread and water, but in addition, a sumptuous meal. In this entertainment, the cruel Syrians were shown that the people of Israel shared something of the character of their God, for they were merciful. This ended, for the time being, the invasions of the Syrians into Israel.

Though the Syrians were the rod used by the Lord to chastise His rebellious people, yet He was continually working to make His name known to them, On this occasion, they were taught that He knew every movement they made, Even the very words they spoke in secret, It has always to be remembered that "all things are naked and opened unto the eyes of Him with whom we have to do" (Heb 4.13), Secrets may be kept from our fellows, but He not only hears what is said, but knows the thoughts of every heart.

When the enemy comes with excessive force, as he does on the "evil day" (Eph 6.13), it is well to remember the forces which are available to help. The young man who was so terrified when he saw the host surrounding Dothan, only needed to see the armies of heaven, and the chariots of fire, to bring an end to his panic, and to steady his nerves. Likewise today, in case of assault there is real comfort in realizing that greater is He that is for His own, than he that is against them. Apart from God's help, no one is a match for the forces which confront him, but by the help of His Spirit, he can be an overcomer.

The blinded Syrians being led by the prophet, as though he were their general, show that God is in control of wicked men, and wicked nations. At times the success of evil is surprising. However, only part of the picture is seen, for if all was understood it would be seen that God uses wicked men to punish other wicked men. At times, He even uses them to destroy themselves.

Many like the Syrians fail to appreciate mercy, for though they did not continue at this time to invade Israel, they were soon back to their old ways. Not a few sinners, who were brought to the brink of destruction, and rescued, have said they would change their ways, but before long, all the favours shown them were forgotten, and they resumed their former way of living.

If the small remnant in Israel led by Elisha, could be instrumental in making God's mercy known to the Syrians, saints too, in spite of their weakness, have the opportunity from time to time, to show an evil world that despises them, that God is gracious, and that they act in grace, because they are His children.

Verses 24-33
Samaria under siege

In spite of the two occasions when the Syrians were shown mercy by the Israelites (1 Kings 20.31 and vv.22-23), they, and their king, continued to invade Israel. On this occasion they aimed at seizing the capital, and all but succeeded in doing so. Of all the ravages of war referred to in Scripture this is possibly the supreme example of the dire straits that can accrue from it. The enemy had made sure that no food entered the city, so its inhabitants were starving. The extremity they reached, meant that they were eating what, in normal times, would be judged unthinkable. Whether eating an ass's head, or dove's dung, or the body of a child, is considered, the extremes to which the people were driven in this time of crisis become apparent. What is surprising is that Elisha was in the city, yet allowed all this to continue, without intervening, or exercising his power. He might have been expected to have done something before such conditions had developed. What brought the deplorable state to a head was a woman's cry to the king for help. He assumed that she was asking for food, and so replied that he had neither food, nor drink, and that only the Lord could relieve her distress, However, her dilemma was even more serious than he expected, for she proceeded to tell him her trouble. She had shared her killed, and boiled, son with her neighbour on the condition that the neighbour's son would be cooked the next day. When the time came for the other boy to be eaten, he had been hidden by his mother, and was nowhere to be found. This defrauded woman asked the king to intervene and judge the case. On hearing such a repulsive story, the king rent his garment, and in doing so, revealed that underneath it, he was wearing sackcloth. His reply to the woman amounted to a threat to the life of the prophet. Like Ahab before him, he blamed the servant of the Lord for the terrible state of the people in the city, and vowed that before the day was over, the head of Elisha would be cut off.

The elders and the prophet were having a consultation, which most likely was about the terrible circumstances prevailing in the city, when the sound of the approaching executioner was heard. His coming was no surprise to Elisha, for the Lord had forewarned him that he was on the way. Lest the plan to kill succeeded these elders were told to hold the door fast, until the king himself arrived, for he was following hard on the heels of his officer. The evil intended by the king, revealed his character, for he was a murderer, as was his father before him, who had slain the prophets of the Lord, and Naboth, The words of the king, when he met face to face with the prophet, were "Behold this evil is of the Lord; what should I wait for the Lord any longer?" This question may imply that he had been told to continue to wait God's time of deliverance, but in his judgment there was no need for further delay. The reply of the prophet was the announcement that on the next day the desired deliverance would be granted. Both fine flour and barley would be so plentiful, that they would be obtainable at very low prices. The officer and attendant of the king was full of unbelief, and thought the claim so ridiculous that it could no more happen than the opening of the windows of heaven to pour down needful supplies, He was sternly told that he would see the prophecy fulfilled, but would not share in the food himself.

When the warnings of Moses were given regarding eating the flesh of children in a siege (Lev 26.29; Deut 28.53), few thought that the day would come when this cannibalism would actually take place. Here, and in the siege of Jerusalem (Lam 2:20) it was indeed solemnly experienced. The survival of the older, at the expense of the young and tender is an evil principle, and goes against the laws of nature, as well as against the laws of God.

Scarcity of spiritual food is as painful to the soul, as scarcity of ordinary food is painful to the flesh. If the enemy shuts God's people up into exclusive camps, famine conditions in their souls will soon prevail. We cannot survive in isolation, but need the help of other saints. Few have developed spiritually, who have refused the ministry of those whom God gifted to feed His own.

The passage perhaps emphasizes the need to wait on God in all distress. The king may have had sackcloth on his body but perhaps it was not a true reflection of his heart before the Lord.

Notes
6 The word "cut down" (KAHTZAU - 7094) means to "clip", and is translated "shorn" in the only other place where it occurs (Song of Songs 4.2). Some have deduced from this word that Elisha shaped a handle that entered the iron before it floated. This is most unlikely, for there was nothing wrong with the original handle, except that it was not tightly fitted to the iron.

25 The ass was unclean and not to be eaten, and its head was the part of it with the least meat upon it. The silver paid for it was about

£500 of our money. The "dove's dung"(DUSYOHNEEM - 1686) may have been just that or is possibly the name of "seed pods" (NIV), or "wild onions". The "cab" (KAV - 6894) was about half a pint. The word is found only here.

CHAPTER 7, Verses 1-2

Elisha prophecies that food would be cheap in Samaria

These two verses really belong to the previous chapter, and give the response to the king's complaint in ch 6.33. Some change of heart must have come over him when he thought over what he had earlier ordered his officer to do with Elisha. The siege had done its work in bringing down the citizens of Samaria to a state of repentance, and to where they really felt their need of God and His servant. The fact that Elisha sat with the elders, would indicate that they were approaching him to intervene, and that they, like the king, had come to realize that what the city was enduring was indeed allowed by the Lord. Never did more welcome words leave the lips of Elisha, than when he announced the news that fine flour and barley, two kinds of meal essential for making bread, "The staff of life", would be on sale at such a low price on the following day. So amazing must this statement have been, that had it not been prefaced by, "Thus saith the Lord", no one who heard it, would have believed it to be possible. The exclamation of the attendant to the king, regarding the unlikelihood of such a thing, must have been the uppermost thought in the minds of most who heard it. Obviously there was no hope of obtaining these essentials from the surrounding fields, nor could they be brought in through the ranks of the surrounding army. Even though the sky above their heads were to open, this lord thought that such supplies could not be rained from heaven, and come down like the waters of the flood. His incredulity proved to be costly, for the prophet, who had just told of the relief that was nearing, also foretold the fate of this man. He would see the prophecy fulfilled, but it would not benefit him, because it would be the cause of his death. He was one of the first to hear the good news, and so was like the Jews and the Gospel. They also were the first to hear the message but through unbelief, they missed the blessing. What was a savour of life to the people of the city, was a savour of death to him, and what was a savour of life to many Gentiles, was a savour of death to many Jews (2 Cor 2.16).

Verses 3-20
The siege of Samaria ends

If the promise of cheap and plentiful flour was wonderful, the means the Lord used to work the change, and the instruments He used to bring the news to the city were no less amazing. Surely, 'God moves in a mysterious way His wonders to perform". Four leprous men, because their disease had made them unfit for society, were sitting outside the city at one of its gates. Although not besieged in the city itself, their lot at its gate was little different, for they confess that to remain where they were would mean death. Likewise, to return to the city, from which they had been banished, would be no better, so they decided to take a chance, and venture to the camp of the enemy, with the hope that some mercy would be shown them, They did this, even though they knew that Syrians were not noted for tenderheartedness. With a deadly disease, a city beside them in starvation, and a powerful enemy encompassing them, they were indeed in a pitiable state. They made an early start, and attempted to reach the enemy camp before they could be distinctly recognized. As circumstances turned out all their timidity and apprehensions were groundless, for not a soldier was in sight. A miracle had occurred, for the Lord had caused the Syrian army to be deluded by sounds of what they thought were the prancing of horses, and the rattling of chariots. If the leprous men talked to each other (verse 3), the Syrians too, conversed together, and concluded that a mighty force was coming against them, one which had been hired by the almost exhausted Israelites. How a starving people could hire other nations to fight their cause, is beyond human reasoning but when people panic, reason seems to leave its throne. At the very time when the lepers were leaving the gate, the hosts of the Syrians were leaving their camp. The lepers left nothing at the gate, but the camp of the fleeing soldiers was left as it was, full of all the provisions required by an army.

The hungry four were quick to have their own appetites satisfied by eating and drinking what they found in the first empty tent. Their eyes must have sparkled, when they saw, not only food, but silver, gold and clothing. They valued this treasure so much that they hid it, lest someone else would come along and claim it. The second tent was also a treasure chest, so more stuff was seized by them, and more was hidden. At length their consciences began to smite them, and they concluded that their selfish handling of the trove was not good, so they decided to return to the city and tell the king's household what they had discovered.

The gate of the city was manned, so that none could go out, or go in, without being checked. When the lepers came and told their story, the porter passed it on to other porters, and these in turn told the king and his household. The suspicious mind of the king could only think that the move was a hoax of the enemy to draw the citizens out of the city and then to enter it when its defences were unmanned. To confirm the report messengers on horseback were dispatched, and these followed the trail of the fleeing soldiers until they reached the river Jordan. All the way was strewn with spoil that had been abandoned by the terrified host. On the return of these messengers and their report, the people who were so hungry, made their way to the deserted tents of the Syrians, and satisfied their hunger. With such supplies as were found, the quantity of meal was so plentiful, that the words of the prophet were proved to be true, for a measure of fine flour was sold for a shekel, and two measures of barley for the same price.

With the rush for such cheap food, as was then being brought into the city, the concourse at the gate must have been dense. The king appointed the lord upon whom he leaned, to take charge of the gate, and to control the hungry crowds, but the crush was so great that he was knocked down, and the people walked over him. Thus he died in the hour of deliverance. An excited mob is all but impossible to control, and those who would wish to stop and help the fallen are pushed on against their will, and are helpless to prevent such a tragedy. Just as sure as the prophecy of plenty was fulfilled, so sure was the prophecy of this man's death.

One feature of this part of Elisha's history is that it is not what he does that is mentioned, but what he said. In a sense the whole story of deliverance was miraculous, yet he did not take any outward part in it, nor do we read of him handling the spoil, or even going with the people to the enemy camp. The king and people of Samaria were made to feel that all the gods in whom they trusted were helpless to deliver, and that only the Lord could rescue them from the disaster they feared. Not until they were really at the point of despair, did deliverance come. This is often God's way with men, for even the sinner in conversion has to learn his helplessness before he will put his trust in the Lord.

Another principle demonstrated in this story is that God uses the least important instruments to do His service. Of all in Israel, these four lepers were among the most despised. They could take no credit for the great way in which the need was met, for it was not they who chased the Syrians, nor did they fight for the food they first ate. There will always be surprises in the work of God, for He is sovereign in the instruments He chooses, and often uses those who are considered to be the least amongst His people. Even Paul, whom we think was a great man, viewed himself differently, for he wrote, "Unto me, who am less than the least of all saints, is this grace given, that I should preach among the Gentiles the unsearchable riches of Christ" (Eph 3.8).

The sovereignty of God in his dealings with men is also exhibited in these verses. He not only caused the Syrians to hear noises which alarmed them, but deluded them to think of things which never happened. In this there is taught the lesson that the most wicked men on earth are not outside the control of God. He can in a short time change men to act in ways thought to be impossible. He not only struck the camp of the Syrians with panic, but overruled them, so that they left behind the very necessities the starving city required. Further, He even caused them to forsake the very treasures they had obtained by plunder, and those things which they previously had thought were really precious. Just as the Egyptians gave freely their treasures at the redemption of Israel, and enriched them with material which afterwards was used in the Tabernacle, so here, in a smaller way, the starving people were not only fed, but enriched as well.

The wrong of hiding good news has often been illustrated from the experience of the lepers. There were times when hiding was a virtue, such as when the parents of Moses hid him as a babe (Heb 11.23), and when Jehoshabeath hid Joash in the Temple (2 Chron 22.11). However, to hide what others are in dire need of having is not only selfish, but criminal. Those who have the treasure of the Gospel have a duty to make it known to their fellows, who are now in the same plight as they were in, before they were delivered.

The city of Samaria at this time is a picture of the siege of Jerusalem in a coming day. At the time of the Great Tribulation, it too will be surrounded by enemies, but the Lord descending upon the Mount of Olives, will bring deliverance (Zec 14), His coming will bring to an end the oppression of Israel by the nations and, as happened on this occasion, the wealth of the Gentiles will be brought through the gates of Jerusalem (Is 60.5,11).

Had the promise of cheap meal been made by a mortal man, then an excuse for unbelief could be expected, but for anyone to question the Lord's promise, is indeed a serious evil. The death of the officer on whom the king leaned demonstrates the seriousness of it. Many promises given to God's children seem to be all but impossible to fulfil. One example of this is the sudden resurrection of the saints at the Lord's coming, and the translation, at the same moment, of thousands of living saints to meet Him in the air. Who can explain how the commotion, which will inevitably ensue, will be overruled? The scoffer views such promises as fantasy, but as in this Lord's case, those who mock at these promises, will never share in the blessings which others, who do believe, will enjoy.

Notes

2 God had already opened the "windows" (AROOBBAH - 699) of heaven, when He poured out His judgment at the Flood (Gen 7.11). He also promised the returned remnant, that He would open the windows of heaven, and pour them out a blessing (Mal 3.10).

9 The word "good tidings" (BSOHRAH - 1309) is only here and in two other passages. (2 Sam 4.10; 2 Sam 18.20, 22, 25, 27).

CHAPTER 8, Verses 1-6
The Shunammite and the famine

Quite often troubles do not come singly, for the Shunammite woman had just passed through the ordeal of the death of her son (ch.4), and now she is faced with another trial, for a famine was nearing. This meant she had to leave all, and live for the duration of the famine, in a strange land. Being a "great woman", she probably owned quite a large establishment, so leaving it and its adjoining lands was no small trial. Furthermore, from this account the conclusion can be reached that in the meanwhile her husband had died, for he is not mentioned in this narrative. Life for this woman, who had been so good to the man of God, was full of changes. There was no such thing as her settling down and resting at ease.

The prophet, who had helped her in every difficulty, was concerned about her welfare during the approaching famine. He had assurance not only of its coming, but also of the time of its duration. Seven years was a long time, but God was punishing Israel for the constant drift to idolatry that prevailed. Both king and people were devoted to Baal worship, and just as Elijah had closed the heavens from raining for years, so now another period, this time of seven years duration, was approaching, when the land would likewise be without rain. While Elisha was not directly instrumental in bringing about this famine, yet its coming, and its duration were revealed to him by the Lord. The pity about this form of judgment is that it hits both the righteous and the wicked. The good-hearted Shunammite, as well as the prophet himself, would have to suffer the same trial as the rest of the nation.

His counsel to her was that she leave her estate, and find sustenance in some other land. He did not tell her where to go, but she chose to go to the land of the Philistines. Apparently this area was not affected by the drought, and apart from rain the mists and dew coming from the Mediterranean Sea would relieve the difficulty. No information is given regarding her experience while away, but as soon as she returned, she found herself in difficulties. Her estate had been taken over during her absence, and the new tenant was reluctant to return to her what was indeed her inheritance. A serious matter like this could only be resolved by the intervention of the king, so to him she made her appeal. Again we are shown the sovereignty of God, for just at the time of her arrival before the king, he was in deep conversation with Gehazi, the servant of Elisha. Whether for curiosity, or for some other reason, the king was anxious to learn all about Elisha's miracles, and none could tell him of these so clearly as Gehazi, for he was present when many of them were performed. His presence here, and intimate contact with the king, have caused many to think that what is said here took place before the healing of Naaman. If this is correct, the history is not written in strict chronological order. For a leper, as he undoubtedly was after the cleansing of Naaman, to be in intimate contact with the king, would be scarcely thinkable. As has been pointed out, some have kept to the chronological order, and assumed that Gehazi had been forgiven, and restored to health, but of this there is no information.

Just as Gehazi was relating the story of the resurrection of the dead boy, the mother and her son, who had been raised, came into view. The king was not only told the strange story, but now had the living proof of it before his eyes. However, the woman had not come to show the king her son, but to plead for the return of her lost property. Without hesitation the king arranged that a eunuch accompany her, to see that she not only had her estate returned, but that she would be compensated for all that it produced during her absence.

It could be imagined that those who are faithful stewards of what the Lord has entrusted to them, would be free from distress and annoyance, but this is not so. The Psalmist had this problem in Ps 73, and it has remained a difficulty until this present time. Sometimes the wicked seem to be enjoying better circumstances than the righteous. Those who advance in the school of God, discover that the higher they rise, the more difficult life becomes. They also prove, as this woman did, that in the trials of life, God is faithful, and provides for them in His own unexpected way. She feared that by obeying the prophet's advice, she was going not only to lose the produce of her estate, but the property as well, yet the Lord who took away her son, and gave him back again, gave her back both the estate and the value of the crops which it produced during her absence. Obedience to God's will may seem costly, but He is no man's debtor, and always works deliverance for His tried people.

What the world speaks of as mere coincidences, the child of God rightly views as the work of His overruling hand. He can time His providential workings in such a way that they are just available when needed. The ram was on the lonely mountain when needed by Abraham (Gen *22),* the fish was at the side of the ship to swallow Jonah (Jonah 1), and another fish had the stater in its mouth to pay the tax money for Peter (Matt 17). Similarly Gehazi was so controlled that he was speaking to the king concerning the raising of the boy, at the very moment when this same boy arrived with his mother. God can not only work, but time His work with precision.

Verses 7-15
Elisha visits Damascus
After the humiliation of the Syrian army by the hand of Elisha (ch.6.16-23*),* it is surprising that he would venture near Damascus the capital city. His presence there was opportune, for the king of Syria, Ben-hadad, was ill at this time, and like most people who are seriously sick, he was anxious to know whether he would recover, or die. He had absolute confidence in the word of the prophet, so having learned that he was visiting his city, he sent to him his servant, Hazael, to obtain the desired information. From the days of Saul, it was customary when anyone was seeking advice from a prophet, to bring a present. On this occasion the gifts were lavish, for they consisted of everything that was valuable and precious. These gifts were borne by forty camels, so they must have been considerable, even though each animal may only have carried a small quantity. Naaman, likewise brought lavish gifts (ch.5). When the question of Ben-hadad was put

to Elisha, "Shall I recover of this disease?" The answer was twofold. As regards the sickness it would not be fatal, but as regards his life, this was at an end, for the Lord had shown the prophet that the king would surely die.

Having announced the solemn verdict, there came into the prophet's mind, no doubt by divine revelation, the terrible consequences of the hour. The man who stood before him would be the future king of Syria, and would in his wars with Israel, execute the most heinous and cruel crimes upon the people. The burden of this coming disaster was so heavy that the prophet burst into tears as he grasped the reality of it. What he said that Hazael would do to his people was so outrageous that even Hazael himself thought only a dog, which was the lowest of animals, could stoop to such barbarity. As the vision of all these evils crossed the mind of the prophet he wept. This experience of the prophet was like Lord when He looked over the city of Jerusalem, and foreseeing its future, He wept (Luke 19). Likewise the gruesome sight of the ravishing of Elisha's people was heart-breaking for him.

When Hazael returned to the king, he told him only part of what the prophet had said, so deceiving him to think he would soon be well. However, the next day, he, by means of a wet cloth, smothered the king, and so fulfilled the latter part of Elisha's prophecy. This left Hazael free to take the kingdom, and apparently he was not confronted by any rival.

If the Ben-hadad here is the same man throughout these chapters, he must have now been an old man. He was a contemporary of Ahab who was twelve years dead at this time. Some think that "Ben-hadad" was a dynastic name like that of "Pharaoh", and that this was Ben-hadad the second, but no hint of this is given in the history.

CHAPTER 8.16-29

THE KINGDOM OF JUDAH   (A Parenthesis)

Verses 16-24

The reign of Jehoram

At this juncture the historian breaks his history of the deeds of Elisha, and turns his thoughts to Judah. He will return to his main theme at the beginning of the next chapter, so the present section can be viewed as a kind of parenthesis. It might be wondered what was going on in the southern kingdom during all the events that are narrated in the northern kingdom, so here is given a summary account of some of the happenings in Judah at this time. There has been no reference of these in this second book, but here the story is taken up from 1 Kings 22.50.

There is much confusion as to how long Jehoram actually reigned, for apparently the title "king" was conferred upon him while his father was alive. Sometimes his reign is counted from one date, and sometimes from another. He may have reigned eight years, but two of these could have been in conjunction with his father. The one great mistake in his life was his choice of Athaliah, the daughter of Ahab and Jezebel, to be his wife. This meant that the evil of Baal worship was introduced into Judah, and all the idolatrous evils associated with it. This marriage was, as has already been noticed, the means of bringing the two kingdoms together, so the sad spectacle of the good king Jehoshaphat joining affinity with the evil king Ahab is recorded. With an influential wife, as evil as her mother, there is no surprise in the statement that "Jehoram did evil in the sight of the Lord". Details of his evil ways are given in Chronicles, but not developed here. But for God's covenant with David, the kingdom would have been destroyed at this time, for the warning given by Moses (Deut 28.15-37), was not mere scaremongering, but was a sincere threat and prophecy of the sad consequences of turning to idols. The history of the nation proved these threats of judgment to be true. The light of David was still to shine, even though the wind of idolatry had almost blown it out.

Up until the reign of Jehoram, the Edomites had been under the sway of Judah, but this submission came to an end in his time, for they revolted, and put a king on their throne. In the days of David, Joab had conquered the Edomites (1 Kings 11.15), and though they revolted again, Jehoshaphat subdued them and appointed a governor over them (1 Kings 22.47). It is likely that Jehoram thought that he also could bring them into subjection, so he made an attempt to do this, which is recorded here. In the fight he was surrounded by the Edomites, and only managed to escape by breaking through their ranks in a night effort. They proved so powerful at this time, that his army left the battlefield, and returned to their homes. This brought to an end, any attempt by the kings of Israel or Judah to subdue Edom. Because of this, Libnah, another neighbouring country on the borders of Philistia, followed Edom's example, and also rebelled against Judah. In the days of Joshua, Libnah had a king (Jos 10.30), and its territory was allotted to Judah, and until this time it seemed to be content to be ruled by the house of David, but now this came to an end. With a brief reference to Jehoram's death, and burial, the historian ends his short account of this wicked king. In Chronicles there are more details of how he died, and as to where exactly he was buried (2 Chron 21).

Verses 25-29
The reign of Ahaziah

Like earlier kings, the exact time of the commencement of Ahaziah's reign is not easily settled, for here it is given as in the twelfth year of Jehoram, king of Israel, whereas, in chapter 9 we read that it was in the eleventh year (v.29). It could well be that he jointly reigned with his father for a year during his father's illness. His time on the throne was short, being only one year. He partook of the character of his mother, Athaliah, who was a granddaughter of Omri, the famous king of Israel, who built Samaria. His mother-in-law was Jezebel, wife of Ahab, so he was surrounded by the influence of Baal worship. Therefore we are not surprised that "he walked in the ways of the house of Ahab".

Like his grandfather, Jehoshaphat, he attempted along with the king of Israel to fight against Hazael, king of Syria, at the famous battleground, Ramoth-gilead. Jehoram, king of Israel, was wounded in the fight, and retired to Jezreel to recover from his wounds. With the principal king out of the war, the other naturally retired, so the fight was ended at this time. The king of Judah, as could be expected, went to Jezreel to visit his wounded fellow king, and the sequence of this visit is recorded in the next chapter.

The main lesson that can be learned from the brief history here given of these two kings is the evil of the "unequal yoke". That a son of Jehoshaphat would have sought a bride in the home of a wicked man like Ahab, is indeed amazing. This union was the root cause of many of the failures already considered. The sad consequences of Christians marrying unsaved partners are painful to consider. Those who venture on such a course of disobedience, bring trouble, not only into their own lives, but also into the lives of others. One thing made plain in these histories is that bringing Athaliah into the house of David, did not change her to be a true worshipper of the Lord, but her influence turned her partner into an idolater. He may have argued that she was an Israelite, and that he was not going to the Gentiles for a wife, but though she was a child of Abraham, she was not one of his daughters, for she was destitute of faith in God. The snare to many true believers is the possibility of entering the unequal yoke, by wedding a mere professor, and learning later of the deception.

Another striking fact most impressive in the history of the kings of Israel and Judah, is that whatever ventures they combined to make, these all ended in failure. Surely God was demonstrating that He cannot bless the efforts of those who worship Baal, even though they are accompanied by those who worship the Lord.

Notes

4 The fact that Gehazi here is spoken of as "the servant of the man of God" seems to strengthen the idea that this famine was over before the healing of Naaman (ch.5).

8 The idea of paying the prophet for information seems to have begun in the days of Samuel (1 Sam 9.7), yet it is significant that he is the one prophet, who claimed that he had not enriched himself by taking from the people (1 Sam 12.3).

19 "light" (NEER or NEHR - 5216) means a "lamp", which is a centre of light. See 1 Kings 11.36; 15.4; and 2 Chron 21.7.

26 Just as David was the outstanding name in Judah, so apparently Omri was the most famous of the kings of Israel. This may explain why Ahab his son is passed over, and his daughter is referred to as the daughter of her grandfather.

CHAPTER 9, Verses 1-13
Jehu is anointed king over Israel

After the brief review of the history of Judah under the reign of Jehoram, and the reign of Ahaziah, the historian returns to his leading theme. He proceeds to tell us of yet another prophetic mission emanating from Elisha. This is the last reference to the prophet's ministry until we come to chapter 13 where we learn of his closing words as he lies on his deathbed. All that intervenes is the fulfillment of his message given here, and is recorded to show that what he predicted, did really come to pass. In a sense, he is here completing the work of Elijah, for the commission given to Elijah to anoint Jehu king over Israel (1 Kings 19.16), was not executed by him personally, but was ordered to be done by his successor. Likewise Elisha instead of doing it himself, directed one of the sons of the prophets to go to Ramoth-gilead, and perform this important duty. The son of the prophet, after some searching, found Jehu surrounded by his brethren, just as he had been told he would find him. However, the anointing was to be done in private, so he took Jehu out of their midst, and into an inner chamber, where he emptied the flask of oil upon his head, and said to him, "Thus saith the Lord God of Israel, I have anointed thee king...over Israel". The purpose of his anointing was not only that he should rule the nation, but also that he would be instrumental in removing for ever the house of Ahab. God had patiently borne with the evil deeds of that wicked house, but the time of its judgment had come, and all the threats uttered against it were about to be executed. The cruel treatment of God's servants, and the fostering of the worship of Baal in the land, so that only a remnant was serving the true God, and doing so at the risk of their lives, had filled the cup of Ahab's house, and left it ripe for destruction.

When Jehu returned from the inner chamber into the presence of his court, he was questioned about what had happened. His army judged the son of the prophets to be mad. Obviously his boldness, and hasty demands, seemed to them to be the characteristics of one out of his mind. Jehu concluded that the captains already knew what had taken place, and that there had been some collusion between his servants and the young man who had just fled. They denied this, and said that it was a false idea. When satisfied that they knew nothing of the transaction, he openly confessed to them that he had been anointed king. Their response was unanimous, and without further questioning, they took off their outer robes, folded them as a cushion, and set him on the stairs as a makeshift throne, blew their trumpets, and loudly proclaimed in his ears, "Jehu is king".

Just as the evils of Jeroboam and the house of Baasha had been removed from the throne of Israel, so at this time the house of Ahab was likewise to be destroyed. The passing of time had not wiped out the memory of the past evils, for though God may appear to be slow to act, yet He does fulfill His words in His own time.

It might be imagined that only God-fearing men would be employed by God to execute His will, but this is not so. Jehu, who had much zeal for the Lord, and would at times appear to be aware of the divine will, was not a true servant of God, for he worshipped the golden calves which Jeroboam had made. He was less wicked than Ahab and Jezebel, yet seemed to have a zeal for shedding blood, and a pleasure in executing the wrath of God upon the guilty. It should have dawned upon him, that God was no respecter of persons. If He judged the evils of past kings, He would not pass over the evils of those who were the instruments used to administer the Judgment. Here it is shown that dealing with the evils of others in any sphere (even in an assembly), in no way excuses doing evil of a less serious character. While Jehu avenged the innocent blood shed by Ahab and his sons, yet the blood he shed was likewise avenged (Hos 1.4).

Like all former kings of Israel who had contact with the prophets of God, he never sought the help of Elisha in his administration of the kingdom. He ruled as though God did not exist, and as though His servants were of no value to him. Once the oil was upon his head, Jehu was happy to let the prophet go away without even asking him for guidance or help in the execution of the prophecy concerning the annihilation of the house of Ahab.

Verses 14-29
Jehu assassinates Joram and Ahaziah

As soon as Jehu was anointed king, and acclaimed by his captains, he proceeded to execute the prophecy against the house of Ahab. He was most anxious that none of the inhabitants of Ramoth-gilead would slip out of the city and go to Jezreel, because Jehoram the king was in that city, recovering from his wounds.

He was afraid lest someone should tell the king of his anointing. Well he knew that his success lay in taking the sick king by surprise, and reaching him before any opposition could be assembled. In haste to execute his warrant to slay the king he left the city in the hands of his trusted officers, mounted his chariot, and began the journey to Jezreel where the one he sought was dwelling. No doubt he was followed by his host of charioteers, for it would seem that the entire retinue, like their master, were carried in chariots.

Ahaziah, the king of Judah, who was an nephew of the king of Israel was no doubt interested in the recovery of his uncle, and had gone to visit him in Jezreel (ch.8.29). This meant that, in the providence of God, the two kings were together at the time when Jehu approached Jezreel. They had been fighting together at the time when Joram was wounded, and now they are about to die together. Neither of them suspected any danger when first informed of the approaching host, nor did even the second messenger, who also was prevented from returning to them, arouse any grave suspicions in their minds. They probably assumed that Jehu was coming with some special news about Ramoth-gilead, or to tell them of some fresh attack of the Syrians. In their simplicity they mounted separate chariots, and went out to meet the approaching army. Again the providence of God is seen in that this meeting took place beside the plot of ground which Ahab had taken from Naboth. It must have been near to the king's palace.

Just as the messengers had inquired "Is it peace?", so when the kings met Jehu they too asked the same question. The answer they received, was sufficient to alert them to the danger they had encountered. Jehu's words, "What peace, so long as the whoredoms of thy mother Jezebel...are so many?" The treachery was at length discovered, and their only hope was to attempt to escape. Though the chariot of Jehoram was turned, yet he was not spared, for Jehu lifted his bow and fired a dart into his heart, so he sank into the well of his chariot and died. The king of Judah likewise sought to escape, and made some progress in doing so, but he too was overtaken and severely wounded. He was taken to Megiddo where he died, and thus suffered the same fate as his fellow king.

There was a distinct difference in the way the two dead bodies were treated. As for Joram, his remains were cast into the field of Naboth where the dogs could devour it. This was in fulfillment of the words of Elijah, for though the threat was made to Ahab, yet it was suspended until his son's death, because the former had shown some remorse for his evil deeds (1 Kings 21.29). The king of Judah was treated differently. His body was carried in a chariot to Jerusalem and buried in one of the royal tombs with his fathers.

While Jehu had no direct warrant to execute the king of Judah, yet in killing him, he was still dealing with the house of Ahab, for his mother was a daughter of Ahab, and he followed in her ways. In this part of Israel's history there is shown the sad consequences of the marriage of a daughter of the king of Israel to one of the kings of Judah. The unequal yoke ended the war between the two parts of the nation, but it brought a harvest of sorrow that no words could fully tell. As already pointed out, not one of the joint efforts of the two kingdoms working together ever was successful. God seemed to show them that He was not prepared to bless the northern kings, and wink at their wicked idolatrous practices, just because they were accompanied by kings who feared Him.

Verses 30-37
Jezebel is killed

It seems likely that Jehu in person pursued Ahaziah to the hill of Gur, and gave the order to the soldier who fired the arrow which fatally wounded him. All this must have taken several hours to accomplish. Here the words "when he was come to Jezreel" show that he returned to where he had slain Joram. This was more than sufficient time for the tragic news to have spread throughout the palace. Jezebel was no doubt living with her son at this time of his illness. No doubt her hope was that he would recover from the wounds he had received when fighting the Syrians. Jehu was intent on entering the palace and taking possession of all that formerly belonged to Joram. As he entered the gate, Jezebel looked out at him, through an open window. She had decorated herself for the occasion, but for what reason, is difficult to say. Some have suggested that by painting her eyes, and arranging her hair, she was seeking to captivate Jehu and win his affection, but this is highly improbable. Others think that she was expecting that when he saw her he would show her some pity and spare her. Possibly her intention was to let him see that she was not mourning the loss of her son, nor sitting in sack-cloth. She stood in bold defiance, and as brazen as it was possible for her to be. Her words to Jehu were far from conciliatory, "Is it peace thou Zimri, thy master's murderer?" (RV). She can see that Jehu was repeating the doings of Zimri, and calls him by that name. Full well she knew that there was no hope of any pity being shown to her by the usurper. As soon as she had called out, Jehu shouted, "Who is on my side?" Then two or three eunuchs, who looked out of the same window, responded by obeying the call to throw her down. She fell down, the palace wall was splashed with her blood, and some of it was sprinkled on the horses of Jehu's chariot. Without the slightest respect for her dead body, the chariot rode on and the horses trampled underfoot her mangled remains.

After such a heavy day of action Jehu must have been feeling hungry, and somewhat exhausted, so he entered the palace and satisfied his hunger and thirst. When he had eaten and drunk, he remembered the body of the dead queen and gave orders that it should be buried. This action was not because of her personal virtues, for she had none, but because she was the daughter of a king. However, when her corpse was sought, nothing could be found but her skull, hands, and feet. The dogs had devoured the softer parts, and only those pieces, which had little to offer them, were allowed to remain. The skull which contained the brain where her evil devices were framed, the hands which wrought wickedness, and the feet which trod her wicked way, were all that could be gathered up. Her unparalleled end brought back to the mind of Jehu the prophecy of Elijah, and caused him to repeat what the prophet had said, and to develop it with details which do not occur in the account given in 1 Kings 21.23.

Jezebel must be one of the most evil women mentioned in Scripture. She not only devised evil, but was successful in executing it. Innocent blood flowed freely at her command, and servants of the Lord filled early graves through her persecutions. She evidently had not won the respect of her closest servants, for they threw her out, as though they were glad to be rid of her. Much of the cruel activity of Ahab was instigated by her, and though he was also wicked, yet he was made more so by her influence. When the Lord rebukes the church at Thyatira for its idolatrous tendencies, He uses her name to mark out, under the figure of a woman, those in it who were seducing His servants. No doubt she is symbolic, and represents the principle of corrupt teaching manifested in the church of Rome, where idolatry and Christianity are mixed together. Just as Israel was ruled by Jezebel, although Ahab was King, so the church rules the Romish system, even though the name of Christ is included in it. Just as she was a persecutor of the faithful, so the church of Rome has slain thousands of the faithful throughout the present era. Even to this day, the Gospel is opposed in many lands where Rome holds sway, so Jezebel in her modern form has not repented, but continues with her evil ways.

Notes

3 Just as David was anointed privately before he was publicly proclaimed king, so Jehu was anointed in secret. He had not as long to wait as had David, for he was immediately accepted as king by those surrounding him. Not all kings in Israel were anointed. It would appear that only when a new dynasty was taking power, or when the throne was in dispute. was this ceremony performed. The "box" or "flask" (PACH - 6378) here used was the same type of vessel as Samuel used when anointing Saul (1 Sam 10.1).

11 the term "mad" (SHAHGAG - 7696) means to "rave" or "play the fool". A special example of its use is in the case of David, when he played the fool before the Philistines (1 Sam 21.14-15). It occurs three times in these verses.

20 Jehu drives "furiously" (SHIGGAHGOHN - 7697) or as a "madman". The word is akin to the word "mad' v.11.

22 The twin evils of Joram and his house were idolatry and witchcraft. The former is here called "whoredom" because it was spiritual unfaithfulness to the Lord. The latter was the "unlawful communications" which was closely associated with idolatry. The word "witchcraft" (KSHAHPHEEM - 3785) comes from a root meaning "to whisper", and is found also in Is 47.9,12; Mic 5.12; and Nah 3.4.

30 Jezebel most likely painted her eyes with black dye. This was thought to increase their brilliancy. Her hair was given due attention and made "good looking". The word translated "tired" (YAHTAV - 3190) simply means "good" or "well", so we cannot tell from it what treatment she gave her hair.

CHAPTER 10, Verses 1-11

The destruction of the house of Ahab

Jehu having gained supremacy in Jezreel, proceeded to gain the same authority in Samaria. As it was the royal city, and the centre of administration in the nation, there was one essential, if he was to reign as king. His authority must be established in the palace where the throne was situated. Though both the king of Israel, and the king of Judah were at Jezreel, this was more like a holiday home, where they could relax, but it was not the capital city, nor was it the real seat of power, so its capture was of limited significance. He did not go directly to Samaria, and show his power there, as he had done at Jezreel. His plan was to avoid any conflict with the heirs to the throne, for this would have meant a civil war, and one that could have been costly in the loss of life. He therefore, sent a letter to Samaria, and in it made a challenge to the rulers to set upon the throne the most suited successor to the slain king. In it he flattered them by stressing the resources at their disposal which would enable them to accomplish this feat. They were in a defenced city, they had chariots and horses, and all that would equip an army for battle. However, the men of Samaria were cowards, and concluded that they had no hope of defending themselves against a man who had slain two kings. They never took into account that the two kings were slain by treachery, and that they did not go out prepared for battle, at the time when they met Jehu. The letter sent in reply contained all that he desired, for it was in fact a statement of complete surrender. A second letter from Jehu followed, which demanded the heads of the seventy sons of Ahab to be brought to Jezreel the next day. They were granted no time to consider the matter, so, in their plight, they began immediately to execute these princes, and to collect their heads into baskets. These were brought to Jezreel where they were piled in two heaps at the gate of the city. Thus in the most public place, the gruesome sight of these two heaps, would confront all who entered the city.

Jehu in a subtle way sought to exonerate himself from all responsibility in slaying these seventy, for this was the implication of his question, "Who slew these?" While he did not actually execute these princes, yet they were slain at his demand, so he slew them with the swords of the elders of Samaria. As in his other occasions of destruction at this time, he was careful to point out that all this shedding of royal blood was in fulfillment of the word of the Lord through Elijah.

Without stating how many friends and priests were slain at this time, the historian, in a summary way, shows that all who had either blood relationship, or were merely friends of the house of Ahab, were put to death. His priests were included in the toll, so that his religious leaders, as well as his rulers, were wiped out.

Verses 12-14
The princes of Judah are slain

On the journey from Jezreel to Samaria Jehu met the princes of Judah, who were on a friendly visit to Samaria. They may not have been aware of the happenings in the capital at this time, or they may have been coming to it to learn the true state of things. Frankly they declare the purpose of their journey, and are immediately taken prisoner. However, when they reached the pit of the shearing house, they were slain, and treated as though they were of the kings of Israel. Because they were related to Ahab through his daughter, Athaliah, who was their mother, they had to suffer the same fate as those who lived in Samaria. Some of these forty-two men may have been grandsons, for Ahaziah would hardly have had so many sons.

Verses 15-17
Jehonadab joins Jehu

Whether Jehonadab went on a special errand to meet Jehu, or whether the meeting was unexpected, is not stated, but both leaders were evidently pleased with each other. The former was the leader of an ascetic tribe which had accompanied Israel from the time of Moses. It would seem that Hobab, who said he would not go with Israel into Canaan, must have changed his mind at the request of Moses (Num 10), for throughout the nation's history these people were sojourning in it. They had certain laws which they obeyed, even until the time of Jeremiah. They abstained from wine, from cultivating the land, and lived in tents (Jer 35). Obviously these people had no regard for Baal, nor for the ways of the house of Ahab, for they appeared to appreciate the man who would rid the land of these evils. A respected man like Jehonadab was an asset to Jehu, and would help to build the confidence of the people in the new ruler, causing them to think of him as a true reformer. When Jehu asked "Is thy heart right?" he desired to learn if there was true harmony between them, and that his zeal for the Lord had the approval of this important leader. Upon hearing an affirmative answer. Jehu took his friend by the hand, and caused him to ride with him in his chariot.

There must have been some remaining in Samaria of the house of Ahab, for here a further slaughter is mentioned. Possibly this included the female members of it, who like Athaliah, in the southern kingdom, were supporters of the regime of Ahab. When we consider the influence of Jezebel, and note that she was so influential in the kingdom, we can well understand that even the women, if spared, could prove dangerous to the new ruler.

Verses 18-28
The destruction of the worshippers of Baal

Closely linked with the house of Ahab was the worship of Baal. His wife had brought this idolatry from her own land, and had gone to great lengths to establish it as the national religion of Israel. To allow this corrupt form of worship to continue would have been a memorial to those who had introduced it. Jehu was determined to rid the land of all such idolatry, and also of the priests who were its chief supporters. In order to exterminate the whole system, he announced a special day of celebration of Baal, thus bringing together the entire band of worshippers. No one could commend the deceitful way in which he sought to bring this about, for he gave the impression that he himself was a devout worshipper of the idol, and that all the resources of the kingdom would be at the disposal of those who would likewise be worshippers. With all the pomp and vestments which normally mark worldly religion, the house of Baal was crowded, and the burnt offerings were offered. Just then the army of Jehu moved in, and slew the entire company. Not one was spared. However, before the executions, great pains were taken to assure that there were none amongst the crowd, who was not a worshipper of Baal. On such spectacular events there is ever the possibility of someone slipping into the company, out of mere curiosity. With the solemn consequences, which were involved on this occasion, the risk that any such was present, had to be carefully avoided.

Not only were the worshippers of Baal put to death, but his house, or temple, and all its contents were destroyed. There were pillars erected to his honour, which were probably made of wood, and these were burnt. One special pillar, which was erected outside the house, may have been a stone structure, so it was broken down and destroyed. What was formerly the seat of worship became the receptacle of all the waste and filth of the city. While other forms of idolatry may have risen in the northern kingdom, yet there is no mention of Baal worship being practised during its remaining years.

Verses 29-36
Jehu's reign and his failings

Although Jehu reigned twenty eight years, yet only a brief summary of his history is given, and one which emphasises his failings. His destruction of the house of Ahab was appreciated by God, and as a reward, he was promised that his seed to the fourth generation would sit upon the throne of Israel. Thus his posterity was the only one in Israel that was allowed this favour. The longest of the other dynasties in Israel extended to three generations, and lasted about half the time of his. Although he executed God's judgment on the house of Ahab, this in no way proved that his heart was right with the Lord. Indeed his ruthless killing seemed to be gratifying to his soul. While he claimed zeal for the Lord, yet he acted in a very callous, and at times, deceitful manner. His entire reign was destitute of anything constructive, or commendable, and shows that God can use instruments to fulfill His purpose, even some who are not sanctified, nor in fellowship with Him.

Jehu destroyed one form of idolatry, but turned to another which, to him, did not appear to be as evil, for it claimed to have some relationship with the God of Israel. He should have known, however, that the calf worship of Jeroboam was hateful and sinful in the eyes of the Lord, for a prophet of the Lord had denounced it, and even put a curse upon it (1 Kings 13.2-5). The calf worship of Jeroboam was more alluring to one who was reared in idolatry. It did imitate some of the features of the worship of the Temple at Jerusalem, and at the same time provided what every idolater desires, a visible object of worship.

It is one thing to destroy evil rule, but quite another to establish a good and prosperous kingdom. Jehu did well in removing the corruptions of the house of Ahab, but had he walked in the fear of God, and in submission to His will, he would have been a tower of strength in the nation. He should have learned from what befell Ahab's house, that the God of Elijah, whose prophecies he often quoted, is to be feared, and obeyed. Instead of his reign being a time of prosperity in Israel, it was the occasion for it to be cut short. The enemy on the north, Syria, had been successful in sweeping down through the land and claiming possession of the territory east of Jordan. The loss of such fertile land, and the helplessness of Israel to resist the invaders were the result of Jehu's disregard for the law of God, and his confidence in his idols. Although he was a mighty man, and had proved this in his early days, yet he was no blessing to the nation, nor was he as prosperous as might be expected. He left behind him a greatly reduced kingdom, so his son, Jehoahaz, while retaining the throne, had much to discourage him.

A look back over the story of Jehu would bring to mind some serious lessons. One of these is that it is important to carry out God's judgment as He demands, but at the same time to do it in the right spirit. It is sad when any one finds all his pleasure in putting down what is wrong. Quite often when those who have demanded that evil should be dealt with, are put into a place of responsibility, they become guilty of some other evil, perhaps not so heinous, yet nonetheless grieving to the

Lord. It is possible to do the will of God in dealing with others, and at the same time not to be careful to obey His will in one's own life. Again it can be noted in this story that the might of any man is useless in defending the inheritance, unless he is supported by the Lord. Had the Lord been with Jehu in his conflicts with Hazael, his kingdom would have remained intact.

Notes

1 The "sons" here must include his descendants such as grand-sons. The expression "rulers of Jezreel" appears to some to be a mistake, for "rulers in Samaria", but these officers were probably from Jezreel, and at this time were living at Samaria.

14 "The pit of the shearing house" may have been a "cistern" or "well" which provided water for the sheep which were gathered there for shearing. Possibly the bodies of the slain friends of Ahaziah were thrown into it, as was the case in Jer 41.7.

19 "Jehu did it in "subtilty" (GOKBAH - 6122) used only here. It means to act in trickery.

22 The use of the word "vestry" (MELTAHGHAH - 4458), implies that there was a "wardrobe" connected with the temple of Baal where the vestments of the priests were kept. The word is used only here.

27 A "draught house" (MOHTZAHOHTH - 4163) from a root meaning "going forth", so here it has the meaning of "sewer", The only other occurrence of this word is in Mic 5.2, where we read, "whose 'goings forth' have been of old".

CHAPTER 11, Verses 1-3

Athaliah slays the seed royal, but Joash is rescued

For a second time, the historian turns his mind from events at Samaria, and directs it to the happenings at Jerusalem. Elisha is still alive at this time, but plays no part in these things. His ministry was mainly confined to the northern kingdom. The death of the young king, Ahaziah, was a heavy blow to the southern kingdom, and one specially felt by his mother. She no doubt expected him to continue the reign of the house of David. Her wicked heart decided that if he had been swept from the throne, none of his brothers would fill his shoes. In her rage, she rose up, and slew all the seed royal, and placed herself on the throne. This was the first, and only occasion, when a woman was queen of Judah. Her reign was short, but it did last for six years. Those slain by her must have been of her own kindred, and many of them quite young. Such children should have been precious in her eyes, but she had inherited the character of her mother, Jezebel, so blood-shedding, and cruelty were in keeping with her inherent nature. In these massacres she was, unknown to herself, helping to exterminate the house of her father, Ahab.

It was a sad day for Judah when Jehoram married a daughter of Ahab and Jezebel, for it resulted in the house of David being corrupted with the idolatrous practices of the northern kingdom. In her slaughter of these descendants of David, there was an attempt by Satan to exterminate the line which led from him to Christ. This would have meant that the promise made to him, that the throne would always be filled by one of his descendants, would have been broken. However, God would not allow such a thing to happen, so He, in a providential way overruled and prevented it, as shall be seen in the story. It must have been beyond the dreams of any in Israel that the time would come when one of the house of Ahab would sit on David's throne, and do so, with supreme authority. For six years she wielded the sceptre, and advanced the worship of Baal, which she and her late husband had introduced into Judah. With a temple for Baal and its images, together with a priesthood officiating at its worship, the distinction between the religious beliefs of the two kingdoms was almost obliterated. It must be concluded that good Jehoshaphat, when he joined affinity with Ahab, and sanctioned the marriage of his son to Athaliah, could not have foreseen the dreadful harvest which had to be reaped from this sowing.

It is all but needless to stress the seriousness of the "unequal yoke", but if some think lightly of it, this story should prove to them that it is by no means a trifling matter. There were good and faithful men in Jerusalem at this time. None of these had the slightest influence on the mind of Athaliah. She changed many in Judah, but none in Judah was able to convert her to the God of Israel. Over the course of Israel's history, Gentiles were brought into sweet relationship with the nation, such as Rahab, and Ruth, both of whom were married to Israelite husbands, but they were converted to God, before they were taken as wives, so this made all the difference.

There is always something thrilling about the overruling hand of God, especially at a time of great crisis. He never fails to have His instruments ready and willing to act in fulfillment of His purpose. Athaliah may have thought that all the house of David was destroyed, and that the promise made to him, that he would perpetually have an heir on the throne of Israel, was at length proved to be an empty dream. However, she was truly mistaken, for God preserved a little infant in the secrecy of His house, who would be spared to rule, and fill an honoured place in the history of the nation. In Athaliah's attempt to wipe out the house of David, there is shown that behind her cruel scheme was Satan, who ever seeks to resist the purposes of God for His Son.

In the providence of God, the high priest, Jehoiada, had married a daughter of king Jehoram, who was a brother of Ahaziah. Her name was Jehosheba, and she was the chosen instrument ordained of God to save the situation at this time. In direct opposition to Athaliah's scheme, she stole a little infant son of her brother, or half brother, Ahaziah, (for she was a daughter of Jehoram, but not of Athaliah) and hid him, together with his nurse, in the house of God. Because she was the wife of the high-priest, she had access to the sleeping accommodation of the Temple, and had no difficulty in concealing her treasure from the cruel hand of Athaliah. As long as the priests were favourable to her, she had no fear from any other quarter, for none but those of the house of Levi were permitted into these bed-chambers. It was a unique experience for a child and his nurse to be imprisoned for six years, for this meant that they were cut off from society. However, there is no mention that this secretive and unnatural mode of nursing had any detrimental effect on the child's health.

Verses 4-12

Joash is anointed king

Jehoiada and his wife Jehosheba must have thought the time long as they waited patiently for the day to arrive when the true king would be enthroned. Athaliah probably never suspected that her position as queen was insecure. She had not the slightest knowledge of the plot devised by Jehoiada that would bring it to an end. One obvious fact is that her rule had failed to win the hearts of her subjects, and those very men, who should have been her true guardians, were quick to join the insurrection. The high priest, whose normal duties lay in the realm of sacrifices and offering incense, became on this occasion, more like the commander-in-chief of an army. Well he knew that without the help of the army he could not succeed in making Joash king. With little difficulty he secured the help of the royal body-guard, but that was not sufficient to make his scheme a success, so he went throughout the nation and gathered the Levites to the Temple and turned them into a military force. If they were to function as defenders of the young king, they must be armed, so the weapons stored in the Temple, from the days of David, were brought out. These became the equipment of this newly formed guard. The gathering of Levites to the Temple would not have aroused suspicion in the palace that anything unusual was afloat, for their service was normally in the house of God.

At length the day arrived when the great event of the king being crowned took place. With the guards set around the palace, and the Temple guards stretching from wall to wall of its court, the child of seven years was brought out and presented to the great assembly. It can scarcely be imagined how he felt as he stood, for the first time in his life, in the midst of an armed host and all the high officials of the realm. All eyes must have centred on him as he stood at the base of one of the pillars. The oil was poured upon his head, the crown, possibly of gold, placed upon him, and the testimony, part of the Law, put into his little hand. How much a lad of his age would understand of the significance of this ceremony is difficult to assess. All must have been like a dream to him, especially so, as he had been kept in seclusion all his life. It speaks well for his nurse, that in spite of his abnormal ordeal at this time, not a hint of any faltering on his part is mentioned.

There are a number of typical suggestions which appear in this story, for like all past history, it foreshadowed things to come. The hidden king is a reminder of the One at God's right hand, the true heir to the throne, but not yet revealed. Only those in the Temple saw the crowned king, so the glorified Christ is not seen on earth, but at God's right hand. The influence of the high priest at this time, speaks of the Melchisedec character of Christ's rule, for "He shall be a priest upon His throne" (Zec 6.13). Just as the wicked rule of Athaliah preceded the rule of the rightful king, so the Antichrist will hold sway in Jerusalem before Christ comes to claim His kingdom. The host around Joash is a picture of the "ten thousand of His saints" (Jude 14), who will accompany the Lord at his coming. From the birth of the king, until his enthronement was a period of seven years, or a week of years, so before Christ sits on David's throne there will be a special week of years (Dan 9), and during this period the faithful will be persecuted. The link between the "crown" and the "testimony" suggests that the rule of the true king will be in accordance with the word of God, for every matter in the coming kingdom will be decided by what is written therein.

There are some links between this passage and Rev 12. There a child is brought forth who is to rule all nations, yet the dragon was ready to devour the child as soon as it was born. Likewise here we have a ruler who was almost destroyed as soon as he was born. Just as Joash was hidden and nourished in the Temple, so the man-child was caught up into heaven, and remains hidden there until the time of His manifestation.

Verses 13-16
The death of Athaliah

The palace where Athaliah dwelt was close by the Temple, so there is no surprise that the noise and excitement surrounding the new king was heard by her. When she came to investigate what was in progress, she was met by a surprising sight. Standing beside the pillar, where he had been anointed, was young Joash with the crown on his head. She immediately realized what had transpired, and screamed out in her distress, "Treason, treason". Jehoiada, who was in charge of the proceedings, gave orders that she be conducted outside the Temple precincts, and that her blood be not spilt on its holy ground. If any dared to take sides with her and followed her, they were sentenced to death, but apparently not one of her guards, or servants moved to her defence. She was led to the ramp where the horses entered the stables of the palace, and there slain. Her end, like that of her mother, was indeed sad, but nonetheless justly deserved, for she had been instrumental in bringing much evil into the kingdom of Judah.

It would be reasonable to expect that when Athaliah had heard of all that befell her parent's house in Israel at the hand of Jehu, she would have seen that Baal was a helpless god, who could in no way defend his worshippers. The God of Israel could protect the life of a helpless infant. Her god could not shield her from the sword of her own officers, even though she was in full vigour. Idolaters are slow to learn the impotency of their gods, and cling to them as though they were realities.

Verses 17-21
The covenant of Jehoiada

When Baal worship was introduced into Judah, the relationship between the Lord and the nation had been gravely weakened. Jehoiada felt that a new covenant should be made to re-establish the nation into normal fellowship with the true God. In this, he was following the example of Joshua, who, at the time of his end, made a covenant with the nation, that they would serve the Lord only (Josh 24.25). Conditions in Jerusalem were returning to normality. With the heir of David as king, with the word of God obeyed, and with judgment executed on all that was contrary to Him, the recovery was indeed a thing of wonder.

If the covenant with God was to be kept, then the destruction of Baal worship was essential, so the people of the land destroyed the house of Baal, slew Mattan the priest of Baal, and smashed the images which were in the house. All of the Zidonian idolatry which Athaliah had introduced in Jerusalem, and which her mother had brought into Israel, was cleared out, and the Lord alone acknowledged as the God to be worshipped.

When Athaliah, and all that she represented, had been removed, the time had arrived when it would be safe to establish the young king in his palace. The captains and leaders of the land brought him down to the royal house, and sat him upon the throne. He was now no longer a king in hiding, but publicly occupying the highest seat in the land. Most likely this was the same throne as the one made by Solomon, so he was filling a post of great responsibility, as well as one of great honour. The entire country was thrilled with what had transpired, and even the city, where the insurrection had taken place, was calm. The corrupt queen killed, and the rightful heir on the throne, marked a turning point in the nation, and in this case, a turning in the right direction.

One fact made plain in these verses, and one which at times is overlooked is that if there be a desire to establish what pleases God, it must include the destruction of what is contrary to Him. To allow the evil worship of Baal to continue would have left a strong temptation for some in the nation to go back to it. True love of the Lord, means to truly hate what He hates. Grace may be sought to tolerate the weaknesses in one another, but to allow this principle to operate with reference to gross evil, would be the road to disaster.

Just as the time arrived for Joash to sit on the throne, so the time is coming when Christ, the hidden king, will come down from heaven and sit on His throne. The words of His Father "Yet have I set My King upon My holy hill of Zion" will then be fulfilled (Ps 2.6). He will rule, not only over Israel, but He will hold universal sway, so that His name will be known to the ends of the earth.

Notes

5-7 The five companies of soldiers were distributed to their respective duties. Three were posted at strategic points around the palace, and two were in charge of the Temple, where the young king was in hiding. The expression "that it be not broken down" (v.6) is difficult. The word "broken down" (MASSAHCH - 4535) occurs only here, but the idea of "guarding", or "defending" the house seems to be the most probable meaning.

8 The defence of the king was paramount in the mind of Jehoiada. King Solomon is viewed as having his body guard of sixty warriors, all armed with swords, and experienced in battle (Song of Songs 3.7-8). Had any harm come to the child, all the organizing of the revolt would have been in vain. In the parallel passage in Chronicles, the Levites played a major part in the defence of the king, but they are not mentioned in these verses (2 Chron 23.7-8).

10 The "shields" (SHEHLET - 7982) were stored in the Temple where much spoil taken from the conquered enemies was deposited for safe keeping. It is improbable that these shields were the brass ones made as a substitute for the gold ones, for they were more for display, than for practical purposes (1 Kings 14.26). A different word is used for them.

CHAPTER 12, Verses 1-3

Joash reigns in Jerusalem

A brief summary of the reign of Joash (also called Jehoash) is given in these verses. He was contemporary with Jehu, but no mention here is made of any relationship between the divided nation. Without mentioning the sad failures of the latter part of his reign, the historian simply tells us that he did well during the life-time of the high priest, Jehoiada. As has been already seen, the chief influence in the early days of the young king was this godly man. Unlike his father and grandfather, who were influenced by evil women, he was favoured to be in good company, and preserved from idolatry by it. Perhaps he leaned too much on the old man, and this meant that when the prop was removed, he fell down.

Earlier it has been noted that it was almost impossible for even good kings to remove the high places of worship. These were not idolatrous high places, but were erected to save the people travelling to the true centre and worshipping God in His appointed place. Toleration of these was probably viewed as of small importance, for the sacrifices offered in them were to the Lord, as was also the incense.

It is obvious from these verses the importance of, and the indebtedness to, good company. The high priest had not been swayed by the Baal worship of the king and his wife. He had sought to carry on when much was against him, and left behind a fragrant testimony, one which all should seek to emulate. Likewise it is shown here, that those who can be influenced for good, can also be influenced in the wrong direction. Only when those upon whom men depend are removed, do they manifest their true convictions, and, as was true in the case of Joash, their weaknesses.

Verses 4-16
Joash seeks to have the Temple repaired
It would be expected that Jehoiada the priest would have been concerned about the state of the Temple, and that he would have been foremost in having it repaired. However, it was rather the young king who undertook this work, and persisted with it, until it was completed. The fact that it was his home in his infancy may have influenced his thinking, or the fact that it was the scene where the Levites and priests were his chief supporters when he was crowned, may have made him feel his indebtedness to them and the house where they served. Whatever his motive, he deserves credit for his zeal in this project.

There were three sources from which the funds to do the renovation could be obtained. Firstly, there was the half-shekel which was paid at every census time (Ex 30.12-16). But as this was very seldom, the amount to come from it was sure to be little. Second the redemption money, which came from the redemption of the firstborn (Num 18.15), and from those who made vows (Lev 27.2-8). Third there were the freewill offerings of the people. The first two sources would have yielded little, so the last collection must have been the chief means of obtaining the needed finance. The damage done to the house must have been extensive, for it is mentioned in 2 Chron 24.7 that "the sons of Athaliah...had broken up the house of God".

For reasons not stated the priests had not shown much zeal in the project, nor had the work been done as fast as the king expected. How long had elapsed from the time the instructions had been given until the twenty third year of Joash's reign is not said, though it may have been several years. In any case the results were disappointing. Perhaps the money collected in the Temple was needed to sustain the services, and if so, there would have been hardly any left to use in the repairs. Jehoiada is called by the king to give an account of the delay, with the result that the responsibility for collecting the money was taken from the priests, and an entirely new method was adopted. At the direction of the king Jehoiada procured a chest, and bored a hole in its lid. This receptacle was placed beside the altar, and near the door of the house. Those who would frequent the altar with their sacrifices, could, as they offered, give a portion to the collection by dropping their coins into the chest through the hole in its lid. This new method proved successful, for there was much money in the chest. The officials of the king, together with the high priest, weighed it after putting it into bags. This money was then given to the workmen who were employed in the repair of the house. Although there were enough funds to do the repairs, there was none left for the purchase of silver and golden vessels. While every care was taken in counting the money involved, yet there was absolute confidence that those in charge of the workforce would handle honestly the funds put into their hands, so there was no necessity to keep a close check on their administration of the finance entrusted to them.

Not all the money brought to the Temple was used for repairs, for the priests had a portion that was not taken from them. When any trespassed, he had to repay for the loss sustained, and add a fifth part. When the trespass was against the Lord, then the recompense could go to the priests, who were His representatives. This money was still to be retained by them, and not put into the chest. In the case of anyone offering a sin offering and giving the priest a gift for his services, then this money also was to be retained, and not used for the repairs.

Verses 17-18
Hazael is bribed by Joash
Very little is recorded in this history of the forty year reign of Joash, and nothing is written that in any way discredits him. In 2 Chronicles the failings of the latter part of his life are exposed. The threatened invasion by the king of Syria, was God's judgment upon him for his wrong-doing, but this is not mentioned in these verses. There is quite a gap between v.16 and v.17. Jehoiada was alive when the repairing

of the Temple was in progress, but is now dead. The history here refers to events toward the end of Joash's life. Hitherto, the Syrians were always seen as attacking Israel, but Judah escaped, for in fact the northern kingdom lay between Syria and Jerusalem, so it was constantly in the front line of defence. On this occasion the Syrian king had ventured south into Philistine territory, and succeeded in taking Gath, a heavily fortified city once famed for its giants. Having conquered this stronghold, he had in mind to proceed with his campaign, and repeat his success by capturing Jerusalem. To prevent this attack, Joash took all the treasures which were stored in the house of God, and sent them to Hazael as a bribe to buy off the feared assault. From the days when the sword of Goliath was stored in the Tabernacle until this time, the sacred dwelling place of the Lord was considered the safest store-house for treasures. Here it is not the enemy sacking the house, but the king himself, emptying it of all that his forefathers had carefully put therein. Not only were the precious metals taken from the Temple, but even the palace was stripped of its valuables. The nation, which once was the richest on earth was reduced to poverty. The lavish gift was accepted by Hazael, and caused him to turn his face away from Jerusalem.

It must be appreciated that had Joash kept right with the Lord, and not turned aside, the invasion of Syria would never have been a threat. Likewise, in this day, when those who lead the saints, drift away from God, the result is the same, for spiritual poverty is sure to ensue. To avoid trouble, many are prepared to give up precious truths, which like the treasures of the Temple, were prized by those who had gone before them. It is much easier to part with treasures, than to gather them.

Verses 19-21
The death of Joash

Only in Chronicles can the full story of Joash be learned, but it is not the purpose of the historian here to go into it in detail. Why he passes over the terrible happenings at the close of the life of this king, is not apparent, nor does he say why such a good king who in his early days did so much for the Temple, had such a tragic end. His death came through his servants, who slew him in the house of Millo. This was the strongest fort of Jerusalem, and the one place where he might have thought he was safe. As an infant, his life had been preserved, but at the end of his days, when he again was in great weakness because of illness, he was no longer shielded by the Lord, because of his evil ways, and especially his cruelty in slaying Zechariah, son of Jehoiada. He was buried in the city of Jerusalem, but not in the tombs of the kings, because of his evil doings (2 Chron 24.25). We cannot but feel sad that one who showed so many good qualities at the commencement of his reign, and for some time afterwards, should have such a deplorable end. Were it not for the fuller account of his history in Chronicles, he would be included among the best kings of Judah.

The one outstanding lesson that can be learned from the history of Joash is that those who act properly solely because they are influenced by good men, are in danger of acting badly when the good influence is removed, and when they are influenced by evil men. He was like water, which takes the shape of the vessel into which it is poured, for he conformed to the conditions which were around him. Like many of the recoveries in the history of Israel, the revival under Jehoiada, was not as it appeared outwardly. Though the evils which developed after his death, were suppressed by him, yet when the day came that there was no restraint, these were soon revealed.

Notes

1 Evidently Joash (Jehoash) was born just when Jehu began to reign, so both the northern and southern kingdoms were ruled for a time by men, who were opposed to the worship of Baal. However, this form of idolatry continued for six years longer in Judah, than in Israel. The mother of Joash, Zibiah, was not an idolater, as was his grandmother, Athaliah.

9 The "chest" (AHROHN - 727) was a box most probably made of wood. The word is translated "coffin" (Gen 50.26), and is elsewhere used only for the Ark of the Covenant.

10, 11 The money was "told" (MAHNAH - 4487), or counted in v.10, and "told" (TCHEHLETH - 8504), or weighed in v.11. Much of the money in ancient times was not in coinage, so it was weighed, and in that way its value was ascertained.

20 The reign of Joash began with a conspiracy, and ended with one. The words "which goeth down to Silla", are difficult to understand, (they are omitted in the LXX), but possibly were included to show exactly where the king died. The meaning would have been quite clear to the first readers.

21 The king "buried with his fathers" might seem to imply that his body was put into one of the royal sepulchres. This was not so. Even though he was buried in Jerusalem, he was not buried in the tombs of the kings. In contrast to him, was his counsellor, Jehoiada, for though he was a priest, he was buried with the kings (2 Chron 24.16).

CHAPTER 13, Verses 1-3
The reign of Jehoahaz king of Israel

The historian, having turned for a time his attention to Jerusalem, now returns to his main story, and continues his account of the northern kingdom. After Jehu had died his son, Jehoahaz began to reign and did so for seventeen years. Like his father, he had no time for Baal worship, but was perfectly happy to continue the calf worship introduced by Jeroboam. As has already been seen, this corrupt form of idolatry, which associated the Lord's name with it, was more deceitful, and tolerated by many as though it were pure in the sight of God. These kings could see the blatant evil of Baal worship and clear the land of it. What they practised may have appeared to them as true devotion to God, but in reality it was no less obnoxious in His sight.

As a result of this false form of worship, the Lord judged Israel, and allowed the king of Syria, Hazael, and his son, Ben-hadad, to oppress it. In the midst of this oppression, the king besought the help of the Lord. This shows that in spite of his wrong association with calf worship, yet he believed that divine power alone could deliver him at this time. The grace of God is seen in His providing a deliverer for His people when they showed any sign of repentance, even though they were most unworthy of His mercy. It is not stated here how the deliverer brought about their relief, but most probably an attack from other nations, possibly an Assyrian attack on Syria, diverted attention from the subjugation of Israel, for a time. This relief meant, that, for a while, the people could leave the scenes of battle and return to their own homes.

After the parenthesis, of vv.5-6, the story of the Syrian oppression is resumed, and the humiliated state of the nation revealed. Almost the entire military strength, of what was once a powerful people, was crushed to the dust, so that only fifty horsemen, and ten chariots, together with a small army of ten thousand footmen were left. By leaving the Israelites in such a weak state, the Syrians made sure that their domination could not possibly be resisted.

It is obvious from v.8 that the detailed history of Jehoahaz is not given here but can be found in another composition, here called "the chronicles of the kings of Israel". How he died is not revealed, but how long he reigned is given as a period of seventeen years. Possibly three of these were with his father in his old age, and if so, he reigned alone only fourteen years. That was about half the time of his father. Like the rest of the kings of Israel, he was buried in Samaria. There is no direct statement that there was a special burial place for these kings in the city, as there were the royal tombs in Jerusalem, but such an arrangement is most probable.

Just as the reformations in Judah, did not end the worship in the high places, and the destruction of Baal did not end the worship of the calves, so it has to be confessed, even in the Reformation, many of the wrong teachings and practices of the church of Rome such as "baptismal regeneration", and "confirmation" were allowed to continue. There has, and ever shall be, great difficulty in eradicating false religion, especially if the Lord's name is linked with it.

Verses 10-13
The reign of Joash

In a brief summary the reign of Joash, the grandson of Jehu, is recorded. More will be said of him later, but here the length of his reign, sixteen years, his likeness to his forefathers, his worship of the calves, introduced by Jeroboam, his warring with Amaziah, and his burial in Samaria, are all the facts mentioned. Clearly he was a repeat of his father and, except for his conflict with the king of Judah, was content to follow his example. Later more of his war with Judah is recorded (ch.14.8-14).

Verses 14-19
Elisha's deathbed prophecy

Although Elisha was not always prominent in the history of Israel, yet for many years his influence and communications from the Lord were an important force in the nation. In these verses the final scenes of his life are recorded. In them is shown that the kings of Israel realized the vital role he played in the nation. This was so, even though for many years they carried on with little regard for him. At this time he must have been advanced in years, for he had represented God for over sixty years, and witnessed many changes on the throne of Israel.

This is not the first time he was visited by a king, for earlier, Jehoshaphat and the king of Edom had gone to him for advice (2

Kings 3.12). It was more normal for prophets to visit kings, but on these two occasions the reverse obtained. This meeting was a sad one, for never again would the favour of the man of God be enjoyed, as he was at his end Joash felt the sorrow so much that he wept, and even allowed the tears to fall on the prophets face. He had vivid recollections of the words used by Elisha when his master, Elijah, was carried up into heaven, and quotes them here. "Oh my father, my father, the chariot of Israel and the horsemen thereof". In this confession the king owns the indebtedness of the nation to the prophet who was now on his deathbed. Perhaps it is only when men are about to lose, or have lost, true friends, that they really value them.

Like most of the events in Elisha's life, the use of varied means was a noted feature. This occasion was no exception. The king was asked to take a bow and arrows, and as he put his hand upon it in order to shoot, the prophet put his frail hand on the king's hand. The window toward the east was opened, and the command was given to shoot. The demonstration was the symbol of the defeat of Syria by Joash. This first shot was followed by further instructions to shoot toward the ground, but the number of the shots was left to the king, He failed to take full advantage of the open offer and smote the ground three times only. This angered the prophet, who said, "Thou shouldest have smitten five or six times". Had he used his full quiver, the Syrians would have been wiped out completely. Because of his limited number of shots, this nation, which had been the constant invader of Israel for centuries, was not mastered by it. The Assyrians were the people who not only conquered Syria, but Israel as well, as will be seen later. While it was no small encouragement for Joash to learn that he would have three victories over his worst enemies, yet it was disappointing for him to be told that these successes would not consume them.

As the history of the northern kingdom throughout the days of Elisha is reviewed, it leaves a definite impression that God had great compassion for His people. Whenever there was evidence of some return to Him, He was ever willing to come to their help. Joash was not a good king, yet his tenderness and tears were sufficient to show that, in spite of his indulgence in calf worship, he still had some confidence in the God of Israel, and in the man who represented Him. This suggests that there are still those who disobey the word of God, yet at the same time know, what and who are pleasing to Him. Another lesson in this closing scene of Elisha that when God gives a free offer, it ought to be taken to its full advantage, and unbelief not allowed to limit enjoyment of it. Few would profess to have taken full advantage of the promise, "Whatsoever ye shall ask the Father in my name, He will give it you" (John16.23).

Verses 20-21
The miracle in the grave of Elisha
The Moabites, like the Syrians, seem to often invade the northern kingdom, and plunder anything they could find from its fields. The time was, when they had to pay an annual tribute to Israel, but now the weakness of the nation, left it a prey to its neighbours. At the time of Elisha's death one such invasion was taking place. The funeral of another man was in progress when the band of invaders was spotted. Such was the fear of the mourners, that they had to abandon their original plan, and push the dead body of their friend into Elisha's grave. To the amazement of all, the corpse, as soon as it had contact with the body of the prophet, stood upright, and returned to life. This miracle is unique, and demonstrates that the power of God which operated in the prophet while he was alive, was still present in his dead body. There can be some understanding of how the warmth of the living could pass to the dead, as it did in the raising of the boys (1 Kings 17.21; 2 Kings 4.34), but that life could be imparted to a corpse by touching the bones of the dead, surpasses all comprehension.

No one can read this narrative without thinking of Rom 6, where it reads "Buried with Him by baptism into death: that like as Christ was raised...so we also should walk in newness of life". This man was buried with the prophet, but raised to live a new life. In this strange instance there can also be seen an illustration of the great truth taught in the NT, that it is contact and relationship with Christ, who was crucified for His own, that is the assurance of their resurrection with Him. If at the rapture of Elijah there is given a glimpse of the rapture of the saints at the Lord's coming, so at the grave of Elisha, there is given a sample of the raised saints at the same coming. Just as those who were about to bury the man, were taught the lesson that contact with the prophet was the secret of life, so in the future day, the nation of Israel in its dead state, like the dead man these men were burying, will come to life again, when they will contact the One whom they pierced (Zec 12.10), The restoration of Israel in the future is likened to the raising of the dead (Dan 12; Rom 11)

CHAPTER 13.22 - CHAPTER 17.41

THE CLOSING YEARS OF THE NORTHERN KINGDOM

After the death of Elisha the days of the northern kingdom were numbered. Even though it struggled on for a number of years, yet its rebellion against God was so persistent, that His patience became exhausted. He allowed the Assyrians to carry into captivity a great many of its people.

For more than sixty years the wonder-working prophet had witnessed for God, and helped some of the kings to achieve victories over the Syrians. With all his efforts, the people still cleaved to idolatry and, while acknowledging God when it suited them, they mixed His name with the calves of Jeroboam. In these chapters is seen the reluctance of God to give up His people, and this specially because they were the descendants of His friend, Abraham. The historian will go out of his way to stress that the disaster which ended the nation was reluctantly allowed by God, and was brought about only when His patience was exhausted.

Verses 22-25
Elisha's prophecy is fulfilled

These verses link the history with vv.3-7, and stress the compassion of God for His people, even when allowing them to suffer under the hand of Syria. They deserved to be destroyed, but were spared, because God remembered His covenant with their fathers. The years which are about to be considered are the interval between the death of Elisha, and the end of this nation, While relating the mercies of God to Israel the death of one of her greatest enemies, Hazael king of Syria, is recorded. The appointment of his son, Ben-hadad, to reign in his place is also mentioned. He is probably the third man with this name, or perhaps it might be called a title.

The success of Joash over this new king is the beginning of the promise made to him by the prophet Elisha (vv.16-17), Certain cites had been overrun by Hazael, and though no account of this campaign is recorded, it is possible that it occurred toward the end of his reign. Here however, the tables are turned, for the cities are re-captured by the king of Israel. Even though this kind of victory was repeated three times, yet parts of the land still remained under Syrian sway, and were not freed until the reign of Jeroboam 2 (ch.4.25).

Notes

1 If v.10 is compared it will be seen why some change the year there to thirty nine to make it fit with this date, but the answer to these apparent discrepancies is that the reigns were at time co-regencies, so a king's reign could include the end years of his father.

3 Possibly Ben-hadad had led the army during his father's life-time.

14 Elisha had prophesied from the days of Ahab, but was much in the shade during the latter years of his life. Some think that little is known of him for over forty years. He is not mentioned after ch.9.1 until this time. The fact that the king here can quote the words of Elisha when Elijah was taken from him "The chariot of Israel and the horsemen thereof" shows that records were kept and that the young king had access to them. These words were spoken more than sixty years earlier, and therefore before the king was born.

17 "Aphek" is the name given to three cities, a city north of Zidon (Josh 19.30); a city of Asher (Jud 1.31); a city of Sharon (Josh 12.18); a city near to Jezreel, to which Ben-hadad retreated, and where the wall fell (1 Kings 20.26-30); and where Joash was here promised to be the scene of his victory over Syria.

21 Because the word "revived" (GHAHYAH - 2421) is used here it does not mean that the man had only "swooned", and was being buried by mistake. The word means "to live" (ch.20.1), When the man was "let down" he was simply put into the tomb, unlike our graves, which usually are several feet below the surface.

23 There are three terms used here to show the Lord's attitude toward Israel. "Gracious" (GHAHNAN - 2603) means "to bend down in kindness to an inferior"; "compassion" (RAHGHAM - 7355) "to show love": and "respect" (PAHNAH - 6437) which means "to turn towards", or "regard". Had the nation received what it deserved it would have been destroyed and cast from His presence.

CHAPTER 14, Verses 1-20
The reign of Amaziah

Again the historian turns to the king of Judah, and narrates the three important actions in his lifetime. Perhaps the reason for turning to the southern kingdom was because of the war between it and the northern kingdom. Though the main subject of the book of Kings is the kingdom of Israel, the sister kingdom is dealt with when there is some involvement with the northern kingdom. In this case the war between the two nations was sufficient reason for the history of both to be given here. When the kings of Judah are mentioned, then the names of their mothers, as well as of their fathers are also given. The mother of Amaziah was "Jehoaddan", but nothing more of her is said, except that she dwelt at Jerusalem. His history was like his fathers in that he did right in the sight of the Lord, but still tolerated the "high places".

The first important matter which demanded the attention of Amaziah was to avenge the murder of his father. Apparently he was unable to do this until he was well established in his kingdom. Unlike many of the avengers we have considered, he did not kill the children of the murderers, but adhered to the Law as given in Deut 24.16. This regard for God's word shows that he must have read the Law, as all kings were expected to do (Deut 17.18-19).

The next great achievement of this king was the victory he gained when fighting with Edom. He slew ten thousand, captured a chief city, and changed its name from "Selah" (rock), to "Joktheel" (subdued of God). During this campaign he seems to be responsive to the word of the Lord through the prophet, and conscious that it was the hand of God which enabled him to have such success. Apparently this victory gave him a proud heart, and the remainder of his life was disappointing. However, the fuller story is given in 2 Chronicles so cannot be developed here.

The third episode mentioned in this king's history was his attempt to war with his sister kingdom then reigned over by Jehoash. He sent messengers to him that he wanted both kings to "look one another in the face". This was not an invitation to meet in a friendly way but a challenge to engage in conflict. There is no reason given here why this conflict was sought, but in Chronicles it is shown that the Israelite army which was sent back and not allowed to help in the war with Edom, was so enraged that it smote several cities of Judah, and took much spoil (2 Chron 25.13). To avenge this evil, Amaziah dared to issue this summons to war. The reply to these messengers was couched in parabolic form. The implication of it was that the king of Judah was like a thistle which could easily be trampled down by a wild beast, and was in no way comparable to the lofty cedars of Lebanon. For the king of Judah to attempt to fight with the king of Israel was sure to be disastrous for the former who would be well advised to remain at home, and not bring his people into defeat. Even though Jehoash was not a God fearing man, yet he could discern that at the back of the threatened attack was pride generated by a previous victory.

One outstanding feature of the kings of Judah was that often their earliest days were the best. In measure this was also true of their father, David. Most would naturally think that experience, and development of mind would bring wisdom, and understanding into the heart, but alas! in many cases the opposite is the result.

Amaziah was not the first, nor the last king to be ruined by pride. That evil weed, the root of which is in every heart, can easily spring up, especially if it is watered by success. Even though the triumph over enemies is due to God alone, (which in Amaziah's case, the changed name of the city implied) there is the danger of men taking some of the glory to themselves. Divine blessing and help when experienced, must always be accepted with a humble mind, and with a realization that without its aid, nothing would have been accomplished.

When the messengers of Amaziah returned with their warning, it was rejected by him, so the threatened war between the two kingdoms began. It was fought at Beth-shemesh in Judah, which was a Levitical town on the borders of Dan, and the place where the Ark was brought by the cows (1 Sam 6). It was a sad day in the history of the nation of Israel, when one part of it was fighting with the other. Obviously the king of Judah had no idea of the weakness of his army, for it deserted him as soon as the superiority of the opposition was discovered. As long as it was victorious, it stood by the king, but when defeat was encountered, then all courage failed, and flight from the scene of battle became the only way to escape. The king himself was taken prisoner by Jehoash, who proceeded to Jerusalem, broke down a long portion of its walls, and plundered the Temple. Perhaps there was not a large quantity of treasure in it. Some gold and silver together with precious vessels were there, and this was brought away to Samaria. The palace was also robbed of its valuables, and those who served in it were taken as hostages.

The death of Jehoash may have some relationship with the release of Amaziah, for the latter was spared some fifteen years after the former's death. If Jehoash died soon after the war, this would mean that the war was fought somewhere near the middle of Amaziah's twenty nine year reign. Like some other kings, his worst enemies were his own officials. They conspired against him, and slew him, even though he fled to Lachish in a bid to escape their sword. However, they were honourable enough to give him a respectable burial, for they carried his body on horses, and buried it in the royal tombs at Jerusalem.

Verses 21-22
The reign of Azariah

Even though the officers of the court killed the king, yet none of them attempted to seize the throne, but put his young son, Azariah, on it. More about this new king is given in chapter 15, but here only one of his achievements is mentioned, His reign was much longer than most of the kings considered, but the latter part of it was spent in seclusion because he was smitten by leprosy. It is noteworthy that no mention is made of the new king punishing those who had slain his father. This may suggest that the murderers were closely associated with the young prince, and that he agreed with what they had done.

Azariah's outstanding success in defeating Edom and recapturing the city of Elath, which was the seat of one of the chiefs, is here mentioned. This city had been taken from Edom by David, but was re-taken by the Edomites for a time. Now he rebuilt it, and restored it to Judah. Possibly it had been reduced to ruins during the wars between Edom and Judah, so it had to be not only captured, but rebuilt. Its importance lay in the fact that it was on the trade route from north to south, so all Arabian and Egyptian caravans were passing it on their missions.

Verses 23-29
The reign of Jeroboam

Again the historian returns to the northern kingdom and deals with the reign of Jeroboam. He was the second Jeroboam and followed the former Jeroboam in his idolatry. He was spared to reign for forty one years, and was the third generation of Jehu to be crowned. This was in fulfillment of the promise made to his great grandfather that his children to the fourth generation would sit on the throne of Israel. Although he began to reign in the fifteenth year of Azariah, yet he was dead before him. However, this was one period in the history of the two kingdoms when both thrones were for over forty years filled by the same two men. As we might expect, this new king in Israel followed closely the evils of his namesake, Jeroboam, for the usual comment is made of him. "He departed not from all the sins of Jeroboam the son of Nebat, who made Israel to sin".

In spite of his unworthiness to receive any help from the Lord, yet he was sent a message of encouragement through the prophet Jonah. This not only assured him of success, but directed him to the area where this would be achieved. He recovered much of the lost territory from the northern border of the land to the Dead Sea in the south. In his favour was not only the prophecy of Jonah, but also during his reign, he had the help of Amos, and Hosea, who were also prophets. These later two are not mentioned in the history, but both of them condemned the nation for its evil ways at that time. The fact that Jonah came from Gath-hepher, which was in Galilee, shows how wrong the Pharisees were, when they said to Nicodemus, "Search and look: for out of Galilee ariseth no prophet" (John 7.52). Had they searched, they would have discovered that Jonah came from a place north of Nazareth.

A brief parenthesis is given to show why such an unworthy king should have been so successful in restoring the prosperity of the land. It was because God pitied Israel in its low estate, and because He had never said that He would blot it out of existence. The same eye which saw the bondage in Egypt and provided a deliverer in Moses, was now seeing His people in deep distress, and used Jeroboam to be their saviour.

There should ever be thankfulness for the mercy and pity of God, even to those of His people who are disobedient to His word. He does chastise, and humiliate them, but at the same time His heart goes after His own and grants them blessings which they rightly feel they are unworthy to receive. Even the most devoted saints are free to confess that all the blessings they receive from God are on the principle of His grace, and are not granted for any merit in the receiver.

The success of Jeroboam was indeed extensive, for he not only recovered the territory which had been taken from Israel, but entered Syria, and took possession of its capital, Damascus. David had conquered it (2 Sam 8.6), but for most of the time, the northern kingdom, Syria was a nation of considerable power, and Israel's chief enemy.

Apparently Jeroboam died of natural causes, and had a longer reign than any other king in Israel. At his death, Zachariah his son took the throne, this was the forth generation of Jehu, and so fulfilled the promise made to him that his seed to the fourth generation, would reign in Israel (ch.10.30).

Notes

4 The "high places" were sometimes places where God was worshipped, but away from the true centre at Zion. In most cases they were shrines of idolatry which good kings destroyed. Those used for the worship of God were symbols of division. Those who worshipped at them may have despised the Temple, and the priests who served in it.

9 The use of parabolic language recalls Jotham's parable (Jud 9.8 -15), He too refers to the cedars of Lebanon, and bramble, or thorn. Here the word "thistle" (GHOHAGH - 2336) can also be translated "thorn" (Job 41.2; Song of Songs 2.2).

The expression "Give thy daughter…" implied that the king of Judah expected that the king of Israel would be as subject to him, as a wife is to her husband.

11 Beth-shemesh here is a city of Judah, and to be distinguished from the place of the same name in Naphtali (Judg 1.33).

26 The expression "not any shut up, nor any left" is quoted from Deut 32.36, where it implies a complete depopulation of the people, so that there would be none either in bondage or at liberty. Here, however, it means that the numbers were greatly reduced.

CHAPTER 15, Verses 1-7
The reign of Azariah

One notable feature of the history of the kings, as given in these chapters, is its brevity. This is especially strange in the case of Azariah, for quite a detailed account of his achievements, especially in his earlier days, are recorded in 2 Chronicles, but here, his fifty-two year reign is covered in seven verses. In the remaining verses of this chapter the history of no less than seven kings is given, so only a condensed summary of their reign is recorded. In most of these cases the same refrain is repeated, the death of the king brought about by the cruel hand of an assassin.

Already there was a brief reference to Azariah, and his work at Elath (ch.14.21-22). Here his mother's name which was "Jecholiah of Jerusalem" is given. As in most other cases of these mothers, nothing more is said about her. This king reigned longer than most, but part of this may have been with his father, and the latter part, of ten years, with his son, Jotham. Thus, the fifty-two years of his reign were not all as sole regent, but some of them, as a co-regent, His leprosy prevented him from fulfilling the full duties of a monarch during the time of his isolation. Like his father, he did what was right, and like him also, he tolerated the high-places. Nothing is said here as to why the Lord smote him with leprosy, but in Chronicles the reason is given. It was due to his daring to act the part of a priest in attempting to burn incense in the Temple (2 Chron 26.16). His son Jotham took charge of the Palace, and likewise fulfilled the duty of a king in judging the important matters of controversy in the state. Being a leper, meant that when he died his body was buried in the field near to the tombs of the kings, but not in the royal sepulchre.

One lesson which can be learned from the story of Azariah is, that with prosperity and blessing there is ever the danger of pride entering the heart. Perhaps it is not easy for fallen man to keep humble when all he touches is blessed with success. Ahaziah entered the kingdom when it was at a very low condition, and at the time when it was dominated by the power of the northern kingdom. From this humble start, he saw the whole scene change, and the southern kingdom regain its dignity and strength. What he and all who are singularly blessed should keep in mind is that their achievements are not the result of their personal worth, but of the power of God. The problem of pride lies in the variety of ways it can appear. Some can be quite humble in many ways, yet as proud as peacocks in some other way. Perhaps men only realize wherein they are proud, when wounded. Few can conceive that for anyone to attempt to do what God has not fitted him to do, as Ahaziah did, is evidence of pride. Everyone should be aware of their limitations.

The prophets Isaiah, Hosea, and Amos began their ministry during his lifetime, The former of these prophesied to the southern kingdom, but the later two were the special messengers to the northern kingdom. The king's death seemed to leave an impression on Isaiah's mind, and it, together with the vision of the Lord on His throne, led him to cry out, "Woe is me" (Is 6). The lessons learned by the prophet at this time were vital for his wonderful life of service.

Verses 8-12
The reign of Zachariah

The historian once again turns his thoughts to the northern kingdom, and in a brief way mentions the various kings who ruled in it. All of these, except one, died by assassination. It is a story of deep decline, and one of lawlessness plaguing the land. The first king mentioned, Zachariah, was the last of the line of Jehu to fill the throne, thus fulfilling the promise made to him, that his seed to the fourth generation would sit on the throne of Israel. Alas! The fourth one had a very short reign, just six months. He copied his forefathers in his evil ways, and the usual refrain is made concerning him regarding his worship of the calves. One of his officers, Shallum, conspired against him and slew him. In his tragic death is seen the fulfillment of the threatened judgment against the house of Jehu for the blood of Jezreel, spoken of by Hosea (Hos 1.4). Those who followed him on the throne were unworthy of the name of "king", for, like Shallum, they stole the throne by treachery, and later reaped what they had sown, for they too, were slain.

Verses 13-16
The reign of Shallum

Shallum had scarcely sat down on the throne until he was slain, for he ruled but a month. In Tirzah, the former capital of the northern kingdom, there was an important army general named Menahem. He travelled to Samaria and slew Shallum, the usurper. There is no mention of the place where he was buried. Many were put to death by Menahem, together with the king, for in his uprising he dealt cruelly with all who dared to oppose him or refused to submit to his authority. Nothing was more like the heathen than the way he treated the women with child. To rip up such helpless people, especially when they were part of his own nation, was the lowest rung of the ladder of depravity.

Verses 17-22
Menahem rules Israel

Unlike some who went before him, whose reigns were short, Menahem ruled somewhat longer, for his reign lasted ten years, and at the end, he died of natural causes. He was not different from the others, for the same refrain, regarding the calf worship is used of him. It must be remembered that none of the kings of Israel ever attempted to overthrow the false worship introduced by Jeroboam.

The threatened invasion by Pul king of Assyria during the reign of Menahem is the first mention by the historian of the great Assyrian empire, the famous world power, which for a time, ruled from Babylon to Egypt. Although on this occasion the evil day was averted, yet it was eventually the instrument used to bring to an end the northern kingdom. It was the rod of God's anger, and the agent of His wrath in judging His people for their evil ways (Is 10.5).

When Menahem was confronted by this foreign power, he devised a way of averting the pending disaster. Like all those threatening invasion, the one object before their minds is to become wealthy at the expense of those they conquer. At this time it was thought wise to give the riches, rather than wait for them to be seized. The king of Israel gathered from all who could afford it the large sum of a thousand talents of silver, and this he gave to Pul. These acted not only as a bribe to halt the invasion, but as a present to win his support in establishing his own position. In spite of the many upheavals in the land, and the poor standard of rule by the kings there must have been quite a few who were sufficiently wealthy to be able to pay the tax imposed upon them. The plan worked, for Pul left off the invasion and turned elsewhere. There was a time when David and Solomon were bringing the wealth of the surrounding nations into the land, but, now at the end of the kingdom, the wealth is departing from it. Later when there was no more wealth to plunder, the people will also go as slaves to provide cheap labour for their enemies.

What brought about Menahem's death is not stated, but apparently it was from natural causes and not the result of rebellion. He was able to pass on the throne to his son, Pekahiah.

The principle of averting trouble by bribery may appear, as in this case, to succeed, but quite often it is like giving salt water to a thirsty person, and only aggravates the desire for more. Not too long after this the Assyrians returned, and did what they threatened to do at this time. Sometimes to avert trouble, precious truths have been surrendered, but invariably this leads to more demands, so eventually all that is worth possessing is forfeited.

Verses 23-26
The reign of Pekahiah
Although Pekahiah, being the son of the deceased king, was evidently the rightful heir to the throne, and did not reach it by usurpation, this did not exempt him from attack. After two years the

assassin entered his palace and slew him there. Like earlier kings, he fell by the sword of one of his trusted officers. During his brief reign he had no regard for the Lord, and as with his predecessors, the pattern of his religion was copied from Jeroboam the son of Nebat.

There appears to be no motive for the slaying of this king except ambition. The wording of verse twenty five is somewhat confusing, but the simplest understanding is to see Argob and Arieh as associates of the king, who were with him in the palace. They suffered the same fate as he did. The fifty men of Gilead were the helpers of Pekah in his evil deed.

Verses 27-31
The reign of Pekah

Although the history of Pekah is only briefly given here, yet more about him is said in 2 Chron 28, and in Is 7. His twenty year reign was full of adventures, some of which he may have assumed to be successes. However, it was during his reign the Assyrian king, Tiglath-pileser, invaded the land and carried away inhabitants to be captives in his own land. The names of the places over-run are given, but generally speaking they were situated in the north of the land, in what was later known as Galilee, and in Gilead, on the eastern side of Jordan. This was the area where the two and one half tribes were located. The invasion at this time greatly reduced the northern kingdom, and took from it some of its most fertile land.

Just as he obtained the kingdom by slaying Pekahiah, so he himself was slain by Hoshea. The principle of sowing and reaping was manifested in his case. There is some apparent confusion in the dates at this time, and this because some of the reigns were as co-regents, so these years when added to the actual time given as the period of sole reigning harmonizes the years stated. Some have thought that there was a period of about eight years between the slaying of Pekah, and the reign of Hoshea, his successor, so a state of anarchy may have prevailed during this time. Others see no need for any such interregnum.

The closing years of the northern kingdom were times of change, especially as to rulers. In this is demonstrated that departure from God always leads to confusion. People become like the object they worship, so along with idolatry there is the absence of reverential fear. Idols, being lifeless, could not judge evil. This was why the prophets were bold in denouncing the besetting sin of Israel, and warned those to whom they spoke of the solemn consequences of turning to false gods. Godly rule is vital in any company of saints, and when men turn away from God and His word, the result is seen in weak leadership and in the constant desire for change, but often the change is for the worse. None of these latter kings of Israel seemed to have any thought of inquiring after the Lord, Not even when the enemy was approaching did they turn to Him for help, nor did they perceive that the disasters which befell them were the result of their sinful ways.

Verses 32-38
The reign of Jotham

Once again the historian turns our thoughts to Judah, and gives a brief account of the reign of Jotham. Like his fellow kings in Jerusalem we are told the name of his mother, and the length of his reign. She, being a daughter of Zadok, may have been of a priestly family, and if so, she may have helped his father in the days of his prosperity. The sixteen years of his reign excludes about ten years when he reigned as regent, so the reference is to "the twentieth year of Jotham" (v.30). Like his father, he feared God, and had a deep interest in the defence of Jerusalem. The danger in his day was expected from the north, so he built the upper gate of the house of the Lord, and according to 2 Chronicles he built extensively throughout Judah.

There were others in Judah who during his reign were also builders, but they were not interested in the Temple, or the city, but in establishing places of worship. Whether these were idolatrous places of worship or places where sacrifices were offered to the Lord is not stated, but in Jotham's day no attempt was made to remove them. The corruption amongst the people was developing at this time, and it may have been the reason why God allowed the invasion by the two neighbouring kings.

Jotham died of natural causes at the age of forty-one, and was buried with David his father in one of the royal sepulchres.

Evidently Jotham continued the work begun by his father, and to a great extent copied his way of life. The one lesson which can be learned from him is that while it is good to imitate those leaders, who have lived their lives for the advancement of God's kingdom, yet their failings must not be imitated nor should their errors be adopted. He learned from his father the costliness of acting wrongly, and was preserved from repeating the same mistake. Those kings in Judah who walked in the ways of David, and were praised for doing so, were never guilty of copying his behaviour with Bath-sheba.

Notes

5 A "several" (GHOPHSHEETH - 2669) house, was one which was kept "free" from close contact with others. The word is from a root meaning "free", and is used only of this house. It may have been built specially for the king, and is here distinguished from the palace. To live in isolation must have been a distressing experience for Azariah, for it meant that he was separated from all the luxury and honour of dwelling in the royal palace, and from sitting upon the throne where he could meet his subjects, and judge the important cases which would from time to time, arise in his domain.

13 Azariah was the Uzziah in Chronicles, Isaiah, Hosea and Amos.

15 The word "conspiracy" (KEHSHER - 7195) occurs eight times in 1 & 2 Kings, and is translated twice "treason" (2 Kgs 11.14). Its verbal form (KAHSHAR) occurs fourteen times in these two books, This shows that rebellion was a feature of the nation during this period.

16 "Tiphsah" and "Tirzah" were evidently two adjacent towns which resisted the rule of Menahem, even though he came from the latter. The former was not likely to be the same as the town on the Euphrates which had the same name (1 Kings 4.24).

19 Pul, King of Assyria is the same as Tiglath-pileser. Possibly the former was his original name, and he assumed the grander title when he secured the throne.

37 The invasion began in Jotham's day, and continued during the reign of his son, Ahaz.

CHAPTER 16, Verses 1-20
Ahaz reigns in Judah

From the days of Athaliah the throne of Judah was filled with relatively good kings, but Ahaz, who copied the kings of the northern kingdom, was different, for he was one of the most depraved of the descendants of David. Unlike most of the kings of Judah, his mother's name is not given. Could it be that she had some influence in turning him to idolatry? Even though he copied the kings of Israel yet one of his chief opponents was Pekah, the contemporary king of Israel. Only those steeped in the lowest depths of idolatry would cause their sons to be burned as sacrifices. This was one of the evils of Canaan prior to Israel's entry, and one for which its inhabitants were cast out, yet

Ahaz made his son to pass through the fire. That one of David's seed, possibly an heir to the throne, would be cruelly treated in this barbaric way is an inexpressible horror.

Instead of repairing the Temple, or enriching it with gifts, he had no regard for it, and spent his energies in building high places, and in erecting shrines under the shade of trees. Whatever doubts may arise about some of the other high places, one thing is sure, these were built for idolatrous purposes. The earlier kings were blamed for tolerating the high places, but he went further, for he participated in worship at them.

Two nations which had warred with each other for centuries, Syria and Israel, on this occasion joined hands to fight with Judah. Their aim was to capture Jerusalem, dethrone Ahaz, and set the son of Tabeal on the throne (Is 7). Isaiah was fully aware of their scheme and assured Ahaz that they would not succeed. Possibly the fortifications erected by his father and grandfather had strengthened the city, and made it too strong for them to capture. Though they failed to reach their target, yet they did have great success, for they captured Elath, which was a city of Edom, and once the seat of one of its dukes. It had been taken by David (2 Sam 8.14). The Edomites recaptured it, but Azariah rebuilt it and restored it to Judah (2 Kings 14.22). Now it was captured by the combined forces of Syria and Israel, and became the possession of Syria. A Jewish garrison had been placed in it by Azariah, but this was driven out so that an important stronghold was conquered at this time. According to the Chronicles passage some more outstanding victories had been won by this combined force, and the army of Judah practically wiped out, before the help of Assyria was sought (2 Chron 25.5-8).

In spite of the counsel given to Ahaz by Isaiah, to trust in the Lord, and not seek for foreign help, he proceeded to procure the aid of Assyria. In order to secure the assistance needed a large amount of gold and silver was taken from the Temple, and sent as a present to Tiglath-pileser. Along with the bounteous gift, an assurance was also given to him, that Judah would become a submissive state over which he would rule, and that the people would be his servants, or slaves. It was indeed a great price to pay for deliverance from neighbouring enemies, and an altogether needless one for had Ahaz relied on the Lord, instead of leaning on a foreign power, he would have been delivered without this expense.

The appeal of Ahaz was accepted, and the forces of Assyria made an attack on Damascus the capital of Syria and took possession of it. Rezin was slain, and the people of the city were taken to Kir. There was a city of this name somewhere in Moab (Is 15.1), but whether this was the place to which these captives were deported cannot be confirmed. It would appear improbable that they would be placed in a land so near to their home country. Perhaps it is best to admit that its exact location is not known. It was a feature of the Assyrians and the Chaldeans that wherever they conquered, they transported the populace to some distant country. Their thinking in this matter would appear to be that when people are removed from their native surroundings, and faced with new customs, this will so upset them that they will be easier to control.

When all was quietened at Damascus the king of Assyria called together a meeting of the heads of the countries he had subjugated. Amongst these was Ahaz. It was important that the conqueror should become acquainted with the heads of the states over which he was then ruling. Apparently the visit to Damascus lasted for a considerable time. While there, an altar was seen by the king of Judah which appealed to him as being superior to the altar in the Temple in Jerusalem. He immediately decided to have one produced like it and with this in view he sent to Urijah the priest at Jerusalem a detailed pattern, and ordered him to have one made exactly the same.

This priest was willing to obey the king, even though he must have known that what he was asked to do was nothing short of sacrilege. His submission was very different to that of the priests who withstood his grandfather, king Amaziah (2 Chron 26.18). He executed the king's command, so when the king returned to Jerusalem from Damascus, the altar was ready for service. Just as Solomon had offered on the original altar when it was brought into use, so Ahaz dedicated this new altar with the various offerings. In order to give the supreme place to it, the brazen altar made by Solomon had to be removed from the front of the Temple, and placed in a more remote quarter, on the north side of the house, From this time onward, all sacrifices, which normally had been offered on the brazen altar had to be offered on this new altar. The brazen altar was not to be entirely discarded, so, for a time, it was left, possibly to see what could be done with it. The expression "the brazen altar shall be for me to inquire" would give us the impression that when he was inquiring of God he would approach it, but this is an unlikely meaning. The idea may be that he would consider later to what use he would put it.

Ahaz, not content with his new altar carried out further innovations. The portable layers were next given his attention and he stripped them of their side panels, and of their layers, leaving nothing but the frames. Thus he rendered them useless in the court. Another important vessel, made by Solomon, was the large laver, or sea, which was upheld by twelve oxen. This was the next object with which he meddled. He had it lifted off the oxen and set on a base of stone. What advantage this was to the laver or to the king is difficult to perceive, but it looks like making changes for the sake of change. Perhaps he needed the copper, salvaged from these oxen, to enable him to pay the tribute demanded by the king of Assyria.

The next great change that he made is more difficult to understand. There was some kind of covered area, either in the Temple court, or on some of the ways from the palace to it. Whatever it was the king and his retinue used it every sabbath, and on feast days. This was removed, together with the entrance gates of the ascent which led from the palace to the Temple. All this was in some way a concession to the king of Assyria. Again these structures could have been made of metal, so their removal may have been for the same purpose as the former changes. Some have thought that all these alterations were demanded by the king of Assyria to facilitate the erection of an idol which this king worshipped but we have no proof of this.

The day came when Ahaz went to the full limit, and actually shut the doors of the Temple (2 Chron 28.24). With so many alterations it would have been difficult for any faithful priest, or any of the people to continue with the worship as God had directed them to do, Not only at Jerusalem did he make changes, but throughout the entire land, he erected shrines for the offering of incense to idols. Little wonder the anger of the Lord was burning against him, and his subjects.

The life of this evil king was cut short for he died at the early age of thirty six. Even in his burial the stamp of dishonour was upon him, for instead of putting his dead body amongst the kings, he was buried in a common grave in the city. Like Jehoram before him (ch.21.20), he was judged to be unworthy of lying beside the faithful sons of David.

In the history of Ahaz there is demonstrated the sad fact that good men do not always rear good sons. If all were known, his mother, may have had more influence upon him than his father. The fact that her name is not given may suggest that she was not a godly woman. The king would be so occupied with the kingdom that he would have had little time to spend with the family. His short reign is a reminder that it is much easier to pull down than it is to erect. Paul was amazed that the Galatians were "so soon removed from Him that called" (ch.1.6). The footsteps of those who are bent on departure are never slow.

What can likewise be learned from this history of Ahaz is that good men, and good ministry do not always prevent departure. To have a prophet of the status of Isaiah actively prophesying in the land, and Hosea and Micah prophesying in the northern kingdom, was no small privilege. Nothing these servants of God said seemed to have had any effect upon him. It is surprising that some who have turned aside from the ways of God, do so, in spite of the good ministry they have heard.

When rulers depart from God they bring those whom they govern into great distress. The judgment of God fell upon Judah at this time, and many of its subjects were slain. God's people, may do wrong, but they cannot escape the consequences. When His hand is upon them, they are tempted, as was Ahaz, to seek help from sources totally opposed to Him.

Paul reminds us, "If any man defile the temple of God, him shall God destroy (1 Cor 3.17). Here we have a king, defiling the sanctuary by his actions and even closing its doors. It is little wonder he filled an early grave. He was, like many in this day, very religious, but all his zeal was in advancing idolatry. There are those who teach that as long as one is sincere in his religion it matters little what he believes, but this is a delusion. Ahaz showed much zeal, but it was always in doing wrong.

The king's son had to suffer for his father's belief. This is a solemn reminder that corrupt religion, not only ruins those who practice it, but also the next generation. It is in connection with idolatry that the words are used, "Visiting the iniquity of the fathers upon the children" (Ex 20.5).

The evil of the unequal yoke has often been demonstrated in the books of Kings. Here the help of Assyria which Ahaz sought, was the linking of the house of David, with a world power which shortly afterwards destroyed the northern kingdom, and later devastated the greater part of Judah. If Christians put their trust in worldly persons, or worldly things, they will not only suffer needless loss, but put themselves into bondage.

Imitating what is seen in the world's religion has always been a snare to God's people. The pattern given to David, and executed by Solomon, had divine sanction, but this was recklessly changed by

Ahaz. God has given His people the pattern, for their gathering, and expects them to be satisfied with it. Some, like Ahaz are bent on exchanging this pattern for what they see in religious circles, and they even try to convince themselves that this is much to be preferred. The setting aside of the brazen altar may suggest failure to value the sacrifice of Christ, and the shedding of His blood as the basis of approach to God. The layers being stripped and the sea being lowered would speak of reducing the standard of purity expected in those who draw near to God. Just as the evils of this king ended with the shutting up of the Temple, so departure from divine principles can culminate in the closing of an assembly.

Urijah the priest is an example of those who will freely help forward what is wrong. The king found a ready helper in the priest, and like most others, who assist evildoers, one who showed much zeal in his work. It is very strange that when Josiah sought to repair the house the priests were dragging their feet, but when this destructive work had to be done, it was accomplished expeditiously. It is sad to think that sometimes those who are worldly put more zeal into their evil work, than saints put into the work of God.

One final lesson to be learned from this sad story is that those who turn aside, quite often try to put the blame on others. Ahaz may have claimed that what he did was to please the king of Assyria. However, had he not invited him to come to his help, he would not have been obliged to cater to his tastes. There is no excuse for interfering with that which God has ordained, and anyone who deviates from His pattern, must bear his own burden.

Notes

10 The fact that there was an altar at Damascus indicates that it was not only the capital city, but the centre of idolatrous worship. In the RV it is "the altar".

15 The word "inquire" (BAHKAR - 1239) comes from a root meaning to "plough", so "to delve into", or "inquire". It is used by David, "to enquire in his Temple" (Ps 27.4). It has also the meaning of "search" (Lev 27.33; Ez 34.12), so here it may mean that he would "inquire" or "search out" what he would do with it.

18 The "covert" (MEHSACH - 4329) or "portico" is another word found only here. The LXX translators thought that it was a reference to a canopy over the throne, but the throne was not in the courts of the Temple.

CHAPTER 17, Verses 1-6
The reign of Hoshea

At this time in the history of the northern kingdom the kings who reigned were under the dominion of the Assyrian power. Hoshea, who was the last of them, was allowed nine years on the throne. As already noticed in ch.15.30, there is some confusion in the chronology at this time, for the twelfth year of Ahaz here, is said to be the twentieth year of Jotham. We are told that Jotham reigned sixteen years (ch.15.33), so the longer period of twenty years mentioned in ch.15.30 must include the time when he jointly shared the throne with his leprous father. Otherwise, the date may be counted from the beginning of Jotham's reign, and if so, this twentieth year of Jotham would actually be the fourth year of Ahaz. If according to ch.17.1 Hoshea did not begin to reign until the twelfth year of Ahaz some have concluded that there was a period in Israel of eight or nine years when no king was on the throne. Most now are convinced that this is a mistake. If all the facts were known it would be seen that all the dates harmonize. That Hoshea was less evil than some of the kings before him may have been because he allowed the faithful in his realm to go to Jerusalem in response to the invitation of Hezekiah at the time of his passover (2 Chron 30.1).

One thing made clear in these chapters is that if Israel sought help from foreign nations, it was not given without payment. The Assyrians, under king Shalmaneser came up against Hoshea, and in order to escape their mighty hand, he gave them presents. This tribute money was the evidence that Hoshea was reigning only as a vassal of Shalmaneser, and that any attempt to withhold it would be viewed as rebellion. The time came when he no longer sent the tribute money, for he had secret talks with Egypt, and by the aid of this great power, he presumed to resist the domination of Assyria. However, Hoshea was let down by Egypt, and left to defend Samaria by his own strength. For three years the siege was resisted. Eventually the city was entered, the king arrested, and the inhabitants carried off to Media, The places mentioned here, to which they were taken, may all have been reasonably near each other, and were all, including the river Gozan, in Mesopotamia.

Verses 7-23
The reason for Israel's captivity

Occasionally throughout the books of Kings the historian indicates why certain evils befell the nation of Israel. In these verses we have his most extensive justification of God's dealings with it and the clear explanation of why the captivity by the Assyrians was permitted to occur. In them there is no history, but rather the reason is given why the history is the sad tale it has proved to be. The historian adopts the role of a religious teacher, or of one of the prophets, and leaves on record this solemn warning for all to heed. God may tolerate departure for a time, but eventually it will result in dire judgment from His hand.

The history of Israel from the time they left Egypt had been stained with sin, especially the sin of idolatry (vv.7-12). The warnings against copying the ways of the nations of Canaan, given in Deuteronomy, were ignored, and the very corruptions of these nations, which provoked God, and caused Him to send Israel into their land as His instrument of judgment, these same evils were practiced by His people. Not only did they worship Gentile gods, but they obeyed the teachings associated with idolatry. Since these gods were powerless to defend the Canaanites, the people who knew the true God, should have known their worthlessness. All the high places, the groves, the images were reproductions of what they saw around them. Added to these temptations were the idolatries imposed upon them by wicked kings, such as the calves of Jeroboam, and the Baal worship of Ahab.

It was God's intention that the nation should be one and that the Temple should be the only centre of worship for all the people. However, instead of gathering to His house, the people built high places in almost every quarter, whether it was a city, or a small isolated area. They erected pillars, planted groves, and set up shrines under green trees, so that the land was studded with religious stations where idols were worshipped. Associated with these centres was not only the offering of animal sacrifices, but also the burning of incense. The golden altar was the place for this, but instead of it ascending as a sweet savour to God it filled the air around these shrines as it was offered in honour to idols. It is no wonder that the Lord was angry, when He saw what was due to Him alone being offered to these worthless objects.

The second great reason for Israel's rejection is indicated in v.13, and stresses Israel's refusal of the prophets sent to them with God's message. It is amazing that so many servants of God were directed to the different kings with suitable messages. The two most outstanding, were perhaps Elijah and Elisha. Some of these prophets were not named, but were simply referred to as "men of God". Along with those mentioned in Kings there were the prophets whose writings still remain, such as Isaiah, Hosea, Amos and Micah. As the end of the kingdom drew near the prophets were increased, so that when the judgment fell, they could not claim that it came without warning. Like their fathers before them, who did not believe God, they resisted His words with the stubbornness of an intractable animal (v.14).

The third part of this treatise, which commences at v.16, is a restatement of the various evils which made Israel ripe for judgment. When the people forsook the commandments of God, they proceeded to make molten images. A notorious example of these was the gold calves positioned at Dan and Bethel. Still not satisfied with these the people in addition planted groves and filled the land with shrines where incense was burnt in honour of their false gods. This was followed by the worship of the hosts of heaven, and by the worship of Baal. The crowning evil, as we have seen, was the cruel burning of the children on the altars of Molech. Furthermore the seeking of information from evil sources was an evil which was hateful to God. The employment of enchantments and divination was possibly not as openly practiced as the idolatry, but were no less seen by God. Jehu refers to the "witchcrafts of Jezebel" (ch.9.22), and Micah speaks of the day when God "will cut off witchcrafts out of thine hand", and thou shalt have no more soothsayers" (5.12). The anger of the Lord was entirely justified, and His casting them out of His sight was what they deserved.

The closing portion of this solemn dissertation begins at v19. It includes a warning to Judah, for if the remaining part of the nation copies the evils of Israel the outcome will be the same. Israel copied the nations and Judah copied Israel, especially in the days of Athaliah. If this continues the remainder of the people will also be carried away. The rending of the ten tribes of Israel from the house of David was the beginning of their downfall. The pattern of idolatry, set up by Jeroboam, was followed by all in his kingdom until there was no remedy. The worst feature of the Assyrian captivity was that there was no recovery from it. Those who were carried to Babylon were not so ill-fated, for a remnant of them did return to the land of their fathers.

The sad story of these verses sounds the trumpet warning to God's people to-day. If they, like Israel, turn away from Him, they cannot expect His blessing to be upon them. The one "besetting sin" of Israel was idolatry, so they should have been deeply exercised lest it would appear in their midst. They were given the appetite for it in Egypt, and were never completely free from it throughout their history.

Weaknesses ought to be detected and the help of the Spirit of God sought in order to overcome them. The world, typified by Egypt, is a constant temptation to the saints, and the evil of copying its ways is constantly a grave danger to them.

Just as Israel neglected the words of the prophets, so there is always the possibility of letting slip the ministry of the Word of God which is heard. Those who teach the saints are responsible to bring to their notice the truth they need to hear, but if no heed is paid to this then departure is sure to develop. God has made rich provision for His people in this present age, for they not only have His complete Word, but He has gifted His servants to minister it to them in words they can understand.

Another principle obvious in these verses is that one step of departure leads to another. Possibly Jeroboam, when he made the calves, never thought that the day would come when his people would be casting their living sons and daughters into the fire. The slippery slope of evil can descend to depths never imagined by those who begin to slide. Some, who once were satisfied with the divine centre, which corresponds to the Temple, have left for other places, and almost forgotten the truths they formerly enjoyed.

Possibly the most solemn lesson here is that when serious departure from God's ways occurs the hope of recovery is quite remote. Very few who turn away from what they had revealed to them in the word of God, are ever restored to the fellowship they forsook. Some, like the remnant referred to, do return, but these are the exception, rather than the rule. While there should always be thankfulness for restoration, yet preservation is by far the greater blessing.

Verses 24-28
The new inhabitants in Samaria

Sargon was a king too shrewd to leave a fertile land like Canaan stripped of its inhabitants, so he put into it the peoples of other countries which he had conquered. Just as the Israelites were transplanted to Media, so they were taken from their own lands and placed in Samaria. The area from which most of them came was the valley of the Euphrates, the one exception being "Hamath", at the northern border of Syria. Settling in a new country must have been as troublesome to these people, as the land of Media was to the Israelites. There was however this one important difference. The land of Canaan was God's land, and while His people were exiled from it, this did not mean that He had given over its ownership. All who lived in it were but tenants, and if some were evicted, because they refused to pay the respect the owner demanded, this meant that the new tenants would not be allowed to do as they pleased.

God has said "every beast of the forest is mine" (Ps 50.10), so they are at His service whenever needed. In this case the lions, which were allowed to increase in numbers due to the absence of humans to destroy them, were the instruments used to punish these colonists for their absence of the fear of God. They were quick to detect the reason for such judgment and concluded that it fell upon them "because they knew not the manner of the God of the land". To overcome this problem, Sargon sent one of the captive priests back, who was to instruct these new inhabitants to fear the Lord. Whether he was a priest who served in the Temple, but lived in the northern kingdom, or one of the priests of Bethel, we are not told, but whatever his character, he knew enough of the unseen God, to reverence Him.

Verses 29-41
The religion of Samaria
Just as Daniel and his fellows brought with them their knowledge of the Lord to Babylon, so these nations brought into Samaria their religions. While all of them were idolaters, yet they worshipped different gods. They had no trouble building new shrines, for the Israelites had these in every place so it was merely a matter of changing the gods and putting theirs into the places where the idols of Israel had been raised and worshipped. When the Israelites for their idolatry were carried down to Assyria and Babylon they were brought to lands full of idols, so these nations who came to Samaria found all they needed by way of miniature temples to accommodate their idols. The variety of gods mentioned here is all strange and not mentioned elsewhere in the Scriptures, but one fact is all too familiar, the burning of the children. It was the most heinous and detestable practice of all. After reading these verses it is easy to understand the words of John 4.9, "The Jews have no dealings with the Samaritans", for with such corrupt religious practices no enlightened Israelite could have anything in common with them. What made this muddle of religious practices even more detestable was the fact that it synchronized idolatry and the name of the Lord. In no way did they part with their beliefs, but they acknowledged that there was a supreme Lord, and to Him they gave honour. The woman at the well (John 4) knew about the fathers,

and about the true place of worship, but she, true to her environment, still thought that the Mount Gerizim was the right place for her to worship. In one place it is said "they feared the Lord" (v.33), and in another "they feared not the Lord" (v.34). Outwardly they owned the existence of the Lord, but they did not fear Him enough to obey His commandments and observe His laws. In the NT some believed, yet later they proved not to be true believers (John 2.22-25).

The historian turns his thoughts to the requirements of the Lord which were given when first the children of Israel came out of Egypt. These included the warning to have nothing to do with idolatry, but worship and sacrifice to the One whose power they had witnessed in their deliverance from Pharaoh. He had also given them statutes, ordinances and commandments, so their obedience was demanded. He had made with them the covenant of Mount Sinai, and they had promised to keep it. Coupled with their obedience to Him was His promise to deliver them from all their foes. The fact that they were now slaves of Assyria was proof that they had not obeyed God.

The nations who then settled in the land, continued to fear the Lord, and to worship as they had done in their own land, even until the time this book was written. This was, at least, one hundred and fifty years after the captivity. Even in NT times little change had come to Samaria, but the Lord's visit, and the testimony of the woman at the well, who had been given the living water, seemed to bring blessing even to these unworthy people. In apostolic times the visit of Philip to Samaria was another time of blessing, for his work there brought great joy to that city.

In one sense the new inhabitants of Canaan were no better than the people who were carried away from it. However there was an important difference in that the new dwellers had not the light enjoyed by the Israelites. Here again the principle is taught that, "Unto whomsoever much is given, of him shall be much required" (Lk 12.48). God tolerated conduct from these heathen people which He would not allow in His own people. Another lesson which can be learned from these verses is that false religious belief passed on to children is likely to stay with them. All would have been very different had the Israelites been as true to their God-given religion, as these nations were to their false beliefs. Our fallen nature will ever take a keen interest in that which is evil. Just as the Lord is mentioned as being feared along with the idols it has to be remembered there is scarcely a "cult" but which in some way brings the Lord into its doctrines. His holy name is linked with many of the corrupt religious theories promulgated throughout the world.

Notes

3 The word "present" (MINGHAH - 4503) here is the word used often for the "meat offering", and occurs first in Gen 4 where we read that Cain and Abel both brought an "offering", or "present" to the Lord. Here it is used for "tribute" given to a foreign king. When the tribute stopped (v.4) then the assault on Samaria began.

15 the emptiness of idols is stressed in the words 'vanity" (HEHVEL - 1892), and "vain" (HAHVAL - 1891). Moses first uses "vanities" for idols in Deut 32.21. Here is taught that men become like the object they worship, for the idolater becomes "vain". The noun is a key word in Ecclesiastes.

17 The word "divination" (KEHSEM - 7081) is here only in Kings and means to determine in a supernatural way what is otherwise unknown. It is used of the prophecies of Balaam (Num 22.7; 23.23), and of the rewards given him for his services. The word "enchantments" (NAHGHASH - 5172) is sometimes translated "divine" as in Gen 44.5,15; and also in a good sense, "learned by experience" but it mostly refers to the sinister practice of using words to invoke the aid of evil spirits, in order to produce supernatural effects on man, or other objects.

24 The name Samaria has been until now used for the city. which was the capital of the northern kingdom. Here and in v 28 it refers to the area of the province.

26 The "manner" (MISHPAHT - 4941) is the ordinary word for judgment and here means what God has decreed or decided concerning the land.

29 This is the only mention of the word "Samaritans" in the OT.

30 The idol "Succoth-benoth" worshipped by the Babylonians may have been another name for Marduk. The idol Nergal was the god of the burning sun. The idol Ashima is only mentioned here, and nothing more is known of it. The idol Nibhaz may have been an Elamite divinity, but again nothing is known of it. The god Tartak is mentioned here only. The Sepharvites worshipped Adrammelech, and sacrificed their children to it. It is thought that this was the same god that the Syrians worshipped, but called Hadad. It would appear that every country selected a god of its own, and while some of the worship may have been alike, the object to which it was offered had a different name. With all this confusion in the Gentile world, it was a wonderful favour for the nation of Israel to be allowed to serve the living and true God. The greater wonder is that those so privileged, ever thought of turning to idolatry.

CHAPTERS 18-25 THE KINGDOM OF JUDAH

THE REIGN OF HEZEKIAH CHAPTERS 18-21

CHAPTER 18, Verses 1-8
The prosperity of Hezekiah

Until now in 2 Kings the historian has been looking at the history of two kingdoms. The northern kingdom of Israel, with all its idolatry, and the southern kingdom of Judah with its mixture of good and evil. From now onward we will be considering the southern kingdom only, for the northern one has ceased to exist. Over one hundred and thirty years passed before the fate which overtook Israel became the portion of Judah. In spite of at least two revivals the southern people mainly followed the evils of the sister kingdom, and suffered the same downfall. It might be thought that, when the people of Judah saw the dreadful consequences of turning away from God to idols, they would have acted so as to avoid a similar disaster. This was not so, for, in spite of many prophets being raised up amongst them and all the warnings given them, they still went on headlong to their destruction.

The unique feature of the history of Hezekiah is that it is recorded in three books. Here, in 2 Kings, in 2 Chronicles chs.29-32, and in Isaiah chs.36-39. The reason for the triple record of this king is that while all the records of the kings are actual history, yet his story is also a prophecy. His experiences were a foreshadowing of his people's trials in a future day, especially the time of tribulation, when the faithful remnant will be brought to the point of extinction. The effort made to recover what was of God, illustrates what it will do in a future day. His powerful enemies were a foreshadowing of the fierce opposition that will confront it when the Antichrist is on the throne. Hezekiah's sickness, coming in the midst of his trouble, is a preview of the helplessness, even to the point of despair, which will be felt in those terrible, and the sign of the sundial moving backwards, is an indication that there will be notable signs granted to encourage and strengthen the faith of those who will be faced with severe trials.

When Hezekiah began to reign the nation was under the heel of Assyria, for his father had become a servant of its king, Shalmaneser. How he was so different in character from his father is difficult to understand, except that, as in other cases, the influence of his mother may have been the secret, for she was a daughter of Zechariah. It could be that her father was the same man who accompanied Isaiah (Is 8.2), and if so, she was reared in a good family. Unlike some of the kings, he was fully matured when he ascended the throne at the age of twenty five, so he could commence, without delay, the projects he had in mind. He was one of the kings who walked in the ways of David, and unlike his father, was not swayed by the example of Israel. Most likely he was influenced by Isaiah, for although his father gave little heed to the prophet, yet he himself was in constant contact with him. The nation must have been surprised that he would dare to destroy the high places, the idols, and the groves. Many of these were in existence for years, and were centres of worship for his forefathers. One thing he had learned was that David had no time for these abominations, nor did he allow any to be in the land in his day. Returning to the true head-line was his wisdom, and having no compromise with idolatry was his settled conviction. Among the objects of worship he discovered was the ancient brazen serpent, that had been made by Moses, and had been the object used in the wilderness for the healing of the bitten in Israel. It had been turned into an idol. Doubtless this antique masterpiece was prized as a relic of the great man Moses, but to turn it into a god, was something its maker would have abhorred. To end its misuse, it had to be smashed in pieces, and instead of esteeming it as being something precious. Hezekiah called it "Nehushtan", which means "a piece of brass".

The secret of Hezekiah's life was his trust in the Lord. and in this respect he eclipsed all the kings of Judah who went before him. Later we will learn of another king, Josiah, who excelled all who went before him (ch.23.25), but perhaps the virtues of the one, were not identical with those of the other. Like all who trust in the Lord, his faith was tested, and at times seemed to be about to fail, but it stood the tests. Even when all natural hope had fled, he discovered that the Lord was ready to save (Is 38.20). Coupled with his faith in God, was his obedience to His word. He was conscious that the path of faith must also be a path walked in submission to all that God had revealed. The result of his devout way of living was that God prospered him, so that he dared to refuse submission to the king of Assyria. In 2 Chronicles we are given an extensive account of all his achievements, but these are not detailed in the record in Kings. However, one feat is mentioned, that of his defeat of the Philistines, when he penetrated into their land, and took Gaza, one of their chief cities. In this campaign he not only smote the larger centres, but even the remote and solitary places, so that "the watch towers", did not escape. Gaining control of Philistia greatly improved communications between Judah and Egypt, something upon which Hezekiah later wrongfully depended.

Verses 9-12
The fall of Samaria

In these verses we have a repeat of what has already been considered. (ch.17.9-12). Perhaps the reason for this repeat was that it was the most important crisis in the history of the nation, for it brought to an end the northern kingdom, which had been founded by Jeroboam. Another reason for these verses is that the cause of the disaster, here again mentioned, was disregard for God and His word. This evil is set in sharp contrast to the obedience of Hezekiah.

Verses 13-16
The first invasion of Judah by Sennacherib

These verses relate to almost the middle of Hezekiah's reign, and many of his successes and reforms are passed over. The victory over the northern kingdom, increased the appetite of Sennacherib to do the same in Judah. He almost accomplished his purpose, for he took all its fenced cities. Of course, the supreme prize was Jerusalem, for once it fell to him, this would end the southern kingdom, as the fall of Samaria had ended the northern kingdom.

What disappoints here is, that instead of trusting in God, Hezekiah does what others had done. He tries to bribe the invader, so that he would turn away from him. The cost was tremendous, for no less than 300 talents of silver, and 30 talents of gold were demanded, and given. Once again mention is made of the stripping of the Temple, and of its treasures going into the hands of the heathen. What makes this episode particularly painful is that the very gold-work, which the king had done in early life, was now stripped down. It was doubtless a great joy to him to see the gold restored to the Temple doors, and to see them opened, after his father had closed them for years, but now all their glory was gone, as was the glory of the pillars. Had this payment ended the conflict, he may have claimed that it was well worth the cost involved, but, as in former cases, it only delayed the evil day, and was to no avail.

The experience of many of God's servants is that days of blessing and prosperity are often followed by days of testing. Many think that those who obey God, and labour to restore His testimony, as Hezekiah did the Temple, will live their lives, in peace and prosperity. However this story demonstrates, that no such experiences are guaranteed. Few conceive that devotion to God is often the way to trial. Those who trust Him, are brought into circumstances in which they feel their helplessness, and are made to lean upon Him. Like the king on this occasion, many of them were tempted to yield to the demands of the enemy. It is easy to say that Hezekiah should have trusted God, and let the temple remain as it was, but anyone in his shoes, might have acted as he did. The exhortation is, "resist the devil, and he will flee from you" (Jam 4.7). but too often men yield to his dictates, and are the poorer for doing so.

It is always sad when men, under pressure, pull down the truth which they built up in earlier days. They may claim that it is done in order to secure peace, and that to stand firm would mean disaster, but God can be trusted to defeat the enemy, and to protect those who obey him. Many leaders among God's people have painfully let go what was dear to them, and justified their action by saying that if they had held on to their convictions, the whole company would have disintegrated. Just as the Assyrian invasion was only temporarily halted, so yielding to demands concerning the truth, will not be a permanent remedy.

Verses 17-37
The threat of Sennacherib

As already noted the costly bribe sent to the king of Assyria, only halted the invasion for a short time, for here a fresh attack upon Jerusalem, and the hosts of Assyria gathered around it in a most terrifying manner. The aim was to obtain the surrender of the city without a fight. Well did the Assyrian generals know, that it took them three years to capture Samaria, it would take them even longer to master the walls and fortresses of Jerusalem. All this could be costly, and even mean the loss of some lives as well. In these verses can be seen one outstanding example of the use of propaganda in the arena of war. Every conceivable argument was propounded to break down resistance, and to have the entire city handed over intact, without a bow being drawn, or a dart fired.

Possibly a period of two or three years passed from the time the bounty and the captives of Judah were carried away to Nineveh, until this second attack took place. The three officials who were commissioned to mount the assault, were anxious to negotiate a settlement, and withheld their army from making an assault, until they had tried to bring about a surrender. The names given these men seem to be titles. "Tartan" was the commander-in-chief, "Rabsaris" was the chief eunuch and "Rabshakeh" was chief butler, or cupbearer. These great men were accompanied by a large army, and halted at the well known place, the aqueduct of the Upper Pool". This spot is referred to as the place where Isaiah and his son were to meet Ahaz, when he was confronted with the united attack of Syria and Israel. The prophet assured him that he was not to fear the two tails of smoking firebrands (Is 7.3-4). It would appear that this site was a vantage point where the city could be viewed from a plateau. Hezekiah had done great work in securing an underground water supply to the city from this pool, so that in the case of a siege, the inhabitants would not die of thirst. The fullers spread their cloth on the fields around, and used the water of the pool in their bleaching process.

Neither the king of Assyria, nor the king of Judah, was directly involved in the negotiations, but just as the enemy had three representatives, so Hezekiah appointed three of his officials to speak to them. Firstly, Eliakim, who had recently been appointed head of the household, and had replaced Shebna the scribe as chief treasurer. Secondly, Shebna the scribe, who though not in the high post which he once held, was still a man of importance. Thirdly, Joah the recorder, who would keep a record of all events. Rabshakeh, although not the chief of the delegation, was their spokesman. Possibly he was the most fluent speaker, for later it is implied that he could speak in at least two languages. In Isaiah 38-39 he is the only one of the three mentioned. It is difficult to imagine how the three weaklings from Jerusalem felt as they listened to the arrogant speech of this orator. Their master was just plain Hezekiah, with no titles attached, but he was speaking on behalf of "the great king".

The oration made by Rabshakeh was calculated to demoralise the people of the city. One argument after another was accumulated in such an impressive fashion that for them to attempt any resistance, would seem to be the height of folly. His first point was to demonstrate the army of Hezekiah to be so insignificant that any confidence in it, was sure to prove disappointing. When consideration is taken of the heavy losses sustained in the various wars in the land, and the recent numbers taken into captivity by this enemy, there is no difficulty in believing that all the forces that could be mustered in Jerusalem, would be no match for the powerful army which was attacking. Secondly, Rabshakeh alludes to the possible support which Hezekiah might find in the great power of Egypt. He shows that the land which was famous for its reeds, was like a reed, and any who would lean upon it would be pierced through. Thus the hope of finding assistance in Egypt were also dashed to pieces. A reed may appear stately and strong, but once it is leaned upon, it breaks down, and proves worthless. Rabshakeh implies that any trust in Pharaoh would be as vain as their confidence in their small army. His third argument attacks Hezekiah's trust in the Lord his God, and again he shows this to be a hopeless idea. How could the king expect to be helped by the God whose high-places he had destroyed, and whose altars he had broken down. Rabshakeh's fourth challenge implies that Hezekiah could resist the attack if only he had the help of cavalry, so he offers to supply the horses, if Hezekiah could find men able to ride upon them. It was never God's intention that His people should trust in horses, so the armies of Israel were mainly composed of infantry. If no such men could be mustered, what hope was there for the handful of defenders of the city, who were facing the might that was arrayed against them? Rabshakel claimed that even the soldiers of a single province would be enough to conquer the city. His fifth claim was even more threatening, for it implied that the invasion was inspired by the Lord, and he was simply obeying what he was directed to do. Whether he had heard of what the prophet had written when he spoke of the invasion of the land by Assyria, and called it the "rod of mine anger" (Is 10.5), or whether he was merely pretending to be directed by the Lord, is not known, but one thing is sure, his statement would have been the most devastating for the people to hear. Well they knew that if the Lord was against them, their hopes which were set on Him, had all vanished. It is understandable why the request of the envoy from Hezekiah that the Assyrians should speak in the Syrian language, and not in the Jew's language, for they knew that the faith of the king was much stronger than that of the people. Rabshakeh was shrewd enough to know that if he could terrify the people, then he had his aim almost accomplished. If the populace surrendered, the king could not hold out. To drive home the hopelessness of the situation, he described the extremities of a siege, when people would attempt to relieve their hunger and thirst by partaking of what was the foulest fare.

At the close of his speech Rabshakeh raised his voice, so that all could hear, and stressed in eloquent terms, the wonderful advantage the people would have if they would surrender. He speaks on behalf of the "great king" of Assyria, but refers to the king of Judah by his personal name, and never calls him king. Only two possibilities remained for their deliverance. One was that they would fight and overcome the invaders. This he shows to be impossible. The second, and most important was that the Lord would deliver. He went to great lengths to remove this prop, and to show that it was a forlorn hope. He adopts the attitude of a benefactor, and paints a rosy picture of the kind treatment they would receive as captives, and promises that they will be spared to enjoy a land similar to their own. The best of conditions awaited them if only they would come out and make an agreement with him, and accompany it with a present. The result of this surrender would be that, instead of the horrible conditions of a siege they would be living in peaceful conditions with all the fruits of the land at their disposal to enjoy. These good things, however, were not to be theirs in the land of Canaan, but in some foreign land, to which they would be brought.

The final note struck was that a glance at the previous successes of the king of Assyria in overcoming all the gods of the nations, would let the people of Jerusalem see that dependence upon the Lord, as Hezekiah had enjoined them to do (2 Chron 32.6-8), was a deception. His argument here would have been unanswerable if the Lord had been as helpless as these other gods. To his mind all gods were alike, but he must never have known, or else had forgotten, the mighty doings of the Lord, from the days of the founding of the nation. Possibly he also had in mind that the northern kingdom spoke of the same Lord as the people of Jerusalem. Samaria was already conquered, so the folly of trusting the same power to defend this city, would end in disappointment. No god had until now been able to resist the force of the Assyrian army. His mistake was to put the Lord into the same category as local gods

The people listened in silence, as they had been advised by the king to do, but the envoys returned with rent garments. These were an outward symbol of their inward distress, and they rehearsed to the king the words of Rabshakeh. There was little comfort in their report, but to the ear of a spiritual man like Hezekiah, it contained one glimmer of hope. The defiance of the living God by these Assyrians, he knew would rouse the anger of the Almighty. When God's name is dishonoured, and His claims disowned, He will always prove to His enemies that He is all that He claims to be.

There is a possibility that the power of propaganda is underestimated, for many have been swept off their feet, in the spiritual realm, by the forcefulness of words, especially if they come from an eloquent speaker. All ought to be wary of any speech which attempts to weaken trust in the Lord. Much that Rabshakeh said when speaking of Egypt, the prophet Isaiah would have accepted as true. Likewise his statement regarding the helplessness of the gods of the nations was equally supported by the prophet, but when he sought to level the Lord with these false deities, then he was totally mistaken.

Another lesson which can be learned from this oration is the importance of fortifying the minds of saints against Satanic attacks. Hezekiah had the simple people of the city warned of what was coming, and assured them that the Lord was able to deliver. He had confidence in God, but he made sure that his confidence was shared by the people. It would have been a delusion on his part to assume that because he had faith in God, the people were also believers. Leaders must make sure that those they lead are not depending on them, but on the Lord.

The enemy, through the voice of his spokesmen, would to this day extol the benefits of surrendering the truth. Many companies of saints can testify that when they gave in to the demands of the younger people, they thought this would be an end to all strife. Alas they learned that the more they yielded, the stronger were the demands made. The dream of sitting under vine and fig trees, with a well beside them, was indeed most attractive, but what was not at that point stressed was that they would be doing so as slaves in a strange land. The Assyrians had not the welfare of the Jews at heart, nor has the devil and his hosts any good in store for those who listen to his insinuations.

Notes

31 The word "present" (BRAHCHAH - 1294) is almost always translated "blessing", or "present" (ch.18.31),but here it possibly has the idea of "peace" (NIV), which was considered a blessing. If they surrender to him, this will be a blessing. The clause occurs only here. The eating of the fruit trees and drinking "the waters of his cistern" are in contrast to v.27.

34 "Hamath" was a city about one hundred and twenty miles north of Damascus. It was captured by Solomon (2 Chron 8.3-4). "Arpad" was a city close by Hamath, "Sepharvaim" was a city of Babylonia, "Hena" was a town on the Euphrates; and "Ivah" was possibly a town in the northern border of Assyria. These were meant to show the scope of the Assyrian victories. They reappear in the threat to Hezekiah (ch.19.13).

CHAPTER 19, Verses 1-8
Hezekiah's message to Isaiah, and its results

The heavy tidings brought to Hezekiah by his envoys drove him to God and to Isaiah the prophet. Little wonder that his heart was broken, and his spirit distressed, for the words of Rabshakeh were calculated to drive from him any faint hope of deliverance he may have entertained. Solomon in his prayer, at the dedication of the Temple, had anticipated that some may be in distress, and that in their extremity, even should they be in a strange land, if they would turn to the Temple, then the Lord would deliver them (1 Kings 8.33). The king took advantage of this and went into the house of God. Conscious also that Isaiah the prophet was God's representative at that time, he sent Eliakim to him. He would give the prophet a first hand account of all that had been said at the upper pool. The picture he used to illustrate his plight was most impressive, for a woman in travail, and not able to bring forth, would surely die, unless early relief would be granted to her. Similarly, unless something was to be done quickly for Jerusalem, its end was certain. As has already been pointed out, Hezekiah knew that God would defend His own name, and that the blasphemy of the king of Assyria, would not go unchallenged.

The prophet was not in the slightest perturbed at the distressing news, but tells the king's envoys to say to their master "Be not afraid of the words which thou hast heard". Four things are about to happen to the king of Assyria. First, God will put a spirit in him, second, he will hear news, third, he will leave Jerusalem and go back home and fourth, he will be slain. This brief statement was the balm the heart of Hezekiah needed. The God Who controls the heavens, and has at His disposal the armies of heaven, can soon bring about circumstances that upset the plans of wicked men. Just as sure as the prophet had said it, the battle ground was transferred from Jerusalem to Libnah. Possibly part of the army of Sennacherib withdrew, so the storm was over for this time, and the imminent danger of an attack halted.

Tests of faith in God are not imaginary ills, but are real trials, sufficiently severe that when they come, even the stoutest heart is shaken to its foundation. God may, at times, allow his servants to reach the brink of despair, but He sits watching over the furnace, and controls the heat, so that they are able to bear it. Sometimes news is anxiously awaited, and when it is heard, the hearts of the hearers sink in despair, but the delight of God is to grant deliverance even in an unexpected way. Hezekiah could never have imagined how simple it was for God to frustrate the intentions of the invaders.

Like most history, there is a typical aspect to the story. As has been suggested already, this siege of Jerusalem is a preview of a greater siege, when again the same city will be surrounded by world powers, and even part of it will be captured. Then the Lord will come, and, as in this case, deliverance will be wrought in a miraculous way (Zec 14.2-4). The figure of a woman in travail used by the messengers sent to Isaiah by the king is one which the prophets use when speaking of Israel's future crisis (Jer 4.31; 6.24). Her lack of strength to deliver is the prominent thought. Unless a mother in such pains is soon delivered, her own life, and the life of her expected offspring, would end. The daughter of Zion was in such a plight, but God, the great midwife as it were, would not be slow to act, and show his ability to deliver.

As has already been stressed, the one encouraging feature of the ultimatum from Rabshakeh was his outlandish reproach of God. This meant that the conflict was not between the powerful Assyrians, and the weak defenders of the city, but between the Lord and idolatry. The king was almost certain that the Lord would defend the honour of His own name. With this in view, the prophet could well afford to lift up his prayer to God for the weak remnant that still remained in the city, and have confidence that it would be spared in spite of the threatenings of Rabshakeh.

The alarming news of the messengers in no way disturbed Isaiah so he calmed their spirits, and told them to tell their master not to be afraid of all that he had heard, nor of the blasphemous speech which had so troubled him. The blast from Jehovah will soon change the situation, for news will reach the camp of the king of Assyria, which will cause him to return home. Instead of bringing with him the spoil of the city, and a host of captives, he will return to end his days, by being slain even in the idol temple. Perhaps some twenty years elapsed before he was slain, nevertheless, the word of the Lord was fulfilled (v.37).

When the spokesman, Rabshakeh returned to the camp, all had changed since he left. Instead of the army preparing to attack the city, it had been diverted to another battleground named Libnah. There is some uncertainty as to where exactly Libnah was situated. It must have been somewhere near Lachish, but whether it was nearer to Jerusalem is not known. Possibly Lachish had been captured by Sennacherib before the war at Libnah, but whatever happened, the threatened danger to Jerusalem was ended, at least for that time, and this must have been no small relief to Hezekiah. The clouds he so much dreaded had blown away, and the storm which he feared, had never materialized.

Can it be that the greater part of human distresses are purely in the mind, and do not really occur? This in no way means that they do not cause deep concern, especially when, in the dilemma, there is no apparent way of deliverance. Hezekiah could never have guessed how he would be relieved at this time, but God made great changes, and did so in a simple way. All high-handed actions against God should strengthen faith, and make the tried ones more confident that He will act to defend His great name, and do so in His own time and way.

Verses 9-14
The Assyrian letter to Hezekiah

Lest Hezekiah should imagine that the diversion of the strength of the Assyrian army to Libnah meant that the threat to Jerusalem was over, a letter was sent to him to assure him that the attack would be resumed as soon as the war in Libnah was ended. What induced the king of Ethiopia to wage war against the Assyrians is not stated. Perhaps he thought that if Judah were overrun, the aggressor would turn south and conquer Egypt. On the other hand, he may have felt it his duty to assist Hezekiah in his day of distress. Whatever the motive, it was ordained of God and fulfilled the purpose of deflecting pressure from Jerusalem, at least for a time. The letter recounted the successes of Sennacherib in conquering the different places he had attacked, and demonstrated the helplessness of their gods to protect them from his power. Most of these victories were of recent times, and were well known throughout the world. The first four places mentioned here were all in the upper Euphrates valley, or near one of its tributaries, thus they were really an early part of the Assyrian empire. The next places mentioned have already been referred to in ch.18.34. When the letter was read to Hezekiah and given to him he took it to the house of God and spread it out before the Lord. In this he was, as it were, asking the Lord to read it for Himself.

Verses 15-19
Hezekiah's prayer

In verse 4 Hezekiah asked Isaiah to pray for the remnant, but here he, himself undertakes to pray, and spread out before the Lord his supplications. The prayer may be divided into four parts. First there is a confession of God's greatness (v.15), second, a plea for God to look and hear the reproaches of Sennacherib (v.16), third, an acknowledgement that the claims made by the king of Assyria were true (vv.17-18) and fourth, a request for salvation at this time (v.19). In extolling the greatness of God he mentions four great factors. He refers to Him as the "The Lord God of Israel". In this he is reminding the Lord that He has ever associated His name with the nation, and has shown the nation His power, especially when He delivered it from Egypt. The king followed this statement with the fact that in the holiest of all the Lord sits enthroned between the cherubim, and so has communicated His mind to His people. This sacred spot was the place where revelations were given to Moses. Then he states that the Lord is alone, so He has no rival, and concludes this confession by stating that unlike the false gods, who were local, the Lord is the universal God, Who has a right to rule, because He has made heaven and earth. Having established the greatness of the One to whom he speaks, he proceeds to request Him to take heed to both the oral and written reproaches of Sennacherib. In this plea he is using the strongest possible argument before the Lord, for he expected One so great to defend His own honour, and prove that the blasphemy of a mere mortal, will not go unpunished. In the next part of his prayer, he acknowledges the claims of the Assyrian king were indeed no empty boast. These victories had been won, but the conquered had no God to help them, but were depending upon gods which could be burnt in the fire. Such were not able to save themselves, and therefore, could do nothing for their worshippers. Finally, his plea for salvation out of the hand of the invader, if answered, would not only be the deliverance of Jerusalem, but would spread the fame of the Lord throughout the kingdoms of the earth.

When speaking to God in prayer men must ever bear in mind the greatness of the One to whom they speak. Though so mighty, yet He is pleased to bend His ear to the cries of His needy people. Likewise they must not forget that He will ever display His power, when its existence is questioned by man. Pharaoh may say "Who is the Lord?" (Ex 5.2), but he received an answer in a way that could not be questioned. Blasphemy and reproach may still be hurled against the Almighty, but He does not need any mortal to defend Him, for He can safeguard His own honour. When praying to Him, the intercessors must not be afraid to face facts, and confess the reality of their problems. Prayers should be such, that when answered, the Lord will be glorified, and the fame of His name spread abroad. When threatenings were made against God's servants in Acts 4 they prayed that signs and wonders might be done through Jesus. Their prayer was heard and the fame of the Lord spread abroad (Acts 5.12).

Verses 20-34
The Lord's answer through Isaiah

Hezekiah had not long to wait until confirmation of the answer to his prayer was given him by the prophet Isaiah. In these verses, after the assurance that his prayer was heard he was told of what the Lord had to say to Sennacherib, vv.21-28. Then the Lord's message to himself follows in vv.29-34. These two messages are in poetic form, and are almost verbatim with the record in Isaiah (ch.37). Like the prayer of vv.15-19 this account of Isaiah's prophecy is not in 2 Chronicles. The entire song is couched in figurative language, which exhibits more vividly the statements of the oracle.

The message concerning Sennacherib in the song could be divided into five parts. First there was the scorn of the people of Jerusalem v.2, second the slanderous words he spoke against the Lord vv.22-23, third the successes of which he boasts v.24, fourth the sovereignty of God in what he had done vv.25-26 and fifth the sentence passed upon him vv.27-28. Though the words of his letter were meant to terrify the people of Jerusalem, yet their response was one of scorn and derision. The city, viewed as a virgin daughter is one who will not be defiled by the corruptions of idolatry, and will not fall for the enticement offered by the invader. She will not open her arms to his army, nor allow it into her streets. She shakes her head, as one who says "no", or as one who mocks and derides. Sennacherib, through his spokesman Rabshakeh, had spoken of the Lord as though He was like one of the gods of the nations, and looked down upon Him, as though he was His superior. He had forgotten that the One whom he so treats is "the holy one of Israel". In his boasting, he reproached the Lord, and took all the honour to himself. He imagines that his successes were due to his chariots, and that he has reached heights and uninhabited terrain, which none other has ever been able to attain. Even the forest of Lebanon with its tall trees was not out of his bounds, nor did he hesitate to fell its lofty cedars. The vital necessity for warriors in the Middle East is a supply of water. He claims to dry up the water, and to deprive his enemies of what was essential for their existence. He has dug wells, even in places where water was never found before, so that his own troops would have ample supplies of this vital commodity. Thus he claimed to have complete control of natural resources. However, he had failed to grasp, that what he gloried in as his own achievements, were in fact the doings of the Almighty, and were purposed before Sennacherib had any part in them. It never dawned upon his mind that he was but a tool is in the Lord's hand, to execute His judgment upon sinful nations, and that this is why he found them so easy to defeat. They had fallen under him like dust, and had disappeared like a bunch of grass on the top of a thatched house, which the burning sun soon withers away. His folly lay in not realizing that the God who punished these nations would not spare him, especially because of his blasphemy, which had reached unto heaven. The judgment pronounced upon him was severe, for he would return to his own land like a wild beast taken captive by a hook in its nose. It was an Assyrian custom to put a ring through the upper lip and nose. To this ring they attached a rope, and led their prisoners, especially kings, into the presence of their king to be sentenced by him. The retirement of Sennacherib from Jerusalem will be such a humiliating experience for him, that it will be as if he were returning home a prisoner.

The prophecy changes from addressing the king of Assyria to speech directed to Hezekiah (v.29). He was offered a sign, which would prove that the city was not going to fall, as he had feared. The invasion had prevented the sowing of crops, so the following spring the growth of the crops was to be as they were in the year when the land rested during the Sabbatical year, and only what sprang from the seed in the ground would be reaped. The next year would be better, for some seed could be kept from the scanty supply and sown, but in the third year all will be back to normal, so that the vineyards, as well as the fields of grain, will yield all that could be desired of them. Using the figure of planting and bearing fruit, the prophecy continues to show that the remnant, as well as the crops, will increase. No doubt the invasion of the Assyrians had reduced the population of Judah to a low level, but when the siege is over, the people will leave the city, and spread throughout the land again. The king of Assyria will not enter the city, nor will he even begin an attack. The city will be defended by the Lord, who will do this for His own name's sake, and for David's sake.

These precious promises from the Lord through Isaiah must have brought great relief to the heart of Hezekiah, and left him with calm expectations for the immediate future. He was not told how the Lord would bring them about, nor could he have imagined the way they would be fulfilled. This, however, was not his concern, but had to be left to the Lord who had promised. There can be little doubt that these things are typical of a future day, as has already been pointed out. Possibly they give a hint that the wondrous prosperity of the Millennium kingdom, so well described in Is.35, may not come suddenly. There will possibly be some time elapse before the fullness promised for that period, will be experienced. In the deliverances wrought in the present age in answer to prayer, there may also be a period before the full enjoyments of them are realized.

Verses 35-37
The destruction of the Assyrian army, and death of Sennacherib

The historian leaves the poetic form and returns to prose. The sudden destruction, by the angel of the Lord, of one hundred and eighty five thousand soldiers of the Assyrian army, all in one night must have sent a shudder through the spine of their king. Apparently this disaster took place the very night that Isaiah had delivered his prophecy. There is no mention of what exactly was the cause of so many deaths, but the Angel who smote the firstborn in Egypt, could easily smite the Assyrian army. Not all were slain, but those spared witnessed, not merely men sick and dying, but men already dead. The king of Assyria lost no time in retreating to the capital of his empire, Nineveh.

Some eighteen or more years passed before the sons of

Sennacherib conspired to slay him. Why they turned against their father is not told, but their action was most unnatural. Their foul deed was done while he worshipped in his temple. In this atrocity, the lesson is obvious, that the idols are helpless in protecting their worshippers This is because they are "no gods". Neither Adrammelech, nor Sharezer, who killed their father, was able to seize the crown, but it was given to another son, called Esarhaddon. As for the murderers, they fled to the land of Armenia or Ararat, and nothing more is said of them in this book. Why thy chose Ararat as their place of shelter may have been that it was a mountainous area which was most difficult to reach, even though it was the resting place of Noah's ark.

Most likely Hezekiah was not spared to hear of Sennacherib's death, but it has a message for all blasphemers. It sounds the warning note in their ears, that all they say is heard in heaven, and will be given the answer it deserves. Pharaoh, Nebuchadnezzar, Belshazzar, or Herod, all of whom were guilty of speaking proudly, as though they were God, all suffered His judgment as a consequence. There is a great contrast in the empty boasting of these kings with the One Who was truly God manifest in flesh, who said, "I am meek and lowly in heart" (Matt 11.29). The persecutors of God's people in this age may seem to escape His wrath, but this is only for a time, for, unless they repent, their day of reaping will come.

Notes

3 The three words. "trouble" (TZAHRAH - 6869), "rebuke" (TOHCHAHGHATH - 8433), and "blasphemy" (NAHTZAH - 5007) show us respectively the day was one of distress for the city, one of chastisement for failure, and one of reproach or disgrace.

7 The "blast" or "wind" would blow him off course, and this would come about through a "rumour" (SHMOOGAH - 8052) or "report" which he will hear. Most commentators, however, prefer the RV which translates "blast" as a "spirit in him". The meaning then would be that a spirit of cowardice would enter into his soul and this would cause him to return to his own land. The idea that the "blast" (7307) is external is supported by Ex 15.8,10; and Is 25.4.

9 Tirhakah called here the king of Ethiopia, was one of the Pharaohs, though born in Ethiopia. In Sennacherib's own history he claims to have defeated this king and to have taken his son captive, but the king himself escaped to Ethiopia.

21 The idea of "shaking" (NOOAG - 5128) the head in scorn occurs in Job 16.4; Ps 22.7; 109.25; Lam 2.15 and Zep 2.15.

31 The word "corpses" (PEHGER - 6297) is translated "carcases" (Gen 15.11); "dead bodies" (Jer 31.40).

37 Nothing is known of "Nisroch his god", but the name may only refer to the temple where he worshipped. Perhaps he had a personal god, which was known to others by a different name. Apparently Esarhaddon was Sennacherib's favourite son, and the two sons who murdered their father were angry at his partiality. The new king was, according to the records, very successful in extending the power and influence of the Assyrian empire. He placed in Judah those whose descendants sought to help in the rebuilding of the Temple, but their help was refused, because they were enemies (Ezra 4.2).

CHAPTER 20, Verses 1-11
Hezekiah's sickness and recovery

The first thirteen years of Hezekiah's reign were comparatively calm, for though the king of Assyria was heavily engaged in the destruction of the northern kingdom, Judah was left to prosper. However, the storm broke in the fourteenth year when the cities of Judah were captured, and even the city of Jerusalem was in grave danger. It was in that same year that this terrible life-threatening illness became the lot of Hezekiah, so, as already noticed, troubles seldom come alone. In Chronicles it is only briefly mentioned, but in Isaiah all is developed, for not only is the illness reported, but a detailed account of the prayer, or song of praise, which he offered during it is also recorded. The sickness in itself may not have been too distressing to the king, but when Isaiah visited him, and pronounced the death sentence, "thou shalt die, and not live" then the seriousness of his plight was brought home to him. In other difficulties he had sent for the prophet, or sent news to him, but on this occasion, the prophet arrived without any invitation. To bring such sad news, to the God-fearing king, must have placed a heavy burden on the prophet's heart. The fact that Hezekiah at this time had no son to fill the throne made the news even more painful for him to bear. Little wonder he turned away from all his attendants and gazed into the wall. As in all his troubles, he poured out his heart to the Lord, and pled with Him for deliverance. He based his prayer on his past record, for he had lived in the fear of God, and had kept from idolatry, or any other form of evil. He is not claiming sinless perfection, for in Isaiah he confessed that God "cast all his sins behind His back" (ch.38.17). Apparently, he modelled his plea on the example of David, who often used similar language when pleading for his life (Ps 63.8). He was being cut off in the midst of his life, for he had not reached forty years at this time. The clouds were black, and not a star was in sight.

Before he had time to "set his house in order" or make his will, the scene was changed, for the prophet, who had delivered the heavy tidings, was halted on his journey. Just as he was leaving the precincts of the palace he was directed back to the king with an entirely different message. This time it was to assure him that his prayer was heard, his tears were seen, his sickness was going to end, he would go back to the house of God and the city would be defended from the Assyrians. Like waters to a thirsty soul, these words ended his distress, and relieved his spirit. The God of David, would do all this, and prove to His people that the passing of time had not changed Him, and that what He did for His servant at the beginning of the kingdom, He was willing to do when it was almost at its end.

Some have wondered how two messages so very different, could come from the Lord at almost the same time. The same principle can be seen in the message to Nineveh by the mouth of Jonah. In all God's threats of judgment, there is room for repentance, and where this is genuine, it is a bar to its execution. Just as David's repentance saved him from the penalty his sin deserved, so his son, Hezekiah, was spared at this time.

His cure was not instantaneous, nor was it without a natural remedy. The fig poultice applied, with God's blessing, brought about the healing. The same principle is seen in the anointing with oil, and prayer (Jam 5.13-15). The mention of "the third day" suggests the thought of resurrection. One, as good as dead, going up to the house of God on the third day is an illustration of that great truth.

Like many in Old Testament times, Hezekiah sought some proof that what he had heard would be fulfilled. He is not rebuked for his unbelief, but a sign is given to him, which confirmed the promise he had heard. He was given a choice of whether the shadow would move forward or back. He chose the latter, for he considered it to be the greater wonder. Thus, as he lay at the window looking out at the sundial of Ahaz, he witnessed the great miracle, for the shadow on the dial moved ten degrees backward.

Just as surely as the siege of the city was a foreshadowing of the future siege of Jerusalem so this sickness of the king is another symbol of that future day. In his sickness is illustrated the soul agony of the repentant remnant, which will accompany their plight, when they will be surrounded by their enemies. In that "time of Jacob's trouble" there will be great searching of heart, for with deepest sorrow they will mourn every family apart when they realize the enormity of their sin, in rejecting Christ (Zec 12.11-13). Likewise, in the great song of repentance, Isaiah 53, the state of the nation there described is that of a people formerly in sickness who confess that, by the stripes of the One they once rejected, they have been healed. Just as the king returned to the Temple on the third day, so will the nation he symbolizes, be healed, and raised up on the third day (Hos 6.1-3).

There are practical lessons in this story which should not be neglected. God may bring to the brink of despair before He delivers. Likewise, he allows, on occasions, not only one trouble, but several troubles to converge at the same time. The greatest wisdom in such circumstances is to do what Hezekiah did, take the humble place before God, frankly confess sin, even though nothing specific is known that has offended Him, and trust Him to deliver in His own way. Experiences like that of the king are painful at the time, but they can often increase the knowledge of God's ways, and the appreciation of His mercy and grace. It is not becoming in this period of full revelation to ask for signs, but often a word from the Scripture can come home in power to the heart, which gives calm assurance.

Verses 12-19
The Babylonian visitors to Hezekiah

Quite often a special time of blessing and of great deliverance is followed by a severe test. Few men can accept miraculous intervention on their behalf, without being in some measure inflated. God's dealings in mercy ought to leave men humble, and filled with a sense of unworthiness, yet the history of the past, and what all have witnessed, demonstrates that the weed of pride can grow in what was considered humble soil. Hezekiah, with all his experience, when left to himself, proved his weakness, and lack of wisdom, when the princes of Babylon came to visit him. Their visit was more dangerous than the armies of Assyria, but he was totally unaware of this. These agents of Berodach-baladan king of Babylon, brought with them letters, and a present. Their letter differed greatly from the one sent by Sennacherib, and the present with it, was a sharp contrast to the threatening which his contained. However, the Assyrian letter, shows the enemy as a "roaring lion", whereas the Babylonian letter, reveals the same enemy as "an angel of light". The sad feature of this story is that Hezekiah was left to himself at this time, for the Lord left him to prove him, (2 Chron 32.31). Perhaps he did not feel his need of God when such apparent friends came to see him, for, as is often pointed out, there is no reference to him praying at this time as he did in other crises.

The reason for the interest of the king of Babylon in the king of Judah is not in doubt, for "the wonder done in the land" had aroused the interest of the astrologists of his kingdom. The sign would have been more important to them, than the miraculous healing of the king. They doubtless would desire to learn more about the man, for whose benefit the sun had returned ten degrees backward. The fact that he was the subject of Assyrian attack, would also have the king of Babylon's sympathy, for he, himself, had suffered from the same enemy.

Hezekiah's chief failure at this time was his display of his entire possessions to the Babylonian ambassadors. He evidently wanted to impress them with his power to withstand attacks, as well as with the treasures which he and others before him, had gathered from defeated enemies. In doing this, he took all the glory, and failed to assure his visitors that all of his wealth came to him by the hand of the God he worshipped. Those visitors were very different from the Queen of Sheba, for she came to Solomon, and brought him presents, but went home with the knowledge of the true God in her soul. There is not a hint that they became converts to the God of Israel.

The aged prophet Isaiah brought his final message to Hezekiah at this time, one which told him of the sad consequences of his folly. When questioned about the visitors, and how he had treated them, he replied in an honest manner, for until then, he did not think he had done wrong in giving these friends access to his possessions. The words of the prophet must have fallen like thunder on his ears, for they told him that all his wealth would be carried to Babylon, and worse still, that his descendants would be carried away with it, and that his sons would become eunuchs in the palace of that foreign king. Daniel and his friends were the fulfillment of this. The only good feature which he could detect in this sad prophecy was that the evil would be delayed until after his death. He humbly submitted to the threatened judgment, and felt relieved that he would be allowed to end his days in peace. Perhaps there is a tinge of selfishness in his remarks, but at least he was relieved that no immediate judgment fell upon him for his mistake.

There is one great principle taught in this story which must ever be borne in mind. The friendship of the world, especially the religious world which Babylon typifies, is enmity with God. When it comes as a pretentious friend, it is much more subtle than when it appears as a foe. Nothing has been more injurious to many testimonies, than when they have been blessed by the Lord, but instead of keeping humble, they have gloried in their spiritual stature. It is most important that those who are gathered to the Lord's name should have discernment to enable them to distinguish between an honest enquirer, like the Queen of Sheba, and the enemy's agents, like those men from Babylon. The truths of Scripture, like the treasures of Judah, have been stolen by the religious world, and used in a way the Lord never intended them to be used. "Baptism", "church", "priest", "Christian", "bishop"; these truths and many others have an entirely different meaning in the world to what they have in the word of God.

Verses 20-21
The death of Hezekiah
Once again the historian directs attention to the book of Chronicles where, if any desires to learn the full extent of the achievements of Hezekiah, they will find it fully recorded. (This is not a reference to the books of Chronicles which follow this book, for they were not written at this time). Before he does so, he makes special mention of one great engineering feat which Hezekiah accomplished for the city of Jerusalem. This was the conduit connecting the well, or Virgin spring, in the Kidron valley, to the reservoir in the inner city. The purpose of this water supply was to meet the needs of the city, especially at a time of siege. Survival of its inhabitants in such a crisis, would depend largely on them having this vital commodity.

When the king died, he was not put into the royal tombs, probably because they were full by this time, but into a grave close by, which, according to 2 Chronicles, was in a lofty position. By the time of his death he had a son of twelve years old, so Manasseh was born three years after the king's sickness, and as far as is known was his only heir.

Notes
5 It is rather unusual for the king to be called "captain" (NAHGEED - 5057). Only four kings, in these books of Kings, are so entitled. Solomon, (1 Kings 1.35), Jeroboam (1 Kings 14.7), Baasha (1 Kings

16.2) and Hezekiah here. Its primary idea is "to go in front", so to be a "commander", or a "leader". See Is 55.4.

7 The "boil" (SHGHEEN - 7822) was the same as plagued Egypt (Ex 9), and could be leprous (Lev 13.18-23). It was the lot of Job to be covered with boils (Job 2:7).

11 The "dial" (MAHGALAH - 4609) was a set of stairs, or steps on which the sun shone so that the shadow cast, denoted the time of day. This apparatus was the invention of Ahaz, who may have seen such an arrangement in Syria, and had it copied in Judah, as he did regarding the altar which he saw there (ch.16.10-11).

12 "Berodach-baladan" or "Merodach-baladan" was the king who established, in spite of much opposition, and at times defeat, the kingdom of Babylon. The fierce opposition he suffered from Assyria gave him a common lot with Hezekiah. Many think the visit, and present were more than an expression of sympathy, but were designed to form a league with Judah, and so unite against a common foe. In showing the treasures, especially the "house of his armour", Hezekiah may have been displaying his resources for future conflicts.

20 Of all the works of Hezekiah, which were many, only one is mentioned here at his end, that of bringing water into the city. In the historian's view this was his major achievement. The water was brought from the well of the virgin in the Kidron valley in a tunnel cut through the rock, and collected in the pool. This pool was probably the Pool of Siloam. In 1880 an inscription was discovered on the walls of the tunnel. Some of the letters were washed off, but what remained indicate that the excavations were begun from opposite ends, and that they met in the middle as desired. The pool is rectangular, and measures fifty-eight feet long, eighteen broad, and nineteen deep.

CHAPTER 21, Verses 1-9
The evil reign of Manasseh

The history of the kings of Judah is like the land they reigned in, for it is a series of hills and valleys. The story rises up to great heights, telling of good kings, and then descends into the valley, recording the doings of evil ones. In no case does it descend so low as in the history of Manasseh. He reached depths of evil which the worst of previous kings never sounded and, what is even more difficult to understand is, that he was allowed longer on the throne than any other of Judah's kings. Although his reign extended to fifty five years, yet possibly five of these were spent in captivity in Babylon. A persistent question in many minds is, "How could such a good king, as Hezekiah undoubtedly was, produce such a wicked son?". Most answer that he was so young when his father died, that he was little influenced by him. Others claim that the court officers, who surrounded him were totally different in character to his father. Even though they served in the court, they were merely tolerating Hezekiah's strict way of life. When he died they felt free to turn to their own idolatrous ways. It was their example and pressure which drove Manasseh to his evil ways. Perhaps the terrible reality of human depravity is not easy to accept. The best of men can only transmit their fallen nature to their offspring, and whatever good is in them is only by the grace of God. One thing is clear, he resembled his grandfather, Ahaz, much more than he did, his father.

Manasseh seemed to have special delight in undoing all that his father had done. He set himself to revive the idolatry and corruption which had plagued Judah and which had been purged during the early years of Hezekiah's reign. Even the Baal worship, which seemed to have been purged from the land, was again practiced. The very sins which caused the destruction of the seven nations of Canaan, he freely re-introduced. The worst feature of his ways was his desecration of the Temple. Evil king Ahaz, who stopped the worship, and closed the Temple doors, did not go so far as this king. Manasseh removed the ark, and used the sanctuary, which was built as God's dwelling, as an idol's temple. He installed a graven image of Asherah in the most holy place, so the priests had to carry the ark again on their shoulders (2 Chron 35.3). The Palace, in which God had chosen to place His name, became the habitation of demons. The worst forms of idolatry he practiced, and even went the length of putting his sons into the fire. Along with idolatry there was its companion evil of spiritism. The craze for knowledge derived from the realm of demons became a marked feature of his life. The depths of evil to which he sank were lower than nations whose evils were once viewed as the worst possible. He not only did these wicked things himself, but he pressurised the people to join with him in his corrupt practices. They seemed to be willing to obey his evil dictates, and few, if any of them seemed to resist his corrupt ways. It is possible that the strict rule of Hezekiah had become irksome to them, and that they considered the new freedom to worship whatever god they chose, as a great boon.

When Uzziah attempted to offer incense in the Temple, he was smitten with leprosy, but apparently Manasseh could go into the same place, and suffer no harm. Could it be that when the ark was withdrawn, the sanctuary had been stripped of the symbol of God's presence, so in a sense, had become like an ordinary building?

Verses 10-15
The Lord's message to Manasseh

Although God tolerated the evil ways of the nation and its king, yet he was observing all that was transpiring. As might be expected, He was careful to warn them of the consequences of what they were doing. There is no information as to who the instruments were, whom He used at this time to bring His message to the people, but Isaiah was not amongst them, for by this stage he was dead. Because the nation had sunk to a level lower than the Amorites, it was ripe for judgment. The wrath of God, when it breaks forth, can be very alarming. When news of His judgment on Judah reaches those who will hear about it, their ears shall tingle with the noise of it. The same treatment measured out to Samaria, was about to fall upon Judah, for God was provoked to wipe it clean, and empty it out like a plate turned upside down. The climax of their departure had been reached. Though it began shortly after they were redeemed out of Egypt, and continued throughout their history, yet at this time it had reached its limit, so that nothing but a complete removal to captivity was sure to be their lot.

Verses 16-18
The death and burial of Manasseh

The mention of the crowning evil of Manasseh, which was his slaying of the innocent, is reserved until the end of his history. The persecution of those who resisted his idolatrous ways was pursued by him with the sternest measures. His flooding of Jerusalem with blood was something that God could not pass over, and is later given as the main reason for the Babylonian captivity (ch 24.4).

The history of Manasseh in this book closes without any mention of his captivity in Assyria, or his repentance at the end of his life. These are given in 2 Chronicles. Perhaps he is the greatest example in the OT of the words, "Where sin abounded, grace did much more abound" (Rom 5.20).

Apparently Manasseh died of natural causes, and though not buried in the royal tombs, he was laid in a private grave in the garden of his palace. He must have had sad memories on his deathbed. He may have regretted his former evils, but no sorrow of his could undo them.

Verses 19-26
The short reign of Amon

Most likely Amon was not the eldest son of Manasseh, for usually when sons were given to pass through the fire, the firstborn was sacrificed. Though spared to wear the crown, his reign was shorter than any of the kings who went before him. Little can be said regarding his mother, for the place from which she came has not been definitely identified. Whatever change may have come to his father, one thing is sure, Amon himself followed with zeal the evils he saw practised in his early life. There is not a hint in the story that he repented, or even turned his thoughts to the God of his forefathers.

Unlike his father, who lived until his late sixties, Amon was a young man of twenty-four when he was slain by his servants. Possibly he attributed the long life of his father to the idols he worshipped, but his gods proved their powerlessness in that they could not safeguard him, not even when in his own house. He was not the only king of Judah to suffer from the hands of conspirers, for Joash, and Amaziah suffered the same fate.

This conspiracy of his servants does not appear to be due to religious beliefs, but must have been for personal matters. The people punished the murderers, so they must have sanctioned the king's way of living. They did not give the crown to one of the conspirers, but set it on the head of the slain king's son, Josiah, who at that time was only eight years old. One of the features of the royal family was the early age at which the sons married. If Amon was twenty four when he died, then he must have been married as a lad of fifteen. As has already been pointed out, the royal tombs of David were full for quite a time before this, so the murdered king could not be buried in one of them. He, nevertheless, was given an honourable burial, when his body was placed beside that of his father, in the garden of Uzza.

Notes
9 Manasseh "seduced" (TAHGAH - 8582) or 'caused to err' the people, and so was like Jeroboam who made Israel to sin.

12 When ears "tingle" (TZAHLAL - 6750), they shake, or rattle, as it were, because of the news they have heard. The word occurs again in 1 Sam 3.11; Jer 19.3; Hab 3.16.

13 God is about to put the same tests to Jerusalem as he had put to Samaria. The "line" was to measure; the "plummet" was to gauge their uprightness. The former city had become as bad as the latter, which was already destroyed.

CHAPTER 22, Verses 1-2
Josiah is made king
After reading the sad story of Manasseh and Amon, it is a great relief to read of one more king who feared God and sought to restore his people to the right ways of the Lord. He was one of the few, who were named before they were born, for the men of God out of Judah, prophesied that there would be a child born into the house of David, Josiah by name (I Kings 13.2). Thus some three hundred years before he was born his name was settled. Whether his parents knew they were fulfilling prophecy when they so named him is not known, but God overruled in their choice. His grandmother came from Boscath, which was in the south of Judah. He moulded his life on the pattern of David, as all good kings of Judah did, and not on the example of his father, or grandfather. While many of the good kings had turned aside in their latter life, he was different, for he "turned not aside to the right hand or to the left". Who influenced him in his tender years, for he began to reign when only eight years old, or who caused him to be so different from his parents, and the officials who surrounded him, is not revealed. Possibly Hilkiah, the high priest played a part in his early education. Jeremiah and Zephaniah were both prophesying during his reign, but not until he was several years on the throne, so they could not have been the moulders of his lifestyle.

Verses 3-13
The Temple repaired, and the book of the Law found
Like all good kings in Judah, Josiah took a deep interest in the Temple, for they could not be right with the Lord, and not be concerned about the house where He dwelt. He had reigned eighteen years before he was able to turn his attention to this matter. With all the corruption introduced into it by Manasseh, and continued by Amon, there was much cleaning up to be done inside its walls, and many repairs to be carried out before it was back to its original condition. All know that it is much easier to destroy, than to repair, so the work was indeed a great task. Not only so, but it could not be done without expense. The king through the scribe Shaphan sent word to the high priest Hilkiah

that the money collected by the priests from those who offered sacrifices should be used for acquiring the materials essential for the repairs of the house. The standard of righteousness in the nation had risen to a high level, for no check was thought necessary on the money given to the workmen. They were so devoted to their duty that they would not have thought of embezzling the funds for their own use.

During the extensive work in the Temple a great discovery was made. Somewhere in its precincts the copy of the Law, which had originally been laid up beside the ark, was discovered. Probably the idolaters who were setting the idol in the most holy place, had thrown it aside, as of no importance. God, in His sovereignty, had watched over His book, and preserved it from destruction. Possibly not many in Israel at this time could read, so the priest brought the book to Shaphan the scribe, and allowed him to read it. Apparently he was not much moved by its contents, but felt it his duty to bring it to the king, and read it to him. The tender heart of the young king was greatly moved by what he heard, so that he tore his garments in evidence of his grief. In all probability the warnings at the close of Deuteronomy were most alarming to him. He knew well the solemn fact that all which was threatened by God, would be executed, and equally well, that the nation had failed in the very way which would bring upon it the threatened Judgments.

Verses 14-20
The message from Huldah the prophetess
In light of the revelation learned from the book of the Law, and the warnings of wrath for the evils which both priest and king knew, were prevalent at that time in the land, it was rightly judged by them that the mind of the Lord should be sought from a prophet. On this occasion the channel of communication was a prophetess named Huldah. In almost all occasions when 'prophetesses' appear conditions in the nation were at a low ebb. The record tells of 'Deborah' (Jud 4), or 'Noadiah' (Neh 6) or 'Anna' (Lk 2). All of these, like Huldah, prophesied in a dark day. Why the king did not go to Jeremiah at this time is not revealed. His home was at Anathoth, which was only two and a half miles from Jerusalem, so his help could have been obtained, but perhaps the prophetess, who lived in the lower part of the city, was nearer to hand, and so, even more convenient to contact. The fact that he sent a delegation of five high ranking officials indicated the gravity of the situation in Josiah's view.

Her message from the Lord was a confirmation of the king's fears. She told the messengers that all the book had threatened was about to be experienced. The gross idolatry prevailing in the land had indeed provoked the Lord, and had made it ripe for judgment. At this late stage, nothing could quench the kindled fires of God's wrath, which were about to burst into flames. In spite of this pending doom, a special message of mercy was sent to the king that must have eased the pain of his heart. Because he had humbled himself and expressed, in every way possible, his deep sorrow, he would be allowed to die in peace. The word 'peace' had ever a sweet sound in the ears of an Israelite, but on this occasion, it must have been like music to him, for it removed his suspense, and replaced it with tranquility. However, his joy must have been somewhat diminished when he thought that though he had been spared himself, his sons and subjects would suffer the threatened judgments. The painful experience, which was threatened will inevitably come, yet it will not be witnessed by him, for he will be gathered to his fathers, before it occurs.

Josiah's response to the word of God should be emulated by all who lead the saints. In his repentance, the way to avert judgment can be learned. Only those who are tender hearted are prone to feel the full weight of the warnings of Scripture. "To this man will I look, even to him that...trembleth at my word" (Is 66.2) is a promise one and all should heed.

Notes

3 Shaphan had four sons mentioned in Scripture: Ahikam (Jer 26.24); Elasah (Jer 29.3); Gemariah (Jer 36.10); and Jaazaniah (Ez 8.11); also a grandson, Gedaliah (2 Kings 25:22). The first three of these were good friends of Jeremiah, but the fourth one turned to be an idolater. The grandson of Shaphan was made ruler over Judah by Nebuchadnezzar, but he was soon slain.

14 The word 'wardrobe' (BEHGED - 899) does not refer to a receptacle for clothes, but to the garments themselves. It is translated 'clothes' v.19. Whether these garments were worn by the priests or by the royal household is not stated, but the latter is the more probable.

The word 'college' (MISHNEH - 4932) means 'second'. Here it is used for the second part of the city. (See Zeph 1.10 'second quarter' RV.)

17 The figure of fire which cannot be 'quenched' (KAHVAH - 3518), for the wrath of God, is used in Is 34.10; Jer 7.20; 17.27; Amos 5.8.

20 The fact that Josiah died in 'war' and not in 'peace' as here stated, has presented some with a problem. Though he was slain in battle, he had an honourable burial, and was the last of the kings of Judah to be buried in Jerusalem. The promise given by the prophetess, "Thou shalt be gathered into thy grave in peace" may be a reference to his burial only.

CHAPTER 23, Verses 1-24
Josiah's great reformation

Having experienced the effects of hearing the Law, the king proceeded to bring the entire people into the same frame of mind as himself. He believed if they heard the message of the book they, too, would repent, and this could avert, at least for a time, the threatened disaster. The venue of the Temple was chosen as the place most suitable for the great congress. The priests and leaders, together with the common people assembled to hear, many of them for the first time, the words of the book of the Law.

Like Joshua (Jos 24), Jehoiada (2 Kings 11), and Asa (2 Chron 15), Josiah made a covenant that he and his people would keep all that was contained in the book of the Law. The departure from it had been so great, that a new start was needful, as though they were coming into relationship with God for the first time. They willingly accepted their responsibility, and consented to stand to the covenant with all their hearts.

There would have been no reality in their acceptance of the covenant, if they, at the same time, had allowed to continue the idolatrous worship and all the paraphernalia that had been brought into the Temple. Hilkiah, the high priest, with the help of priests and door keepers, was ordered by the king to purge the Temple of all its corrupt images and idolatrous objects. These were to be destroyed by burning them in the fields of Kidron, but instead of throwing the ashes of these into the brook, as was the custom, they were taken to Bethel. In his dealing with idols, he seemed to have the example of Moses before him, who destroyed the golden calf, and ground it to powder. One special object in the Temple was the "grove" or "Asherah" which had been placed where the ark normally rested. It was taken out and burned also at the Kidron, but its ashes were cast over the graves of the common people.

Along with idolatry is always immorality, so he had to remove all the places where sodomy and other such evils were practised. As far back as the days of Rehoboam, idolatry and sodomy had been introduced into Judah, and these twin evils were still in existence at almost the end of the kingdom.

Even in the revival of Hezekiah, the high places were allowed to continue, but in this revival, they too, were destroyed. The craze for them had become so great, that two were erected in different gates of the city. These were given the same treatment. When high places were in use, the priests, the sons of Levi, officiated at their altars, so when they were destroyed, the priests, who served at them, were unemployed. They were made to return to the city, but were not allowed to serve in the Temple worship. Nevertheless, they did not starve, for they were given the unleavened bread which was offered along with certain sacrifices and this was their sustenance. Thus they were treated like a deformed priest, who was prevented from approaching the altar, but was allowed "to eat the bread of his God" (Lev 21.22).

The most wicked form of idolatry was centred in the valley of the children of Hinnom, for there children were to pass through the fire, when they were being offered to Molech. The high place of Tophet was built in it, and both Ahaz, and Manasseh caused their children to pass through its fire. After it was destroyed, the offal of the city was burnt in it, and it became a type of hell and the lake of fire. The word "Gehenna", which is derived from Ge-Hinnom, the valley of Hinnom, came into use as a name for hell.

Some of the nations thought that the sun was driven across the sky by horses, so they dedicated to it, horses and chariots. These had been introduced by Manasseh at one of the entrances of the house of God. How they were used in sun worship is not known, but they may have been driven in processions, when special offerings to the heavenly bodies were being presented. Solomon, though a lover of horses, would never have thought that they would be given a favoured place in the precincts of the Temple, even at the side of Nathan-melech's chamber, who was the chamberlain of the house. These horses were removed, and the chariots burned. This implies that the chariots were made of wood, so differed from war chariots, which were usually made of iron.

From the days of Ahaz through to the days of Amon extra altars were built for the worship of idols. Some of these were placed on the roofs of houses for sun worship. Also in the courts of the Temple, new altars were in use for the different form of idol worship, and these, too, had to be destroyed. Probably the new altar which had been made at the command of Ahaz (2 Kings 16.11), was one of these.

Having cleansed the Temple and its courts, the king turned his attention to the hills around Jerusalem, and purged them of the many high-places which were dotted over them. Some of these were in use from the days of Solomon, who had them built to accommodate the idolatrous worship of his foreign wives. From the list given here, it is obvious that almost all the gods of the surrounding nations had been introduced into Judah, and worshipped there. When any strangers came to live in the land, they had no need to be concerned about leaving the religion of their fathers, for all they desired in that respect was already in use in it. How wonderful was the case of Ruth, for she not only left her own land, but left her Moabite religion behind her.

Unlike the revivals of former kings of Judah, Josiah extended his cleansing programme right into the area of the former northern kingdom. At Bethel was the long established religious centre where the golden calf was worshipped. It was to Israel, what Jerusalem was to Judah. He passed over the border, and began to do at Bethel what he had done at Jerusalem. All that Jeroboam and the kings who followed him had erected, he totally destroyed. Even the best kings of Israel, though they destroyed other idolatrous shrines, were careful not to touch the great centres of Dan and Bethel. When involved in this destruction, his eyes rested on the tombs in the hillside where the worshippers of the calf had been buried. He immediately took the bones which were in them and burnt them on the altar that was there. This defiled it, so that it could no longer be used for sacrifices. At that time a tombstone was discovered by him. It appeared to him to be distinctly different, and upon making enquiry, he learned it marked the tomb of the man of God from Judah. He had prophesied, some three hundred and fifty years before this, that these things would happen (1 Kings 13). Thus the word of the Lord, had been fulfilled by the very man who was named so long before his birth. The bones of the man of God were not disturbed, and his tomb left as a silent witness to the faithfulness of his testimony. Close by this tomb were buried the bones of the prophet who came out of Samaria (1 Kings 13.31). The respect shown to the bones of the man of God was exercised toward them so they too were left undisturbed.

Having cleared up Bethel, Josiah proceeded to other centres of idolatry which were scattered throughout the cities of Samaria, and purged them of all those structures which provoked the anger of the

Lord. It is very probable that in this passage "Samaria", being the capital city of the kingdom of Israel, stands for the entire country. These other centres were given the same treatment as Bethel so for the first time since the kingdom was founded the entire domain was cleared from idolatry, its persistent evil. There would not have been a complete end to idol worship if the priests who officiated at the high places had been left to continue their evil work. They might soon have re-erected altars, and burnt incense upon them, so the king slew them on the very altars on which they sacrificed. The severity of his dealings with then priests, is a contrast to his mild treatment of the priests of Jerusalem. The slain here were idolatrous priests, whereas the priests of ch.23.9 were priests of Levi who had served in centres other than the Temple.

It is never enough to destroy the wrong, and fail to establish what is right, so Josiah gave commandment that the entire nation should keep the Passover. This feast, which commemorated its deliverance from Egypt, was one of special interest to every Israelite. Hezekiah had kept a remarkable Passover which eclipsed all before it, but this one went even further, for it included the people of both kingdoms. What is rather surprising is that it was held in his eighteenth year. That was the very year of his destruction of idolatry. All that he did must have been done with zeal and determination. The book which had been found must have given him the urge to keep this feast, and enabled him to embrace something of its importance. While in Kings there is only a brief reference to it, in 2 Chronicles it is dealt with at great length.

There remained yet another evil in the land, the seriousness of which the king had learned from reading the book. It too was an abomination to the Lord and was closely associated with idolatry. It was the sin of witchcraft. The desire to communicate with the evil spirit world is one which has marked fallen man throughout the history of the world. Spiritism continues to this day, even in lands enlightened by the Gospel, and can be most deceptive, in that those who may have imagined that it was all a delusion are surprised to discover its reality. God has ever jealously guarded His right as the One who alone can reveal the future. Only those, who, like Saul, have turned away from Him, would wish to enquire at the mouth of His enemies. There were times in Israel when such wizards had to keep hidden lest they be slain, but before Josiah's day, they appear to have been able to practise their evil trade, without any fear of danger. He had no trouble searching these out, and putting them to the sword.

After this long list of Josiah's efforts to stamp out idolatry, the conclusion might be reached that the land had, for the first time for many years, been truly purged from idols and all that went with them. Alas! This conclusion would be a mistake. It was one thing to take the idols out of the land, yet quite another, to remove idolatry from the hearts of the people. Had all the population been like their king, all would have been well. However, the prophet Jeremiah makes plain that not all was as well as might have been expected. The reformation was mainly outward, and superficial, but not one which gave God pleasure. While there was no resistance to Josiah's judgment on idolatry, yet his actions were only reluctantly tolerated by the vast majority of the people. They were not rending their garments, nor was there any inward conviction of the evil of their ways. Without true repentance, all reformation counts for little with God. The Baptist at Jordan was not impressed by the Pharisees and Sadducees who came to his baptism, so he warned them to "Bring forth fruits meet for repentance" (Matt 3.7-8).

Verses 25-27

The character of Josiah

The historian pays tribute to Josiah, and speaks of him as being outstanding among the kings of Judah. His heart turned to the Lord without reservation, and he obeyed the word of God with all his soul and might. To earn a commendation like this, especially in the dark days, in which his lot was cast is no small achievement. This lets all see that God can enable His servants to please Him, no matter how bad the conditions may be in which they have to live. Most are inclined to blame their own shortcomings upon the general decline of godliness, but the story of Josiah demonstrates that light can shine in the midst of darkness, and not be dimmed by it.

In sharp contrast to the commendation of the king is what is said about the people he ruled. God's anger was still burning toward them. The wickedness of Manasseh was a fire too great for the reformation of Josiah to quench. The depths to which he brought the nation were so low, that no effort of his grandson could lift it out of them. The threat from the Lord that Jerusalem would become like Samaria, was not uttered merely for past sins, but was the just punishment of a people who had angered Him with their evil ways. Both the city and the Temple were about to be destroyed and all the efforts of Josiah, and his admirable work, could not avert the threatened disaster.

Verses 28-30
The death of Josiah

In a brief way the historian tells of the death of this worthy king. A full account of it is given in 2 Chronicles, but here it is condensed into one verse. There were about twelve or thirteen years between his cleansing of the land, and the time of his death. These are passed over, both in Kings and Chronicles. Not until the thirty-ninth year of his life did he encounter any invasion from the nations around him. Great changes were taking place internationally, one of which was the rise of the Chaldeans, and with it, the end of Assyrian domination. The terror of the then known world had become associated with the power of Babylon. The Egyptian king Pharaoh-Nechoh attempted to halt the progress of the king of Assyria, or king of Babylon, for as in Ezra 6.22 even the Persian king is still called king of Assyria. Whether the king mentioned here was the last of the Assyrian kings or whether the empire had already fallen and was ruled by Nabopolassar, the father of Nebuchadnezzar and founder of the Babylonian empire, cannot be decided. The land over which the latter ruled was originally the land of Assyria. This territory though taken over could be still called by its old name. The Egyptian king attempted to pass through Canaan, on his way to confront the Chaldean army, but Josiah felt it was his duty to stop this expedition. Accordingly, he mustered his army, and ventured to make war with the trespasser. The battle was fought in the valley of Megiddo, but even though he disguised himself, he was fatally wounded and died on his way to Jerusalem. He acted against the advice of the Egyptian king, and what was even more serious, without seeking counsel from one of the prophets. He may not have had full confidence in the words of Nechoh, nevertheless, he should have been sufficiently concerned about them, to make sure they were not a spurious message dressed up in religious garb. He was the only king of Judah to be slain in war, and the last of the good kings to sit on the throne of David. He had been told by Huldah that he would be "gathered into his grave in peace" (ch.22.20), yet he died in war. For the answer to this apparent contradiction, see the note on that verse. He was buried in his own tomb, which was one of the tombs near to where Manasseh and Amon were buried. In Chronicles is shown the great mourning by the people for him.

Jeremiah in a special way lamented his death. The mourning for him was so great that it is viewed as a sample of the mourning of the future remnant of Israel. When the Lord returns to establish His kingdom those who will see His wounds will be convicted of the wrong done to Him at His first coming, and will retire into solitude where they will mourn in deepest sorrow (Zec 12.11-14).

After reading the story of this good king, the question might be asked, why is there no reference to contact with Jeremiah during his reign? All are aware that both men were alive at the same time, and that they lived sufficiently near each other to allow both to converse together. How different was the relationship between Hezekiah and Isaiah, for that king, in almost all his trials, went to the prophet for help. Josiah, as far as the record goes, never sent for Jeremiah, nor did the prophet go to him with any message. In the prophecy of Jeremiah, the dreadful state of the nation is exposed, whereas in the pages of this book which cover the same period, there is every encouragement to think that conditions were greatly improved. Could it be that Josiah really believed that the people he ruled over were one in heart with him in his reformation, but in this assumption, he was mistaken? Perhaps the prophet had a deeper insight into the reality of the situation and knew that beneath the outward zeal in destroying idolatry, there was still a hankering after it in the hearts of the people. If all were known, perhaps the tears of Jeremiah were not only because of the wrath that his people would have to endure, but also because they were not really repentant of the evils which were bringing it upon them. A lesson can be learned from all this. There have been times when sincere men thought they were seeing a great work done for God, but in the course of time it all melted away, and proved, beyond doubt, that it was only a sham. The danger of acting presumptuously is another important matter illustrated in this story. To take needless risks is not in keeping with the path of faith. Satan told the Lord to cast Himself down, and He would be preserved, but the Lord refused to tempt God (Matt 4.6-7).

Verses 31-34
The reign of Jehoahaz

At the end of v.30 it is stated that the people anointed Jehoahaz to be king, even though he was not the oldest son of Josiah, but possibly the fourth (1 Chron 3.15). The reference to him being anointed suggests that there was some difficulty in his appointment, for only when something unusual was involved, did this particular ceremony become needful. His three months reign was sufficient to reveal his character, which was moulded, not after the pattern of his father, but after the example of his fathers, Manasseh and Amon. He was, like them, an evil king. Nechoh took him prisoner, and eventually brought him to Egypt where he died. Moreover, a tribute was levied on the land by the king of Egypt of no less than one hundred talents of silver, and one talent of gold. The new king of Judah was not chosen by the people, but by the king of Egypt. He was Eliakim, but Nechoh later changed his name to Jehoiakim. He was the second oldest son of Josiah.

It is interesting, yet sad, to see the contrast between the story of Exodus and the one here. There, the Passover was observed at the time when Israel was freed from Egypt, and this same deliverance was celebrated by this king's father. Most likely he was alive at the time, and helped to share in the celebration, but now he is taken prisoner to the very land from which his people were freed. When Israel left Egypt they brought with them treasures of silver and gold, but now the descendants of the people then enriched, are sending their wealth back to the very place from which their forefathers had obtained it.

The people may have thought they were doing Jehoahaz a favour in making him king, but in reality they were putting him into danger. Whatever made them choose him, instead of one of his older brothers, we may not know, but in the end, it proved to be a short lived honour, for it would have been better for him, if the crown had never been put upon his head.

This king's short reign is not without its lessons. One of these is that popular choice of leadership may make a man think highly of himself, but no matter what position one may be given by men, if he cannot hold it, then he would have been better without it. The power of Egypt, which is a type of the world, was too much for him. Since his day many have found the power of the world too much for them to overcome. Just as Egypt was seeking after the treasures of the land, so the world would desire to strip the saints of the enjoyment of all the riches they have through redemption. It is indeed sad to see saints using their gifts and energies to advance worldly projects, and neglecting the work of God, which ought to be their priority.

Verses 35-37
Jehoiakim reigns in Judah
Although Jehoiakim was a son of Josiah, yet he was only a half-brother of Jehoahaz, for the two kings had different mothers. His first duty was to satisfy the demands of Nechoh, who had made him king. This meant the land had to bear the burden of supplying the silver and the gold which was demanded. In order to obtain this, the people had to be heavily taxed. Unlike Menahem in Israel, who exacted the silver from the wealthy (ch.15.20), in this case the entire population had to share the burden.

Notes
5 The word translated "idolatrous priests" (KMAHREEM - 3649) occurs also in Hos 10.5 and Zep 1.4. It is the name given to the priests of the high-places.

10 This is the first mention in scripture of "Topheth" the place where the children were burned in the fire. It is referred to by Isaiah who speaks of it as "being ordained of old" (30.33), and by Jeremiah (7.31-32; 19.8-14). Some think the name was derived from the sound of the drums which were used to dull the noise of the cries of the children being offered

17 The "title" (TZEEYYOON - 6725) is translated "waymarks" (Jer 31.21), and "sign" (Eze 39.15). It occurs nowhere else.

21 The passover was kept at this time, but there is no record that it was so kept annually, as it ought to have been. Both Hezekiah and Josiah kept it in a national way, but whether this continued, we do not know. Probably some faithful souls in Israel kept it, even in the darkest days of Israel's history.

29 Megiddo was the fortified city at whose waters Barak earlier defeated Sisera (Judg 4), and where Ahaziah died (ch.9.27). It was of strategic importance, since it commanded the pass through the mountains between the plains of Sharon and Esdraelon. In a future day, just prior to the Lord's coming, the kings of the world will gather to its mountain, Armageddon, where they will wage war against "the King of kings" (Rev 18.18; 19.19)

CHAPTER 24, Verses 1-7
Jehoiakim ruled by Nebuchadnezzar
During the eleven year reign of Jehoiakim great international changes took place, for the extensive power of Egypt, which troubled

him during the early years of his reign, was defeated by the Chaldeans. Because of this change, he had to submit to a new master. For him, this meant "out of the pan, and into the fire". He tolerated Nebuchadnezzar the king of Babylon for three years, but likely due to his underestimating the power of his oppressor, he rebelled against him. Evidently Nebuchadnezzar, because of other commitments, was not able to deal directly with him for his rebellion, but other adversaries, such as Syrians, Moabites, and Ammonites combined with Chaldean forces to destroy his land. The nations which were once mastered by David, and had become his subjects and servants were now the instruments used by God to punish his descendant and are doing so, because of the sins of Manasseh. The special cruelties of this king, and the depth of evil to which he sank, are constantly mentioned as the reason why Judah was so humiliated at this time. The fact that bands of invaders could penetrate into the kingdom at will, demonstrates how weak it had become, and how helpless was the power of its king.

Much can be learned of Jehoiakim in other writings, such as Jeremiah's prophecy but in this history little is said of him, except that he did evil. There is no clear historic evidence of how he died, but according to Jeremiah's prophecy (even though here it is said that he slept with his fathers) he was not to be granted an honourable burial. The prophet foretold that "He shall be buried with the burial of an ass, drawn and cast forth beyond the gates of Jerusalem (Jer 22.19).

The boundaries of the new world power were extensive, for they reached from the River of Egypt, which was the south-west border of Canaan, to the river Euphrates. Once the Chaldeans took over this vast territory, there were no more attacks from Egypt. Throughout the history of the kingdoms of Israel and Judah the Egyptians made quite a number of raids into the land, and were always a power to be either dreaded, or depended upon for help. As far as help was concerned, Egypt often proved disappointing to those who put their trust in it.

There is evidence in the book of Revelation that at the end times, false Christianity, typified by Babylon, will dominate the social world, typified by Egypt. The former will, for a time, control the Beast, until he will reject it (Rev 17). Neither Egypt, nor Babylon were true friends of Israel, and the world, whether socially or religiously, is always opposed to God and His people.

Verses 8-17
Jehoiachin reigns in Judah

Although Jehoiachin's reign was a very short one of only three months, yet it was a most momentous one. During it, the great captivity of Judah took place. He, himself, together with his mother and wives, were taken to Babylon, where he died. Like all the kings at the end of the kingdom, he did evil in the sight of the Lord. More will be said about him at the end of this book, but here his captivity at the siege of Jerusalem, brought to a swift end his time on the throne. Instead of holding out for as long as he could, he decided to go out to the attacker and surrender to him. He himself, together with all the officers of his kingdom went forth to the king of Babylon. This meant they were prisoners, but unlike some others who were brought to this king, they were spared, and allowed to live out their days. Jehoiachin outlived his captor, and did so, in spite of his thirty seven years in prison, so he must not have been too cruelly treated while in it.

Before this time, the smaller gold vessels and other valuables had been carried to Babylon. On this occasion the population of Judah, as well as all the gold that was on the vessels of the sanctuary were the spoil that was seized and taken to it. Only the poor were left, but all men of skill or ability, who were judged to be useful for the army, or for slavery, were also taken to the same city. The number of trained soldiers made captive at this time was ten thousand, and they were accompanied by seven thousand skilled workers. A thousand other men were also taken, who are described as "smiths". These would be useful in making weapons, and also in forming vessels from the gold which accompanied them. The poor people left behind, had nothing valuable to give, so they were allowed to eke out an existence as best they could. However, there were still princes in the land, captains of forces, and men of war (Jer 38.4,25,27; 40.7; 52.7).

The plundering of Jerusalem had occurred so often, the wonder is, that anything worthwhile remained in it. The Temple was a grand storehouse, so was the palace. Both of these were constantly replenished with fresh supplies of gold and silver, but the wealth in them at this time, must have been but a fraction of the amount that was there in Solomon's day. However, the gold which covered the vessels, such as the ark, the incense altar and the tables, still remained, and this, together with any remaining vessels of gold were collected together and transported with the captives. For many years, at the end of the kingdom, no spoils had been taken from surrounding enemies, so the flow of wealth from them into these houses, during this period, must have almost dried up.

For reasons not revealed, the king of Babylon made Mattaniah, the youngest son of Josiah, king of Judah, so that the throne was filled by the uncle of the exiled king. Just as Nechoh changed the name of Eliakim to Jehoiakim, so Nebuchadnezzar changed the name of Mattaniah to Zedekiah. Possibly both kings had in mind, when doing so, that these viceregents, whom they had made kings, were no longer linked with their old way of life, but had become the property of their masters, and must wear the names they gave them. In both cases, the name of Jehovah was included in the new name, so they were unlike the changed names given to the youths in Babylon. They were names linked with idolatry (Dan 1.7).

Verses 18-20
Zedekiah's reign

The time was when to be king of Judah was no small honour, but when the throne was given to Zedekiah, all was changed. Kingship then was but the stepping stone to a life of misery. He was, when he began to reign, about three years older than his nephew had been, and must have been very young when his father was killed, perhaps about ten years of age. He did not copy his father's ways, but was as wicked as his nephew. He was only thirty two years old when he became a blind prisoner, so life for him was sad and disappointing. Even though he sat on David's throne, and was the last man to do so, yet he bore no resemblance to his forefather, nor was there the slightest indication in his ways that he had any inclination toward obedience to the word of God. Even the prophet Jeremiah, who did his best with him, could not influence him to obey it.

When Nebuchadnezzar made Zedekiah king, he made him swear that he would be submissive to the terms agreed between them. After nine years on the throne, despite his oath, he rebelled. Ezekiel strongly condemned him for this breach of faith, and prophesied of his captivity and death at the hand of the Chaldeans (Ez 17.18-21). At this time he made a covenant with Egypt and obtained help from Pharaoh, so that for a time the Chaldeans had to withdraw from Jerusalem (Jer 37). He must have felt relieved that such a time of respite was granted, but alas! it was short lived, for at the eleventh year of his reign, all that he feared came upon him.

A consideration of Zedekiah's history, especially as seen in

Jeremiah, would make clear the seriousness of swearing. Even though in the case of this king, the oath was to a heathen dictator, yet it was in the name of the Lord, and should have been kept. The reason why he broke the covenant is made clear by the prophet. It was because of the weakness of his character. The princes could sway the king whatever way they wished, and even though he knew that he was doing wrong, yet he yielded to them. One of the greatest failures of any ruler is to have no convictions of his own, but, be like water, which fits the surroundings into which it is poured.

There is a great difference between being temporarily relieved, as he was, and being completely delivered. A respite may be granted by the Lord, in order to give time for repentance, but in Zedekiah's case, the years he had been allowed to reign in peace, brought no change in his attitude toward the Lord.

Notes

7 The verse implies, that the Chaldeans had defeated the Egyptians, something which secular history confirms. It resulted from the battle of Carchemish in 605 B.C.

8 Jehoiachin, Jeconiah, and Coniah are three names referring to the same king. In the second form a kindred root is employed, and the component parts are transposed. The latter name is a contraction of the second one (1 Chron 3.16; Jer 22.24,28; 37.1). He is the last of the kings mentioned in the genealogy of Christ in Matt 1.

Elnathan is mentioned in Jeremiah as one who went down to Egypt to bring Urijah to Jehoiakim, who then slew him (ch.26.22-23). He was also one of those who sought to prevent Jehoiakim burning the roll, but the king would not listen (ch.36.25).

12 "Eighth year of his reign". This is the first time the history dates any event in Judah by the reign of a foreign king. The times of the Gentiles are beginning. Jehoiachin's captivity is in the eighth year of Nebuchadnezzar's reign.

13 The term "cut in pieces" (KAHTZATZ - 7112) is translated "cut off" (ch.16.17), and in this case may mean the stripping of the gold off the sides of the vessels of the sanctuary. The smaller vessels were not cut up, for they were used for drinking out of by Belshazzar (Dan 5.3).

18 Jehoahaz and Zedekiah were brothers of the same mother (ch.23.31).

CHAPTER 25, Verses 1-25
The fall of Jerusalem

This closing chapter is the saddest one in this book, for it brings to a climax the partial destruction of Jerusalem, which has already been mentioned by the historian. Much said here is also found in Jeremiah, and in 2 Chronicles. One special feature of this section is the four references to exact dates. Throughout the book, the year in which events occurred is stated, but here the very day is given (vv.1, 3, 8, 27). The rebellion of Zedekiah brought to a head the destruction of Judah, for the armies of Nebuchadnezzar surrounded Jerusalem, and built forts around it, so that no supplies could enter it. The plan was that the siege would bring its inhabitants to their knees by starvation. They were able to hold out for one year and one half, before the king deserted the city, and thought to escape through the plains of Jericho. The terrible famine conditions which then existed are vividly described by Jeremiah, especially in Lamentations. At the time when the king and his servants were fleeing the city, the Chaldean army was entering it from another direction. He may have thought he could escape under the cover of darkness, without detection, but the watchers in the turrets detected his movements. The army pursued him in the plains, where his men had forsaken him, and having captured him, they brought him to their master at Riblah, for judgment. His two sons were with him, and they were slain before the eyes of their father, who looked on in total helplessness. They were only lads at this time, so life for them was short. The reason for their slaughter was to make sure that no heir of Zedekiah would ever sit on the throne of Judah. Having slain his sons they proceeded to put out his eyes, so that he would be blind until the end of his days. Being the last sight he ever saw, the slaughter of his two dear sons would fill his mind for ever. He was then taken in fetters to Babylon and put in prison. This meant that two kings of Judah were imprisoned in Babylon, Jehoiachin, and his uncle. How long he was spared is not recorded, but apparently he died of natural causes. Unlike Jehoiakim, who was buried like an ass, he had an honourable funeral (Jer 34.5).

A month elapsed between the taking of the city and its destruction. This period would allow for all the prisoners to be sorted out, and all the dwellings to be searched, lest any should be hiding in them. When all was cleared, then the Temple, the palace, and all the dwellings of the wealthy were set on fire. This final work of destruction was entrusted to Nebuzar-adan, who was captain of Nebuchadnezzar's body guard, and was given instructions by him as to how the city should be treated. The handiwork of the house of God was of the highest standard, and all its timber was of the best quality. The huge amount of cedar in the roof, the planks of cedar lining the walls and the cypress floor would all be combustible material. After four hundred years in a warm climate the wood must have been tinder dry, and so would burn fiercely. The stone, being of a calcium nature, would have crumbled under the intense heat. Even the foundation stones, which were exceedingly large, must also have melted, for a new foundation had to be laid by Zerubbabel and his helpers, when they were rebuilding it (Ezra 3.10).

Not only was the Temple burned at that time, but the remains of the Tabernacle which were stored in it, were also burned, so the two former dwelling places of God were consumed at one, and the same time. Seldom, if ever, was there so much sacred material destroyed, and so much skilful workmanship counted as of no value.

The outstanding defence feature of Jerusalem was its walls. These had been breached several times, but nevertheless, they were a symbol of strength, and had for many years been a barrier between its people and their enemies. When destroying the property within them, and removing the captives which they had shielded for a time, the captain decided that they too should be demolished, and their gates removed. Most likely the entire wall was not tumbled, but gaps were made in it, and these left it useless as a defence. The book of Nehemiah tells how those breaches were rebuilt, and how the gates were also repaired.

The poor of the land, who must often have envied their rich brethren, and their grand houses, were allowed to remain, and to cultivate their own soil. These poor people were considered to be worthless to Babylon, for if they had not been prosperous in their own land, it was concluded that they would not be likely to enrich their captors. The captain could see that these could do him a service in their own land, for they could attend to the vineyards, and so produce grapes for the making of wine. This would eventually help to supply the needs of Babylon for this special commodity. Possibly the wine at the feast of Belshazzar as well as the vessels from which he and his lords drank was produced in the land of Israel.

With the gold and silver secured, the palaces burned, the prisoners rounded up, and the poor allocated their vineyards, the captain's work was almost completed. However, there was a massive amount of another valuable material with which he had to deal. It was the brass

327

or copper which could not be burned, and was too precious to leave behind. The weight of the pillars and of the sea which were made of this metal was so great that they could not be hauled to Babylon in their original form, so these were broken up into pieces in order that this difficulty could be overcome. The entire stock of brass, whether in vessels or in these larger structures was collected together, and made ready for transport. The weight of this vast amount of metal was beyond calculation, and could not be stated.

Special mention is made of the pillars, for they were the most ornate, and possibly the greatest of the works of brass. The height of eighteen cubits refers to the stem of the pillars, and the three cubits refer to the square frame of network which was upon them. In 1 Kings and in Jeremiah the height of these is said to be five cubits, but here the lily work may not have been included. There is no mention here of the twelve oxen which upheld the great sea, but they are mentioned in Jeremiah, and so were still in existence, even though they had been removed from their original position by Ahaz (ch.16.17).

The destruction of the Temple is a solemn reminder of the well known fact, that a few days can destroy what it took years to build. The Psalmist describes the havoc wrought at this time as like men in a forest cutting down trees. The roaring of the breakers, and the sound of the axes and hammers, were a sharp contrast to the notable silence at its construction (Ps 74.3-7).

Not only did Nebuzar-adan destroy the precious buildings in the city, but he went further, and brought the chief men in it, together with sixty other persons, to his master at Riblah. They were all treated as rebels and slain. The chief priest at that time was Seraiah, who was a grandson of Hilkiah (1 Chron 6.13, 14), and an ancestor of Ezra (Ezra 7.1). He would be considered by the captain as a man of influence, not only in the religious sphere, but also in the secular affairs of the people. His helper, Zephaniah, the second priest was also taken, and also the three keepers of the doors or gates. What happened to the other twenty two keepers is not stated, but possibly they had given up their post before this time.

With the religious leaders, the captain also arrested those who had responsibility in the army. The commander at this time was an eunuch, so he would have been considered as the chief enemy opposing the surrender of the city.

The five men mentioned were closely linked with Zedekiah, and were viewed as his advisers, so they had to be taken. The "scribe of the host" who was responsible for gathering together the army, and keeping the records of its personnel, was also taken prisoner. Exactly why the sixty mentioned at the end of the list, were taken prisoners, is not stated, nor is it said why they were singled out to go along with the army officers, but they may have been influential in the defence of the city. Although Zedekiah himself was spared, yet neither his sons, nor his supporters were granted any mercy, for these prisoners, when brought to Nebuchadnezzar, were all slain.

One of the great marvels of OT revelation is that God was pleased to dwell with His people. The symbol of this was the cloud of glory which descended both on the Tabernacle and the Temple. However, His presence with His people was conditional, for after centuries of departure, and worshipping false gods, they became so corrupt that He had to forsake them and His dwelling. While He dwelt in it, no enemy could touch it, but when it was forsaken by Him, it became like any other structure, and so could be destroyed. The warning given to the church at Ephesus, that the lampstand would be removed, is a solemn reminder, that in this age, when the local assembly is God's sanctuary, a like fate could befall it. As happened to the Temple, it too could be removed (Rev 2.5). If the account of the destruction of the material Temple is such a sad story, how much more sad is the account of the removal of a spiritual sanctuary.

Verses 22-26
Gedaliah made governor of Judah
No matter how poor, and unimportant people may be, they are in need of someone to govern them, and deliver them from anarchy. The captain of the guard knew well that if the land was to produce the fruits expected of it, and the Chaldeans were to obtain from these the tribute they demanded, someone must be put into the position of responsibility for the accomplishment of these aims.

Previous appointments to the throne were selected from the royal seed, but in this case, only a governor was needed, so the seed of David was passed over, and Gedaliah was given the post. This man was probably one of those who sought to influence the people to serve the king of Babylon. His appointment may have been his reward for this service. Instead of ruling from Jerusalem, as all the kings of Judah did, he made his headquarters at Mizpah. It is evident that quite a few of the army of Judah had escaped the Chaldean net, and either hid in the land, or in its fields (Jer 40.7), or slipped into the territory of surrounding nations, until the clearing up operation was over. Those living in any country know the hiding places, better than any stranger, who is searching for them. These men, wherever they may have been, ventured out of their hiding places, and came to Gedaliah, who assured them that they were safe, provided they submitted to serve the Chaldean officials, who were under him. In less than two months after the destruction of Jerusalem, Ishmael the son of Nethaniah, and ten others with him, came to Mizpah, and after being entertained by the governor, rose up and slew him (Jer 41.1-2). All the Jews who were with him were also slain. He had been warned by Johanan that his life was in danger by the man whom he trusted, but he did not take seriously the threat, nor would he allow Johanan to secretly slay Ishmael. Had he taken the warnings given him, the plot on his life would never have been successful (Jer 40.13-16).

There were two influences behind this cruel act of Ishmael. One was that Baalis, the king of Ammon was pressing him to do it, and the other was that he was of the seed royal, and could not bear to see one, who was not of the seed of David, being made governor of the Jews.

After the murder of Gedaliah and his associates, the perpetrators dare not remain in the land, so they escaped into Egypt, thinking perhaps, that there they were beyond the reach of the Chaldeans. However, Jeremiah was quick to let them know that the one they dreaded would soon set his throne in the place to which they had fled (Jer 43.10). They were not going into safety, but into disaster. It would seem that Ishmael and some of his men went to the children of Ammon, where they would be welcome, because their king had been behind the assassination of Gedeliah.

Much of the history of Hezekiah is given almost verbatim in the book of Isaiah, and this closing part of Kings is also given verbatim in the book of Jeremiah. Notwithstanding the great part Jeremiah played in the events of this time, he is never named in this book. Some think this was because he is the author of the books of Kings, and like John in his Gospel, he keeps his name out of the history.

The fact that Judah was carried captive to Babylon and Egypt respectively, is not without significance. All know that the father of the nation came from Ur of the Chaldees, so his descendants returned to the land he had left. Likewise all know that the nation of Israel was born in Egypt, so those who went there, were back to where their forefathers had left. There is in this the lesson that those believers, who drift away from the Lord, often return to the very ways, which they left when they were first converted. Both Babylon and Egypt were noted centres of idolatry. The main cause of the captivity was the worship of false gods by the king and his subjects. In the sovereignty of God the captives were brought to lands where they would be surrounded with idols, and thus they would be satiated with the very evil which they had hankered after for many centuries. The returned remnant of Jews had many failings, but idolatry was never again introduced among them so the seventy years in the midst of idolatry, proved to be the antidote to that plague.

Verses 27-30
The liberation of Jehoiachin
At the end of the dismal history of Israel and Judah, with all its revelation of the failure of the most favoured people in the world, it is good to see a glimmer of light shining in the midst of the darkness. The historian in this closing paragraph, leaps forward to the death of the famous king Nebuchadnezzar, and to the successor to his throne. A period of thirty years is passed over in silence, but the release of Jehoiachin from his prison cell is considered important enough to be mentioned. A common practice of new kings is to commence their reign with some magnanimous gesture such as an amnesty for criminals and captives. Even in the first year of Evil-merodach's reign he, not only released Jehoiachin, but gave him a seat at his table, here called a "throne". To leave off the rags worn in prison, to be dressed in royal apparel, and to be treated with respect by all around, was no small change of circumstance for him. The pity of it all was, that the most of his life was gone before these favours were his lot.

The kindness of God to the house of David, is seen in this incident, and also in it there is a hint that the captivity of the people he represented, would likewise come to an end. The experience was a little shadow of their future.

None can read these verses without recalling the treatment granted to Mephibosheth by David (2 Sam 9). The reason why David acted as he did is given, for it was done for Jonathan's sake, but what moved the king of Babylon to exalt the king of Judah, is not revealed.

Notes

18 The high priest Seraiah was the father of Jehozadak, who was carried into captivity; he was also the grandfather of Jeshua, who was highpriest after the Exile. He was also an ancestor of Ezra (1 Chron 8.14; Ezra 3.2; 7.1). Zephaniah the second priest had brought messages from Jeremiah to king Zedekiah (Jer 21.1), and had shown the prophet the letter that Shemaiah had sent to the people of Jerusalem (Jer 29.29).

22 Ahikam was one of men who went to Huldah the prophetess (ch.22.14) He protected Jeremiah when priests and false prophets demanded his death (Jer 26.24). Shaphan the grandfather of Gedaliah, had three other sons, Elasah (Jer 29.3), Gemariah (Jer 36.10), and Jaazaniah (Ezek 8.11).

30 His allowance (AROOGHAH - 737) was probably a daily portion of food. The word, in the other three places where it occurs, is translated "dinner" (Prov 15.17), "victuals" (Jer 40.5), and "diet" (Jer 52.34).

Appendix A

CHRONOLOGY OF THE BOOKS OF KINGS

One outstanding problem, which has confronted students in the study of the books of Kings is the chronology. The historian is careful to mention the length of time each king reigned, and during the divided kingdom he often mentions the corresponding time of the contemporary kings. Even when a king reigned only part of a year, he tells the duration of it in months. One has only to consult the various "Tables of Chronology" to see how they differ, for scarcely two of them are in agreement. Of the two very important dates mentioned, one is the date of the building of the Temple (1 Kings 6.1), and the second is the nineteenth year of Nebuchadnezzar (2 Kings 25.8). If these two dates could be settled, then the intervening years would be less difficult to sort out. The former date was about 966 BC and the latter about 586 BC. If the first three years of Solomon's reign be added, because he began to build in the fourth year of his reign, then the total number of years from the reign of Solomon to the destruction of Jerusalem was approximately three hundred and eighty three years. The sum of the years of the kings as recorded in Kings amounts to four hundred and thirty five. This clearly shows that the duration between Solomon and the destruction of the Temple can never be settled by adding together the years of each king's reign. The solution to this apparent discrepancy lies in the fact that part of a year of a king's reign was counted as a whole. This meant that the same year was counted for two kings. Another obvious practice was that when there was a co-regency the years were counted to both kings. If the full facts were known, the problems would disappear.

There were about one hundred years between the death of Hezekiah and the destruction of Jerusalem (686-586 BC). The sum total of the reigns of the various kings of this period reaches one hundred and eleven years. Some have suggested that Manasseh was about twenty four when he began his sole reign, having already reigned eleven or twelve years with his father, However, it is most improbable that he had twelve years reigning with his God-fearing father, and then turned so suddenly to his own wicked ways. At the age of twelve, as stated in the text, he would have been much more susceptible to the influence of the evil court officials who surrounded him.

The following table gives an approximate chronology of the reign of the kings in both kingdoms. With the light now available, it is impossible to say dogmatically that these dates are correct.

Judah or Southern Kingdom		Israel or Northern Kingdom	
Ruler	Date BC	Ruler	Date BC
Solomon	970 - 930	Jeroboam	930 - 909
Rehoboam	930 - 913	Nadab	909 - 908
Abijah	913 - 910	Baasha	908 - 886
Asa	910 - 869	Elah	886 - 885
Jehoshaphat	870 - 848	Zimri	885
Joram	850 - 842	Tibni	885 - 881
Ahaziah	842 - 841	Omri	885 - 874
Athaliah	841 - 835	Ahab	874 - 853
Joash	835 - 796	Ahaziah	853 - 852
Amaziah	796 - 767	Jehoram	852 - 841
Uzziah	792 - 740	Jehu	841 - 814
Jotham	750 - 735	Jehoahaz	814 - 798
Ahaz	735 - 719	Jehoash	798 - 781
Hezekiah	719 - 698	Jeroboam	793 - 753
Manasseh	697 - 642	Zechariah	753
Amon	642 - 640	Shallum	752
Josiah	640 - 609	Menahem	752 - 742
Jehoahaz	609	Pekahiah	741 - 740
Jehoiakim	609 - 598	Pekah	740 - 732
Jehoiachin	597	Hoshea	732 - 722
Zedekiah	597 - 586		
(Gedaliah)	586		

Appendix B

IDOLATRY IN ISRAEL

The one evil which plagued the nation of Israel throughout the period of the kings was idolatry. Closely linked with this sin and indeed the source of it, was Israel's desire to be associated with the nations around. God had purposed that His people should be separated unto Himself, and that He would be their only object of worship. He is a jealous God and cannot bear a rival. The land which Israel left when redeemed was notorious for its idols, and the land into which God brought them was likewise full of idolatry. In the human heart there is a deep rooted desire to have a god that can be seen. Therefore, to have confidence in a God who cannot be seen by the natural eye is not appealing to man's nature.

It would not be helpful to look intently into the different forms of idolatry mentioned in Kings, but a brief look at the main objects of worship mentioned throughout its pages may be of some interest. One feature of David much valued by the Lord was that he never turned to idolatry. Sad to say his descendants failed in this realm. His wise son Solomon married strange wives who brought their idolatry with them, and while he may never have bowed down to their gods, yet he facilitated these women by erecting shrines for their gods on the hills near Jerusalem.

Perhaps Baal worship was the most ancient form of idolatry in the Middle East. Baal was thought to be the male generative power of all life. Closely linked with him was "Ashtoreth" which was thought to be the female producer of life. As early as the days of Balaam and Balak, Israel was tempted by this form of idolatry (Num 22.41). In the times of the Judges it was introduced into Israel, and altars were erected in the land for Baal (Judg 2.13; 6.28). Ahab's marriage to Jezebel, who brought Baal worship with her from Sidon, resulted in it becoming the chief religion of the northern kingdom. Elijah confronted its prophets on Mount Carmel, and exposed its helplessness by the fire of the

Lord consuming his offering. Though Baalism sustained a heavy blow at this time, it continued in the nation a long time afterwards. When Jezebel's daughter, Athaliah, married Jehoram, she brought Baal worship with her into Judah. She had a temple for it in Jerusalem (2 Kings 11.18). Jehu was instrumental in destroying the altars of Baal and its worshippers. Though it almost disappeared for a time, it still existed in the closing days of the kingdom (2 Kings 23.4).

As early as the days of Saul "Ashtoreth" was worshipped by the Philistines. She is called the "goddess of the Sidonians" (2 Kings 11.5). Much of the prostitution and sexual corruption associated with idolatry was practised in devotion to this goddess. She was thought to be the queen of heaven, and her devotees imagined that the captivity was the result of the nation failing in its offerings to her (Jer 44.18).

One of the neighbouring nations which had close relationships with Israel was Moab; though descended from Lot who had a knowledge of the true God, yet it was a nation of idolaters. Ruth, David's ancestor had to leave her gods as well as her country when she came to Bethlehem and later married Boaz. The first high place for idolatry built by Solomon was for "Chemosh the abomination of Moab" (1 Kings 11.7). There appears to be a close relationship between this idol and Molech, the god of the Ammonites. Both demanded the sacrifice of the children of their worshippers (2 Kings 3.27). As Ammon and Moab shared common descent from Lot, it is not surprising that their objects of worship would be similar.

Moses warns Israel regarding the offering of children to "Molech" (Lev 18.21), The name means "reigning one" or "your king". Throughout the days of the kings this idol had a place. Solomon built a high place for this abomination of the Ammonites (1 Kings 11.7). At almost the end of the kingdom Manasseh caused one of his sons to pass through the fire as an offering to this god. Topheth, in the valley of Hinnom, on the south side of Jerusalem, was the famous centre in Israel for this cruel practice. Later the place was turned into a refuse dump, and eventually became a symbol of the lake of fire.

Often mentioned in Scripture as an important idol is the Canaanite goddess "Asherah". For some reason, possibly because of the translation of the LXX the word is always translated "Grove" in the AV. She was considered to be the mother of the gods, and the queen of heaven. Possibly the trunk of a tree with its branches cut off, or an upright pole was used as her symbol. Some of these idols were made of stone. Mention is made of these poles sixteen times in the books of

Kings. Manasseh put one in the Temple which Josiah later brought out and burnt at the brook Kidron (2 Kings 23.6).

The gold calves made by Jeroboam are considered by many to be a reproduction of Apis, the sacred bull of Egypt. Of all the idolatrous objects in Israel these seemed to last the longest. They remained at Bethel and Dan until the destruction of the kingdom by the Assyrians. The high places erected for them remained until the days of Josiah. None of the previous reformers attempted to destroy these. The main reason for tolerating them was that the name of the Lord was linked in some way with them. Those who worshipped at these shrines may not have admitted that they were idolators, and even today, many who bow to images, claim that they are not worshipping the objects, but the person whom the image represents.

Perhaps the strangest object of idolatrous worship in Israel was the brazen serpent made by Moses in the wilderness. He could never have imagined that the day would come when incense would be burned to it. How it was preserved is not stated. It could have been stored in the Tabernacle and transferred to the Temple. Those bitten by the serpents who looked toward it were healed, but this was by the power of God and not because of any virtue in it. Hezekiah had it broken in pieces, so this ended its unlawful use (2 Kings 18.4).

When the Assyrians planted people from different nations in Samaria this brought together a mixture of idolatry never before experienced in Israel. Blended with this confusion was the Scriptural teaching of a priest specially sent by Shalmaneser to instruct these idolaters regarding the law of the Lord. The woman at the well (John 4) made clear that a certain amount of truth was known in Samaria. Whatever they may have known of the true God, they were in no sense worshippers of Him. They persisted in their idolatrous ways.

There is a solemn lesson to be learned in the evident proneness of the people of Israel to turn to idolatry. The very nation favoured by God was the one which repeatedly turned to other gods for help. There was no excuse for their apostasy, for He had on many occasions demonstrated to them His power. In turning away from Him, they not only lost His help, but brought upon themselves His fierce wrath. The human heart does not change, and would still turn to objects for help which are as powerless as the idols of old. Any object which displaces God in the heart is an idol. "Flee from idolatry" (1 Cor 10.14), and "Little children keep yourselves from idols (1 John 5.21), are two exhortations still to be heeded.

Appendix C

THE PROPHETS

A feature of the books of Kings is the many references in them to the messengers of God, and equally significant is the amount of space in these books occupied with their activities. A number of names are used for these servants of God which are worthy of attention. Sometimes they are mentioned by their personal names, such as Nathan, Ahijah, Elijah, and Elisha. Sometimes they are anonymous such as the "old prophet" (1 Kings 13.11). Quite often the term "man of God" is used (1 Kings 13.1; 20.28). On one occasion in Kings the term "seer" is used (2 Kings 17.13), When God is speaking regarding the prophets He often calls them "My servants" (2 Kings 17.13; 21.10; 24.2). It does not appear that any in Israel addressed them as "servants of God". The "sons of the prophets" is a term used quite often. It first occurs in 1 Kings 20.35. These were not the literal children of the prophets, but were their disciples. Apparently Samuel was the first to have such a school of prophets around him (1 Sam 10), Both Elijah, and Elisha had them. They called their respective masters "father". The use of this title of respect helps to explain the use of the term "sons".

In the darkest days of Israel's history God was pleased to use His messengers to convey to the people His thoughts of them. Delivering messages to those who had no ear for the word of the Lord was a difficult task. At times the prophets were sent with tidings to kings who were so resentful that the messengers who delivered the message were exposing themselves to grave danger. Because of the threats of Ahab and especially of his wife, Jezebel, Elijah had to flee to Horeb (1 Kings 19).

One notable feature of Kings is that most of the prophecies mentioned were shown to have been fulfilled. This is so different from the major prophecies, such as Isaiah, for some of his writings were fulfilled after hundreds of years, and some of them are yet to be fulfilled. When Elijah told Jeroboam that the kingdom would be rent (1 Kings 11), this was fulfilled in his day. When Elijah said it would not rain, this too was immediately fulfilled, and when the destruction of both kingdoms was foretold this too was seen to occur. In one case the prophecy of the man of God concerning Josiah was not fulfilled for three hundred years after it was spoken, nevertheless, even in this case, it was fulfilled during the history of the kings. If the people failed to lay to heart the words God sent to them through His servants, they had no excuse, for they had knowledge of former prophecies being accurately fulfilled.

Sometimes the prophets came to the kings and people without being invited. At other times the kings sent for them, or sent messengers to hear their words. One thing is clear, and ought to have been appreciated, they were always available. Except for the time when Elijah was at Zarephath, and later at Horeb, he could be found when required. There appeared to be no difficulty in finding God's messengers when they were sought. In a special sense it could be said of the nation, "The word is nigh thee". God was pleased to have His messengers living in the midst of the people they served, whether or not the service rendered was appreciated. There is a principle involved in this fact, for until the present day, it is still the mind of the Lord that His servants dwell among the people they serve. Paul was conscious that his example was as important as the message he carried.

Appendix D

THE NATIONS OPPOSED TO ISRAEL

Without dealing with the smaller nations which from time to time attacked Israel, there were four larger ones, which at different times, invaded the land and wrought havoc. It is solemn to consider that these were God's instruments to chastise His people. Had the nation kept right with the Lord, no enemy could have dared to wage war against it. The first of these was "Syria", the second was "Egypt", the third was "Assyria" and the fourth was "Babylonia". One might ask why these nations were so prone to invade Canaan. The answer is that through the conquests of David and Solomon it had become one of the richest countries of that time. All the invaders knew that if they could overcome it, they would increase their wealth tremendously. Their selfish greed made them yearn to possess what to them was a choice prize. The incalculable amounts of gold, silver and copper taken from Israel from time to time indicate the enormous wealth which was stored in it. When the books of Kings are ended, all of value had gone, and only a poor remnant was left to occupy and cultivate the land.

Syria

The first and most powerful nation to attack Israel, especially the northern kingdom was Syria. Being on the north coast of the land, with no natural barrier between, meant that an army could march over without too much expense. Damascus was its capital city. Three kings bearing the name "Ben-hadad" at different times attacked Israel. The first, during the reign of Baasha invaded the northern kingdom at the behest of Asa king of Judah and captured the cities west of the lake of Gennesaret (1 Kings 15). The second, fought against Ahab (1 Kings 20), but was defeated twice. The third, was the son of Hazael (2 Kings 13.22), and he was defeated by Jehoahaz three times, He recovered from him the cities which the king of Damascus had earlier captured in Israel (2 Kings 13.22-25). While Syria was a thorn in the side of Israel, and did at times do much harm to the nation, yet on the whole, its campaigns against it were limited in success. There was one man in Damascus who was told by the prophet Elijah that he would be king before the reigning king was dead. He was Hazael, a courtier of Ben-hadad, who was sent to enquire from the prophet if the sick king would recover. He was told that the king would recover, and that he would reign in his stead. He murdered the king and sat on the throne of Syria, during the period between Ben-hadad 2 and Ben-hadad 3. At the close of his reign, and during the reign of Jehu he attacked Israel. He not only oppressed the northern kingdom, but invaded Judah. Jerusalem was spared when a bounteous present from the treasures of the Temple was given to him (2 Kings 12.17-18). Rezin was another king of Syria who troubled Israel. He joined with Pekah king of Israel in an attempt to capture Jerusalem (Is 7). Though he failed to capture the city, yet he managed to take the town of Elath from Judah (2 Kings 16.6). He was overcome by the Assyrians who slew him (2 Kings 16.7-9).

Egypt

From the days of Moses Egypt from time to time proved to be an enemy of Israel. During the reign of Solomon the possibility of any trouble from that quarter was averted because Pharaoh's daughter was his special wife. In his son's day, however, this close relationship came to an end, for in the fifth year of Rehoboam's reign about 925 (BC) Shishak king of Egypt invaded Judah. He was the founder of Egyptian dynasty 22. He is the first king of Egypt to be mentioned in Scripture by name, rather than by the title "Pharaoh". He removed the shields of gold, sacked the Temple and the palace. This was the beginning of a series of raids which stripped from the palaces the treasures stored by David and Solomon. Other nations followed this example and similarly despoiled Israel. Closely associated with Egypt, and at times identified with it was Ethiopia. During the reign of Asa an invasion by the Ethiopians was repelled and routed. At this time the southern land, Ethiopia, was predominant, yet it was one with its sister Egypt.

The temptation for Israel was to think that Egypt was a sincere friend. When trouble arose in the nation, the tendency was to turn to Egypt for help. The prophets sought to warn the people of the folly of this, and the history proved how disappointing was the outcome of reliance on such a fickle nation. When the Assyrians invaded Israel in the days of Hoshea help was sought from So king of Egypt, but this was not forthcoming, so the king of Israel was shut up in prison (2 Kings 17.4).

At almost the end of the kingdom of Judah Pharaoh-nechoh king of Egypt engaged in war with Assyria against the rising power of Babylon (2 Kings 23.29). Josiah king of Judah took sides with Pharaoh, and went to the battlefield at Megiddo. The former king was slain at that time, and Judah, over which he had reigned, became subject to Egypt. Later Nebuchadnezzar subdued Egypt, so all invasions from that quarter ended (2 Kings 24.7).

Assyria

For quite a time a fierce enemy of Israel was Assyria. If Egypt was the southern enemy, this one was from the opposite direction, for it was northerly. Its people descended from Shem. The original land was elevated, but with conquests it extended into the rich valleys below and included Babylon. Tiglath-pileser, also named Pul (2 Kings 15.19) was the first Assyrian king to attack Israel. He was satisfied to end his campaign when Menahem the king of Israel gave him a thousand talents of silver (2 Kings 15.19-20). In the days of Pekah he came again into the land, and not only conquered it, but took the people from its northern and western parts as captives (2 Kings 15.29). Ahaz sought the help of the king of Assyria when Rezin king of Syria fought against Israel, and paid him well for his assistance (2 Kings 16.7-9).

Shalmaneser succeeded Tiglath-pileser as king of Assyria (727-722 BC). He invaded Israel and, like his predecessor, was given tribute by Hosea the king. Later when this tribute was withheld, he took Samaria, and carried the people of the northern kingdom into Media (2 Kings 18.9-11). It took him three years to overcome the defences of Samaria. When he did succeed, he was most cruel with the surviving inhabitants, and slew many of them. The patience of the Lord with the evils of Israel became exhausted, so He sold it into the hand of its enemy. The kingdom lasted about two hundred years, but at no time was it free from idolatry. There were souls in it who worshipped the Lord alone, and at times some of these made their way to the true centre at Jerusalem, but the threatened disaster came, and Shalmaneser was the instrument employed to bring it about.

Another king of Assyria not mentioned in Kings was Sargon (722-705 BC). It is thought by many that he became king during the siege of Samaria. According to Isaiah 20, the general of his army fought against Ashdod and took it. His success was chiefly in Egypt and Ethiopia where he shamefully treated the captives which he took. In this prophecy Israel was taught that the lands, on which they leaned for support, were not able to protect themselves.

For a little more than twenty four years (705-681 BC) the throne of Assyria was filled by Sennacherib, son of Sargon. He was the special enemy of Hezekiah. In spite of the payment of a huge sum by the king of Judah, he proceeded to capture the cities of Judah, and would have taken Jerusalem, had not the Lord intervened. The long struggle at Samaria had taught him that laying siege for years is a costly business, so he sought the surrender of Jerusalem by negotiation. The plague that smote his army at that time ended the siege and left a time of peace for Hezekiah. Sennacherib was slain by his two sons. Eventually the Assyrian empire was taken over by the Chaldeans, following the capture of Nineveh (612 BC), and Harran (609 BC).

Babylonia

Toward the end of the kingdom of Judah the Babylonian empire rose to its zenith, and was the final enemy mentioned in the books of Kings. Nebuchadnezzar became king after his father, Nabopolassar, died, and became the "head of gold" in the great image which represented the "times of the Gentiles" (Dan 2). He reigned from 605-581 (BC), and extended the kingdom of Babylon until it was a world power. He invaded Judah in the days of Jehoiakim who became his servant. After three years the king of Judah rebelled against him (2 Kings 24.1). Soon afterwards in 598 BC, he came to Jerusalem and captured it. Jehoiachin was taken prisoner together with all the princes of Judah and carried to Babylon (vv.10-16). Ten years later, because Zedekiah had rebelled, he returned to Jerusalem and captured it. Zedekiah was taken prisoner and made blind after his two sons were slain before his eyes. After a two year siege, the city and Temple were burnt by Nebuzar-adan captain of the guard under Nebuchadnezzar. This ended the kingdom of Judah, and left the land denuded of all its wealth.

It is interesting to note that these enemies of Israel had links with the fathers of the nation. As for Syria, it was where Jacob found his two wives, so the mothers of the nation were Syrians. Egypt had also close links with Israel, for Joseph was its saviour during the seven years famine, and his wife was an Egyptian. The nation was born there in the days of Moses. Abraham was called out of Ur of the Chaldees, which was south of Babylon, so that nation had links with the father of the nation of Israel.

Perhaps these enemies of Israel represent the enemies of the Lord's people until this day. Syria and Assyria were closely related, and remind us of the danger of worldly ambition. By aiming for worldly fame some of the saints have become captivated until they are virtually spiritual slaves. It was in Syria that Jacob had to serve, and was in danger of losing his life. "A Syrian ready to perish was my father" (Deut 26.5). Egypt has often been viewed as representing the world in its social luxury. Some believers have become ensnared by worldly pleasures and try to convince themselves that there is no harm in such engagements. Babylon represents the world in its corrupt religion. When false Christianity is being exposed in the book of Revelation, Babylon is the symbolic name given to its headquarters. The call to be obeyed in a future day, "Come out of her, My people" (Rev 18.4) is one that should be obeyed today with regard to the religious world. Perhaps the most subtle of the saint's enemies is the world in a religious garb. A large number of worldly pursuits are in some way garnished with a sprinkling of religion. Had Israel kept right with the Lord, not one of her enemies would have harmed her, so if believers walk in the power of the Spirit of God, they will be overcomers (Gal 5.16).